# Mastering Book-Keeping

**Visit our How To website at www.howto.co.uk**

At www.howto.co.uk you can engage in conversation with our authors – all of whom have 'been there and done that' in their specialist fields. You can get access to special offers and additional content but most importantly you will be able to engage with, and become a part of, a wide and growing community of people just like yourself.

At www.howto.co.uk you'll be able to talk and share tips with people who have similar interests and are facing similar challenges in their lives. People who, just like you, have the desire to change their lives for the better – be it through moving to a new country, starting a new business, growing their own vegetables, or writing a novel.

At www.howto.co.uk you'll find the support and encouragement you need to help make your aspirations a reality.

How To Books strives to present authentic, inspiring, practical information in their books. Now, when you buy a title from How To Books, you get even more than just words on a page.

An accredited textbook of
The Institute of Certified Bookkeepers

# Mastering Book-Keeping

A COMPLETE GUIDE TO
THE PRINCIPLES AND
PRACTICE OF BUSINESS
ACCOUNTING

## Dr Peter Marshall

**how**to books

Published by How To Books Ltd,
Spring Hill House, Spring Hill Road,
Begbroke, Oxford OX5 1RX. United Kingdom.
Tel: (01865) 375794. Fax: (01865) 379162.
info@howtobooks.co.uk
www.howtobooks.co.uk

First edition 1992
Second edition 1995
Third edition 1997
Fourth edition 1999
Fifth edition 2001
Sixth edition 2003
Seventh edition 2005
Reprinted 2006
Eighth edition 2009
Ninth edition 2010

British Library Cataloguing in Publication Data
A catalogue record for this book is available from the British Library

ISBN: 978 1 84528 446 6

Produced for How To Books by Deer Park Productions, Tavistock, Devon
Typeset by PDQ Typesetting, Newcastle-under-Lyme, Staffordshire
Cover design by Baseline Arts Ltd, Oxford
Printed and bound by Bell & Bain Ltd, Glasgow

# Contents

# Contents

# Contents

# Contents

# Preface

This book was inspired as much by educational science as by book-keeping. Having had a dual role of business studies writer and educational researcher I have been particularly interested in the way educational science can be applied to this subject, which has, hitherto, been largely missed by the research community.

Other books teach book-keeping in a spatial way assuming that if students understand the page layouts they will naturally understand how to enter them. That is so for people with relatively spatial learning styles, such as accountants tend to have, but it is not the case for those with a more sequential learning style, such as book-keepers so often tend to have. This is a cause of much communication difficulty in classrooms. This book tackles this problem head-on by teaching in a sequential—'set of rules'—manner.

Although this book aims to teach readers the principles of double entry accounting, it must be acknowledged that there are many small businesses (corner shops, cafés, hairdressers, etc) which do not use this. This edition includes a short section on the kinds of deviations from conventional accounting which a reader may encounter.

This book has been designed to cover the requirements of all the principal book-keeping courses, including ICB, IAB, AAT, the GCSE and A level courses of AQA, OCR, Edexcel, Pitman, LCCI and all the various Open College syllabi in the subject. Moreover, this edition contains a wealth of examination material. In this enhanced and fully updated edition it will provide students with all they need to achieve success in their courses.

*Peter Marshall*

*ICB examination papers and model answers are reproduced by kind permission of the Institute of Certified Bookkeepers. AQA examinations questions are reproduced by kind permission of The Assessment and Qualifications Alliance. OCR questions are reproduced by kind permission of Oxford, Cambridge and RSA Examinations. AAT questions are reproduced by kind permission of The Association of Accounting Technicians. IAB examination papers and model answers are reproduced by kind permission of The International Association of Book-keepers.*

# 1   A period of transition

With the increasing globalisation of trade and industry at all levels it is becoming increasingly necessary to achieve some degree of harmony in accounting practices between countries. The standards that applied in the UK since 1970 i.e. Statements of Standard Accounting Practice (SSAPs) and Financial Reporting Standards (FRSs)) are being gradually phased out and replaced by International Accounting Standards (IASs) and International Financial Reporting Standards (IFRSs). All companies listed on EU Stock Exchanges already use the international standards and in time they will be used by all UK businesses.

Here are some examples of the changes in terminology with which you will have to become familiar. In the international standard terminology, instead of turnover the term *revenue* is used, instead of stock the term *inventory* is used, and debtors and creditors are called *accounts receivable* and *payable*. Provisions tend to be referred to as *allowances*, the profit and loss account is known as the *income statement* and any profit that is brought down to the balance sheet is termed *retained profits*. Debentures are known as *loan notes*, fixed assets are called *non-current assets* and long-term liabilities are called *non-current liabilities*.

## 2 The role and significance of the professional association

One of the distinguishing characteristics of all professions is the existence of professional associations. Such bodies maintain and improve the reputation of the profession by the regulation of conduct, the improvement of skills and the validation of qualifications.

The Institute of Certified Bookkeepers is based at 1 Northumberland House, Trafalgar Square, London WC2N 5BW, under the Royal Patronage of His Royal Highness Prince Michael of Kent GCVO. The other professional association for book-keepers is The International Association of Book-keepers (AIB), whose registered office is at Burford House, 44, London Road, Sevenoaks, Kent TN13 1AS.

Book-keeping became a regulated profession under the Money Laundering Regulations of 2007. As a result of this book-keepers now have special legal duties imposed upon them, and failure to comply with them has serious legal consequences. All practising book-keepers must be registered with a supervisory body. Both professional bodies mentioned here are Treasury Appointed Supervisory Bodies under the Money Laundering Act and, as such, will monitor, guide and supervise members to ensure compliance.

In addition, membership also provides proof of proficiency which is recognised worldwide. It offers assistance with career development, not only through the provision of training and qualifications, but also though notification of job vacancies, updates on legislation and advice and guidance on private practice. Members also get the opportunity to meet and associate with others in the same profession in local groups and forums.

Making you count™

THE INSTITUTE
OF CERTIFIED
BOOKKEEPERS

Annual Conference

Regional Seminars

Introduction

The Lucas 2009

About Us ▶

Membership ▶

Members Area ▶

Money Laundering
Regulations

Syllabuses ▶

Examinations ▶

Where To Study

Exemptions

Find a Bookkeeper

FAQs

Shop

Contact Us

**Website login**

Email Address:

Password:

Login

Forgotten Password?

Join online today

Membership of the
Institute of Certified
Bookkeepers is awarded
in recognition of
professional
qualifications and
experience. Membership
offers a wide range of
useful benefits.
Click Here

**News Headlines**

InVOICE April 2010

April's Regional Seminars

The cheque's in the post

Minimum Wage set to rise from
October

Sick notes change to Fit notes
from April 2010

Welcome

## The Institute of Certified Bookkeepers

A message from our Patron:
**His Royal Highness Prince Michael
of Kent GCVO**
Sound financial management is the
crucial factor, not only in the survival
of new businesses but for making
business more efficient, and sound
financial management starts with
effective book-keeping. The Institute
of Certified Bookkeepers, ever since
its inception, has contributed
significantly to good business
practice, particularly amongst small
and medium sized enterprises, and I
am delighted to support this in my
role as Patron.

00:00/01:59

## What is a Bookkeeper?

**Bookkeeping is a growing profession - it is demanding, exciting, challenging and above all, rewarding. It is about
understanding how a business works and then providing accurate figures that enable the business to know
exactly how well it is doing. For men and women of all ages and from all backgrounds it provides outstanding
career opportunities.**

The basic system of double entry bookkeeping was invented more than five hundred years ago by a Cistercian monk called
Luca Pacioli. His system still endures today and is used throughout the world, making bookkeeping a truly international
profession. This website will give an understanding of how to train to become a bookkeeper and how to become a member of
the Institute. It will also help those who already have a qualification or have been working as a bookkeeper for many years
but now want the support of a professional organisation to enhance career prospects.

**A CAREER IN BOOKKEEPING**
Every business, no matter how large or small, is required by law to 'keep books'. This involves the recording of the financial
transactions of a business, whether manually into ledgers or by entering everything onto a computer. So, if you are well
organised and methodical, like working through documents and enjoy seeing a set of figures add up properly, bookkeeping
could be the career for you.
People of all ages are becoming bookkeepers: Young people fresh from school or college can achieve a professional
qualification that opens up a whole new world of business to them or may become the first step to becoming a qualified
accountant. More mature people bring years' of experience to their role and are in great demand from businesses who want a
safe pair of hands. Many are mothers wanting to find a well-paid career running a bookkeeping business from home whilst still
bringing up their family.

**YOU AND THE INSTITUTE**
The Institute of Certified Bookkeepers was established to provide a series of professional qualifications that reflect the needs
of business and the aspirations of people wanting to enter the profession. It exists to represent bookkeepers at all levels and
to promote the professionalism of bookkeepers to business, government and the general public.
Becoming a member of the Institute is like joining a club. You will receive strong on-going support from a team of qualified
professionals. You will have access to free legal and technical advice. You will have the opportunity to meet other bookkeepers
and to update your skills through continuing professional development seminars.
The Institute has more than 150,000 students and members spread across more than fifty countries, making it the largest
bookkeeping institute in the world.

HQ: 1 Northumberland Avenue, Trafalgar Square, London WC2N 5BW
T: 0845 060 2345 E: info@bookkeepers.org.uk

www.bookkeepers.org.uk homepage reproduced by kind permission of The
Institute of Certified Bookkeepers.

www.iab.org.uk website page reproduced by kind permission of The International Association of Book-keepers.

## 3　Data security and the Data Protection Act 1998

When a business keeps a substantial number of personal details in computerised accounting records it may be obligated to register with the Information Commissioner. The person who decides how data will be used and for what purpose is referred to in the Act as the data controller while a person on whom data is kept is referred to as a data subject. It is essentially so that the data subjects are aware of what is held and how it is used.

It is not necessary to inform the Information Commissioner if:

- the data controller is only using the data for sending and receiving invoices and statements;
- the data subjects are companies and no individuals can be identified in them;
- the data is only used to process payroll and prepare statutory returns.

However, if a data controller is going to make accounting data available to management or any other department for non-accounting purposes, e.g. marketing, statistical, planning or control purposes, it must register. It must disclose the kind of data held, the purpose for which it will be used and how subjects can access their own data.

### LEGAL OBLIGATIONS IN RESPECT OF PERSONAL DATA

Businesses registered under the Data Protection Act 1998 must comply with certain standards of practice contained in Schedule 1 of the Act. These require that the personal data shall:

- be obtained only for specified and lawful purposes and must not be used in any manner incompatible with such purposes;
- be relevant and adequate but not excessive for the purpose for which it has been collected;
- be accurate and kept up to date;
- not be kept for any longer than necessary for the purpose for which it was collected;
- only be processed in accordance with the subject's rights under the Act;
- be protected by appropriate organisational and technical measures against unauthorised and unlawful use, or accidental loss or damage;
- not be taken outside of the country to any country where there is not adequate legal protection of the rights and freedom of data subjects in respect of the processing of their personal data.

In many businesses today accounting information *will* be used for non-accounting purposes so it is very likely that anyone who controls such data will need to register and comply with the Act. To access the full text of the Act click on www.opsi.gov.uk/ads/ads1998/19980029.htm. The Information Commissioner's general website is on www.ico.gov.uk.

# 4  The flow of documents and processes

This chapter outlines the paper trail between buyer and seller in a typical business transaction and the processes within each firm that each document triggers.

## Estimate or quotation

Sometimes it is not possible to give a precise quotation and an estimate is regarded as the best that can be done. The quotation must be for an exact figure while an estimate is only a rough figure. However, the final costs of work or supplies are expected to be within 10% of the estimated figure and courts are likely to be sympathetic to the purchasing party in actions where this figure has been exceeded.

## Request for quotations

Often when a business wishes to purchase goods and services from another requests for quotations will be sent out to a number of potential suppliers. Any company interested in competing to supply goods to the business will begin to calculate the lowest prices at which it is prepared to supply the goods or services. It will then prepare a quotation or estimate (according to whichever was requested) and send it to the potential customer.

When the customer receives the estimates or quotations they will compare them all on the basis of prices and perceived quality of the goods or services being offered, taking into account such things as delivery dates and past experience of dealing with that particular supplier.

## Purchase order

When a final selection is made the buyer will normally issue a purchase order. This will state the quantity, type of goods, prices and the special conditions of the contract, such as the terms of business, the timescale in which payment is agreed to be made, e.g. strictly 30 days. Delivery instructions and any other special conditions which may apply will be included, e.g. there may be a penalty clause for late completion of work, entitling the buyer of services to compensation of a specific sum, or a specific percentage of the total.

## Delivery note

If the supplier accepts this purchase order then a delivery note will normally be made out and sent with the goods. This will normally be in at least triplicate form and will specify the goods.

Some multipart, carbonised sales forms contain three copies of the delivery note and two copies of the sales invoice. The delivery notes, being the bottom two copies, may have the cash columns blocked out. In certain aspects these invoices and delivery notes will be the same, including the boxes for name and address, order number and details of goods, but the cash details will normally be omitted on the delivery notes.

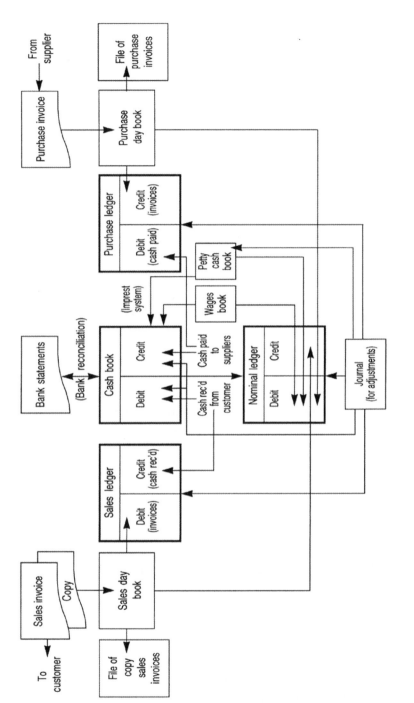

Fig. 1. An overview of business accounts records. Note: The actual records are shown in the boxes. The arrows show the flow of information between the various records. The boxes shown in bold are divisions of the ledger. There is an additional month-end information flow between ledger divisions when cross-referencing is made in folio columns.

7

The delivery note will be passed to the stores, where it will trigger the packing and shipment of the goods to the customer. At the same time the stock records will be adjusted to show the goods have been booked out from stock and have become the responsibility of the delivery driver and remain so until he or she returns a signed delivery note confirming they have been received by the customer in good order.

## Where the order is for services

If the purchase order is for services rather than goods, e.g. building work, then a job order sheet may be produced by the supplying firm and passed to the works department for the manager to allocate the job to a worker or workers.

## Customer signs to confirm delivery

When the goods arrive a copy of the delivery note is signed by the customer after he or she has checked the goods are those that were ordered and have been received in good condition. There will usually be a second copy for the customer to file. These retained copies are source documents for updating the stock records, which at the end of the year, after verification against a physical stock check, will be used in the balance sheet as one component of the current assets section (Closing Stock).

## Production of an invoice

The signed delivery note will be passed to the sales office of the supplier, where it will trigger the preparation of an invoice. This may have already been prepared as part of a quadruplicate or quintruplicate set and sent to the customer with the delivery note, or it may be sent by post once a signed delivery note is received to confirm the goods it is charging for have been received by the customer.

In a manual system one copy of the invoice will go to the accounts department where its details will be entered into the sales day book. In a fully computerised system the sales day book may automatically be updated with the invoice details when the invoice is produced on the system.

## Purchase returns note

Sometimes goods are returned by agreement with the supplier, because they are faulty or not what was ordered. In such a case a purchase returns note will be created by the buyer, which is essentially the opposite of a delivery note, describing the goods being returned and the reason.

## Production of a credit note

The receipt of this note will normally, after checking it is justified, trigger the production of a credit note at the supplier's end (which is essentially the opposite of an invoice). When the customer receives this it will be entered in the purchase returns day book and this, in turn, will be posted to the debit side of the relevant bought ledger account to reduce the indebtedness of the company to that particular supplier.

## Production of a statement

At the end of the month (or sooner if it is the firm's policy) the sales day book details will be posted to the ledger divisions—the sales account in the nominal ledger and the personal account details in the sales ledger. The ledger divisions will be balanced and the resulting balances will be reproduced in statements and sent to customers, informing them of the amount they owe, whether they are overdue and when they should be paid by. These will also include any interest or penalties that have been agreed for late payment and details of any early settlement discount the customer can claim.

Often these will be age-analysed, i.e. stating which parts of the total amount have been outstanding for one month, which parts of it have been outstanding for two months, and so on. If the debt is overdue for payment a strong demand will normally be annotated, such as *This account is overdue for payment. Please settle by return.* Such demands may become increasingly strong the older a debt becomes.

Statements will not normally give details of the goods or services supplied. Their purpose is merely to deal with the financial indebtedness of the customer, but some statements may show such details.

Often a remittance advice slip will be included with the statements (attached or as a separate slip). It will give the necessary details for the cashier to tie up the payment with the relevant account. This is partly for the convenience of the customer to save them preparing a covering letter to accompany the cheque.

## Production of a cheque

The receipt of the statement by the customer is usually what triggers the production of the cheque payable to the supplier and any remittance slip that came with the statement will be filled in and sent with it to the supplier.

The details from the cheque stub will be entered into the cashbook to credit the bank with the funds it is transferring to the supplier and if any early settlement discount has been received it will be posted to the discount received account. The other side of each part of this transaction will be posted to the debit side of the supplier's personal account in the bought ledger, to record that the business has been settled by bank funds, less any discount the suppliers have allowed.

Figure 2 provides a schematic illustration of the flow of documents in a single business transaction and the processes which are triggered by each.

## Symmetry of the processes of purchases and sales

This same flow of documents takes place in respect of goods supplied by the firm as for goods supplied to the firm. The roles are just reversed.

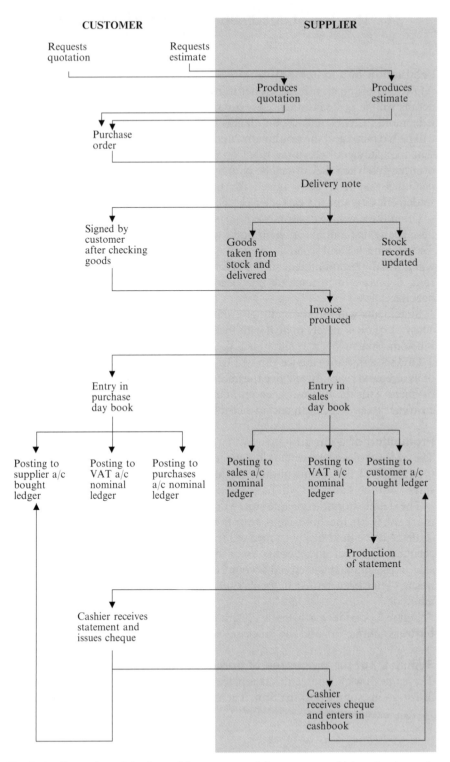

Fig. 2. An illustration of the flow of documents and the processes which each triggers in a transaction between two businesses.

## 5   What is double entry book-keeping?

### Debit and credit
All transactions have two sides, a **debit** and a **credit**. When a firm sells a TV and sends a bill for payment, for example, on the one hand it has made a sale (which is a credit entry). On the other hand it has gained a liability from the customer (debit entry). That customer is liable to the firm for the money.

### The need for two records
Both these transactions need recording separately, because we need:

- a total of sales figures for tax computation and management purposes (to make sure the business is working to plan)

- a cumulative total of money owed by each customer.

### A check of accuracy
There is another important advantage of double entry book-keeping. If both sides of each transaction have been recorded then, at any time, if the sums have been done correctly the debit entries will equal the credit entries. It provides a check of accuracy. An example is as follows:

*Example*
Suppose A. T. Office Supplies made the following transactions:

Purchased 6 tables for £60.00 from seller A
Purchased 10 chairs for £40.00 from seller B
Sold 1 table for £15.00 to customer A
Sold 1 chair for £24.00 to customer B
Received cheque for £15.00 from customer A
Paid cheque for £60.00 to seller A

The entries would be:

| DEBIT | £ | CREDIT | £ |
|---|---|---|---|
| Purchases | 60.00 | Seller A | 60.00 |
| Purchases | 40.00 | Seller B | 40.00 |
| Customer A | 15.00 | Sales | 39.00 |
| Customer B | 24.00 | | |
| Bank | 15.00 | Customer A | 15.00 |
| Seller A | 60.00 | Bank | 60.00 |
| | 214.00 | | 214.00 |

## JOURNAL

| Date 200X | Particulars | Dr. | Cr. |
|---|---|---|---|
| Jan 1 | Sundries: | | |
| | Factory premises | 69,500 | |
| | Fixtures and fittings | 1,000 | |
| | Printing machine | 18,000 | |
| | Motor van | 5,000 | |
| | Bank | 6,500 | |
| |   Capital | | 100,000 |

| Dr. | | | *Factory Premises* | | | Cr. |
|---|---|---|---|---|---|---|
| Date 200X | Particulars | Totals | Date 200X | Particulars | | Totals |
| Jan 1 | Opening balance | 69,500 | | | | |

| Dr. | | | *Fixtures & Fittings Account* | | | Cr. |
|---|---|---|---|---|---|---|
| Date 200X | Particulars | Totals | Date 200X | Particulars | | Totals |
| Jan 1 | Opening balance | 1,000 | | | | |

| Dr. | | | *Printing Machine Account* | | | Cr. |
|---|---|---|---|---|---|---|
| Date 200X | Particulars | Totals | Date 200X | Particulars | | Totals |
| Jan 1 | Opening balance | 18,000 | | | | |

| Dr. | | | *Motor Van Account* | | | Cr. |
|---|---|---|---|---|---|---|
| Date 200X | Particulars | Totals | Date 200X | Particulars | | Totals |
| Jan 1 | Opening balance | 5,000 | | | | |

| | | | *Capital Account* | | | |
|---|---|---|---|---|---|---|
| Date 200X | Particulars | Totals | Date 200X | Particulars | | Totals |
| | | | Jan 1 | Opening balance | | 100,000 |

## CASH BOOK

| *Receipts* | | | | | *Payments* | | | |
|---|---|---|---|---|---|---|---|---|
| Date 200X | Particulars | Discount | Cash | Bank | Date Particulars | Discount | Cash | Bank |
| Jan 1 | Opening balance | | | 6,500 | | | | |

Fig. 3. An example of the journalising and posting to the ledger of the opening figures.

# 6 Opening the books of account

## Assets, liabilities and capital

When opening the books of a new business for the first time we need to list:

- all its assets

- all its liabilities.

By taking away the value of the liabilities from the assets, we can tell how much **capital** the business has at the beginning. In other words:

assets – liabilities = capital

Or to put it another way:

assets = capital + liabilities

## Accounts as an equation

The accounts of a business always represent such an equation, in which one side is always exactly balanced by the other side. This balancing list of opening assets, liabilities and capital should then be posted to (i.e. entered in) the relevant ledger accounts, by way of a very useful account book called the **journal**. We will see how to do this when we come to the journal and ledger sections a little later on.

The page on the left shows a typical first page of the journal of a new small printing business, working from a small workshop, and owning a printing machine and delivery van. As you can see, the firm's assets are £100,000, made up of such things as premises, equipment, and £6,500 cash at bank. We keep a separate account for each of these assets—factory premises account, fixtures and fittings account and so on. The cash account we record in the ledger (cash book division); in the example (bottom left) you can see the £6,500 entered in as an 'opening balance'.

```
┌─────────────────────────────────────────────────────────────┐
│                          Invoice                             │
│                                                               │
│  D. Davidson (Builder)              Delivered to:             │
│  1 Main Road                        Broad Street              │
│  Anytown                            Anytown                   │
│  Lancs                              Lancs                     │
│                                                               │
│  P356   20/12/200X                                            │
│                                                               │
│  20  bags of cement                10.00     200.00           │
│  15  5 litre tins of white emulsion  1.00      15.00          │
│  32  bags of sand                    5.00     160.00          │
│  40  metres of 100mm x 50mm pinewood 1.00      40.00          │
│                                               ──────          │
│                                               415.00          │
│                    VAT @ 17½%                  72.63          │
│                                               ──────          │
│                                               487.63          │
│  E&OE                                         ══════          │
└─────────────────────────────────────────────────────────────┘
```

Fig. 4. Example of an invoice.

```
┌─────────────────────────────────────────────────────────────┐
│                        Credit Note                           │
│                                                               │
│  D. Davidson (Builder)              Delivered to:             │
│  1 Main Road                        Broad Street              │
│  Anytown                            Anytown                   │
│  Lancs                              Lancs                     │
│                                                               │
│  P3756   20/01/200X                                           │
│                                                               │
│  60  Door hinges                    0.50       30.00          │
│                                                ──────         │
│                                                 30.00         │
│                     VAT @ 17½%                   5.25         │
│                                                ──────         │
│                                                 35.25         │
│  E&OE                                          ══════         │
└─────────────────────────────────────────────────────────────┘
```

Fig. 5. Example of a credit note.
E&OE stands for errors and omissions excepted.

### Recording daily details: books of prime entry

Double entry accounts are kept in the ledger, but daily details of transactions are not normally entered directly into it; it would become too cluttered and difficult to use. For convenience we first of all enter all the day-to-day details of transactions in other books, called **books of prime entry**. In modern accounting these books are the:

- purchase day book

- purchase returns day book

- sales day book

- sales returns day book

- journal

- cash book

- petty cash book.

### Day books or journals

This group of books can also be called either **day books** or **journals**. We will use the term day books here for the four which are identically ruled and most often referred to as day books, that is the purchase day book, purchase returns day book, sales day book and sales returns day book. The word journal we will keep for the journal proper, because of its individual ruling and the others we will call 'books of prime entry'. It is the four day books as defined here, that we will explain in this section.

### Source documents for the book-keeper

The sources of information we need to enter into the day books are invoices and credit notes. When a firm receives invoices or credit notes for goods it has purchased they are known as purchase invoices and credit notes inwards respectively. When it sends them out, they are called sales invoices and credit notes outwards. Whether the documents refer to sales or purchases, their format is basically the same. After all, what is a purchase invoice to one party in the transaction is a sales invoice to the other, and similarly for credit notes.

> The production of invoices is usually triggered by receipt of signed delivery notes for *goods sold* and by time sheets or some kinds of job completion docket for *services rendered*. Except in very small firms, where such details may be known by heart, product or service descriptions, codes and prices are sourced from sales, or service catalogues, trade terms are dictated by company policy and any special terms which are allowed to particular customers may be listed in a customers special terms file.

**DEBIT NOTE**

P Donague                     Delivery Address:        6 Broad Street
1 Main Road                                            Anytown
Anytown                                                Lancs.
Lancs.


Credit note number CN 200X/12/28 – 3


Undercharge of invoice number p356 20/12/200X          10.00

VAT                                                     1.75

Total                                                  11.75

Fig. 6. Example of a debit note.

## Debit notes

Sales office clerks occasionally make mistakes and undercharge a customer for goods, so firms usually print the term E&OE on their invoices, which means errors and omissions excepted. This means the firm reserves the right to ask for more money for the goods if they realise they have inadvertently undercharged. If this has to be done the document they use is known as a debit note. An example is given in Figure 6 opposite.

## Book-keeping and confidentiality

Book-keeping and accounting technicians have a duty to treat all information to which their job exposes them in strictest confidence, disclosing details only to those who have a professional right to know them. Examples are:

- employers, or employees who need the information to carry out their professional role;

- professionals outside the company who work on behalf of the company who need the information to carry out their function;

- any other person to whom their employer, or officer senior to themselves instructs them to disclose information, since it must be assumed that the employer or senior officer will also be working within the confines of such confidentially rules.

# PURCHASE DAY BOOK

| Date | Supplier | Inv. No. | Fo. No. | Net.Inv Value | VAT 17½% | Stationery | Books | Calculators |
|---|---|---|---|---|---|---|---|---|
| 200X | | | | | | | | |
| Apr 1 | Morgan and Baldwyn | 4/1 | BL6 | 80.00 | 14.00 | 80.00 | | |
| 3 | " | | | 200.00 | 35.00 | | | 200.00 |
| 15 | S. Jones | 4/2 | BL5 | 70.00 | | | 70.00 | |
| 21 | A Singh Wholesale | 4/3 | BL9 | 160.00 | | | 160.00 | |
| | | | | 40.00 | 7.00 | 40.00 | | |
| 30 | Morgan and Baldwyn | 4/4 | BL6 | 150.00 | 26.25 | 150.00 | | |
| | | | | 700.00 | 82.25 | 270.00 | 230.00 | 200.00 |

Fig. 7. How to write up purchases into the purchase day book.

A. Frazer, a retail stationer, makes the following purchases during the month of April 200X:

200X

| Apr 1 | Morgan and Baldwyn | 20 Geometry sets @ £4 |
|---|---|---|
| 3 | " | 40 Calculators @ £5 |
| 15 | S. Jones | 20 Assorted books @ £3.50 |
| 21 | A Singh Wholesale | 40 Assorted books @ £ £4 |
| | | 80 Bottles of ink @ £0.50 |
| 30 | Morgan and Baldwyn | 25 De-luxe writing cases @ £6 |

Figure 7 shows how he writes up the transactions in the purchase day book.

# 8  The purchase day book

The **purchase day book** is one of the day books mentioned. It is where we first enter up all our purchases on credit. The book itself is not part of 'the accounts': it is just one of the sources from which the accounts will be written up later on.

## How to write up the purchase day book
What you need:

- the purchase day book
- the invoices for the period (day, week, etc.).

First, sort the invoices into date order. Next, write or stamp a purchase invoice number on each one. (This is not the invoice number printed on the document when the firm receives it; that is the sales invoice number of the firm which sent it.) The idea is to help the book-keeper find an invoice easily if he/she has to look up details of an old transaction.

Many firms keep a list of consecutive numbers for this purpose. Others use a two-part number made up of the month number and a number from a consecutive list for that month.

## Step by step
1.  Write the year of entry once, at the head of entries to be made for that year. There is no need then to keep writing the year against each individual entry. This helps to keep the page neat and uncluttered. Do the same for the month, and then the day, as in the example on the opposite page:

     | Apr | 1 |
     | | 3 |
     | | 15 |
     | | 21 |
     | | 30 |

2.  Enter the supplier's name, e.g. Morgan and Baldwyn.

3.  Enter your own purchase invoice number e.g. 4/1.

4.  Enter net invoice total, e.g. £80.00. (Net means after deduction of any trade discounts and not including VAT; we will come to these later.)

5.  Enter the VAT, e.g. £14.00.

6.  If analysis columns are in use, also enter the net amount of each invoice under the correct heading, e.g. 'stationery'.

7.  When required (e.g. monthly) total each column. You will then be able to post (transfer) the totals to the ledger.

## S. JONES (WHOLESALE STATIONERY SUPPLIES) LTD
210 Barton High Street, Barton, Barshire

*Credit Note No*: SJ /02206                    10/2/200X

To authorised return of faulty
desk diaries                                         200.00

VAT @ 17½%                                         35.00
                                                      235.00

*Name of customer*
D. Davidson
1 Main Street
Anytown
Lancs.

Fig. 8. Example of a credit note inwards.

## PURCHASE RETURNS DAYBOOK

| Date | Supplier | C/N No | Net Inv. Value | VAT 17½% | Stationery | Books | Cards | Machines |
|------|----------|--------|----------------|----------|------------|-------|-------|----------|
| 200X | | | | | | | | |
| Feb10 | S.Jones | 2/1 | 200.00 | 35.00 | 200.00 | | | |
| 14 | Morgan & Baldwyn | 2/2 | 270.00 | | | 270.00 | | |
| 25 | A. Singh | 2/3 | 230.00 | 40.25 | | | 15.00 | 215.00 |
| | | | 700.00 | 75.25 | 200.00 | 270.00 | 15.00 | 215.00 |

Fig. 9. Example of the same credit entered into the
purchase returns daybook.

# 9 The purchase returns day book

## Returning unwanted goods

When a firm buys goods or services on credit, it records the details in the purchase day book, as we saw on the previous pages. Sometimes, however, it has to return what it has bought to the supplier. For example the goods may be faulty, or arrived damaged. In this case, the firm obtains a **credit note** from the supplier, and the value of the credit note is then entered up in the purchase returns day book.

All the points which apply to the purchase day book also apply to the purchase returns day book. Even the ruling is identical, though of course the transaction details may be different. So once you have become familiar with the ruling of a typical purchase day book, you will also have a picture of the purchase returns day book in your mind.

## Example

Look at the example on the opposite page. We purchased a quantity of desk diaries from S. Jones (Wholesale Stationery Supplies Ltd), and unfortunately found that some of them were faulty. We told them about the problem and they agreed that we could return them. S. Jones then issued us with a credit note for the value of the faulty goods, plus VAT, a total of £235.00. The credit note is dated 10th February. We now enter the details of this credit note in our purchase returns day book as shown opposite.

1. On the far left we enter the date, followed by the name of the supplier.

2. In the third column we enter our own credit note number from our own sequences of numbers, in this case 2/1 meaning February, credit note number one. (We do not enter S. Jones' own number SJ/02206.)

3. In the correct columns we then enter the net amount of the credit, i.e. excluding VAT—£200.00—and the VAT element of £35.00 in the VAT column.

4. If our purchase returns day book has additional analysis columns, we 'analyse' the net amount into the correct column, in this case stationery.

The additional analysis columns can be useful, because they help us to check the value of each category of goods returned.

```
         Entwhistle & Co – Builders Merchants
              Ferry Yard, Anytown, Anyshire

  To: D. Davidson (Builder)        2nd January 200X
      1 Main Street
      Anytown
      Lancs

      INVOICE No:-              501

  100 English facing bricks @ 28p      £     28.00
  24 breeze blocks @ 50p                     12.00
  Assorted cut timber                       320.00
  Screws, nails and ironmongery              40.00
  5 rolls vinyl wallpaper  @ £ 3             15.00
                                            415.00

  VAT @ 17½%                                  72.63

  Total                                      487.63


  Terms strictly 30 days net
```

Fig. 10. Example of a sales invoice.

**SALES DAY BOOK**

| Date | Customer | Inv. No. | Net.Inv. Value | VAT 17½% | Bricklyr Supplies | Carptry Supplies | Decor Supplies | Roofing Supplies |
|------|----------|----------|----------------|----------|-------------------|------------------|----------------|------------------|
| 200X |          |          |                |          |                   |                  |                |                  |
| Jan 2 | D. Davidson | SO1 | 415.00 | 72.63 | 40.00 | 360.00 | 15.00 | |
| 4 | Kahn & Kahn | SO2 | 30.00 | 5.25 | | 30.00 | | |
| 5 | JBC Roofing | SO3 | 250.00 | 43.75 | | | | 250.00 |
| | | | 695.00 | 121.63 | 40.00 | 390.00 | 15.00 | 250.00 |

Fig. 11. The same sales invoice duly entered into the sales day book.

### A. Frazer records his sales

Let us suppose that A. Frazer is a business stationery supplier. He makes the following sales on monthly credit account during the month of June 200X:

200X
Jun 1   Edwards' Garage       150 white A4 envelopes = £4.00
                              150 small manilla envelopes = £4.00
     6  A. K. Insurance
           Services           150 large envelopes = £10.00
     8  J.B.C. Roofing        4 calculators @ £12.50 ea
    30  F. Evans              20 note pads = £21.60

Let's suppose that, like many firms, A. Frazer has his sales invoices pre-printed with numbers in a chronological sequence and that the above sales were billed on invoice numbers 961/2/3 and 4. He would write the invoice dates followed by the names of the customers in the first two columns of his sales day book. In the next column he would enter the net invoice values (i.e. excluding VAT), and in the next the amounts of VAT charged on each invoice. Further to the right, he would then 'analyse' the net amounts into handy reference columns. (This analysis will be useful to him later, as he will be able to tell quickly what value of his sales were for stationery, what for calculators, and what for any other categories which he may decide to have analysis columns for.)

| Date | Supplier | Inv. No | Net Inv. Value | VAT 17½% | Statnry | Calcs. |
|------|----------|---------|----------------|----------|---------|--------|
| 200X | | | | | | |
| Jun 1 | Edwards' Garage | 961 | 8.00 | 1.40 | 8.00 | |
| 6 | A.K. Insurance Servs | 2 | 10.00 | 1.75 | 10.00 | |
| 8 | J.B.C. Roofing | 3 | 50.00 | 8.75 | | 50.00 |
| 30 | F. Evans | 4 | 21.60 | 3.78 | 21.60 | |
| | | | 89.60 | 15.68 | 39.60 | 50.00 |

Fig. 12. Extract from A. Frazer's sales day book.

```
CREDIT NOTE No: 0135                     8 March 200X

To authorised return of                           £   p
5 × 10 litre cans of white gloss paint          50.00
returned as faulty
VAT @ 17½%                                        8.75
                                                 58.75


┌ Name of customer        ┐
│ D. Davidson (Builder)
│ 1, Main Street
│ Anytown
└ Lancs                    ┘
```

Fig. 13. Example of a credit note inwards.

## SALES RETURNS DAY BOOK

| Date | Customer | C/N No | Net Inv Value | VAT 17½% | Bricklayer Supplies | Carpentry Supplies | Decor Supplies |
|------|----------|--------|---------------|----------|---------------------|--------------------|----------------|
| 200X | | | | | | | |
| Mar 8 | D. Davidson | 135 | 50.00 | 8.75 | | | 50.00 |
| 10 | J.B.C. Roofing | 6 | 60.00 | 10.50 | 60.00 | | |
| | | | 110.00 | 19.25 | 60.00 | | 50.00 |

Fig. 14. The same credit note outwards duly entered
into the sales returns day book.

# 11   The sales returns day book

## When a customer asks for a credit

When a firm sells goods or services on credit, it records the details in the sales day book, as we saw on the previous pages. Sometimes, however, the customer has to return what he has bought. For example the goods may be faulty, or arrived damaged. In this case, the firm sends a **credit note** to the customer, and the value of the credit note is then entered up in the sales returns day book.

All the points which apply to the sales day book also apply to the sales returns day book, even the ruling is identical, though of course the transaction details may be different. So once you have become familiar with the ruling of a typical sales day book, you will also have a picture of the sales returns day book in your mind.

## Example

Look at the example on the opposite page. We sold 50 litres of white gloss paint to D. Davidson (Builders) who unfortunately found them to be faulty. They returned the goods to us and we issued them with a credit note for the value plus VAT, a total of £58.75. The credit note is dated 8 March 200X. We now enter the details of this credit note in our sales returns day book as shown opposite.

1.   On the far left we enter the date, followed by the name of the customer.

2.   In the third column we enter the credit note number (this is usually pre-printed on credit notes outwards, but if not it must be allocated from a chronological sequence).

3.   In the correct columns we then enter the amounts of the credit, i.e. excluding VAT— £50.00—and the VAT element of £8.75 in the VAT column.

4.   If our sales returns day book has additional analysis columns, we 'analyse' the net amount into the correct one, in this case *Decorators' supplies*.

The additional analysis columns can be useful, because they help us to check the value of each category of goods returned.

```
A. FRAZER & CO, 10 THE PARADE, ANYTOWN AN1 1YT

Received from   F. Evans
for      Stationery                          £   20–00
Signed           A. Frazer          Date   16.6.0X
```

```
                        BARSHIRE BANK PLC
Barshire House, Barton                    1.6.  20  0X

Pay   D. DAVIDSON

Twenty one pounds only              21.00

                                    A.K. INSURANCE
                                       B. Jones
```

## CASH BOOK

*Dr. (Receipts)*        *(Payments)  Cr.*

| Date | Particulars | Fo. | Discount | Cash | Bank | Date | Particulars | Fo. | Discount | Cash | Bank |
|---|---|---|---|---|---|---|---|---|---|---|---|
| June 1 | Balance | b/d | | 50.00 | 1,750.00 | Jun 1 | Razi & Thaung | BL3 | | | 40.00 |
| 2 | Edwards Garage | SL2 | 2.50 | | 97.50 | 1 | D. Davidson | BL5 | | | 21.00 |
| 8 | Cash Sales | NL2 | | 7.50 | | 9 | A.T. Office Supplies | BL4 | | 100.00 | |
| 9 | C.Jones | SL5 | | | 12.50 | 12 | Cash | ¢ | | | 290.00 |
| 12 | Bank | ¢ | | 290.00 | | 14 | Wages | NL8 | | 240.00 | |
| 15 | J.B.C. Roofing | SL7 | | 110.00 | | 14 | Petty Cash | PCB3 | | 50.00 | |
| 16 | Cash Sales | NL2 | | 20.00 | | 20 | M. Bandura | BL6 | | 30.00 | |
| 24 | Eliot Transport | SL8 | 5.00 | | 200.00 | 22 | L. Cleaves | BL12 | 4.87 | | 190.00 |
| 24 | Morgan & Baldwyn | SL1 | | | 42.50 | 22 | Van den Burgh | BL7 | | | 200.00 |
| 30 | Cash | ¢ | | | 7.50 | 30 | Interest and | | | | |
| | | | | | | | bank charges | | | | 20.00 |
| | | | | | | 30 | Bank | ¢ | | 7.50 | |
| | | | | | | 30 | Balance | c/d | | 50.00 | 1,349.00 |
| | | | 7.50 | 477.50 | 2,110.00 | | | | 4.87 | 477.50 | 2,110.00 |

Fig. 15. Examples of cash book entries concerning money received, and a payment
by cheque.

## What is the cash book?

The cash book is where we record the firm's cash and cheque transactions. In it we record all the payments coming in and all the payments going out. Like the four day books it is a book of prime entry: it is the first place we record a transaction. However, unlike the day books, it is also a book of account, i.e. part of the ledger. The cash book and petty cash book are the only ones with this dual status.

The cashier is responsible for writing cheques to pay bills, banking money received and for drawing funds for petty cash. Most people are familiar with the process of writing cheques, banking funds and drawing cash from banks so no treatment of this will be given here. Similarly most people understand what payments by standing order and direct debit mean. What they may not be familiar with, however is receiving and making payments by electronic means, e.g. BACS and CHAPS transfers. Both are electronic forms of funds transfer for which a form has to be completed at the bank branch. BACS takes around four working days to reach the recipient, but CHAPS payments are usually received same day.

The advantages of making payments by BACS or CHAPS include:

- No need to write individual cheques.
- The payments are more secure, as they are not physically handled in any form.

The advantages of receiving payments in this way, include:

- The funds are available immediately the instruction is received by recipient's bank branch, as no clearance time is needed.
- They are less time-consuming as the need to visit the bank to pay in a cheque is eliminated.
- No bank paying-in slip has to be filled in.
- The payments are more secure as the funds are not physically handled.

## Recording cash and bank transactions

The cash book is where we first record the details of cash and banking transactions. This includes all cash or cheques received from such customers as Mr Jones or JBC Roofing (see opposite) or indeed from anyone else, and all cash or cheques paid out to suppliers or to anyone else (disbursements). Banks debit firms directly for their services—they don't send out invoices for payment of interest and bank charges. The firm must record details of these amounts in the cash book as soon as it knows them, for example from the bank statement which shows them.

## Source documents

To write up the cash book we need:

- Cheque book stubs (counterfoils) and paying-in book stubs (counterfoils) for all transactions which involve the bank account.

- Any bank advice slips, bank statements or other information received from the bank from time to time. This might for example include a letter advising that a customer's cheque has been returned unpaid by their bank owing to lack of funds, or information on standing orders, direct debits or bank charges and so on: anything that tells us about any payments going out from, or receipts coming into, the firm's account.

- Cash purchase invoices, receipts for cash paid out, and copies of receipts given for cash paid in.

- Any payment advice slips which arrived with cheques or cash received: these will show for example whether an early settlement discount has been claimed.

## Entering debits and credits

All the cash and cheques we receive are entered on the left-hand side of the cash book (debits). All the cheques we write, and cash we pay are entered on the right-hand side (credits).

**CASH BOOK**

| Dr. | | | | | | | | | Cr. |
|---|---|---|---|---|---|---|---|---|---|
| Date | Particulars | Fo. | Cash | Bank | Date | Particulars | Fo. | Cash | Bank |
| 200X | | | | | 200X | | | | |
| Mar 1 | Balance | b/d | | 1,500.00 | Mar 28 | S. Jones | BL6 | | 48.60 |
| 19 | Cash sales | NL4 | 81.00 | | 31 | Salaries | NL9 | | 600.00 |
| 31 | Bank | ¢ | 303.16 | | 31 | Cash | ¢ | | 303.16 |
| | | | | | 31 | Wages | NL14 | 384.16 | |
| | | | | | 31 | Balance | c/d | 0.00 | 548.24 |
| | | | 384.16 | 1,500.00 | | | | 384.16 | 1,500.00 |
| Apl 1 | Balance | b/d | 0.00 | 548.24 | | | | | |

Fig. 16. Entering details of cash and bank transactions
into the cash book.

## Cash book entry step by step

1. Turn to your first receipt counterfoil for the period you are handling (day, week, month). Record, in the first column of the cash book on the far left the date of the transaction. To help keep the page neat and uncluttered, just enter the year once at the top of all the entries for that year. Do the same for the start of each new month.

2. Write the payer's name in the second column (cash sales in the example opposite).

3. The third column is for the folio reference which you will enter later. Leave it blank at this stage.

4. In the fourth column (not used in example) enter the amount of any early settlement discount.

5. In the fifth column (cash) enter the amount of cash received, £81.00.

6. Now turn to your paying-in book counterfoils and do exactly the same— except for one small difference: enter the amounts in the sixth (bank) column this time. Enter in the first (date) column the date of the bank lodgement as shown on the front of the counterfoil. The date written in ink by the payer-in (the cashier) might be different from the bank branch stamp on the counterfoil; the paying-in book might have been written up the day before the lodgment, and lodged in a nightsafe at the bank after the close of business, to be paid in properly the next day. Where there is a difference, you should use the date shown on the bank's stamp.

7. Turn the counterfoil for the period over and look on its reverse side. Each counterfoil represents a payment into the bank of a sum of money in cash and/or cheques; it should bear the names of people from whom the cheques have been received (the drawers). Enter in the second column of the cash book (name column) the first name from this list.

8. Again, the third column is for the folio reference, which you will enter later. Leave it blank for now.

9. Enter in the fourth column (discounts) the details of any discount allowed.

10. Enter in the sixth column the actual amount of the cheque.

11. Repeat steps 6 to 10 for all the cheques in the list.

12. Now enter the cash paid in to the bank, if any.

13. Write the word 'cash' in the second column (since it is the cashier who is paying it in).

14. Enter amount in the sixth column (bank column).

## CASH BOOK OF A. FRAZER

| Dr. | | | | | Cr. | | | | |
|---|---|---|---|---|---|---|---|---|---|
| Date 200X | Particulars | Fo. | Discount | Cash | Bank | Date 200X | Particulars | Fo. | Discount | Cash | Bank |

| Dr. Date 200X | Particulars | Fo. | Discount | Cash | Bank | Cr. Date 200X | Particulars | Fo. | Discount | Cash | Bank |
|---|---|---|---|---|---|---|---|---|---|---|---|
| Aug1 | Balance | b/d | | 50.00 | | Aug 1 | Balance | b/d | | | 1,100.00 |
| 2 | Edwards Garage | SL60 | 0.72 | | 27.88 | 30 | Wages | NL8 | | | 800.00 |
| 12 | Razi & Thaung | SL9 | 10.07 | | 392.43 | 30 | A.T. Office | | | | |
| 20 | Morgan & Baldwyn | SL11 | | | 560.63 | | Suppls | BL5 | 5.01 | | 195.50 |
| | | | | | | 30 | F. Evans | BL6 | | | 258.00 |
| 31 | Balance | c/d | | | 1,372.56 | 31 | Balance | c/d | | 50.00 | |
| | | | 10.79 | 50.00 | 2,353.50 | | | | 5.01 | 50.00 | 2,353.50 |
| Sept 1 | Balance | b/d | | 50.00 | | Sep 1 | Balance | b/d | | | 1,372.56 |

Fig. 17. A. Frazer's cash book.

*Notes*

The balance of A. Frazer's cash as at 1st August 200X was £50.00 and there was a bank overdraft of £1,100. On 2nd August a cheque was received from Edwards' Garage for £27.88 in full settlement of its bill of £28.60. On checking, it is found that discount has been properly deducted. On the 12th a cheque was received from Razi and Thaung for £392.43 in full settlement of their a/c in the sum of £402.50, after properly deducting 2½% discount for settlement within 7 days. On the 20th a cheque was received from Morgan and Baldwyn in the sum of £560.63 in full settlement of a/c in the sum of £575.00, after deducting 2½% discount for payment within 7 days. On checking it is found that the cheque is dated 14 days after the invoice date. On the 30th £800.00 cash was drawn for wages, a cheque for £195.50 was paid to A. T. Office Supplies after deducting 2½% for payment within 28 days and a cheque for £258 was paid to F. Evans.

Write up his cash book for the month. (Worked answer below.)

1. No discount has been entered for Morgan and Baldwyn as they were not eligible for the discount they claimed. Only £560.63 would, therefore, be deducted from their ledger account and they would remain indebted to the firm for the remaining £14.37.

2. If the cheque for £195.50 takes into account a 2½% discount then the discount figure will be £5.01, since if £195.50 = 97.5% then 1% =

$$\frac{£195.50}{97.5}$$

= £2.00½ and 100% = £2.00½ × 100 = £200.50, of which 2½% = £5.01

3. It has been regarded as unnecessary to debit the £800 drawn from the bank to cash since it went straight out again in wages; the debit entry has, thus, been made directly to wages account.

# 14 The cash book: money paid out

## Posting to the credit page

Now we need to do our first piece of double entry book-keeping. Since the bank has been debited with the money the cashier paid in, the cashier must be credited with the same amount. Otherwise, the cashier will appear to remain indebted for a sum he/she no longer has.

## Step by step

1. Enter the date of the paying-in slip in the date column of the right hand (credit page) of the cash book.

2. In the second (name) column, enter the word 'bank', since it is the bank which is taking the money from the cashier.

3. In the fifth (cash) column, enter the amount of the payment. You have now given the cashier credit for that amount—and so you should! They no longer have it: they have given it to the bank.

4. Now let's do the other credit side entries. Take the first of the receipt vouchers for cash paid out for the period (day, week, month). Enter the date (taken from the receipt voucher) in the appropriate column of the right hand page (see step 1 on the previous page).

5. In the second column enter the name of the person to whom the cash was paid.

6. Discount details probably won't be relevant here; such discounts arise from early settlement of credit accounts, usually by cheque rather than by cash. If any such account was settled in cash, the cashier would know about it: they would have been the one to arrange payment. In such cases enter the details in the fourth (discount) column.

7. In the fifth column enter the amount of cash paid out.

8. Turn to the first cheque book counterfoil for the period. In the first column of the right hand (credit) page, enter the cheque date.

9. In the second column enter the name of the payee (the person to whom the cheque is payable).

10. In the fourth column enter details of any discount received. You will find this from the copy of the payment advice slip outwards.

11. In the sixth (bank) column, enter the amount of the cheque.

12. When required, total both the debit and credit columns for both cash and bank. Enter balancing items, so that both sides add up to the same figure, narrating them 'balance c/d'.

13. Bring down the balancing items on the opposite sides as the opening balances for the next period, narrating them 'balance b/d'.

```
┌─────────────────────────────────────────────────────────────┐
│                  BANK RECONCILIATION                          │
│                   as at 30 June 200X                          │
│                                                               │
│                                                               │
│  Balance as per cashbook (in favour)              910.00      │
│                                                               │
│  Add customer account                                         │
│    paid directly into the bank:                               │
│                          Watson                   180.00      │
│                                                 1,090.00      │
│                                                               │
│  Deduct dishonoured cheque:                                   │
│                          Davies                    50.00      │
│                                                 1,040.00      │
│                                                               │
│  Deduct standing order paid but not yet                       │
│    recorded in cash book:                                     │
│                     Wilson & Smith                 30.00      │
│  Updated balance as per cash book               1,010.00      │
│                                                               │
│                                                               │
│                                                               │
│  Balance as per bank statement (in favour)        880.00      │
│                                                               │
│  Deduct cheques drawn but not as yet                          │
│    presented for payment:                                     │
│                     Smith      30.00                          │
│                     Jones      40.00                          │
│                     Clarke     50.00             120.00       │
│                                                               │
│                                                               │
│                                                   760.00      │
│  Add lodgement 30 June not yet showing                        │
│    on bank statement                              250.00      │
│                                                               │
│  Balance as per cash book                       1,010.00      │
└─────────────────────────────────────────────────────────────┘
```

Fig. 18. Example of a bank reconciliation.

## 15   Disagreeing with the bank

### Cash book versus bank statement

Every cashier tries to keep the cash book as accurate and up to date as possible. Many receipts and many payments may have to be entered up each day. Then, at regular intervals, the firm receives bank statements from the bank—weekly, monthly or quarterly. Unfortunately, the balance shown on the cash book hardly ever agrees with the one shown on the bank statement! There can be various reasons for this.

### Noting unpresented cheques

When you get the bank statement and compare the balance with that shown in your cash book, you'll see that some cheques you drew have not yet been presented to the bank for payment: they simply don't appear on the bank statement at all, as yet. The cashier enters cheque transactions within a day or two of handling the cheques; but it could be days or even weeks before the payee presents them to your bank for payment.

### Noting bank lodgements

Payments into the bank will have been recorded in the cash book, but if they haven't yet been recorded by the bank they won't appear on the bank statement. This could happen, for example, if a bank statement was sent out between the time the cashier lodged the bankings in the night safe and the time he/she actually paid them in over the counter.

### Automatic payments

Payments by direct debit or standing order may have been omitted by the cashier, but they will still appear on the bank statement.

### Bank charges and interest

A cashier may know nothing about these until the bank statement arrives, containing the details.

### Returned cheques

A customer's cheque may have been returned unpaid—'bounced' in popular jargon. The cash book will show the money having been received, but the bank won't have received funds for the cheque; so the statement will show a contra entry.

### Errors

The cashier could simply have made an error. Bank errors can happen, but they are rare.

## BANK RECONCILIATION AS AT (*date...*)

| | £ p | |
|---|---|---|
| Balance as per cash book | 320.00 | (in favour) |
| Add customer's account | | |
| paid by telephone banking (M. Bandura) | 40.00 | |
| | 360.00 | (in favour) |
| Deduct dishonoured cheque (D. Davidson) | 10.00 | |
| | 350.00 | (in favour) |
| | | |
| Deduct bank charges | 50.00 | |
| Updated balance as per cash book | 300.00 | (in favour) |
| | | |
| Balance as per bank statement | 500.00 | (in favour) |
| Deduct cheque drawn but not yet | | |
| presented for payment: S. Jones | 200.00 | |
| Balance as per cash book | 300.00 | (in favour) |

Fig. 19. Worked example of a bank reconciliation statement.

On comparing A. Frazer's bank balance as per bank statement with his bank balance as per cash book, it is found that the former shows £500 in favour while the latter shows £320 in favour. In looking for the reasons we find that a cheque drawn by D. Davidson in favour of the firm in the sum of £10.00 has been dishonoured, a cheque drawn by the firm in favour of S. Jones for £200 has not yet been presented by his bank for payment, bank charges have been made in the sum of £50 and a customer's (M. Bandura's) bill of £40.00 has been paid via telephone banking and the cashier was not aware of this. Figure 19 shows how we would write up a Bank Reconciliation Statement.

# 16   The bank reconciliation

If a discrepancy arose from just one source it would be easy enough to deal with, but usually there are several discrepancies, some distorting the credit side and some distorting the debit side, and liable to cause confusion.

To remove this confusion, and explain the discrepancies, the cashier draws up a bank reconciliation statement. The cashier, after all, is responsible for the firm's money, so if the bank statement disagrees with the cash book balance, he/she must clearly show the reason why.

There are three ways of reconciling the two accounts:

1. Reconcile cash book to bank statement: starting with the closing cash book balance, and check through step by step towards the bank balance, explaining the discrepancies as we go.

2. Reconcile the bank statement to the cash book: the opposite process (see Figure 19).

3. Correct all the errors and omissions on both the cashier's part and the bank's part, showing how we did it, until we end up with the same balance from both viewpoints. (See Figures 18 and 20.)

The third way is usually the best since it is easier to understand. We'll see how to write up a bank reconciliation statement, step by step, on the following pages.

**What you need**
- the cash book
- the bank statements for the period (week, month, quarter).

Remember, a page of figures can be bewildering to your reader, who may not understand book-keeping as well as you, or have the time or patience to make sense of muddled words and figures. Simplicity and clarity should be your goal. Head all your cash columns £ and p to avoid having to write these symbols against every single entry. Likewise, when writing dates record the month once only, followed by the individual days. Put a clear heading against the left of each line of your figures. You will probably need two cash columns, one for sub-totalling particular types of transactions. For example, if there are three unpresented cheques you would add their values in a left hand column, and place the subtotal in a main right hand column.

## BANK RECONCILIATION AS AT (*date...*)

|                                                         | £      p                  |
|---------------------------------------------------------|---------------------------|
| Balance as per cash book                                | 780.00 (overdrawn)        |
| Add dishonoured cheque: D. Davidson                     | 10.00                     |
|                                                         | 790.00 (overdrawn)        |
| Add bank charges                                        | 50.00                     |
|                                                         | 840.00 (overdrawn)        |
| Deduct customer's account paid by telephone banking: M. Bandura | 40.00             |
| Updated balance as per cash book                        | 800.00 (overdrawn)        |
| Balance as per bank statement                           | 600.00 (overdrawn)        |
| Add cheque drawn but not yet presented for payment: S. Jones | 200.00               |
| Balance as per cash book                                | 800.00 (overdrawn)        |

Fig. 20. Suppose the same circumstances as in the worked example on page 34 were true except that the balance as per bank statement was £600 overdrawn and the balance as per cash book was £780 overdrawn. This figure shows what the bank reconciliation would look like.

## Bank reconciliation step by step

1. Compare the balances of the bank statement and the cash book as at the end of the accounting period you are checking. If they disagree then a bank reconciliation will be needed. Proceed as follows.

2. Can you see on the statement any standing orders (STOs), direct debits (DDRs) or bank charges? These items may not have been recorded in your cashbook as yet. Also, are there any returned ('bounced') cheques? If there are, they will appear as consecutive entries, or at least close together, identical but appearing on opposite sides (Dr and Cr) and will be annotated '₵', 'Contra Entry', or 'Returned Cheque'.

3. Take a sheet of A4 paper and write 'Balance as per cash book'. Place the actual figure next to it on the right hand side of the page. State whether it is 'in favour' or 'overdrawn' (see example overleaf). It is important to use a term such as 'in favour' rather than 'in credit', since 'in credit' is ambiguous here. An 'in credit' bank balance means you are 'in the black', but an 'in credit' balance in the cashbook means you are 'in the red'. The terms 'in favour' and 'overdrawn' overcome this ambiguity, since they mean the same from both viewpoints, the firm's and the bank's.

4. List all the omissions on the cashier's part, in groups, e.g. listing STOs first, then DDRs, then bank charges, etc. Write your additions and deductions as you go to show what difference it would have made to the bank statement if such errors or omissions had not occurred. If you arrive at a figure that is equal to the bank statement balance then the job of reconciliation is done. Write against your final figure 'Corrected balance as per cashbook'. If this does not happen then proceed to reconcile the bank statement to the cashbook as follows.

## BANK RECONCILIATION
### as at 30 June 200X

| | | | | |
|---|---|---|---:|---:|
| Balance as per bank statement (in favour) | | | | 880.00 |
| Deduct cheques drawn but not as yet presented for payment: | | | | |
| | Smith | 30.00 | | |
| | Jones | 40.00 | | |
| | Clarke | 50.00 | | |
| | | | 120.00 | |
| | | | | 760.00 |
| Add lodgement 30 June not yet showing on bank statement: | | | | 250.00 |
| | | | | 1,010.00 |
| Deduct customer account paid directly into the bank: | | | | |
| | Watson | | | 180.00 |
| | | | | 830.00 |
| Add dishonoured cheque: | | | | |
| | Davies | | | 50.00 |
| | | | | 880.00 |
| Add standing order paid but not yet recorded in cash book: | | | | |
| | Wilson and Smith | | | 30.00 |
| Balance as per cash book | | | | 910.00 |

## BANK RECONCILIATION
### as at 30 June 200X

| | | | | |
|---|---|---|---:|---:|
| Balance as per cash book (in favour) | | | | 910.00 |
| Add cheques drawn but not as yet presented for payment: | | | | |
| | Smith | 30.00 | | |
| | Jones | 40.00 | | |
| | Clarke | 50.00 | | |
| | | | 120.00 | |
| | | | | 1,030.00 |
| Deduct dishonoured cheque: | | | | |
| | Davies | | | 50.00 |
| | | | | 980.00 |
| Deduct lodgement 30 June not yet showing on bank statement: | | | | 250.00 |
| | | | | 730.00 |
| Deduct standing order paid but not yet recorded in cash book: | | | | |
| | Wilson and Smith | | | 30.00 |
| | | | | 700.00 |
| Add customer account paid directly into the bank: | | | | |
| | Watson | | | 180.00 |
| Balance as per bank statement (in favour) | | | | 880.00 |

Fig. 21. The bank reconciliation method advised has been chosen for its simplicity and clarity. Above are worked examples of the two alternatives referred to on page 35; use them only if specifically requested by an examiner or employer.

5.  Check off each payment listed in the cash book against the bank statement. Tick each one in pencil in the cash book and on the bank statement as you go. As you will see, items on the credit side of your cash book appear on the debit side of the bank statement and vice versa. This is because the same account is seen from two opposite viewpoints: the cash book from the firm's and the bank statement from the bank's.

6.  Record next on your sheet the words 'Balance as per bank statement' ('in favour' or 'overdrawn', as appropriate) and place the actual figure next to it, on the right hand side of the page. Then list all the errors and omissions on the bank's part, in groups, e.g. listing unpresented cheques first, and then any unshown lodgements. Write your additions and deductions as you go to show what difference it would have made to the bank statement if such errors or omissions had not occurred.

7.  When you have listed all the errors and omissions, if you have done it correctly, the two balances should now match. If so, write against your latest figure 'Balance as per cash book' ('in favour' or 'overdrawn' as appropriate).

## Updating the cash book

The items in the first part of the reconciliation statement, i.e. the one that starts with balance as per cash book, represent items that the cashier had not previously known about. Now that they are known about the cashier can update the cash book by making the necessary entries.

Take the worked example in Fig. 19. Suppose the cashbook of A. Frazer and Co., balanced off for the month, appeared as shown in Fig. 22a. The balance as per cash book shows £320 in favour, while the balance as per bank statement shows £500 in favour. The reconciliation statement shown in Fig. 19 explains the differences. We can update the cash book by making the entries listed in the second part of the reconciliation, as this shows the entries that belong in but have not yet been made in the cash book. This is demonstrated in Fig. 22b.

So much for updating the accounts in accordance with the first part of the reconciliation statement, but what about the second part, the one that starts with the balance as per bank statement? Don't worry about that part. It would only update the bank statement and that is merely a copy from an account that is not ours to update. It is the bank's. We don't include the bank statement balance at all in the accounts. Even in the balance sheet the cash figure comes from the balance as per cash book. In any case, by the time the next statement arrives the figures missing from the current one will have been included.

## CASHBOOK

| | Cash | Bank Dr £ | | | Cash | Bank Cr £ |
|---|---|---|---|---|---|---|
| **200X** | | | | **200X** | | |
| Jun 1 | Balance b/d | 300.00 | | Jun 1 | I. Bodlavich | 80.00 |
| | L. Gregory | 410.00 | | | F. Khan | 120.00 |
| | D. Davidson | 10.00 | | Jun 26 | S. Jones | 200.00 |
| | | | | | Balance c/d | 320.00 |
| | | 720.00 | | | | 720.00 |
| | Balance b/d | 320.00 | | | | |

Fig. 22a. The cashbook before updating.

## CASHBOOK

| | Cash | Bank Dr £ | | | Cash | Bank Cr £ |
|---|---|---|---|---|---|---|
| **200X** | | | | **200X** | | |
| Jun 1 | Balance b/d | 300.00 | | Jun 1 | I. Bodlavich | 80.00 |
| | L. Gregory | 410.00 | | | F. Khan | 120.00 |
| | D. Davidson | 10.00 | | Jun 26 | S. Jones | 200.00 |
| | m. BARDURA £ | 40.00 | | | D. DAvidson £ | 10.00 |
| | | | | | Bank charges | 50.00 |
| | | | | | Balance c/d | 300.00 |
| | | 760.00 | | | | 760.00 |
| | Balance b/d | 300.00 | | | | |

The updates after the bank reconciliation

Fig. 22b. The cashbook after updating.

40

You have now crossed from single entry book-keeping into double entry accounting since the cash book bridges a gap between these two, being both a book of prime entry and part of the double entry system. In most accounts offices the keeping of the cash book is a specialised job. It is the task of the cashier, a position of considerable responsibility and attracting a higher salary than that of a day book clerk. For those of you already working in an accounts office, mastering this section could soon gain you promotion and pay rises.

## PETTY CASH BOOK

| Dr Receipts | Fo. | Date | Cr Details | Rec | Total | Motor exp. | Travlg exp. | Postage | Statnry | Cleaning |
|---|---|---|---|---|---|---|---|---|---|---|
| | | 200X | | | | | | | | |
| 50.00 | CB5 | May 1 | Cash | | | | | | | |
| | | 1 | Petrol | 5/1 | 10.00 | 10.00 | | | | |
| | | 2 | Fares | 5/2 | 3.20 | | 3.20 | | | |
| | | 5 | Petrol | 5/3 | 8.00 | 8.00 | | | | |
| | | 8 | Postage | 5/4 | 9.00 | | | 9.00 | | |
| | | 17 | Stationery | 5/5 | 1.30 | | | | 1.30 | |
| | | 22 | Fares | 5/6 | 1.40 | | 1.40 | | | |
| | | 25 | Fares | 5/7 | 1.40 | | 1.40 | | | |
| | | 26 | Petrol | 5/8 | 7.00 | 7.00 | | | | |
| | | 31 | Cleaning | 5/9 | 4.00 | | | | | 4.00 |
| | | 31 | Fares | 5/10 | 1.40 | | 1.40 | | | |
| | | 31 | Postage | 5/11 | 1.80 | | | 1.80 | | |
| | | | | | 48.50 | 25.00 | 7.40 | 10.80 | 1.30 | 4.00 |
| | | | | | | NL8 | NL9 | NL15 | NL17 | NL18 |
| 48.50 | CB6 | 31 | Cash | | | | | | | |
| | | 31 | Balance c/d | | 50.00 | | | | | |
| 98.50 | | | | | 98.50 | | | | | |
| 50.00 | | Jun 1 | Balance b/d | | | | | | | |

Fig. 23. Example of a completed petty cash book page.

**SMITHS GARAGES, NORTH CIRCULAR ROAD, NEWTON**
**Tel: Newton 0798**

Date: 9/10/0X

To: A, T. Office Supplies

. . . .    . . . .    . . . . £ 1.60

Received with thanks. H. Green

Fig. 24. Example of a simple cash purchase invoice, showing the supplier, goods or services supplied, date, and payment.

# 17 The petty cash book

## The petty cash float
The petty cashier looks after a small float such as £50 or £100 in notes and coins. It is used to pay for miscellaneous small office expenses such as staff travel and hotel accommodation, window cleaning, or small office items needed quickly. The petty cashier keeps account of all such transactions in the petty cash book.

## Using the imprest system
From time to time the cashier will reimburse the petty cashier for the amount he/she has spent on the firm's behalf: the float is replenished to the original amount. This is called an **imprest system**, and the original amount of the float e.g. £50 is called the **imprest amount**.

Without a petty cash book, cash expenditure on lots of very small items would mean making entries in the ledger, for each item of expense. But by using the petty cash book, such items can be analysed into useful columns which can be totalled up monthly, and just these totals—not all the details—posted to the ledger.

## Keeping the petty cash secure
The petty cashier is personally responsible for the petty cash, so he/she should:

- keep it locked away

- limit the number of people who have access, preferably to one person

- reconcile cash to records regularly (petty cash vouchers + receipts + cash = imprest value).

## A helpful analysis
Even if the firm is small, and the cashier keeps the petty cash book themself, it is still a very useful means of analysing and totalling office expenditure. Otherwise all such expenditure would have to be entered in the cash book and later posted individually to the ledger. The cash book, remember, has an analysis facility for double entry book-keeping. The analysis columns of the petty cash book act as a book of prime entry for the expenses in which the petty cashier becomes involved. From here they are later posted to the expense accounts in the ledger.

## Dual status of the petty cash book
The petty cash book, like the cash book, usually has a dual status: it is both a book of prime entry and part of the ledger. However, some firms treat it purely as a book of prime entry, to record transactions involving notes and coins. They then write up a 'petty cash account' in their general ledger. Here, however, we will treat it as part of the ledger. Unless told otherwise, you should do the same.

Like the other books of prime entry, such as the day books, the petty cash book usually has a few helpful analysis columns. But since it is also part of the ledger, it also needs to have both debit and credit columns.

| Dr. | | | | PETTY CASH BOOK | | | | | Cr. |
|---|---|---|---|---|---|---|---|---|---|
| Receipts | Fo. | Date | Details | Rec. no. | Total | Stnry | Trav. exp. | Tel. | Cleang. |
| | | 200X | | | | | | | |
| 50.00 | CB1 | Jan 1 | Bank | | | | | | |
| | | 6 | Stationery | 1/01 | 1.50 | 1.50 | | | |
| | | 17 | Trvlg exp. | 1/02 | 2.00 | | 2.00 | | |
| | | 26 | Telephone | 1/03 | 0.50 | | | 0.50 | |
| | | 28 | Wndw clnr | 1/04 | 8.00 | | | | 8.00 |
| | | | | | 12.00 | 1.50 | 2.00 | 0.50 | 8.00 |
| 12.00 | CB1 | 31 | | | | NL4 | NL6 | NL8 | NL9 |
| | | 31 | Balance c/d | | 50.00 | | | | |
| 62.00 | | | | | 62.00 | | | | |
| 50.00 | | Feb 1 | Balance b/d | | | | | | |

Fig. 25.

1. Suppose A. Frazer has only just started up in business and intends to use an imprest system for his petty cash transactions. (The firm's estimated turnover is below the VAT threshold so it does not intend to register as taxable. There is, therefore, no need to account for VAT in the petty cash book.) The transactions during its first month are as follows. Write up his petty cash book for the month.

Jan 1   Received cheque from cashier £50

  6   Paid for staples and glue £1.50

  17   Paid travelling expenses £2.00

  26   Refunded phone-call expenses 50p

  28   Paid window cleaner £8.00

  31   Received cheque from cashier to replenish the fund to the imprest amount of £50.00

2. A. Frazer is a Taxable firm for VAT purposes; this means that the VAT aspects of its transactions have to be recorded in its books. Suppose the firm's Petty Cash transactions for the month of December 200X are as follows. Write up his petty cash book for the month, using the imprest system. Assume, for the purpose of this exercise, that there is currently only one VAT rate in operation and that is 10%.

Opening balance £100.00, Dec 10 paid travelling expenses £20.00, Dec 15 refunded petrol expenses £10.00 and paid cleaner £16.00, Dec 21 bought parcel tape £1.85, Dec 31 received cheque from cashier to replenish the fund to the imprest figure of £100.00.

| Dr. | | | | PETTY CASH BOOK | | | | | | Cr. |
|---|---|---|---|---|---|---|---|---|---|---|
| Receipts | fo. | Date | Details | Rec. no. | Total | VAT | Trvlg. exp. | Motor exp. | Wages | Stnry. |
| | | 200X | | | | | | | | |
| 100.00 | | Dec 1 | Balance b/d | | | | | | | |
| | | 10 | Trv. exp | 12/01 | 20.00 | | 20.00 | | | |
| | | 15 | Petrol | 12/02 | 10.00 | 0.90 | | 9.10 | | |
| | | | Cleaner | 12/03 | 16.00 | | | | 16.00 | |
| | | 21 | Prcl tape | 12/04 | 1.85 | 0.16 | | | | 1.69 |
| | | | | | 47.85 | 1.06 | 20.00 | 9.10 | 16.00 | 1.69 |
| 47.85 | CB15 | 31 | Balance c/d | | 100.00 | NL11 | NL6 | NL7 | NL5 | NL9 |
| 147.85 | | | | | 147.85 | | | | | |
| | | 200X | | | | | | | | |
| 100.00 | | Jan 1 | Balance c/d | | | | | | | |

Fig. 26.

## What you need
- the petty cash book

- all the cash purchase invoices for the period.

## Preparation: numbering and dating
Sort all your cash purchase invoices (receipts) into date order, and number them. (The numbers already printed on them won't do: they are cash sales invoice numbers of the firms that issued them and no uniformity between them can be expected.) You need to give them consecutive numbers from your own numbering system, so that you can file them chronologically for each period. Many firms keep a list of such numbers for this purpose. Others give them a two part number made up of the month number (e.g. 3 for March) and a number from a consecutive list for that month.

## Value Added Tax (VAT)
The VAT may not be shown as a separate item on cash purchase invoices for small amounts. If not, the petty cashier will need to calculate the VAT content, if any, of each invoice total (see page 179). HM Revenue and Customs publish details of current VAT applications and rates, but a little experience will save the petty cashier having to check this every time. Briefly, if the current VAT rate is $17\frac{1}{2}\%$, the VAT content of such an invoice is worked out like this:

| | |
|---|---|
| Invoice amount: | £100 |
| Equivalent to: | 100% net amount plus $17\frac{1}{2}\%$ VAT |
| Therefore VAT element: | $\dfrac{17\frac{1}{2}\%}{100\% + 17\frac{1}{2}\%}$    or    $\dfrac{17.5 \times 100}{117.5}$ |
| Answer | £14.89 (not £17.50!) |

## Opening a new petty cashbook
When starting a new petty cash system (i.e. opening a new petty cash book) a sum of money will be entrusted as a float to the petty cashier, let's say £50.00. He/she immediately enters this on the debit (left) side, because he/she now 'owes' the cashier that amount.

# PETTY CASH BOOK

| Receipts | Fo. | Date | | Details | | Rec | Total | VAT | Trav. exp. | Stnry | Motor exp. | Post |
|---|---|---|---|---|---|---|---|---|---|---|---|---|
| | | 200X | | | | | | | | | | |
| 100.00 | CB6 | Feb | 1 | Cash | | | | | | | | |
| | | | 1 | Fares | | 2/1 | 5.00 | | 5.00 | | | |
| | | | 2 | Envelopes | | 2/2 | 7.00 | 1.04 | | 5.96 | | |
| | | | 4 | Petrol | | 2/3 | 8.00 | 1.19 | | | 6.81 | |
| | | | 7 | Petrol | | 2/4 | 9.00 | 1.34 | | | 7.66 | |
| | | | 16 | Postage | | 2/5 | 6.00 | 0.89 | | | | 5.11 |
| | | | 18 | Fares | | 2/6 | 3.00 | | 3.00 | | | |
| | | | 19 | Fares | | 2/7 | 3.00 | | 3.00 | | | |
| | | | 25 | Petrol | | 2/8 | 7.00 | 1.04 | | | 5.96 | |
| | | | 26 | Postage | | 2/9 | 4.50 | | | | | 4.50 |
| | | | 27 | Staples | | 2/10 | 2.00 | 0.30 | | 1.70 | | |
| | | | 28 | String | | 2/11 | 3.50 | 0.52 | | 2.98 | | |
| | | | | | | | 58.00 | 6.32 | 11.00 | 10.64 | 20.43 | 9.61 |
| 58.00 | CB7 | | 31 | Cash | | | | NL8 | NL6 | NL14 | NL11 | NL9 |
| | | | 31 | Balance | c/d | | 100.00 | | | | | |
| 158.00 | | | | | | | 158.00 | | | | | |
| 100.00 | | Mar | 1 | Balance | b/d | | | | | | | |

Fig. 27. Example of a completed page in a petty cash book.

46

**Step by step**

1.  Enter in the third column the date that the fund or float was received.

2.  Write in the fourth ('particulars') column the word 'cash' or 'bank' as appropriate, depending on whether the float came from the cashier by cash, or from the bank by cheque.

3.  Write the imprest amount in the first column (debit cash column). Unless the system is being started from scratch, this stage will have been completed previously. The procedure for all other entries will start from step 4 below.

4.  Record from each cash invoice the date, purchase invoice number, purpose of expenditure, gross and net invoice total and VAT, as shown on the page opposite. Enter the net total directly into a suitable analysis column.

5.  Whenever necessary (end of period, end of page) total up the two main columns. The cashier should reimburse the petty cash fund for what has been spent, to restore the fund to its original imprest figure. Then balance the two columns, just like any other ledger account: entering a balancing item (the difference between the two totals) to make each side add up to the same amount. That balancing item should be annotated 'balance c/d' (carried down). The counterpart of that balancing item should then be recorded after the totals as the *opening* figure for the *next* period and annotated 'balance b/d' (brought down).

6.  Next, total up each analysis column and the VAT column and cross check with the gross invoice total column, to make sure there are no mistakes.

**Entering the folio references**
Enter folio references for the debit side in the folio column, e.g. CB (cash book)7. Enter those relating to the credit side at the foot of their respective column totals: it is only the *totals* that will be posted to the ledger, e.g. travelling expenses, folio reference NL6 (Nominal Ledger item 6) in the example opposite.

# THE JOURNAL

| Date | Particulars | Fo. | Dr. | Cr. |
|------|-------------|-----|-----|-----|
| 200X | | | | |
| Feb 20 | Morgan and Baldwyn | SL15 | 25.00 | |
| | Sales | NL1 | | 25.00 |
| | To correct error of original entry | | | |
| 21 | Drawings | PL3 | 70.00 | |
| | Purchases | NL6 | | 70.00 |
| | To record goods taken from stock for private use | | | |
| 22 | Sundries: | | | |
| | Motor van 2 | NL39 | 8,000.00 | |
| | Edwards Garage | BL16 | | 8,000.00 |
| | Asset disposal A/C | NL40 | 3,350.00 | |
| | Motor van 1 | NL10 | | 3,350.00 |
| | Edwards Garage | BL16 | 2,000.00 | |
| | Asset disposal A/C | NL40 | | 2,000.00 |
| | Profit and loss A/C | NL41 | 1,350.00 | |
| | Asset disposal A/C | NL40 | | 1,350.00 |
| | Edwards Garage | BL16 | 6,000.00 | |
| | Bank | CB18 | | 6,000.00 |
| | To record the details of the purchase by cheque of a motorvan with part exchange on old motor van. | | | |

Fig. 28. Example of a complete page of journal entry. Note: You would normally expect provision for depreciation account to also feature in such a combination entry as this, but here it does not in the interests of simplicity.

# 19  The journal

## A general purpose record
A book of prime entry, the journal is simply a place for making the first record of any transaction for which no other prime entry book is suitable. It has debit and credit columns, but they are simpler than those of the cash book and petty cash book. The journal itself is not part of the accounts, merely one of the sources from which the accounts are written up later on.

## Examples of journal entries
Here are some examples of transactions you would need the journal to record:

- opening figures of a new business (e.g. list of assets)
- bad debts
- depreciation (e.g. of vehicles or equipment)
- purchase and sales of fixed assets (e.g. vehicles or plant)
- correction of errors
- goods taken for private use (as against for sale)
- ledger transfer needed if a book debt were sold.

## Information needed for an entry
When entering a transaction into the journal, you need to record these aspects of it:

- date
- accounts affected
- folio references
- amounts (debit and credit)
- reason.

Write a brief explanation against each entry. Separate each new entry from the one above by ruling a horizontal line right across the page (see Figure 28).

Sometimes it is a good idea to make combination double entries, i.e. where there is more than one debit entry per credit entry, or vice versa. This would be appropriate when journalising 'opening figures', which include various assets and liabilities, together with the capital figure to which they relate. A group of entries are recorded on the opposite page with the prefix 'Sundries', which all relate to trading in an old motor van for a new one.

On the next page we will see how to write up the journal step by step.

## THE JOURNAL

| Date | Particulars | Fo. | Dr. | Cr. |
|------|-------------|-----|-----|-----|
| 200X | | | | |
| May 28 | L. Cleese | SL6 | 60.00 | |
| | L. Cleaves | SL10 | | 60.00 |
| | To correct error | | | |
| | of commission | | | |
| 30 | Profit and loss A/C | NL30 | 85.00 | |
| | F. Evans | SL8 | | 85.00 |
| | To write off bad debt | | | |

Fig. 29. Journalising an item in the sales ledger.

1. Journalise the following:
On 28 May 200X it is discovered that L. Cleaves' a/c in the sales ledger has wrongly been debited with the sum of £60. Such sum should have been debited to L. Cleese's a/c instead. Two days later, F. Evans, a debtor of the firm, is declared bankrupt and the firm expects no ultimate settlement of his a/c in the sum of £85.00.

2. Using the following information, calculate the capital, journalise the opening figures and post them to the ledger for A. Frazer, a retail stationer, who started business on 1 April 200X. Cash at bank £1,450.00, cash in hand £50.00, office equipment £1,500.00, land and buildings £54,000, fixtures and fittings £4,000.00, a motor van £3,000.00 and stock £2,000.

## THE JOURNAL

| Date | Particulars | Fo. | Dr. | Cr. |
|------|-------------|-----|-----|-----|
| 200X | | | | |
| | Sundries | | | |
| Apr 1 | Land and buildings | NL1 | 54,000.00 | |
| | Fixtures and fittings | NL2 | 4,000.00 | |
| | Office equipment | NL3 | 1,500.00 | |
| | Motor van | NL4 | 3,000.00 | |
| | Stock | NL5 | 2,000.00 | |
| | Cash at bank | CB1 | 1,450.00 | |
| | Cash in hand | CB1 | 50.00 | |
| | Capital | NL6 | | 66,000.00 |
| | To record opening figures | | | |

Fig. 30. Journalising the opening figures.

50

## Using miscellaneous source documents

There are no routine source documents for this job, as there are for example for the purchase day book (purchase invoices) or for the cash book (cheque counterfoils etc). The journal is a miscellany, and its sources will be miscellaneous. They may be documented by nothing more than a rough note, if indeed they are documented at all. For example, the sales manager may pass a memo to the journal clerk saying that a customer has gone into liquidation, so that its debt to the firm will have to be written off. Similarly a roughly pencilled note from the accountant, saying what depreciation should apply to an asset, may be your only source document for an entry.

## Writing up the journal step by step

1.  Enter the date in column one (the date column).

2.  Enter the names of the ledger accounts which will be affected by this entry, e.g. Motor van account, or Profit and loss account, as in example 1 opposite. Indent the credit entry (usually the second entry). The folio column gives the 'address' of the account in question in the ledger, for example NL (nominal ledger), CB (cash book), PCB (petty cash book) and SL (sales ledger).

3.  Record the amounts against each ledger account name. Note: these last two steps provide the posting instructions for the ledger clerk. Many debit entries may have a common credit entry, as with opening figures. If so, prefix them with the word 'sundries'.

4.  Explain, briefly but precisely, your reason for the entry, e.g. 'To write off bad debt' or 'To record opening figures'.

5.  When you have finished, underline the entry right across the page.

## Filing source documents

When the day books have been written up the source documents should be filed. Bank statements are filed chronologically, purchase invoices alphabetically or numerically (if the latter there is an important caveat). It must be on the basis of a number you allocate, rather than the supplier's invoice number. Sales invoices are numbered by one of the following methods:

-  they are pre-printed with consecutive numbers;

-  the invoice clerk obtains consecutive numbers from a log book;

-  they are given numbers consisting of the year, month and consecutive number of issue in that month in the form of yy/mm/ consecutive number as and when they are produced.

**POSTAGE BOOK**

| Dr. | Date 200X | Particulars | Cr. £ p |
|---|---|---|---|
| 92.00 | Jan 1 | Balance b/d | |
| | 1 | Edwards | 20 |
| | 1 | Bandura | 26 |
| | 1 | Jones | 26 |
| | 1 | Northern Electricity | 1.30 |
| | 1 | J.B.C. Roofing | 20 |
| | 1 | Evans | 20 |
| | 4 | Eliot Transport | 26 |
| | 4 | Morgan and Baldwin | 26 |
| | 5 | Entwhistle | 2.60 |
| | 9 | Davidson | 26 |
| | 10 | A.T. Office Supplies | 20 |
| | 15 | Baker | 26 |
| | 25 | Cleaves | 26 |
| | 25 | Gange | 26 |
| | 25 | Entwhistle | 26 |
| | 28 | Keele Engineering | 20 |
| | 29 | Razi and Thaung | 2.60 |
| | 29 | Eliot Transport | 20 |
| | 29 | Inko | 20 |
| | 30 | Kahn and Kahn | 26 |
| | 31 | Keele Engineering | 1.30 |
| | 31 | Evans | 20 |
| | 31 | Jones | 20 |
| | 31 | Baker | 20 |
| | 31 | Edwards | 20 |
| 12.60 | 31 | $20 \times 36p + 20 \times 27p$ | |
| | 31 | Balance b/d | 92.00 |
| 104.60 | | | 104.60 |
| 92.00 | Feb 1 | Balance c/d | |

Fig. 31. Example of a postage book page.

This book is like the petty cash book, in that it is a subsidiary account book. It gives a useful record of a fund entrusted to an employee, in this case the postage clerk. This person may have several other junior jobs to do within the office, such as reception/telephonist.

The postage book works much like the petty cash book, except that there is no VAT to deal with, and no analysis columns. It, too, is run on an imprest system, whereby the fund is topped up from time to time to its original level (the imprest amount).

One big difference, however, is that the fund is not kept as notes and coins: cash received by the postage clerk is used immediately to buy postage stamps. The fund exists in the form of stamps, not cash.

It differs even more from the petty cash book, and indeed from any of the other books, because it is not even a book of prime entry, providing sources for ledger posting. So it is really on the edges of the accounting system. The real source of postage data for the ledger is the cash book: this records cash paid into the postage fund.

Neverthless, it is a useful financial record for the firm. It provides details of a current asset (even if small) in the form of postage stamps; it is the only source document from which this detail can be gleaned. The postage book also provides a record of the financial relationship between the postage clerk and the firm.

You can buy books specifically designed for this purpose, though any general notebook with cash columns can be ruled up to do the job.

### Writing up the postage book step by step
You will need:

- the receipt slips for stamps purchased (supplied by the Post Office);
- the stamped letters and/or parcels to be sent out.

Suppose the imprest amount was £92.00.

1. Record the date in the date column, with year/month to start.

2. Record the combined value of any stamps purchased, from the receipt slips, in the first (debit cash) column. In the third ('particulars') column record the breakdown of the stamps purchased, e.g. 20 × 36p and 20 × 27p as in the example opposite.

3. List the addressees' names shown on the envelopes or parcels, in the third column ('particulars'), recording against each in the fourth (credit cash) column the value of the stamps affixed.

4. When desired, the cashier can be asked to replenish the fund to the original imprest amount of £92.00. At such times the two columns should be totalled, treating the imprest figure as the balancing item.

## SALES DAY BOOK

| Date | Supplier | Inv. no. | Net. inv value | Stationery | Books |
|------|----------|---------|----------------|------------|-------|
| 200X | | | | | |
| Feb 4 | S. Jones | 2/1 | 200.00 | 200.00 | |

---

CB10

## CASH BOOK

| Date | Particulars | Fo. | Discount | Cash | Bank | Date | Particulars | Fo. | Discount | Cash | Bank |
|------|-------------|-----|----------|------|------|------|-------------|-----|----------|------|------|
| 200X | | | | | | 200X | | | | | |
| Feb 1 | Balance | b/d | | | 9,000.00 | Feb 1 | Petty cash | PC15 | | | 50.00 |
| 28 | S.Jones | SL17 | 10.00 | | 190.00 | 28 | Balance | c/d | | | 9,140.00 |
| | | | 10.00 | | 9,190.00 | | | | | | 9,190.00 |
| Mar 1 | Balance | b/d | | | 9,140.00 | | | | | | |

---

P15

## PETTY CASH BOOK

| Receipts | Fo. | Date | Details | Rec | Total Exp. | Motor Exp. | Trvlng Exp. |
|----------|-----|------|---------|-----|-----------|-----------|-------------|
| | | 200X | | | | | |
| 50.00 | CB10 | Feb 1 | Cash | | | | |
| | | 1 | Petrol | 5/1 | 10.00 | 10.00 | |
| | | 28 | Balance c/d | | 40.00 | | |
| 50.00 | | | | | 50.00 | 10.00 | |
| 40.00 | | Mar 1 | Balance b/d | | | NL9 | |

---

## JOURNAL

| Date | Particulars | Fo. | Dr. | Cr. |
|------|-------------|-----|-----|-----|
| 200X | | | | |
| Feb 21 | Drawings | PL3 | 70.00 | |
| | Purchases | NL6 | | 70.00 |
| | To record goods taken for private use | | | |

Fig. 32. Examples of entries in books of prime entry to be posted to the ledger (see page 58).

# 22　The ledger

## The firm's official record

The ledger is the 'official' record of a firm's accounts. We sometimes speak of the general ledger, the bought ledger, sales ledger and cash book separately—as if they were separate 'ledgers'. But to an accountant the ledger is a single unit, even if it is made up of physically separate books. The ledger is really a 'system' rather than a book. Whatever form it takes—books or computer disks, etc—'the ledger' means the master record of all the firm's financial affairs.

## Divisions of the ledger

We have already discovered two parts of the ledger—the cash book and the petty cash book—which also happen to be books of prime entry. The only difference in the ruling between that and the other divisions we will now deal with is that the latter are simpler. The cash book has three cash columns on each side; the other divisions of the ledger have only one. (However where ledger posting is done on a computer the format involves three columns, a debit and credit column and a running balance column. This is because the running balance can easily be calculated electronically—it doesn't call on the time and effort of the book-keeper. In manual systems, working out such running balances is considered a waste of time.)

The other ledger divisions are:

- the general ledger (often called the nominal ledger)

- the personal ledger, subdivided into bought ledger (or purchase ledger) and sales ledger (or debtors ledger)

- a private ledger is sometimes kept, in which capital items are posted, for example proprietor's drawings. It is sometimes kept away from staff because the proprietor considers such information confidential.

## The nominal and personal ledger

In the nominal ledger the impersonal aspects of transactions are posted, for example purchases, sales figures, wages, stationery and asset purchases. In the personal ledger the personal side of each transaction is posted, i.e. the credit to suppliers' accounts when the firm has purchased something, and the debit to customers' accounts when the firm has sold something.

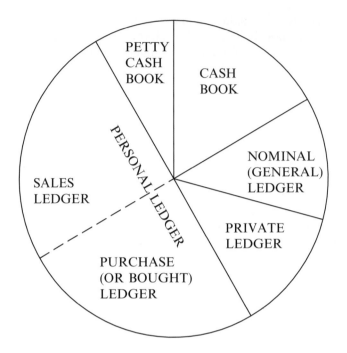

Fig. 33. The ledger.

### Different accounts within the ledger

Each part of the ledger contains a number of different accounts—one for each expense item, revenue asset or liability, as they will appear in the final accounts. For example, there will be an account for purchases, an account for sales, an account for wages, and a separate account for each asset such as Motor car 1 account, Motor car 2 account or Printing machine account, and so on.

### A variety of forms

Though the ruling of each type of book is reasonably standard, both the ledger and books of prime entry are found in a variety of forms. Indeed, they don't have to be 'books' at all. They can be sheets of analysis paper in a loose leaf binder, or written into a computer program so that the rulings appear on a VDU screen. Entries are then made via the keyboard rather than with pen and paper.

In a loose leaf ledger system these divisions (sales, purchases, nominal, etc.) may take the form of cardboard page dividers. If bound books are used, each division may be a physically separate bound book. The personal ledger (purchase ledger/sales ledger) will contain a separate account for each supplier and customer. The arrangement of accounts in each division is flexible.

### Post only from books of prime entry

Nothing should ever be posted into the ledger except from the books of prime entry.

Never, for example, post information into the ledger directly from such things as invoices, bank statements, cheque counterfoils, petty cash receipt slips and so on. These are source documents for the books of prime entry.

### Recording each transaction twice

We have already seen how each transaction in double entry book-keeping has two aspects—a debit and a credit. So each transaction has to be recorded in two separate places, on the debit side and on the credit side. It follows that at any moment in time the total number of debit entries must exactly equal the total of credit entries (unless a mistake has been made). In a small office, one ledger clerk will probably handle all the divisions (except perhaps the cash book). In a large firm there may be a separate bought ledger clerk, sales ledger clerk, and so on.

## SALES LEDGER

| p17 | | | | | | | | |
|---|---|---|---|---|---|---|---|---|
| | | | | *S. Jones* | | | | |
| | | | | 200X | | | | |
| Feb 4 | Sales | NL7 | 200.00 | Feb | 28 | Bank | CB10 | 190.00 |
| | | | | | 28 | Discount allowed | NL8 | 10.00 |
| | | | 235.00 | | | | | 200.00 |

## NOMINAL LEDGER

| p6 | | | | |
|---|---|---|---|---|
| | | *Purchases* | | |
| | | 200X | | |
| | | Feb 21 | Drawings | PL3 | 70.00 |

| p7 | | | | |
|---|---|---|---|---|
| | | *Sales* | | |
| | | 200X | | |
| | | Feb 4 | S. Jones | SL17 | 200.00 |

| p8 | | | |
|---|---|---|---|
| | *Discount Allowed* | | |
| 200X | | | |
| Feb 28 S. Jones | SL17 | 10.00 | |

| p9 | | | |
|---|---|---|---|
| | *Motor Expenses* | | |
| 200X | | | |
| Feb 1 | Petty cash | PC15 | 10.00 |

## PRIVATE LEDGER

| p3 | | |
|---|---|---|
| | *Drawings* | |
| 200X | | |
| Feb 21 Purchases NL6 | 70.00 | |

Fig. 34. Postings to the ledger from the prime entries on page 54.

## 23 Posting to the ledger from the day books

### What you will need
- The ledger in all its parts—all the books or sheets that make up the complete ledger or at least the part you are concerned with, e.g. the purchase ledger.

- All the books of prime entry, or those you are concerned with, e.g. the purchase day book.

### Posting from the purchase day book to the ledger
1. Turn to the start of the entries in the purchase day book as yet unposted to the ledger. Your first job is to post each purchase invoice (gross) to the credit of the supplier concerned, in their personal ledger account. The personal ledger should have an index of supplier's names, telling you on what page in the ledger you will find their account. (If no account exists, you will need to open one. Just head a new page with the supplier's name, and remember to list it in the index.)

2. In the first (date) column, write the date of entry.

3. Write the name of the account to which the other side of the transaction will be posted, in column 2 ('particulars').

4. In the fourth (cash) column record the gross value, in other words including VAT, of the transaction.

5. Now make the dual aspect of these postings: post the column totals for the net amount (i.e. net goods value) and VAT, to the debit of purchases and VAT accounts respectively. The procedure is the same as for posting the personal side of the transaction, following steps 1 to 4.

### Posting from the purchase returns day book to the ledger
This is the reverse of posting from the purchase day book. This time you debit personal accounts in the bought ledger, and credit the VAT account and a purchase returns account in the nominal ledger.

### Posting from the sales day book
This is just like posting from the purchase day book, except that you debit personal accounts in the sales ledger, and credit the VAT account and a sales account in the nominal ledger.

### Posting from the sales returns day book
This is the reverse of posting from the sales day book: you credit personal accounts in the sales ledger, and debit the VAT account and a sales account in the nominal ledger.

| Dr. | | | | A. T. Office Supplies | | | | Cr. |
|---|---|---|---|---|---|---|---|---|
| 200X | | | | | 200X | | | |
| | | | | | May 1 | Balance | c/d | 380.00 |
| | | | | | 26 | Purchases | NL9 | 620.00 |
| May | 28 | Bank | CB17 | 380.00 | | | | |
| | 31 | Balance | c/d | 620.00 | | | | |
| | | | | 1,000.00 | | | | 1,000.00 |
| | | | | | Jun 1 | Balance | b/d | 620.00 |

Fig. 35. Postings to the purchase ledger.

### 1. Postings to the purchase ledger

Suppose that, as at the last day of April 200X, A. Frazer owed A. T. Office Supplies the sum of £380.00. On the 26 May the firm purchased further goods from A. T. Office Supplies for £620. On 28 May the firm paid its April statement by cheque. This is what the ledger postings would look like (*and remember, they have to be recorded in the books of prime entry first*).

### 2. Postings to the sales ledger

Suppose that K. Gange is a customer of A. Frazer, and at the close of last month (January 200X) his a/c balance stood at £2,100.00. Suppose that on 4 February Gange returned goods to the value of £100.00. On 6 February Gange purchased a further £1,000 worth of goods. On 12 February he paid his January a/c, after deducting the returned goods and a 2½% agreed discount for payment within 14 days. Gange then purchased a further £980.00 worth of goods on 18 February and then £220.00 worth of goods on 26 February. This is what the ledger postings would look like:

| Dr. | | | | | K. Gange | | | Cr. |
|---|---|---|---|---|---|---|---|---|
| 200X | | | | | 200X | | | |
| Feb | 1 | Balance | b/d | 2,100.00 | Feb 4 | Sales returns | NL19 | 100.00 |
| | 6 | Sales | NL18 | 1,000.00 | | | | |
| | | | | | 12 | Bank | CB6 | 1,950.00 |
| | 18 | Sales | NL18 | 980.00 | 12 | Discount allowed | NL22 | 50.00 |
| | 26 | Sales | NL18 | 220.00 | 28 | Balance | c/d | 2,200.00 |
| | | | | 4,300.00 | | | | 4,300.00 |
| Mar | 1 | Balance | b/d | 2,200.00 | | | | |

Fig. 36. Postings to the sales ledger.

# 24 Posting to the ledger from the cash book

The cash book entries are, by their very nature, one side of the double entry. All you have to do now is to make the other side of the entry:

## Step by step

1.  Every time you post in the cash book, make an opposite posting to the relevant personal account in the bought or sales ledger as appropriate. The narration against each of these postings will be 'cash' (if the payment was in the cash column of the cash book) or 'bank' (if it was in the bank column). Now you have to post any discounts from the discounts column. Remember, although the cash book is part of the ledger, this column does not have such status; it is a single entry element sitting inside a ledger division, while not exactly being part of it. So the postings from the discounts column must be twofold, just as for any other prime entry source.

2.  Post the discounts to the correct personal accounts, making sure they are to the opposite sides to the ones on which they appear in the cash book.

3.  Post the column totals to the other side of the 'Discount allowed' or 'Discount received' accounts in the nominal ledger as applicable, to complete your dual posting. Use the name of the account to which the dual posting has gone for this purpose in all ledger posting.

## Posting from the petty cash book

The petty cash book may, or may not, be treated as part of the double entry system. If it is, as with the cash book, its entries will themselves already contain one side of the ledger posting; you have only to make the other. However, this one aspect of the dual entry is itself split into various postings to nominal ledger accounts and this is why analysis columns have been used. Their individual totals, together with the VAT column total, provide the figures to be posted to the various accounts denoted by their column headings. The net invoice total column is not posted anywhere.

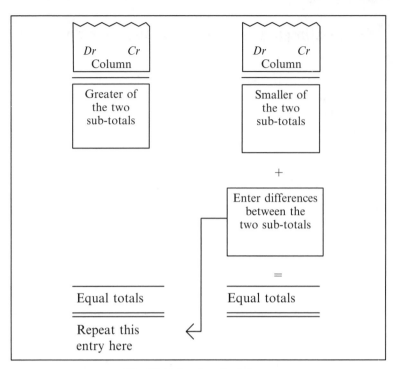

Fig. 37. Balancing the ledger.

Fig. 38. In the above examples of Folio Column entry you will see that each posting is cross-referenced with another. Note also that the Sales Ledger should not be confused with the 'Sales A/C' in the Nominal Ledger.

## 25   Balancing the ledger

Periodically, usually once a month, the ledger accounts are balanced.

### Balancing the ledger step by step
1.   Total up both the debit and credit sides individually. Work out what figure you need to add to the lower figure to equalise the totals. Write against this figure: 'Balance c/d' (carried down).

2.   Rule off. Enter the two equal totals and underline twice, to show they are final totals.

3.   Enter the same figure on the opposite side below the total box: this will be the opening figure for the new period. Write against it: 'Balance b/d' (brought down). Note: you do not need to do this if the account only contains one item; in such a case no lines are drawn, and no dual totals entered.

The word 'balances' as used here simply means differences.

### Completing the folio columns
We have now posted all our entries to the ledger. The next stage before extracting the trial balance is to complete the folio columns against each posting in the ledger. These columns show the ledger 'address' (ledger division and page number) where the counterpart posting has been made. Let's take as an example the folio column beside a posting in the sales account of the nominal ledger; we might perhaps write 'SL8' for the address of a personal account in the sales ledger, i.e. it is on sales ledger page 8. The name of the account in which the counterpart posting has been made is entered in the particulars column of each ledger account, so you could say that this extra cross-referencing is unnecessary. But if the ledger divisions are large, a note of the exact page number could save time. Also filling in the folio columns will help the detection of errors. If the trial balance fails, errors of omission can be spotted by the absence of a folio column posting, because it could mean that no counterpart posting has been made.

### Important points to understand
Of all the things students find difficult to grasp in book-keeping, two in particular stand out.

* The first is knowing whether to debit or credit an account. Which is the debit aspect and which the credit aspect of the transaction? What does it really mean to debit or credit an account?

* The second is knowing which nominal ledger accounts to post the impersonal side of transactions to, i.e.: knowing how to classify expenses and revenues into the right account names in the first place.

As for how to name the overhead expense accounts, with the exception of limited companies (whose final accounts formats are governed by law—see p.137) there is no hard and fast rule. Each firm and each accountancy practice will have defined its own range. The various worked examples of trial balances in this book will give you some idea. The range of asset and liability account names are a little easier to suggest, since the anticipated balance sheet effectively governs the range of accounts which will be set up. There is a good degree of consistency between firms in this respect and the range which tends to be used can be memorised in terms of 4 levels of classification.

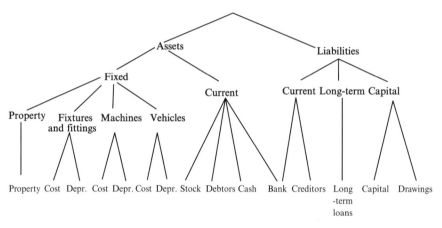

Fig. 39.

You will see that this classification gives us an eventual 15 asset/liability accounts, but there may be more, e.g.: if the firm has more than one machine there will be a separate asset and depreciation account for each of them.

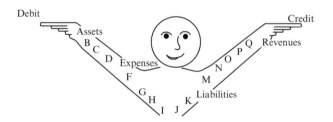

Fig. 40. Let Alf Direct You.

Once you have mastered how to categorise things into assets, expenses, liabilities and revenues then with this simple model in memory you cannot go wrong.

Taking the first point first:

1.  The word debit comes from the Latin verb *debere*, meaning 'to owe'; debit is the Latin for he or she owes. In business, a person owes to the proprietor that which was loaned or given to him by the proprietor.

2.  The word credit comes from the Latin verb *credere*, meaning 'to trust' or 'to believe'. Our creditors believe in our integrity, and trust us to pay them for goods and services they supply; so they are willing to deliver them without asking for immediate payment.

Perhaps this will help a little in personal ledger accounts; but what about the impersonal accounts of the nominal ledger? Whenever an account has a debit balance it means that it 'owes' the proprietor the value of it (and vice versa for credit balances), as if that account were a person.

```
┌─────────────────────────────────────────────────────────────┐
│                 RED HOUSE CEMENT WORKS                        │
│                     Mulvy Island Road                         │
│                    Anytown, Anyshire.                         │
│                                                               │
│   Invoice No:              002345                             │
│                                            £       p          │
│   100 Bags of cement @ £10              1,000.00              │
│   Less 35% trade discount                 350.00              │
│                                           650.00              │
│   Plus VAT                                113.75              │
│   Total                                   763.75              │
│                                                               │
│   Terms strictly 30 days net                                  │
└─────────────────────────────────────────────────────────────┘
```

Fig. 41. Example of the way trade discount may be shown on
a wholesaler's invoice to a retailer.

```
┌─────────────────────────────────────────────────────────────┐
│                                                               │
│   S. JONES (WHOLESALE STATIONERY SUPPLIES) LTD                │
│              210 Barton High Street, Barton, Barshire         │
│                                                               │
│    Invoice No: 00322                       10/2/200X          │
│                                                               │
│    10 reams of typing paper @ £7              70.00           │
│    plus VAT          17½%                     12.25           │
│                                               82.25           │
│                                                               │
│                                                               │
│    2½% early settlement discount                              │
│    Deduct £2.06 if paid within                                │
│    14 days.                                                   │
│                                                               │
│    ┌─────────────────┐                                        │
│    Customer                                                   │
│    Razi & Thaung                                              │
│    15 Bolton Road                                             │
│    Finchester     └────────┘                                  │
└─────────────────────────────────────────────────────────────┘
```

Fig. 42. Example of the way early settlement discount may be shown on an
invoice.

# 26 Discounts

## Trade discounts

A trade discount is one given by wholesalers to retailers, so that the retailers can make a profit on the price at which they sell goods to the public. Example:

| | |
|---|---|
| Wholesale price of 5 litre tin of paint: | £4.00 |
| Trade discount: | £2.00 |
| Recommended retail price: | £6.00 |

In this example, the trade discount is $33\frac{1}{3}$ of the recommended retail price. However, trade discounts have no place as such in a firm's accounts. They are deducted before any entry is made in any of the books. As far as the wholesaler is concerned, his price to the retailer is simply £4.00, so £4.00 is the amount the wholesaler enters in his sales day book, and the amount the retailer enters in his purchase day book.

## Early settlement discounts

These are discounts offered to persuade customers to settle their debts to the firm early. Typically, a discount of $2\frac{1}{2}\%$ might be offered for payment within 14 days. But the details can vary. Example:

| | |
|---|---|
| Building materials supplied: | £200.00 |
| Less 2% discount for settlement within 7 days: | £   4.00 |
| | £196.00 |

Firms offer such discounts for two reasons: to speed up cash flow and to reduce the chance of debts becoming bad debts (the longer a debt remains outstanding, the more likely it is to become a bad debt).

If you write up your day books daily, you will not know whether or not an early settlement discount will be taken. You will know once the actual payment arrives. So you have to enter the figure without any deduction of discount into your sales day book. When the debt is paid, if a discount has been properly claimed, the credit entry to that customer's account will be $2\frac{1}{2}\%$ less than the account shows. You then need to enter the discount as a credit to his account and a debit to 'discount allowed account' in the nominal ledger. This will make up the shortfall. It has the same effect as cash on the customer's personal account—and so it should: the offer shown on the invoice is like a 'money off voucher', and we would expect to treat that the same as cash.

## Discounts and VAT

An early settlement discount is based on the invoice total (including VAT). Whether it is claimed or not will not alter the net sale value or the VAT amount which will be entered in the books.

## CASH BOOK

| Dr. Date 200X | Particulars | Fo. | Discount | Cash | Bank | Cr. Date 200X | Particulars | Fo. | Discount | Cash | Bank |
|---|---|---|---|---|---|---|---|---|---|---|---|
| Mar 1 | Balance | b/d | | 50.00 | 1,000.00 | Mar 13 | Eliot | | 7.64 | | 297.81 |
| 13 | Morgan & Baldwyn | SL5 | 13.71 | | 260.34 | | | | | | |
| 20 | Edwards' Garage | SL7 | | | 193.40 | | | | | | |
| 28 | A. Singh | SL9 | | | 640.39 | 31 | Balance | c/d | | 50.00 | 1,796.32 |
| | | | 13.71 | 50.00 | 2,094.13 | | | | 7.64 | 50.00 | 2,094.13 |
| Aprl 1 | Balance b/d | | | 50.00 | 1,796.32 | | | | | | |

## PURCHASE LEDGER

BL3

| Dr. 200X | | | Eliot Transport | | Cr. 200X | | |
|---|---|---|---|---|---|---|---|
| | | | | | Mar 1 | Balance b/d | 305.45 |
| Mar | 10 | Bank | CB8 | 297.81 | | | |
| | 10 | Disc recd | NL19 | 7.64 | | | |
| | | | | 305.45 | | | 305.45 |

## SALES LEDGER

SL9

| Dr. 200X | | | A. Singh | | Cr. 200X | | | |
|---|---|---|---|---|---|---|---|---|
| Mar | 1 | Balance | b/d | 674.10 | Mar 1 | Bank | CB8 | 640.39 |
| | | | | | 31 | Balance | c/d | 33.71 |
| | | | | 674.10 | | | | 674.10 |

SL18

| Dr. 200X | | | Edwards Garage | | Cr. 200X | | |
|---|---|---|---|---|---|---|---|
| Mar | 1 | Balance | b/d | 193.40 | Mar 20 | Bank | 193.40 |

SL20

| Dr. 200X | | | Morgan and Baldwin | | Cr. 200X | | | |
|---|---|---|---|---|---|---|---|---|
| Mar | 1 | Balance | b/d | 274.05 | Mar 13 | Bank | CB8 | 260.34 |
| | | | | | 13 | Discount All | NL18 | 13.71 |
| | | | | 274.05 | | | | 274.05 |

## NOMINAL LEDGER

NL18

| Dr. 200X | | | Discounts Allowed | | Cr. 200X |
|---|---|---|---|---|---|
| Mar | 31 | Debtors | 13.71 | | |

NL19

| Dr. 200X | | Discounts Received | Cr. 200X | |
|---|---|---|---|---|
| | | | Mar 31 Creditors | 7.64 |

Fig. 43. Recording discounts in cash book and ledger.

## Prime entry of discounts in the cash book

You make your prime entry of discounts in the cash book. But the column you use is unlike the other cash columns: it is not a ledger column, just a prime entry 'lodging place'. Entries in the discount column of the cash book, unlike entries in its other (ledger) columns, are not part of a dual posting; the dual posting is made in the 'discount allowed account' in the nominal ledger for the one part, and the personal customer account in the sales ledger for the other (or 'discounts received account' and supplier account, as the case may be). The postings to the discount accounts in the nominal ledger are, of course, column totals rather than individual items.

## Entering early settlement discounts

Both the cashier and the ledger clerk will be involved in entering early settlement discounts. When the cheques are first received from customers or sent out to suppliers the cashier will check whether they have been properly claimed by reference to the time limit for early settlement discount and then enter the discounts in the cash book when he/she is entering the other payment details. For this step-by-step process please refer to pages 27 and 29.

At the end of each month the ledger clerk will make the dual postings to the ledger accounts for each item in the discount columns of the cash book.

## Step by step

What you will need is the cash book, sales ledger, purchase ledger and nominal ledger.

1. One by one, post each item in the discounts received column to the debit of the named suppliers' purchase ledger accounts.

2. Post the column total for the month to the credit of discounts received account in the nominal ledger.

3. One by one, post each item in the discounts allowed column to the credit of the named customers' sales ledger accounts.

4. Post the column totals to the debit of discounts allowed account in the nominal ledger.

## SALES LEDGER

*Total Debtors Account*

| Dr. | | | | | Cr. |
|---|---|---|---|---|---|
| Balance | b/d | 200.00 | Cheques | | 150.00 |
| Sales | | 300.00 | Balance | c/d | 350.00 |
| | | 500.00 | | | 500.00 |

Fig. 44. An example of a total debtors acount.

## PURCHASE LEDGER

*Total Creditors Account*

| Dr. | | | | | Cr. |
|---|---|---|---|---|---|
| Cash paid to | | | Balance | b/d | 2,000.00 |
| suppliers | | 1,200.00 | Purchases | | 2,200.00 |
| Balance | c/d | 3,000.00 | | | |
| | | 4,200.00 | | | 4,200.00 |

Fig. 45. An example of a total creditors account.

## SALES LEDGER
*Sales Ledger Control Account*

| 200X | | | | | 200X | | | | |
|---|---|---|---|---|---|---|---|---|---|
| Feb | 1 | Balance | b/d | 15,000 | Feb | 28 | Sales returns | | 200 |
| | 28 | Sales | | 10,000 | | 28 | Bank | | 11,100 |
| | | | | | | 28 | Discounts allowed | | 400 |
| | | | | | | 28 | Bad debts | | 300 |
| | | | | | | 28 | Balance | c/d | 13,000 |
| | | | | 25,000 | | | | | 25,000 |

Fig. 46. Example of a more complex sales ledger control account.

# 27 Control accounts

## Useful summaries
A control account is a sort of trial balance for just one ledger division. You write the account at the back of the ledger division concerned. The main idea of control accounts is to subdivide the task of the main trial balance. They also provide useful summaries of data for more effective financial management. For example the boss might want an up-to-date figure for total debtors, to help monitor credit control in the firm. Control accounts are in fact sometimes called total accounts (for example, total creditors account).

## Subdividing the work
In a small firm, where one book-keeper posts all the ledgers, control accounts might be unnecessary. But the double entry system can be quickly expanded if necessary by using control acounts. Individual specialist book-keepers, such as the bought ledger clerk or sales ledger clerk, could balance their own ledger division using a control total, i.e. a balancing item equal to the difference between all their own debit and credit balances. A head book-keeper could then build up an overall trial balance just by taking the control account totals. In large firms today, control accounts are vital to the smooth running of the accounting system. Without them, reaching a trial balance would really be a difficult, time-consuming and messy business.

Control accounts are summaries of ledger balances in a division of the ledger. For example, purchase ledger control accounts contain the sum totals of all VAT inclusive purchases, payments to suppliers and discounts received.

The postings go on the same side as they do in the individual ledger accounts. However, to avoid a duplication on one side of the dual posting either the control accounts, or the individual ledger accounts must be left out of the double entry system. If the individual ledger accounts are treated as double entry then the control accounts are not, in which case they are known as memorandum accounts. If, however, the control accounts are treated as part of double entry system then the individual ledger accounts which they summarise are known as subsidiary ledger accounts and are not part of the double entry system.

Though they are most commonly used for the sales and purchase ledger divisions, control accounts can be used for any ledger divisions, e.g. cash or petty cash. Furthermore, the layout is the same and they are administered in the same way, so once you know how they are used for one type of account you know how they are used for others.

## Advantages of using control accounts
The principal advantage of using control accounts is to reduce the need to deal with many sales, or purchase ledger balances to a single sales, or purchase ledger balance. This way interim and final accounts can be drawn up more quickly.

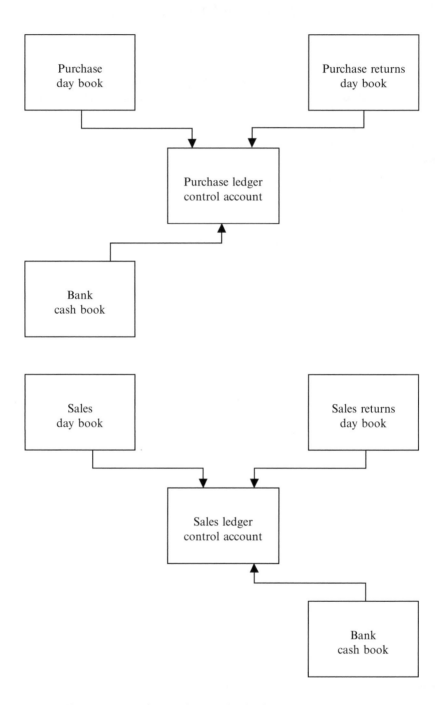

Fig. 47. Sources for purchase and sales ledger control accounts.

A second advantage is that the control account balances can be used as a check on the accuracy of individual ledger account postings, especially if the control accounts are posted by a different book-keeper to the one who posts the individual sales and purchase ledger accounts. This is usually the case in large companies. It is unlikely that the same posting errors will be made by both clerks.

Thirdly, subdividing a ledger means errors are easier to find because each division is self-contained in double entry terms.

Fourthly, fraud is made more difficult. Illegal transfers of money are more likely to be noticed if a different clerk deals with each side of the dual postings.

## Source documents for control accounts

The source documents you need for posting to control accounts are the books of prime entry. But you only need monthly (or other period) totals, not individual entries as with other postings. Each entry in the sales day book, for example, you post separately to a specific account in the sales ledger, but you only post the total of gross invoice values to the sales ledger control account.

The four day books for sales and purchases are well suited to control accounts; column totals are readily available. It may be a good idea to add a gross invoice total column if control accounts are going to be kept. The other day books are not quite so helpful in this respect, since they do not analyse totals of different classes. Take the cash book, for example. From here you take the total of payments to suppliers, but 'purchases' may be mixed up with 'expenses' such as drawings, wages, transfers to petty cash, and other types of payments, all of which must be totalled up for posting to control accounts. Still, while not being quite so easy as posting from the sales and purchase day books, it is not too difficult to use the cash book for control accounts.

| Dr. | | | Sales Ledger Control | | | | Cr. |
|---|---|---|---|---|---|---|---|
| 200X | | | | 200X | | | |
| Sep 30 | Balance b/d | 20,263.60 | | Oct 31 | Sales returns | | 500.00 |
| Oct 31 | Sales | 24,630.70 | | 31 | Cheques | | 22,840.90 |
| | | | | 31 | Discount allowed | | 250.80 |
| | | | | 31 | Bad debts | | 420.50 |
| | | | | 31 | Balance c/d | | 20,882.10 |
| | | 44,894.30 | | | | | 44,894.30 |
| Nov 1 | Balance b/d | 20,882.10 | | | | | |

Fig. 48. A. Frazer's sales ledger control account.

1. Suppose:
The balance of A. Frazer's sales ledger control account as at the end of September 200X was £20,263.60 Dr.

Total sales for the month of October 200X were £24,630.70.
Total payments received for the month were £22,840.90.
Total discounts allowed for the month were £250.80.
Total bad debts written off for the month were £420.50.
Total sales returns were £500.00.

Write up the sales ledger control account for October 200X.

2. Suppose:
The balance of A. Frazer's purchase ledger control account as at 31 August 200X was £1,293.00 Cr.

Total purchases during September 200X amounted to £18,950.
Total payments to creditors were £9,800.00.
Total discounts received were £250.

Write up the purchase ledger control account for the month of September 200X.

| Dr. | | | | Purchase Ledger Control | | | | Cr. |
|---|---|---|---|---|---|---|---|---|
| 200X | | | | | 200X | | | |
| Sept 30 | Cheques | | 9,800.00 | Aug 31 | Balance | b/d | 1,293.00 |
| 30 | Discount rec. | | 250.00 | Sept 30 | Purchases | | 18,950.00 |
| 30 | Balance c/d | | 10,193.00 | | | | |
| | | | 20,243.00 | | | | 20,243.00 |
| | | | | Oct 1 | Balance | b/d | 10,193.00 |

Fig. 49. A. Frazer's purchase ledger control account.

# 28 Preparing control accounts step by step

## What you need
- the ledger (or those parts of it for which you want to operate control accounts)

- the relevant day books.

## Step by step
1. Unless the control account is a new one, your opening balances will already be there. These are merely the closing balances for the previous month. If the control account is created at the start of a year, you can take your opening balances of assets and liabilities from the trial balance.

2. Take each of the four day books relating to sales and purchases. Post the monthly gross invoice (or credit note) totals to the sales or purchase ledger control account as the case may be. Post the totals to the same side as the individual postings were made, i.e. debit customers accounts for sales, and so on. Annotate each posting accordingly, for example 'sales', 'sales returns' and so on.

3. Take each of the other books of prime entry, and extract from them totals for all the classes of transaction that relate to the ledger divisions concerned. Post each of these in turn to the relevant control acounts. Again, the appropriate side is exactly the same you would use if you were posting the items individually. Annotate each posting accordingly, for example 'cash', 'bank' and so on.

4. Total up and balance each control account as you would any other ledger account.

## Note on purchase and sales ledger control accounts
The purchase and sales ledger control accounts can be treated as part of the double entry system, but if they are the individual personal accounts in the purchase and sales ledgers must not be; they must simply be treated as an analysis. One or the other can be included in the double entry system—not both.

## ARMSTRONG ENGINEERING
Trial balance as at 31 March 200X

*Ledger balances*

| | | |
|---|---:|---:|
| Sales | | 100,000 |
| Fixtures and fittings | 15,000 | |
| Freehold premises | 40,000 | |
| Motor van | 8,000 | |
| Debtors | 10,000 | |
| Stock (opening) | 10,000 | |
| Cash at bank | 10,000 | |
| Cash in hand | 50 | |
| Capital | | 63,050 |
| Bad debts | 2,000 | |
| Bad debts provision | | 2,000 |
| Drawings | 6,450 | |
| Depreciation | 2,350 | |
| Provision for depreciation on motor van | | 1,600 |
| Provision for depreciation on fixtures and fittings | | 750 |
| Purchases | 60,000 | |
| Motor expenses | 750 | |
| Heat and light | 800 | |
| Wages | 10,000 | |
| Postage and stationery | 550 | |
| Repairs and renewals | 250 | |
| Creditors | | 12,000 |
| Interest and banking charges | 200 | |
| Carriage | 3,000 | |
| Closing stock | 9,000 | 9,000 |
| | 188,400 | 188,400 |

$=$

| *(debit balances)* | $=$ | *(credit balances)* |
|---|---|---|

Fig. 50. A typical trial balance, listing all the debit and credit balances in the ledger.

## A listing of ledger balances

The trial balance is unlike anything we have seen so far, but it is quite simple to understand and quite simple to do. It is just a listing of all the ledger balances at a particular moment in time. You list the balances in two columns—one for the debit balances and one for the credit balances. If all the ledger divisions have been correctly posted your two columns will balance. Remember, for every transaction there have been two postings, a debit and a credit, so the sum of all the debits should equal the sum of all the credits. See example opposite.

We always talk of 'extracting' a trial balance, or 'constructing' or 'drawing up' a trial balance.

## Summary

The trial balance is:

* a way of checking the accuracy of all previous postings

* a source, in a useful summary form, for putting together the firm's final accounts later on.

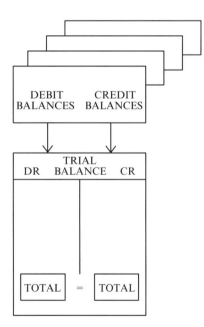

## TRIAL BALANCE: A. FRAZER & CO

|                                    | Dr.        | Cr.        |
|------------------------------------|------------|------------|
| Purchases                          | 28,879.00  |            |
| Sales                              |            | 48,133.00  |
| Bank                               | 981.00     |            |
| Cash                               | 50.00      |            |
| Land and buildings                 | 490,000.00 |            |
| Machinery                          | 100,000.00 |            |
| Fixtures and fittings              | 60,000.00  |            |
| Motor vehicle                      | 80,000.00  |            |
| Stock                              | 3,600.00   |            |
| Debtors                            | 2,010.00   |            |
| Creditors                          |            | 3,190.00   |
| Opening capital                    |            | 178,199.00 |
| Long-term, secured loan creditor   |            | 548,031.00 |
| Heat and light                     | 400.00     |            |
| Motoring expenses                  | 1,480.00   |            |
| Insurance                          | 240.00     |            |
| Wages                              | 6,913.00   |            |
| Salaries                           | 3,000.00   |            |
|                                    | 777,553.00 | 777,553.00 |

Fig. 51. Worked example of a trial balance. Note: there will be pence as well as pounds in a real life trial balance, but we have omitted them to keep things simple.

Suppose the ledger balances of A. Frazer for the month of August 200X were as follows:

Purchases, £28, 879.00 Dr, Sales £48,133.00 Cr, Bank £981.00 Dr, Cash £50.00 Dr, Land and buildings £490,000.00 Dr, Machinery £100,000 Dr, Motor vehicle £80,000.00 Dr, Fixtures and fittings £60,000 Dr, Stock £3,600.00 Dr, Debtors £2,010.00 Dr, Creditors £3,190.00 Cr, Opening capital £178,199 Cr, Long-term, secured loan creditor £548,031.00 Cr, Heat and light £400.00 Dr, Motoring expenses £1,480.00 Dr, Insurance £240.00 Dr, Wages £6,913.00 Dr, Salaries £3,000.00 Dr.

Construct a trial balance as at 31 August 200X.

# 30　How to extract a trial balance

## What you need
- the ledger (including of course the cash book and petty cash book, which are both part of the ledger)

- a sheet of A4 paper.

## Preparation
Make sure that all the folio columns have been entered in all the ledger accounts. Enter them now if necessary.

## Extracting a trial balance step by step
1. Head your blank sheet 'trial balance as at [date]'. Rule two cash columns down the right hand side. Head them, 'debit' and 'credit'.

2. List the balances of every single ledger account, including the cash book and petty cash book. Put each one in the correct column of your trial balance (debit, or credit).

3. Total up the two columns. If they balance, the job is done! If not, proceed as follows.

4. Look for an error of complete omission of an account balance in the trial balance, or of one side of a posting in the ledger. You should spot this if you look for a figure equal to the error.

5. If this fails, look for an error due to something being entered on the wrong side of the trial balance, or to both sides of a transaction being posted to the same side in the ledger. Divide the discrepancy in your trial balance by two, and look for a figure which matches this.

6. If this fails, look for an error of transposition. Is the discrepancy divisible by nine? If so, there could well be such an error. If these methods all fail, the error could be in the totalling up, or in under- or overstating one side of a transaction, or a mixture of errors.

7. Check through the ledger again to look for any folio column omissions.

8. Check off each ledger balance against the trial balance. Have you recorded it on the correct side? Tick each in pencil as you go. If this does not solve the problem, proceed to step 9.

| | Ledger balances | | Adjustments | | Trading profit and loss account | | Balance Sheet | |
|---|---|---|---|---|---|---|---|---|
| | Dr | Cr | Dr | Cr | Dr | Cr | Dr | Cr |
| Purchases | 32,087 | | | | 32,087 | | | |
| Sales | | 48,133 | | | | 48,133 | | |
| Heat and light | 400 | | | | 400 | | | |
| Motor expenses | 1,480 | | | | 1,480 | | | |
| Insurance | 240 | | | | 240 | | | |
| Wages | 6,913 | | | | 6,913 | | | |
| Salaries | 3,000 | | | | 3,000 | | | |
| Stock | 3,600 | | | | 3,600 | | | |
| Closing stock P & L | | | | 4,000 | | 4,000 | | |
| Closing stock B/S | | | 4,000 | | | | 4,000 | |
| Cash | 50 | | | | | | 50 | |
| Bank | 981 | | | | | | 981 | |
| Land and buildings | 490,000 | | | | | | 490,000 | |
| Machinery | 96,000 | | | | | | 96,000 | |
| Fixtures and fittings | 60,000 | | | | | | 60,000 | |
| Motor vehicles | 80,000 | | | | | | 80,000 | |
| Debtors | 2,010 | | | | | | 2,010 | |
| Creditors | | 3,190 | | | | | | 3,190 |
| Capital | | 178,199 | | | | | | 178,199 |
| Long-term creditor | | 547,239 | | | | | | 547,239 |
| | 776,761 | 776,761 | 4,000 | 4,000 | 47,720 | 52,133 | 733,041 | 728,628 |
| | | | | | 47,720 | | 728,628 | |
| | | | | | 4,413 | 4,413 | | |

Fig. 52. Example of an extended trial balance.

### TRIAL BALANCE

| trading, profit & loss account items | | | balance sheet items | | |
|---|---|---|---|---|---|
| | Dr. | Cr. | | Dr. | Cr. |
| Purchases | 28,879.00 | | Cash | 50.00 | |
| Sales | | 48,133.00 | Bank | 981.00 | |
| Heat and light | 400.00 | | Land and buildings | 490,000.00 | |
| Motor expenses | 1,480.00 | | Machinery | 100,000.00 | |
| Insurance | 240.00 | | Fixtures and | | |
| | | | fittings | 60,000.00 | |
| Wages | 6,913.00 | | Motor vehicles | 80,000.00 | |
| Salaries | 3,000.00 | | Debtors | 2,010.00 | |
| Stock | 3,600.00 | | Creditors | | 3,190.00 |
| | | | Capital | | 178,199.00 |
| | | | Long-term | | |
| | | | creditor | | 548,031.00 |
| | 44,512.00 | 48,133.00 | | 733,041.00 | 729,420.00 |
| | | | | 44,512.00 | 48,133.00 |
| | | | | 777,553.00 | 777,553.00 |

Fig. 53. Example of a four column trial balance using the same figures as on page 78.

9. Re-check the addition of all your ledger columns, and balance each account. If this still doesn't solve the problem proceed to step 10.

10. Check that the values in the posting of both sides of each transaction are equal. Start at the first page of the ledger and work through to the end. Tick each in pencil as you go.

If you have carried out all the steps accurately, the trial balance will now balance. Note: a small error need not hold up the preparation of final accounts; you can post the error to a 'suspense account' to save time. When eventually the error is tracked down a 'statement of amended profit or loss' can be drawn up.

### The four column trial balance
A variation of the trial balance described above is the four column version. This is simply one with two debit columns and two credit columns. In fact the page is most usefully split down the middle so that each side can have its own debit and credit columns. On one side you enter all the balances relating to the revenue accounts. On the other side you enter those which relate to the balance sheet. On

each side you total up the debit and credit columns separately to give either a debit or credit balance. If things are right the debit balance on one side will equal the credit balance on the other.

Sometimes these two types of trial balance are combined, side by side, with a balance of adjustments to make what is called an extended trial balance.

We could, if we wished, also show profit (or loss) on this too, since we debit profit and loss account, to close it, and credit capital account, to transfer the balance, at the end of the year.

# 31 The trial balance: errors

## Errors revealed and errors not revealed
The trial balance will immediately show that there is an error if it does not balance. However, it will not guarantee that the posting is error free if it does. In other words, things cannot be right if it does not balance, but can still be wrong if it does! Furthermore, a failure to balance does not tell us where in the posting the error or errors exist. So while the trial balance performs something of an error-checking role, it is not a foolproof one.

## Errors not revealed
1.  Errors of complete omission, where neither debit nor credit has been entered.

2.  Compensating errors, where errors of equal value cancel each other out.

3.  Errors of commision—posting to the wrong accounts, though to the correct sides of the correct ledger division.

4.  Errors of reverse posting: the debit entry of a transaction has been wrongly posted to the credit side, and vice versa. (See also page 171.)

5.  Errors of principle, for example posting of an asset to an expenses account.

## Errors which will be revealed by a trial balance
1.  Errors arising from both parts of the double entry (debit/credit) being posted to the same side (e.g. debit).

2.  Errors of partial omission, for example, where only one side of a transaction was posted, such as the credit side but not the debit side, or vice versa.

3.  Errors in adding up.

4.  Errors of transposition, where digits have been accidentally reversed, for example 54 has been written as 45. See page 168 for how to identify this error.

5.  Errors due to under- or overstating one side of the transaction.

6.  Errors of original entry, for example when making a mistake while entering a sales invoice into the sales day book.

```
                              Electricity
200X                             200X
Mar  1   Balance   b/d   2,100   Mar 31  Profit and loss        2,520
     31  Balance   c/d     420
                         ─────                                  ─────
                         2,520                                  2,520
                                 Apr  1  Balance        b/d       420
```

Fig. 54. Example of an accrual for electricity charges.

```
                              Insurance
200X                             200X
Mar  31  Balance   b/d     230   Mar 31  Profit and loss          120
                                     31  Balance        c/d       110
                         ─────                                  ─────
                           230                                    230
Apr  1   Balance   b/d     110
```

Fig. 55. Example of prepayment of insurance.

1. Suppose A. Frazer's insurance premium of £1,200 is payable yearly in
advance from 1 June, but its accounting year runs from 1 May. By the end
of the accounting year only 11 months of the premium will have been used
up, there will still be an asset of 1 month's prepaid premium to carry
forward to the next year. This is how it will appear in the ledger:

```
                              Insurance
200X                             200X
June  1   Bank           1,200   Apr 31  Profit and loss        1,100
                                         Prepayment     c/d       100
                         ─────                                  ─────
                         1,200                                  1,200
Prepayment        b/d      100
```

Fig. 56. Worked example of the posting of a prepayment.

2. Suppose that aggregate weekly wages of £1,500 are payable on a Friday
and the end of the firm's acounting year falls on a Tuesday. There will be a
liability for 3 days aggregated, unpaid wages to account for in the end of
year accounts. This is how it will appear:

```
                              Wages A/C
200X                             200X
Aug  31  Balance   b/d  77,100   Aug 31  Profit and loss a/c   78,000
     31  Accruals  c/d     900
                        ──────                                 ──────
                        78,000                                 78,000
                                 Sep  1  Accruals       b/d       900
```

Fig. 57. Worked example of the posting of an accrual.

# 32  Accruals and prepayments

## Adjustments to accounts

Accruals and prepayments are adjustments we need to make to the accounts at the end of the year (or other management accounting period).

- Accruals are sometimes called accrued expenses, expense creditors or expenses owing. Accruals are a liability for expenses for goods or services already consumed, but not yet billed (invoiced).

- Prepayments are an asset of goods or services already paid for, but not yet completely used. Prepayments are, therefore, in a sense the opposite of accruals.

## Example of accrued expenses

Suppose we are drawing up accounts for the year ended 31 March. We know there will be an electricity bill for the three months ended 30 April, a month after the end of our financial year. By 31 March, even though we haven't had the bill, we would already have used two months' worth of it, but as things stand the cost of this won't appear in our accounts because it is too soon to have received a source document (i.e. the invoice) from which to enter it. Still, electricity clearly was an expense during the period, so we have to 'accrue' a sensible proportion. For example:

| | |
|---|---|
| Electricity account period | 1 February to 30 April |
| Estimated charge | £630.00 (three month period) |
| Period falling within our accounts | 1 February to 31 March (two months) |

Charged accrued for period: $\dfrac{£630.00 \times 2 \text{ months}}{3 \text{ months}} = £420.00$

## Wages and rent

Other items that often have to be accrued are wages and rent. The firm receives the benefit of work, and of premises, before it pays out wages and rent (assuming rents are payable in arrears; if rent is payable in advance we would need to treat it as a prepayment).

### ACCRUALS

The balance c/d will be a debit one, but the ultimate effect on the expense account (the balance b/d) will be a credit entry.

### PREPAYMENTS

The balance c/d will be a credit one, but the ultimate effect on the expense account (the balance b/d) will be a debit entry.

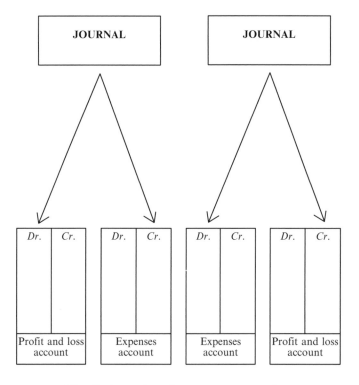

Fig. 58. Accruals and prepayments at a glance.

### Example of prepayment

A prepayment arises, for example, where an insurance premium or professional subscription is paid annually in advance but only one or two month's benefit has been used by the end of the year. We must adjust the figures so that we don't charge the whole amount against profits for the year. Clearly, much of the benefit remains as an asset for use in the next year. Example, again assuming that our accounting period ends on 31 March:

| | |
|---|---|
| Professional subscription for calendar year: | £100.00 |
| Period falling within our accounts: | 1 January to 31 March |
| Period falling into next accounting period | 1 April to 31 December (9 months) |
| Prepaid for next year: | $£100.00 \times \dfrac{9}{12} = £75.00$ |

### Carrying down accruals and prepayments

When these amounts have been calculated or assessed, you place them in the relevant ledger accounts as 'carried down' balances. In this way you increase or decrease the amount to be transferred to the profit and loss account for the year, depending on which side the posting is made. The resulting 'b/d' balances are listed in the balance sheet just like any other balance remaining on the nominal ledger at the end of the year. If they are credit balances (accruals) they are current liabilities. If they are debit balances (prepayments) they are assets.

**THE TRADING ACCOUNT**

1 Sales

2 Purchases

3 Opening stock

4 Closing stock

5 Carriage inwards (and any warehousing and packaging costs)

Fig. 59. Items listed in a trading account. Remember the mnemonic SPOCC.

**TYPICAL PROFIT AND LOSS ACCOUNT ITEMS**

Wages and salaries

Heat and light

Rent and rates

Motor expenses

Bank charges

Bad debts

Depreciation

Insurance

Carriage outwards

There can be many more; it just depends on the type of business.

Fig. 60. Items listed in a profit and loss account.

## The trading account and profit and loss account

The revenue accounts are a pair of ledger accounts called the trading account and the profit and loss account. They are much like any other ledger account except that they are not ongoing (except for limited companies, dealt with later). Also, they are needed by more people outside the firm for example:

- HM Revenue and Customs to assess tax liability
- shareholders to see how the business is doing
- prospective purchasers to value the business
- prospective lenders to assess the risk of lending to the business, and its ability to pay interest.

But we adapt these accounts to a more easy-to-read version. Instead of two main columns we have only one (though we also use subsidiary columns for calculations). The two sides of the accounts are then represented in progressive stages of addition and subtraction. So the revenue accounts forwarded to interested parties don't look like ledger accounts at all.

## The trading account

This shows the gross profit, and how it is worked out:

sales − cost of goods sold = gross profit

To work out the cost of goods sold (i.e. cost of sales):

purchases + opening stock + carriage inwards, packaging and warehouse costs  − closing stock = cost of sales

When transferring the balances to the trading acount, deduct sales returns from sales, before posting in the trading account. After all, they are merely 'unsales' so to speak. The same goes for purchase returns: there is no place for any returns in the trading account.

## Contribution to overheads

Gross profit is not the same things as net profit. Gross profit is first and foremost a contribution to overheads. It is only when they are paid for that any net profit may, or may not be available for shareholders.

## The profit and loss account

The profit and loss account sets out the calculation of net profit like this:

gross profit + other income − expenses = net profit

We know that there must be two sides to every ledger posting: as you post each item in the revenue accounts, make an opposite side posting in the original ledger account from where your balance came. Against such postings just write 'trading account' or 'profit and loss' account. You are now closing down the revenue and expense ledger accounts, ready for a fresh start in the next accounting period.

**TRADING ACCOUNT**

| | | | |
|---|---|---|---|
| Sales | | | 100,000 |
| Purchases | | 58,000 | |
| **Opening stock** | 12,000 | | |
| **Closing stock** | 10,000 | 2,000 | 60,000 |
| Gross profit | | | 40,000 |

**BALANCE SHEET (EXTRACT FROM)**

Current assets
| | |
|---|---|
| **Stock** | 10,000 |
| Debtors | 8,000 |
| Cash at bank | 2,000 |
| Cash in hand | 50 |
| | 20,050 |

Fig. 61. Stock appears three times in the final accounts. Closing stock appears twice (although it is conventional to only use the adjective 'closing' in the trading account to distinguish it from 'opening stock').

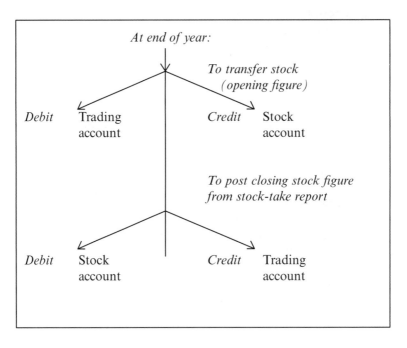

Fig. 62. What to do about stock at the end of the year.

# 34 Stock in the final accounts

## Opening and closing stock

Stock is dealt with three times in the revenue accounts and balance sheet—once as opening stock and twice as closing stock. Suppose we started the year with £1,000 worth of stock; we purchased a further £10,000 of stock during the year, but had none left at the end of it. Altogether, it means that we have sold assets of £11,000 during the year. Purchases and opening stock must be the same kind of asset, since they were both finished goods on the shelf; otherwise we could not have sold them both and had nothing left to sell. Clearly, stock and purchases need to be treated in the same way in the final accounts.

This year's opening stock was, in fact, last year's closing stock. Throughout this year it was an asset, appearing on the debit side of the ledger. So this year's closing stock must also be carried forward to the next year as an asset; it too must stay on the ledger, just like all other assets at the end of the year. The only balances we must transfer out permanently to the revenue accounts are those for expenses and revenues (which of course are not assets).

## Physical stocktake

Closing stock will not even be in the ledger until we have done a stocktake (a physical counting and valuation of the stock in hand). We must then post to the debit side of the stock account in the nominal ledger the actual asset value of stock remaining, and being carried forward into next year.

## Why we need a counter-entry for stock

The counter-entry must be posted to the credit of the trading account. Why? Let us go back to our basic example. We posted opening stock as a debit in the trading account because we assumed it had all been sold, along with the purchases for that year. But what if we bought £12,000 worth but still had £2,000 worth left? We will need to make an entry to the opposite side for this. Closing stock is a credit posting in the trading account.

Another way to look at it is this: if we purchased £12,000 worth of stock but only sold £10,000, it would be as if we had purchased only £10,000 worth for sale during the year. The other £2,000 worth would be for sale in the next year. So we are right to deduct closing stock from purchases.

Remember, a credit posting in the final accounts can also be done as a subtraction from the debit column. You have to do this when converting the ledger format to vertical format (see page 101).

```
TRADING ACCOUNT FOR A. FRAZER
for year ended 31 March 200X
                          £          £          £
Sales                                          90,000
Less cost of sales:
  Purchases                         50,000
  Opening stock         6,000
    Less closing stock  2,000        4,000     54,000
Gross profit                                   36,000
```

Fig. 63. Worked example of revenue accounts.

1. From the following ledger balances draw up the trading account of A. Frazer for the year ended 31 March 200X.

> Sales £90,000
> Purchases £50,000
> Stock (from ledger) £6,000
> Stock (from final stock-take) £2,000

2. From the following ledger balances draw up the revenue accounts of A. T. Office Supplies for year ended 30 April 200X.

| | |
|---|---:|
| Sales | 180,000 |
| Purchases | 100,000 |
| Ledger balance for stock | 6,000 |
| Stock as per final stocktake | 14,000 |
| Heat and light | 1,000 |
| Motor expenses | 1,500 |
| Bank charges | 500 |
| Rent | 3,000 |
| Wages | 37,000 |
| Insurance | 2,000 |

```
TRADING, PROFIT AND LOSS ACCOUNT FOR A.T. OFFICE SUPPLIES
for the year ended 30 April 200X
                          £          £          £
Sales                                         180,000
Less cost of sales:
  Purchases                        100,000
  Opening stock         6,000
    Less closing stock 14,000       (8,000)    92,000
Gross profit                                   88,000

Wages                              37,000
Heat and light                      1,000
Rent                                3,000
Motor expenses                      1,500
Bank charges                          500
Insurance                           2,000      45,000
Net profit                                     43,000
```

Fig. 64. Further worked example of revenue accounts.

# 35  How to compile revenue accounts

**What you will need**

- the trial balance

- the ledger (all divisions)

- details of end of year adjustments to the accounts, such as depreciation, bad debts, closing stock

- the journal.

**Adjustments before you start**

You will need to adjust the trial balance for various end of year adjustments. Remember to enter all your adjustments into the trial balance twice, once on the debit side and once on the credit side. You can achieve the same effect by adding to and subtracting from the same side as, indeed, you would need to with accruals and prepayments. For a prepayment for example, you would debit 'prepayments' in the trial balance, and subtract the same amount from the debit balance of the expense account concerned, e.g. 'insurance'. Check that the trial balance still balances after you have adjusted it: there is no point in starting to put together your final accounts until it is correct.

**Getting the right balance into the right accounts**

It is a good idea to label each balance, to show where it will go in your final accounts. For example against 'sales' write 'T' 'for trading acccount'. Write 'P & L' beside 'rent & rates' to show that it is going into the profit and loss account. Write 'B' beside each asset account, to show you will be taking it into your balance sheet.

Items on the debit side of the trial balance are expenses or assets; those on the credit side are revenues or liabilities. In the revenue accounts we are only interested in revenues and expenses. How do we recognise them?

A revenue is an income; an expense is an outgoing. Neither has to be in cash. If you have more stock left at the end than you had at the beginning of the accounting period, that is just as much a revenue as a sales figure. Another way of putting it is to say that excesses of expenses over revenues are called losses. Expenses represent an outflow of funds within the period. They include such things as electricity, motor expenses, rents paid or payable, and discounts allowed. Items classed as revenues represent incomes within the same period. They include things like commissions, rents receivable, and discounts received.

```
                         A. FRAZER
           TRADING PROFIT AND LOSS ACCOUNT
                 for year ended 31 March 200X

Stock as at 1 April 200X    10,000    Sales                 100,000
Purchases                   60,000    Stock as at
Carriage inwards             3,000    31 March 200X            9,000
Gross profit c/d            36,000
                           109,000                           109,000

                                      Gross profit b/d        36,000

                   Profit and loss account

Wages                        6,000
Motor expenses               2,000
Heat and light                 450
Cleaning                     1,500
Depreciation                 2,550
Net profit c/d              23,500
                            36,000                            36,000

                                      Net profit b/d to
                                      capital account        23,500
```

Fig. 65. Trading profit and loss account in horizontal format in the ledger. This can now easily be transformed into the more useful vertical format shown below.

```
                         A. FRAZER
           TRADING PROFIT AND LOSS ACCOUNT
                 for year ended 31 March 200X

Sales                                                        100,000
Less purchases                            60,000
Carriage inwards                           3,000
Opening stock              10,000
   Less closing stock       9,000          1,000              64,000
Gross profit b/d                                              36,000

Less expenses

Wages                       6,000
Motor expenses              2,000
Heat and light                450
Cleaning                    1,500
Depreciation                2,550                             12,500
Net profit b/d to capital account                            23,500
```

Fig. 66. Trading profit and loss account in vertical format.

# 36 Compiling revenue accounts step by step

Once you have labelled each item in the trial balance according to where it will go in the final accounts you can put together your revenue accounts as follows.

1. Write in the next available space in the 'particulars' column of the journal: 'sales'.

2. In the debit column, enter the balance of your sales account.

3. Beneath the last entry in the 'particulars' column, write: 'trading account' (indenting it slightly).

4. Enter the same figure in the credit cash column.

5. In the next space in the 'particulars' column, write: 'trading account'.

6. Enter in the debit/cash column the balance of your purchases account.

7. Write in the next space in the 'particulars' column (indenting slightly) the name of the account from which you are transferring (in this case 'purchases') and enter the value of purchases in the credit cash columns.

8. Repeat steps 5 to 8 for each of the other categories in the 'cost of sales' equation (see page 89).

9. When you have made all the entries relating to the trading account, write beneath them: 'To close revenue and expense accounts and transfer the balances to the trading account'.

10. Now do the same for any other income accounts (items other than 'trading income', e.g. rents). Debit the accounts concerned. Credit your profit and loss account.

11. Now do the same for each of the overhead expense accounts. Debit your profit and loss account and credit each account concerned.

12. When you have made all the entries for your profit and loss account, write underneath: 'To close expense accounts and transfer balances to profit and loss account.'

13. Now post to the ledger, including a trading, profit and loss account, exactly following the instructions you have just written in your journal. The trading, profit and loss account can be seen as two divisions of the same account, since they are written on the same page. The balance of the fomer is brought down to the latter, and marked: 'Gross profit b/d' (see opposite page, top).

14. Total up and balance all the ledger accounts concerned. This will mean closing all but the trading profit and loss account (except where an accrual or prepayment is present).

15. Mark the balance of profit and loss account: 'Net profit c/d to capital account'.

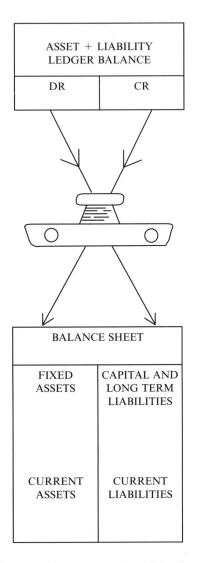

Fig. 67. The balance sheet as a snapshot of the financial affairs.

# 37   The balance sheet

## A financial snapshot

We have already seen standard sorts of statement summarising particular aspects of the business. The bank reconciliation was an example. The balance sheet is another—but a much more important one. Unlike the trading, profit and loss account, the balance sheet is not an 'account' as such. Rather, it is a useful snapshot of the firm's financial situation at a fixed point in time. It sets out clearly all the firm's assets and liabilities, and shows how the resulting net assets are matched by the capital account.

The balance sheet always goes hand-in-hand with the trading, profit and loss account. We need it to show:

- where the net profit has gone (or how the net loss has been paid for)

- how any net profit has been added to the capital account

- how much has been taken out as 'drawings' and whether any of it has been used to buy new assets (stating what those assets are).

## Management data

Accounting ratios can be worked out to help decision-making. For example the ratio of current assets/current liabilities shows how easily a firm can pay its debts as they become due (a ratio of 2/1 is often seen as acceptable in this respect). More will be said about these ratios later.

## Five main components of the balance sheet

The balance sheet tells us about five main categories:

1.  Fixed assets. These are assets the business intends to keep for a long time (at least for the year in question). They include things like premises, fixtures and fittings, machinery and motor vehicles. Fixed assets are not for using up in day to day production or trading (though a small part of their value is used up in wear and tear, and that is treated as an expense—'depreciation'). Property should be valued at net realisable value or cost whichever is the lower.

2.  Current assets. These are assets used up in day to day trading or production. They include such things as stock, debtors, cash at bank and cash in hand.

3.  Current liabilities. These are amounts the business owes to creditors, and which usually have to be paid within the next accounting year. They include trade creditors, and bank overdraft.

## A. FRAZER
### BALANCE SHEET
as at 31 December 200X

| | Cost | Less provision for depreciation | Net book value |
|---|---|---|---|
| Fixed assets | | | |
| Premises | 40,000 | | 40,000 |
| Fixtures and fittings | 15,000 | 750 | 14,250 |
| Motor van | 8,000 | 1,600 | 6,400 |
| | 63,000 | 2,350 | 60,650 |
| Current assets | | | |
| Stock | | 9,000 | |
| Debtors | 10,000 | | |
| Less provision for doubtful debts | 2,000 | 8,000 | |
| Cash at bank | | 10,000 | |
| Cash in hand | | 50 | |
| | | 27,050 | |
| Current liabilities | | | |
| Creditors | | 12,000 | |
| Total net assets (or working capital) | | | 15,050 |
| | | | 75,700 |
| Financed by | | | |
| Capital as at 1 January 200X | | | 63,150 |
| Add profit for period | | | 19,100 |
| | | | 82,250 |
| Less drawings | | | 6,550 |
| | | | 75,700 |

Fig. 68. Example of a balance sheet in vertical format.

## A. FRAZER
### BALANCE SHEET
as at 31 December 200X

| Fixed assets | | | Capital | | |
|---|---|---|---|---|---|
| Premises | | 40,000 | Balance as at 1 January 200X | | 63,150 |
| Fixture and fittings | 15,000 | | Add profit for year | | 19,100 |
| Less provision for depreciation | 750 | 14,250 | | | 82,250 |
| | | | Less drawings | | 6,550 |
| | | | | | 75,700 |
| Motor van | 8,000 | | | | |
| Less provision for depreciation | 1,600 | 6,400 | | | |
| | | 60,650 | | | |
| Current assets | | | | | |
| Stock | | 9,000 | Current liabilities | | 12,000 |
| Debtors | 10,000 | | | | |
| Less provision for bad debts | 2,000 | 8,000 | | | |
| Cash at bank | | 10,000 | | | |
| Cash in hand | | 50 | | | |
| | | 87,700 | | | 87,700 |

Fig. 69. Example of a balance sheet in horizontal format.

4.  Long-term liabilities. A business may also have financial obligations which do not have to be settled within the next accounting year. These include such things as long term loans, for example to buy plant, equipment, vehicles or property.

5.  Capital. This means the property of the owner of the business. He has invested his personal property in the business—cash, any other assets, and profits ploughed back. The business holds the value of all this for him in safe-keeping; it must deliver it up to him on cessation of the business, or earlier if he requires. Capital is, in a way, a liability to the business; but it's a rather different one from the other liabilities, which is why we don't include it with them.

### Postings to capital account
There are four types of posting we may need to make to capital account in the ledger: opening capital, extra capital injections, drawings, and the addition of profit.

### Terminology
'Capital' should not be confused with 'working capital', which is a very different thing (current assets − current liabilities). And do not confuse capital with capital expenditure, which just means expenditure on fixed assets rather than on expenses.

If the books have been written up correctly, the assets and liabilities must balance against capital in the balance sheet, to embody the equation we first saw on page 13:

$$\text{assets} - \text{liabilities} = \text{capital}$$

### What you need
- The trial balance 'adjusted' or 'redrafted' after compilation of the trading, profit and loss account to show the stock figure and the profit or loss.

### Preparation
Make sure that the balances listed on the trial balance that have already been used in the trading, profit and loss account are clearly ticked off. The remaining balances can then easily be spotted for use in compiling the balance sheet.

```
┌─────────────────────────────────────────────────────────────────────┐
│                    BALANCE SHEET OF A. FRAZER                         │
│                      as at 30 June 200X                               │
│  Fixed assets                                                         │
│  Land and buildings                                            200,000│
│  Fixtures and fittings                        50,000                  │
│     Less provision for depreciation           12,000           38,000 │
│                                                                       │
│  Office machinery                            100,000                  │
│     Less provisions for depreciation          15,000           85,000 │
│                                                                       │
│  Motor van                                    50,000                  │
│     Less provision for depreciation           30,000           20,000 │
│                                                                343,000 │
│                                                                       │
│  CURRENT ASSETS                                                       │
│  Stock                                        40,000                  │
│  Debtors                          33,000                              │
│     Less provision for bad debts   1,000      32,000                  │
│                                                                       │
│  Cash at bank                                  3,950                  │
│  Cash in hand                                     50                  │
│                                               76,000                  │
│                                                                       │
│  Less CURRENT LIABILITIES                                             │
│  Creditors                                    35,000                  │
│  Working capital                                               41,000 │
│                                                                384,000 │
│                                                                       │
│  Represented by                                                       │
│  Opening capital                                               347,777│
│     Less drawings                                                9,950 │
│                                                                337,827 │
│  Add profit                                                     46,173 │
│  Closing capital                                               384,000 │
│                                                                       │
└─────────────────────────────────────────────────────────────────────┘
```

Fig. 70. Balance sheet of A. Frazer in vertical format.

From the following details construct a balance sheet as at 30 June 200X in vertical format for A. Frazer (answer above).

| | |
|---|---|
| Land and buildings | 200,000 |
| Office machinery | 100,000 |
| Motor van | 50,000 |
| Fixture and fittings | 50,000 |
| Provision for depreciation on machinery | 15,000 |
| Provision for depreciation on motor van | 30,000 |
| Provision for depreciation on fixtures and fittings | 12,000 |
| Closing stock | 40,000 |
| Cash at bank | 3,950 |
| Cash in hand | 50 |
| Drawings | 9,950 |
| Debtors | 33,000 |
| Creditors | 35,000 |
| Bad debts provision | 1,000 |
| Capital | 347,777 |
| Net profit | 46,173 |

1. Make a heading 'Balance Sheet of [firm] as at [date].

2. Make a sub-heading on the left, 'Fixed assets'.

3. Beneath this, in column three, write the value of any premises. Annotate it; on the left 'Land and buildings'.

4. In column two, list the balance of other fixed assets, in order of permanence. Annotate each one on the far left. Beneath each one record the provision for depreciation, annotating 'Less provision for depreciation'.

5. Subtract the depreciation from each asset and place the difference in column three.

6. Total up column three.

7. Now make a second sub-heading, 'Current assets'.

8. Beneath this, in the second cash column, write the balances of the short-life assets, in the order of permanence, annotating accordingly.

9. Total up these balances.

10. Make a third sub-heading on the left, 'Less current liabilities'.

11. Below that, list, in the first cash column, the creditors figure and the bank overdraft figure, if there is one.

12. Total up this column. Place the total in the second column beneath that for current assets. If there is only one item you can place it directly into the second column.

13. Now rule off this column and subtract the latter total from the former. Place the difference in the third column below the total for fixed assets, annotating it 'Working capital'. Add these two totals and rule off with a double line, annotating it 'Total net assets'.

14. Make a sub-heading below this, 'Represented by'.

15. Enter the opening capital in the third column, annotating it 'Opening capital'.

16. Enter the drawings balance, annotating it 'Less drawings'.

17. Rule off and deduct.

18. Enter the profit in column three, annotating it 'Add profit'.

19. Rule off and add. Underline the answer with double line and annotate it 'Closing capital'.

**Horizontal and vertical formats**

A balance sheet may be shown in horizontal or vertical format. Unless told otherwise, use the vertical format in exams and in practice.

## ARMSTRONG ENGINEERING
### MANUFACTURING ACCOUNT
as at 31 December 200X

Raw materials

| | | |
|---|---:|---:|
| Opening stock | | 10,000 |
| Add purchases | | 102,000 |
| | | 112,000 |
| Less closing stock | | 12,000 |
| Cost of raw materials consumed | | 100,000 |
| Manufacturing wages | | 200,000 |
| Prime cost | | 300,000 |

Overhead costs

| | | |
|---|---:|---:|
| Rent (½) | 10,000 | |
| Rates (½) | 2,000 | |
| Heat, light and power ($^3/_4$) | 8,000 | 20,000 |
| | | 320,000 |

Adjustment for work in progress

| | | |
|---|---:|---:|
| Opening stock | 12,000 | |
| Less closing stock | 15,000 | (3,000) |
| Cost of finished goods | | |
| Transferred to trading account | | 317,000 |

Fig. 71. Simple example of a manufacturing account.

## Part of the revenue accounts

Like the trading account, the manufacturing account is part of the revenue accounts. Its format is similar, but it has quite different components. It is used when we want to show the manufacturing costs involved in the production of goods. This final cost of production is transferred from the manufacturing account to the trading account. For a manufacturing firm this figure is the equivalent of purchases for a purely trading firm.

# 39   Manufacturing accounts

We need to show two important cost figures in the manufacturing account:

- **prime cost**—the sum of the costs of direct labour, direct materials and direct expenses; and

- **overheads**—the sum of all costs which cannot be directly related to output (e.g. factory rent).

Three stages of the production process are shown in a manufacturing account:

1.   Raw materials consumed.

2.   Adjustment for stocks of partly finished goods (work in progress).

3.   Finished goods transferred to trading account.

The cost of raw material consumed is arrived at like this:

| | |
|---|---:|
| Opening stocks | 600 |
| Add purchases | 200 |
| | 800 |
| Less closing stocks | 150 |
| Cost of raw material consumed | 650 |

The prime cost is found by adding the direct wages and direct expenses to cost of raw materials consumed.
   Work in progress is calculated similarly:

| | |
|---|---:|
| Opening stocks | 600 |
| Less closing stocks | 150 |
| Work in progress adj. | 450 |

Purchases do not come into this equation.
   The end product of the manufacturing account is the value of the stock of finished goods (just as the gross profit is the end product of the trading account). This value is then transferred to the trading account, just as the trading account transfers its gross profit to the profit and loss account.

```
┌─────────────────────────────────────────────────────────────┐
│        MANUFACTURING ACCOUNT OF ARMSTRONG ENGINEERING         │
│                 for the year ended 31 October 200X            │
│                                                               │
│                                                               │
│ Stock of raw materials as at 1.11.200X              4,000     │
│ Add Purchases                                      40,000     │
│                                                    44,000     │
│                                                               │
│                                                               │
│ Less Stock of raw materials as at 31.10.200X        5,500     │
│ Cost of raw materials consumed                     38,500     │
│                                                               │
│                                                               │
│ Add Direct labour                                   4,500     │
│ Prime cost                                         43,000     │
│                                                               │
│                                                               │
│ Factory overheads                                   1,600     │
│                                                    44,600     │
│                                                               │
│ Add Work in progress as at 1.11.200X     8,000               │
│                                                               │
│                                                               │
│ Less Work in progress as at 31.10.200X   9,500    (1,500)     │
│                                                               │
│                                                               │
│ Cost of finished goods transferred                            │
│    to trading account                              43,100     │
│                                                               │
│                                                               │
└─────────────────────────────────────────────────────────────┘
```

Fig. 72. Worked example of a manufacturing account.

Suppose Armstrong Engineering is a manufacturer who at the end of the year to 31 October 200X has a stock of raw materials valued at £5,500 and work in progress valued at £9,500. The firm started the year with a stock of raw materials worth £4,000 and work in progress valued at £8,000. During the year it purchased a further £40,000's worth. The factory wages bill was £4,500 and the cost of power used solely in the factory was £1,600.

Figure 72 shows how you would write up its manufacturing account.

1.  Calculate the cost of raw materials consumed. Write the correct heading against each line of your calculation.

2.  Add the figures for direct wages and direct expenses, annotating accordingly.

3.  Annotate the total 'prime cost'.

4.  In a subsidiary column, itemise the various overhead expenses. Note: it may be that only part (e.g. half) of a cost (e.g. rent) can be fairly attributed to the manufacturing process, the other part being more fairly attributed for example to sales. In such a case, only the first part should be itemised. Just mark it like this: 'Rent ($\frac{1}{2}$)'.

5.  Total up this column. Place the total in the main cash column and total that column.

6.  In the subsidiary column write your work in progress adjustment. Write the correct heading against each line of your calculation. Place the resultant figure in your main cash column and add or deduct it from your subtotal according to whether it is a positive or negative figure.

7.  Write against the difference: 'Cost of finished goods transferred to trading account'.

|  | £ | £ |
|---|---|---|
| Cost |  | 100,000 |
| *Less* Estimated residual value |  | 3,000 |
| Amount to be depreciated over 5 years |  |  |
| Provision for depreciation |  |  |
|  |  |  |
| Yr 1  97,000 × 0.2 = | 19,400 |  |
| Yr 2  97,000 × 0.2 = | 19,400 |  |
| Yr 3  97,000 × 0.2 = | 19,400 |  |
| Yr 4  97,000 × 0.2 = | 19,400 |  |
| Yr 5  97,000 × 0.2 = | 19,400 |  |
|  | 97,000 | 97,000 |

Fig. 73. Worked example of depreciation using the straight line method.

1. Suppose a lorry costing £100,000 had an estimated lifespan within the company of 5 years and an estimated residual value at the end of that period of £3,000.

Using the straight line method and a rate of 20% the effect would be as shown in Figure 73.

### When assets drop in value

So far we have recorded figures, analysed them, summed and balanced them, and learned the standard ways of doing so. Now, with depreciation, we will also need to make calculations involving percentages.

Depreciation is the drop in value of an asset due to age, wear and tear. This drop in value is a drain on the firm's resources, and so we must put it in the accounts as an expense. We will need to write down the value of the asset in the books, to reflect its value more realistically. A company car, for example, loses value over time. So do plant, equipment and other assets. All have to be written down each year.

### Methods of calculating depreciation

- straight line method

- diminishing (or reducing) balance method

- sum of the digits method

- machine hours method

- revaluation method

- depletion method

- sinking fund method

- sinking fund with endowment method.

Even this list is not exhaustive. But the first two are the most common.

### The straight line method

This involves deducting a fixed percentage of the asset's initial book value, minus the estimated residual value, each year. The estimated residual value means the value at the end of its useful life within the business (which may be scrap value). The percentage deducted each year is usually 20% or $33^{1}/_{3}$% and reflects the estimated annual fall in the asset's value. Suppose the firm buys a motor van for £12,100; it expects it to get very heavy use during the first three years, after which it would only be worth £100 for scrap. Each year we would write it down by one third of its initial value minus the estimated residual value, i.e. £4,000 per year. On the other hand, suppose we buy a company car for £12,300; we expect it to get only average use and to be regularly serviced. We expect to sell it after five years for £4,800. In that case we would write down the difference of £7,500 by one fifth (20%) each year, i.e. £1,500 per year.

This method is useful where value falls more or less uniformly over the years of the asset's lifetime.

2. Suppose a machine cost £100,000 and it is estimated that at the end of 5 years it will be sold for £3,125. Suppose also that the greatest usage of the machine will be in the early years as will also the greatest costs, for since it is tailor-made for the firm's requirements its resale value is drastically reduced the moment it is installed. The appropriate rate of depreciation on the diminishing balance method will be between 2 and 3 times that for the straight line method, so an acceptable rate will be 50%. (See Figure 74.)

|  |  | £ | £ |
|---|---|---|---|
| Cost |  |  | 100,000 |
| Depreciation provision year | 1 | 50,000 |  |
|  | 2 | 25,000 |  |
|  | 3 | 12,500 |  |
|  | 4 | 6,250 |  |
|  | 5 | 3,125 | 96,875 |
| Residual value after 5 years |  |  | 3,125 |

Fig. 74. Example of depreciation by the diminishing balance method.

## 42　Depreciation: the diminishing balance method

**Diminishing balance method (or reducing balance method)**
This method also applies a fixed percentage, but it applies it to the diminishing value of the asset each year—not to the initial value. It is used for assets which have a long life within the firm, and where the biggest drop in value comes in the early years, getting less as time goes on.

Suppose a lathe in an engineering workshop cost £40,000 to buy. In the first year it will fall in value much more than it ever will in later years. The guarantee may expire at the end of the first year. The bright smooth paint on the surface will be scratched and scarred; the difference between its appearance when new and its appearance a year later will be quite obvious. But the next year the change will seem less; who will notice a few more scratches on an already scarred surface? Nor will there be a great drop due to the guarantee expiring, for it will not have started out with one at the beginning of the second year. And so it will go on; the value of the asset will depreciate by smaller and smaller amounts throughout its life. Most people would agree that a three-year-old machine has less value than an otherwise identical two-year-old one, but who could say that a 16-year-old machine really has any less value than a 15-year-old one? Since the value of these assets erodes in smaller and smaller amounts as the years go by, we use the diminishing balance method of calculation.

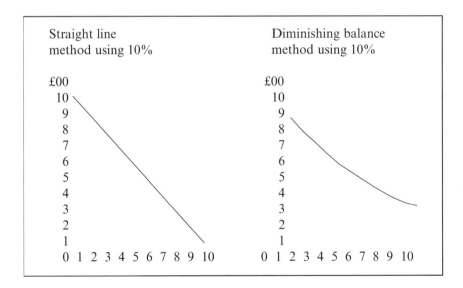

Fig. 75. Common methods of depreciation. The figure of 10% is used in both cases to illustrate the comparison (it is not necessarily the most common percentage to be used).

# 43  Other methods of depreciation

### The sum of the digits method

This method is more common in the USA than in Britain. It works in the opposite way to the diminishing balance method. The latter applies a constant percentage but to a progressively reducing balance, but the sum of the digits method applies a progressively small percentage to a constant figure (the initial cost figure). It is called the sum of the digits method because it involves summing the individual year numbers in the expected life span of the asset to arrive at the denominator of a fraction to be applied in calculating depreciation each year. The numerator is the year number concerned, in a reverse order.

For example if an asset had an expected useful life of 5 years then in year 1 the numerator would be 5, and in year 2 it would be 4 and so on, until year 5 when the numerator would be 1. Supposing an asset was expected to last 10 years before becoming worthless: we would add $1 + 2 + 3 + 4 + 5 + 6 + 7 + 8 + 9 + 10 = 55$. In year one, we would depreciate by multiplying the original value by 10/55, in year 2 by 9/55 and so on until year 10 when we would write it down by only 1/55 of its initial value.

### The machine hours method

We divide the initial cost value of a machine by the estimated number of machine hours in its useful life. The depreciation charge is then calculated by multiplying this quotient by the number of hours the machine has been used within the accounting year.

This method is appropriate wherever the erosion of value of an asset is directly related to its usage.

### The revaluation method

This method means revaluing the asset each year. It may involve observation, and item counting, and taking into account factors such as current market prices.

It is useful in respect of small tools, for example, for which it would be silly to keep a separate asset account and provision for depreciation account for each little item. Revaluing is also useful in dealing with livestock, for their values go up and down; a dairy cow for example will be less valuable when very young than when fully grown, but then its value will decline as it gets old. Throughout its life this rise and fall in value may be further affected by changes in food prices in the market place. If revaluation is used, no provision for depreciation is needed.

### The depletion method

This is used in the adjusting of values of ore bodies, mines, quarries and oil wells. The initial value of the mine, etc is divided by the quantity of ore or mineral that it contained at the beginning; the quotient is then multiplied by the quantity *actually* mined in the accounting year to give the amount of depletion in value.

### The sinking fund method

This method, as well as depreciating an asset's value in the books, builds up a fund for replacing it at the end of its useful life. A compound interest formula is applied to the estimated cost of replacement at the end of the asset's life; it shows how much money must be invested each year (outside the firm) to provide the replacement fund when the time comes. This amount is then charged annually to the profit and loss account as depreciation. The credit entry is posted to a depreciation fund account. The amount is then suitably invested and the asset which thereby comes into existence is debited to a depreciation fund investment account, the credit entry obviously going to bank. This method is not popular now because there is so much uncertainty about inflation and interest rates.

### The sinking fund with endowment policy method

This is similar but uses an endowment policy to generate the replacement fund on maturity. The premium is payable annually in advance.

## JOURNAL

| 200X | Particulars | Fo. | Debit | Credit |
|---|---|---|---|---|
| June 30 | Profit and loss provision for | NL30 | 50,000 | |
| | depreciation on machines | NL8 | | 50,000 |
| | Profit and loss provision for | NL30 | 19,400 | |
| | depreciation on lorry | NL9 | | 19,400 |

## LEDGER

| NL8 | *Provision for depreciation on machine* | | |
|---|---|---|---|
| Dr. | | | Cr. |
| 200X | | 200X | |
| | | June 30 Profit and loss | 50,000 |

| NL9 | *Provision for depreciation on motor lorry* | | |
|---|---|---|---|
| Dr. | | | Cr. |
| 200X | | 200X | |
| | | June 30 Profit and loss | 19,400 |

| NL30 | *Profit and loss account* | | |
|---|---|---|---|
| Dr. | | | Cr. |
| 200X | | 200X | |
| June 30 | Depreciation | 69,400 | |

Fig. 76. Worked example of depreciation accounting. This is how the depreciation in the worked examples on pages 106–108 would be written at the end of the year. The same would be the case for the subsequent years, except, of course, that the values would be different in respect of the machine depreciation.

# 44   Depreciation step by step

## What you need

- the nominal ledger

- scrap paper for your calculations

- the journal.

## Step by step

1.   Decide what kind of asset is concerned, what pattern of erosion applies to it and so which method of depreciation is best.

2.   Calculate the annual depreciation figure for the asset.

3.   In the next available space in the journal, write the date in the date column, and 'profit and loss' in the 'particulars' column. Remember, never post directly to the ledger—only via a book of prime entry (in this case the journal, a useful book for miscellaneous recordings like depreciation).

4.   Enter the amount of depreciation in the debit cash column.

5.   Underneath the last entry in the 'particulars' column, indenting slightly, write: 'provision for depreciation on [name of asset]'.

6.   Enter the same value in the credit cash column.

7.   Repeat for any other assets you need to depreciate in the accounts.

8.   Open a 'provision for depreciation' account for each asset concerned. Record the page numbers in the index.

9.   Make postings to each of these ledger accounts, following the instructions you have just written in the journal.

## Note

A Statement of Standard Accounting Practice (SSAP) was issued in December 1977 and revised in 1981 for the treatment of depreciation in accounts (SSAP12). The student can refer to this for further information if desired.

## SALES LEDGER

p2                                                                                          p2

*H. Baker*

| Date | Particulars | Fo. | Totals | Date | Particulars | Fo. | Totals |
|------|-------------|-----|--------|------|-------------|-----|--------|
| 200X | | | | | 200X | | |
| Jun 30 | Sales | NL6 | 200.00 | Mar 31 | Bad debts | NL20 | 200.00 |

## NOMINAL LEDGER

p20                                                                                         p20

*Bad Debts Account*

| Date | Particulars | Fo. | Totals | Date | Particulars | Fo. | Totals |
|------|-------------|-----|--------|------|-------------|-----|--------|
| 200X | | | | | 200X | | |
| Mar 31 | H. Baker | SL2 | 200.00 | Mar 31 | Profit and loss | NL27 | 200.00 |

p19                                                                                         p19

*Provision for Doubtful Debts Account*

| Date | Particulars | Fo. | Totals | Date | Particulars | Fo. | Totals |
|------|-------------|-----|--------|------|-------------|-----|--------|
| | | | | 200X | | | |
| | | | | Mar 31 | Profit and loss | NL27 | 600.00 |

p27                                                                                         p27

*Profit and Loss Account*

| Date | Particulars | Fo. | Totals | Date | Particulars | Fo. | Totals |
|------|-------------|-----|--------|------|-------------|-----|--------|
| 200X | | | | | 200X | | |
| Mar 31 | Provision for Doubtful debts | NL19 | 600.00 | | | | |
| 31 | Bad debts | NL20 | 200.00 | | | | |

Fig. 77. Accounting for bad and doubtful debts in the ledger.

Not every credit customer (or other debtor) will pay what he/she owes. They may dispute the amounts; some may disappear or go out of business. The debts they owe to the business may be bad, or of doubtful value. If so, our accounts must reflect the fact.

Accounting for bad and doubtful debts, like depreciation, means estimating an erosion of value. But it differs from depreciation because there it is time that erodes the value. Here it is more a product of fate. We can predict what effect age will have on physical assets like motor cars, but we cannot very easily predict which, and how many, debtors won't pay their bills. If we could, we should never have given them credit in the first place! There are no special calculation techniques for bad and doubtful debts as there are in depreciation. You just need to choose a suitable overall percentage, and make specific adjustments from time to time in the light of experience.

When a company becomes aware that a debt is uncollectable, because, for example, the customer has been declared bankrupt, or the company has gone into liquidation, the debt is written off by crediting the relevant sales ledger account and debiting bad debts account. Figure 77 provides an example.

### Postings

We may know a debt has become worthless because the individual has gone bankrupt, or a company has gone into liquidation. Such a debt must then be posted to a 'bad debts account'. This is an account for specific debts we know to be bad. This is quite aside from our provision for a percentage of debtors control account going bad. If bad debts are recovered later on, we will treat them as credits to bad debts account, and a debit to cash account. We do not need to reopen the individual debtor account, since the posting would result in its immediate closure anyway.

Only if a firm is in liquidation, or if an individual has too few assets to be worth suing, do we need to write off the debt to bad debts account. If the non-payer does have sufficient funds, the firm may be able to sue them successfully for the debt.

### Saving tax and being realistic

The reason we need to write down bad or doubtful debts is twofold. First, the firm will be charged income tax on its profits; if the profit figure is shown without allowing for the cost of bad and doubtful debts it will be higher than it should rightly be, and the firm will end up paying more tax than it needs to.

Secondly, the balance sheet should show as realistically as possible the value of the assets of the business. After all, interested parties such as bankers, investors and suppliers will rely on it when making decisions about the firm. Failure to write off bad debts, and too little provision for doubtful debts, will mean an unrealistically high current asset of debtors being shown. Accountants are guided by the principle of *prudence*. This provides that (a) losses should be provided for as soon as anticipated and (b) it is preferable to understate profit than overstate it.

```
                              JOURNAL
Date        Particulars       Fo.        Debit      Credit
200X
Aug 30    Bad debts          NL9        200.00
          Vat                NL8         35.00
          H. Baker           SL5                    235.00
To write off bad debt.
```

```
                         NOMINAL LEDGER
p9                          Bad debts
Dr                                                          Cr
Date                                   Date
200X                                   200X
Aug 30  H. Baker       SL5    200.00
```

```
                         NOMINAL LEDGER
p8                            VAT
Dr                                                          Cr
Date                                   Date
200X                                   200X
Aug 30  Bad debts     SL5     35.00
```

```
                          SALES LEDGER
p5                          H. Baker
Dr                                                          Cr
Date                                   Date
2000X                                  200X
Aug 1                                  Aug 30  Bad debts   NL9   200.00
                                               VAT         NL8    35.00
```

Fig. 78. Worked example of bad debt accounting taking VAT into account.

1. Suppose A. Frazer received information on 30 August that H. Baker, a customer who owed the firm £200, had been declared bankrupt; the appropriate entries in the books would be as shown in Fig. 78.

```
                              JOURNAL
200X       Particulars                   Fo.      Debit      Credit
Mar 31     Profit and loss               NL30     600.00
           Provision for doubtful debts  NL20                 600.00
           To provide for doubtful debts
```

```
                               LEDGER
NL20                  Provision for doubtful debts
Dr.                                                         Cr.
200X                                   200X
                                       Mar 31   Profit and Loss   600.00
```

```
NL30                      Profit and loss
Dr.                                                         Cr.
200X                                   200X
Mar 31   Provision for
         Doubtful debts      600.00
```

Fig. 79. Worked example of provision for doubtful debts (2).

2. Suppose that A. Frazer estimates his necessary bad debts provision for the year ending 31 March as £600; the book-keeping entries would be as shown in Fig. 79.

## Posting to 'provision for doubtful debts account' and 'bad debts account'

You will need:

- the journal
- the nominal ledger
- the sales ledger.

## Step by step

1. Decide the percentage figure and from that the actual amount you will use as a provision for doubtful debts (e.g. 1% or 2%).

2. Write in the next available space in the journal the date (in the date column) and the words 'profit and loss account' in the particulars column.

3. Enter the value of your provision in the debit cash column.

4. Beneath the last entry in the particulars column, indenting slightly, write: 'provision for doubtful debts'.

5. Enter the same value in the credit cash column.

6. Repeat the process when writing off any actual bad debts, but in this case you need to debit the bad debts account and credit the individual debtor accounts.

7. Now post to the nominal and sales ledger, exactly following the instructions you have just written in the journal.

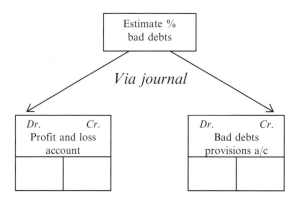

It is now time to change perspective. We are no longer dealing with pieces of the accounting system, but with different types of accounts for different purposes, beginning with accounts for partnerships. Partnership accounts differ from sole proprietor accounts in two ways:

- a profit and loss appropriation account is needed and
- separate capital accounts are needed for each partner.

In every other way, they are the same.

### What is a partnership?

Partnerships are business units owned jointly by more than one person. Such people may have joined in partnership for all kinds of reasons. Perhaps neither had enough capital on their own; perhaps they wished to obtain economies of scale by combining their capitals; perhaps they had matching skills or matching control of the factors of production (e.g. one owned land and buildings while the other had special skills). There are partnerships of solicitors, accountants, building contractors, agencies—in fact of almost any kind of business activity.

Each partner is responsible 'jointly and severally' for all the debts of the partnership. This means that if the business cannot pay its debts, the creditors can hold each and every partner personally responsible. More than that, if one partner has personal assets such as a house and savings, while the other partners have none, creditors can sue the partner who does have assets for all the debts of the partnership—not just for their 'share' of the debts.

There are endless types of financial arrangement in partnerships. For example profits may be shared in proportion to capital invested; or interest may be paid on capital before any residual net profit is shared equally, regardless of capital. Similarly, the partners may agree that interest will be charged on all individual drawings against capital. At the onset, they may decide that each working partner will receive a fixed salary. It is to take care of all such points that partnership accounts have these extra facilities.

Where there is no written partnership agreement, the Partnership Act 1890 (section 24) states that no interest is to be allowed on capital except where provided in excess of any agreement (in which case 5% would be allowed). No interest is to be charged on drawings; no partner will be entitled to a salary, and each will share the profits equally.

Advantages of partnerships over sole proprietorships:

- increased capital
- increased range of expertise
- sharing of responsibilities
- sharing of work
- sharing of risk.

Disadvantages are:

- loss of independent control
- profits have to be shared
- debts, or even insolvency of one partner can negatively affect the other partners.

The appropriation account is just an extension of the trading, profit and loss account. In it, we post the appropriation (i.e. sharing out) of net profit between the partners. We do not need an appropriation account in the accounts of a sole proprietor, because all the net profit goes to the one proprietor's capital account. In a partnership or limited company, things are a little more complicated.

- In a partnership some of the profit may be owed to the partners for interest on capitals they have invested.

- If a partner has drawn money from the business (other than salary) he/she may have to pay interest on it, according to arrangements between the parties. Any such interest payment will have to be deducted from any interest due to them on their capital. We show such transactions in the appropriation account.

- If a partner has lent money to the partnership, however, that is a very different thing. Any interest payable to that partner would be an expense to the business, not an appropriation of profit. Its proper place would be in the profit and loss account.

After deducting these items from the net profit (brought down from the profit and loss account) we have to show how the rest of the profit will be shared out. We will show an equal split, or an unequal one, depending on the profit-sharing arrangements between the partners.

### What you need
- the ledger

- details of interest rate on capital due to partners

- details of interest rate payable by partners on drawings

- details of partners' capitals

- details of partners' drawings

- details of partners' salaries and/or fees

- details of profit-sharing arrangements.

### Preparation
Work out the interest on capital due to each partner. Remember to apply the correct percentage interest rate. Work out the interest payable by each partner on their drawings, again applying the correct percentage interest rate.

*Horizontal format*

## FRAZER AND BAINES
### PROFIT AND LOSS APPROPRIATION ACCOUNT
for year ended 31 December 200X

| | | | | |
|---|---|---|---|---|
| Net profit b/d | | | | 21,000 |
| Interest on capital (10%) | | Interest on drawings (12%) | | |
| Frazer | 2,000 | Frazer | 240 | |
| Baines | 5,000 | Baines | 300 | 540 |
| | | | | |
| Salary: Frazer | 8,000 | 15,000 | | |
| | | | | |
| Share of Residual profits | | | | |
| Frazer (67%) | | 2,180 | | |
| Baines (33%) | | 4,360 | | |
| | | 21,540 | | 21,540 |

*Vertical format*

## PROFIT AND LOSS APPROPRIATION ACCOUNT
## OF FRAZER AND BAINES

| | | | |
|---|---|---|---|
| Net profit b/d | | | 21,000 |
| Frazer | | | |
| Interest on capital (10%) | 2,000 | | |
| Less interest on drawings (12%) | 240 | | |
| | 1,760 | | |
| Salary | 8,000 | 9,760 | |
| | | | |
| Baines | | | |
| Interest on capital (10%) | 5,000 | | |
| Less interest on drawings (12%) | 300 | 4,700 | |
| | | | |
| Share of profits in ratio 2:1 | | | |
| Frazer | 2,180 | | |
| Baines | 4,360 | 6,540 | 21,000 |
| | | | 00,000 |

Fig. 80. Worked examples of partnership accounts.

**Step by step**

1. Make another heading under the completed profit and loss account in the ledger: 'Profit and loss appropriation account'.

2. Bring down the net profit from the profit and loss account.

3. In the credit column record: 'Interest payable on drawings' for each partner, marking it accordingly.

4. In the debit column enter: 'Interest on capitals' for each partner, marking each entry accordingly.

5. In the debit column record the value of individual partners' salaries, marking each one accordingly.

6. Again in the debit column, record the individual profit shares of each partner, marking each one accordingly. Show the proportion, e.g. ½ or a percentage e.g. 50%.

7. Total up and balance this 'account' (the balance c/d will be zero).

**Converting final accounts into vertical format**

You can now rewrite your final accounts in a more useful vertical format. If you do, change the appropriation account in the same way. The figure opposite (bottom) shows how this is done.

The figure opposite (top) shows an alternative, horizontal layout, but remember that vertical formats are much more popular in Britain and you should use them in exams and in business unless told otherwise.

**Example: Frazer and Baines**

Frazer and Baines are partners. Frazer initially invested £20,000 in the business and Baines £50,000. Frazer took drawings of £2,000 during the year and Baines £2,500. It had been agreed at the onset that 10% interest would be paid on capitals, interest of 12% would be payable on drawings and that Frazer, because he, alone, would be working full-time in the business, would receive a salary of £8,000. Suppose, also, that the net profit shown in the profit and loss account at the end of the current year is £21,000. Following the step-by-step instruction given here, the examples opposite show what the appropriation account might look like.

*Before amalgamation*

# A. FRAZER
# BALANCE SHEET
as at 28 February 200X

FIXED ASSETS

| | | | |
|---|---|---|---|
| Workshop and yard | | | 45,000 |
| Machinery | 4,000 | | |
| Less provision for depreciation | 200 | 3,800 | |
| | | | |
| Motor van | 6,000 | | |
| Less provision for depreciation | 2,000 | 4,000 | 7,800 |
| Goodwill | | | 5,800 |
| | | | 58,600 |

CURRENT ASSETS

| | | |
|---|---|---|
| Stock of materials | 4,500 | |
| Debtors | 1,200 | |
| Cash at bank | 150 | |
| | 5,850 | |

Less CURRENT LIABILITIES

| | | |
|---|---|---|
| Creditors | 5,100 | |
| Working capital | | 750 |
| TOTAL ASSETS | | 59,350 |

| | |
|---|---|
| Financed by: | |
| CAPITAL as at 1 March 200X | 57,050 |
| Add profit | 11,300 |
| | 68,350 |
| | |
| Less drawings | 9,000 |
| TOTAL LIABILITIES | 59,350 |

---

*Before amalgamation*

# E. BAINES
# BALANCE SHEET
as at 28 February 200X

FIXED ASSETS

| | | |
|---|---|---|
| Machinery | 3,000 | |
| Less provision for depreciation | 150 | 2,850 |
| Motor lorry | 5,000 | |
| Less provision for depreciation | 1,000 | 4,000 |
| Goodwill | | 2,000 |
| | | 8,850 |

CURRENT ASSETS

| | | |
|---|---|---|
| Stock of materials | 900 | |
| Debtors | 4,000 | |
| Cash at bank | 41,000 | |
| Cash in hand | 500 | |
| | 46,400 | |

Less CURRENT LIABILITIES

| | | |
|---|---|---|
| Creditors | 2,600 | |
| Working capital | | 43,800 |
| TOTAL ASSETS | | 52,650 |

| | |
|---|---|
| Financed by: | |
| CAPITAL as at 1 March 200X | 42,450 |
| Add profit | 10,200 |
| TOTAL LIABILITIES | 52,650 |

Fig. 81. Two balance sheets before amalgamation into a partnership.

## Consolidation

Now we come to a new accounting technique, **consolidation**. The idea is to consolidate or amalgamate the accounts of two separate businesses into those of a single partnership. The method is very simple:

- we just add each of the individual balance sheet items together, after making adjustments in each for any changes in asset values agreed by the parties.

## Making the adjustments

Such adjustments may arise for example because A thinks their 'provision for bad debts' of 5% is reasonable, while B feels it should be 7½%; or B might feel that one of A's machines is not worth what A's balance sheet says it is; and so on. If the amalgamation is to go ahead, the parties will have to settle all such disagreements first.

When we make such adjustments, it is bound to affect the capital figure. So we also need to make the adjustment to the capital accounts, before consolidating the balance sheets by adding all their components together. Indeed, if we didn't adjust the capital accounts, the individual balance sheets would cease to balance, and then the consolidated one would not balance either.

## The 'goodwill' value of each business

The parties may agree that different values of **goodwill** existed in their businesses before amalgamation. Perhaps one business was long-established, while the other one was rather new and had not yet built such a good reputation. In such a case, each business would write an agreed figure for goodwill into its balance sheet before amalgamation. It would post the other side of the dual posting to the credit of its capital account. On amalgamation we then add the two goodwill amounts together, just like all the other assets.

## Writing off goodwill after amalgamation

If it is decided later on to write it off, the one aggregated goodwill figure in the post-amalgamation accounts will be credited to goodwill account; the debit entry to complete the dual posting will be posted to the partners' current accounts, in proportion to their profit-sharing arrangements (unless a different agreement exists between them).

**FRAZER AND BAINES**
**BALANCE SHEET**
as at 1 March 200X

FIXED ASSETS

| | | |
|---|---|---|
| Yard and workshop | | 45,000 |
| Machinery | | 6,650 |
| Motor van | | 4,000 |
| Motor lorry | | 4,000 |
| Goodwill | | 7,800 |
| | | 67,450 |

CURRENT ASSETS

| | | |
|---|---|---|
| Stock of materials | 5,400 | |
| Debtors | 5,200 | |
| Cash at bank | 41,150 | |
| Cash in hand | 500 | |
| | 52,250 | |

Less CURRENT LIABILITIES

| | | |
|---|---|---|
| Creditors | 7,700 | |
| Working capital | | |
| | | 44,550 |
| TOTAL ASSETS | | 112,000 |

Financed by:
CAPITAL ACCOUNTS

| | | |
|---|---|---|
| Frazer | | 59,350 |
| Baines | | 52,650 |
| | | 112,000 |

Fig. 82. Opening balance sheet of the new partnership.

124

On the previous pages we saw that, to amalgamate two businesses into one, we have to consolidate (add together) their two balance sheets. It is quite a simple procedure.

## What you need
- the two balance sheets
- details of any changes (adjustments) to the item values, as agreed between the owners of the two businesses.

## Step by step
1.  Adjust any item values as appropriate, in other words correct the amounts from their original values to the new agreed values.
2.  Take care to amend the capital values, too, so that the individual balance sheets do, in fact, still 'balance'.
3.  Add together the values of each item (other than depreciation). Then write out a consolidated balance sheet for the new partnership.

## Note on depreciation
Provision for depreciation is not carried over into the new partnership, because the business unit has in effect purchased the assets at their already written down value.

## Example
On the facing page we can see the consolidated balance sheet of the businesses of Frazer and Baines (their separate balance sheets were shown on page 122). Notice how the newly amalgamated partnership treats the machinery, motor van and motor lorry. The consolidated value of the machinery is £6,650, representing £3,800 (its written down value in Frazer's balance sheet) plus £2,850 (its written down value in Baines' balance sheet).

## New partner joining
When a new partner is admitted to a partnership their acquisition of a share in the existing value of goodwill means that other partners will lose. Those partners who gain should be charged the amount of their gain and those who lose should be compensated for their loss. Figure 83 shows the four stages in the process.

## Paying for the goodwill acquired
The new partner can pay for their share of goodwill in one of four ways. He/she can pay each partner for the amount of goodwill they have lost in allowing him/her to take a proportion of the total, e.g. in the example most recently used, Able, Bryce and Collins each gave up £3,750 of goodwill to the new partner, so a simple way would be for Dean to pay each of them a cheque for £3,750 which they can bank in their private accounts and no goodwill account needs to be opened.

Alternatively, a sum equal to the combined loss of goodwill (£11,250) can be paid into the partnership's account and this sum credited proportionally to the

| Stage 1 Partners | Old profit sharing ratios % | Share of goodwill | Stage 2 New profit sharing ratios % | Share of goodwill | Stage 3 Gain/loss | | Stage 4 Adjustment required |
|---|---|---|---|---|---|---|---|
| Able | 33 | 15,000 | 25 | 11,250 | 3,750 | Loss | Pay Able or credit his/her capital account |
| Bryce | 33 | 15,000 | 25 | 11,250 | 3,750 | Loss | Pay Bryce or credit his/her capital account |
| Collins | 33 | 15,000 | 25 | 11,250 | 3,750 | Loss | Pay Collins or credit his/her capital account |
| | | | 25 | 11,250 | 11,250 | Gain | Charge Dean or debit his/her capital account |
| | | 45,000 | | 45,000 | | | |

Fig. 83. The four stages of adjustment of the profit-sharing ratios and shares of goodwill on the admission of new partner.

*Goodwill*

| | | | | |
|---|---|---|---|---|
| Able | Capital | 15,000 | Balance c/d | 45,000 |
| Bryce | Capital | 15,000 | | |
| Collins | Capital | 15,000 | | |
| | | 45,000 | | 45,000 |

Fig. 84. An illustration of recording the capital changes resulting from the admission of a new partner.

capital accounts of Able, Bryce and Collins, i.e. £3,750 to each. Again, there would be no need to open a goodwill account in this case.

A third method would be to debit the new partner's capital account with the goodwill share they have acquired and credit the same to the capital accounts of the existing partners in accordance with their profit-sharing ratios. Again, there would be no need to open a goodwill account in this case.

A fourth method is to open a goodwill account and capitalise the existing goodwill shares, i.e. debit the goodwill account with the total value of the goodwill and post the equivalent value to the credit of the existing partners' capital accounts in the proportions of their profit-sharing ratios.

### Example
Suppose Dean joins the partnership of Able, Bryce and Collins. Goodwill is valued at £45,000 and the partners will share profits equally as has always been the case in the past. Their capitals are different, as you will see, but this does not affect the profit-sharing ratios as their capitals are remunerated by interest paid on them. Figure 84 shows the entries that will be made in the ledger to record the changes.

### Writing off the goodwill
After the adjustment has been made the goodwill can be written off by crediting the goodwill account with the full amount to close it down and debiting the partners' capital accounts in the proportions of their new profit-sharing ratios. Figure 85 provides an illustration of this.

### Changes in profit-sharing ratios for other reasons
The admission of a new partner is not the only circumstance in which profit-sharing ratios may change. They may change because a partner ceases to work full-time or his/her skills cease to be as important as those of the other partners. If a partner agrees to take a smaller percentage of profits he/she deserves to be compensated for what they have given up. The financial adjustments can be made by the same methods as for changes in profit sharing as a result of a new partner joining. See Figure 86.

### Death or retirement of a partner
If a partner dies or retires from the partnership goodwill has to be accounted for so that the retiring partner, or their estate if deceased, can be paid a fair value for their share in the business. The process is essentially the same as for a joining partner and once the adjustments to the capitals have been made the goodwill can be written off if desired and the account closed down.

### Example
Suppose Bryce is retiring from the partnership of Able, Bryce, Collins and Dean The value of goodwill has been agreed as £48,000. Their capitals are £50,000,

£30,000, £20,000 and £50,000 respectively, but they share profits equally. Figure 87 shows how this would be dealt with in the accounts.

Bryce's capital account stands at £42,000 now that his share of goodwill has been capitalised, so on retiring from the partnership he will receive this amount.

If a goodwill account had already existed it may have needed updating. It may have been undervalued or overvalued. If a goodwill account is undervalued debit it with the amount by which it should be increased and credit the partners' capital accounts in the proportions of their profit-sharing ratios. If goodwill is overvalued in the accounts then do the exact opposite.

Again, once the adjustments have been made the goodwill can be written off by crediting the account with the full value of goodwill and debiting the partners' capital accounts in the proportions of their post-adjustment, profit-sharing ratios.

*Capital accounts*

| | Able | Bryce | Collins | Dean | | Able | Bryce | Collins | Dean |
|---|---|---|---|---|---|---|---|---|---|
| Balances c/d | 65,000 | 45,000 | 35,000 | 50,000 | Balance b/d | 50,000 | 30,000 | 20,000 | |
| | | | | | Cash for capital | | | | 50,000 |
| | | | | | Goodwill | 15,000 | 15,000 | 15,000 | |
| | 65,000 | 45,000 | 35,000 | 50,000 | | 65,000 | 45,000 | 35,000 | 50,000 |

*Goodwill*

| | | | |
|---|---|---|---|
| Balance b/d | 45,000 | Able — Capital | |
| | | Bryce — Capital | |
| | | Collins — Capital | |
| | | Dean — Capital | |
| | | | 45,000 |

Fig. 85. An illustration of writing off goodwill after the admission of a new partner.

*Capital accounts*

| | Able | Bryce | Collins | Dean | | Able | Bryce | Collins | Dean |
|---|---|---|---|---|---|---|---|---|---|
| Goodwill | 11,250 | 11,250 | 11,250 | 11,250 | Balances b/d | 65,000 | 45,000 | 35,000 | 50,000 |
| Balances c/d | 53,750 | 33,750 | 23,750 | 38,750 | | | | | |
| | 65,000 | 45,000 | 35,000 | 50,000 | | 65,000 | 45,000 | 35,000 | 50,000 |

Fig. 86. An illustration of accounting for a change in the profit-sharing ratios in a partnership.

## Goodwill

| | | | Balance c/d | 48,000 |
|---|---|---|---|---|
| Able | Capital | 12,000 | | |
| Bryce | Capital | 12,000 | | |
| Collins | Capital | 12,000 | | |
| Dean | Capital | 12,000 | | |
| | | 48,000 | | 48,000 |

## Capital accounts

| | Able | Bryce | Collins | Dean | | Able | Bryce | Collins | Dean |
|---|---|---|---|---|---|---|---|---|---|
| Balances c/d | 62,000 | 42,000 | 32,000 | 62,000 | Balances c/d | 50,000 | 30,000 | 20,000 | 50,000 |
| | | | | | Shares of goodwill | 12,000 | 12,000 | 12,000 | 12,000 |
| | 62,000 | 42,000 | 32,000 | 62,000 | | 62,000 | 42,000 | 32,000 | 62,000 |

Fig. 87. An illustration of using the goodwill account to adjust the capital accounts on the retirement of a partner.

# CERTIFICATE OF INCORPORATION
# OF A PRIVATE LIMITED COMPANY

Company No.

The Registrar of Companies for England and Wales hereby certifies that

is this day incorporated under the Companies Act 1985 as a private company and that the company is limited.

Given at Companies House, Cardiff, the

THE OFFICIAL SEAL OF THE
REGISTRAR OF COMPANIES

*Companies House*
—— *for the record* ——

Fig. 88. Certificate of Incorporation of a Limited Company.

# 52    Limited companies

## Public and private companies
The form and extent of the accounts of limited companies are governed by the Companies Act 1985.

There are two main types of limited company:

- **public** limited companies, which have Plc after their name; and

- **private** limited companies, which have Ltd after their name.

Public companies have to disclose more information than private companies.

## The company as a 'person'
The main difference between the company and other business entities is that it is a legal entity or 'person' quite separate from the shareholders. The partnership and the sole proprietorship on the other hand are inseparable from the people involved: if these two businesses cannot pay their debts then the partners or proprietors may be called upon to settle them personally, because 'the business's debts' are in reality 'their debts'. On the other hand a company's debts are its debts alone. The shareholders cannot be called upon to settle the company's debts: their liability is limited to the original value of their shares. In law, a company is a separate legal 'person' (though obviously not a human one), and so has its own rights and obligations under the law.

## Share capital
The capital account has its own special treatment in limited company accounts. The capital of limited companies is divided into shares, which people can buy and sell. A share in the capital of the company entitles the shareholder to a share of the profits of the company—just as a partner owning capital in a firm is entitled to profits.

## Authorised share capital
Authorised share capital is just a statement of the share capital a company is authorised to issue, not what it has issued. The issued share capital is the amount of that limit that it actually has issued, i.e. the shares it has sold. It is only this latter amount that actually represents the company's capital.

The authorised share capital shows the nominal value of the company's shares. That is a rather arbitrarily chosen rounded-figure value at incorporation of the business selected for the purpose of making it easy to divide up the equity of the firm. Suppose a sole proprietor, whose total net assets are £360,000 is incorporating his/her business in order to take in two other investors, but wishes to retain the controlling share of 51%. Allocation of shares representing the net assets would be a messy business unless an easily divisible figure was used to represent the £360,000 net asset value. A figure of £100,000 can be registered as its authorised share capital, divided into 100,000 ordinary shares of £1, each of which represents £3.60 of the actual share capital.

Even if the authorised share capital did reflect exactly the net assets of the business, as might be the case where a new business is incorporated from scratch, five years later the company may be worth twice as much as when it started because of reinvested profits. Therefore any shares still to be issued will be worth probably twice as much as they were when the company started even though their nominal value will still be listed as the same figure as when the company was formed. It is necessary to keep them listed at their nominal value because that reflects the nominal proportion of the share capital that they represent. The difference between the nominal value and the market value is know as **share premium.** The excess over nominal value that is charged for the shares is posted to **share premium account** and shows up in the balance sheet as such.

### Ordinary and preference shares
There is, however, a difference, because limited companies can have different kinds of shares with different kinds of entitlements attached to them, e.g. **ordinary shares**, and **preference** shares.

- Preference shares receive a fixed rate of dividend (profit share), provided sufficient profit has been made. For example it might be 10% of the original value of the preference shares.

- Ordinary shares have no such limit on their dividend, which can be as high as the profits allow. However, they come second in the queue, so to speak, if the profit is too little to pay dividends to both the preference and ordinary shareholders.

Furthermore, a company is allowed to retain part of the profits to finance growth. How much, is up to the directors. Unless otherwise stated in the company's memorandum of association, preference shares are cumulative, in other words any arrears of dividend can be carried forward to future years until profits are available to pay them. Since the Companies Act 1985, a company is allowed to issue redeemable shares, preference and ordinary. These are shares that the company can redeem (buy back) from the shareholder at their request.

### Debentures
Some of the net assets of a company may be financed by debentures. These are loans, and interest has to be paid on them. Since debentures have to be repaid, we have to show them as liabilities in the balance sheet.

*Format 1*

1. Turnover
2. Cost of sales
3. Gross profit or loss
4. Distribution costs
5. Administrative expenses
6. Other operating income
7. Income from shares in group companies
8. Income from shares in related companies
9. Income from other fixed asset investments
10. Other interest receivable and similar income
11. Amounts written off investments
12. Interest payable and similar charges
13. Tax on profit or loss on ordinary activities
14. Profit or loss on ordinary activities after taxation
15. Extraordinary income
16. Extraordinary charges
17. Extraordinary profit or loss
18 Tax on extraordinary profit or loss
19. Other taxes not shown under the above items
20. Profit or loss for the financial year

*Format 2*

1. Turnover
2. Change in stocks of finished goods and in work in progress
3. Own work capitalised
4. Other operating income
5. (a) Raw materials and consumables
   (b) Other external charges
6. Staff costs:
   (a) wages and salaries
   (b) social security costs
   (c) other pension costs
7. (a) Depreciation and other amounts written off tangible and intangible fixed assets
   (b) Exceptional amounts written off current assets
8. Other operating charges
9. Income from shares in group companies
10. Income from shares in related companies
11. Income from other fixed asset investments
12. Other interest receivable and similar income
13 Amounts written off investments
14. Interest payable and similar charges
15. Tax on profit or loss on ordinary activities
16. Profit or loss on ordinary activities after taxation
17. Extraordinary income
18. Extraordinary charges
19. Extraordinary profit or loss
20. Tax on extraordinary profit or loss
21. Other taxes not shown under the above items
22. Profit or loss for the financial year

Fig. 89. Profit and loss account formats under the 1985 Companies Act.

### The profit and loss appropriation account

The appropriation of net profit has to be shown in company accounts, so we need to draw up a **profit and loss appropriation account**. This shows how much of the profit is being set aside for taxation, how much is being distributed in dividends on shares, and how much is being retained in the company for future growth.

### A limited company's statutory 'books'

The law requires a company to keep the following books, as well as its books of account:

- a register of members (shareholders)
- a register of charges (liabilities such as mortgages and debentures)
- a register of directors and managers
- a minutes book.

### Annual audit

It also requires it to appoint an external **auditor**. This person is an accountant, not employed by the company, who checks that the entries in the accounts are all correct, and that the accounts give a 'true and fair view' of the company.

### Special points on company accounts

Limited company accounts differ from those of other business units in several other ways. For sole proprietors and partners, the profit and loss account is closed each year by transferring any balance to capital account. In the case of limited companies, any undistributed profits stay on the profit and loss account as **reserves** along with undistributed profits for all previous periods. However, to avoid showing a high profit and loss account balance, a company will often transfer some of it to a **general reserve account**, when compiling the profit and loss account. These reserves, along with paid up shares, are called **shareholders' funds** because they are owned by the shareholders.

In the balance sheet of a limited company creditors have to be analysed into those falling due for payment within a year, and those falling due in more than a year (e.g. long term loans).

## ARMSTRONG ENGINEERING
## TRIAL BALANCE
as at 31 December 200X

|  | £ | £ |
|---|---|---|
| Sales | | 308,000 |
| Opening stock | 15,000 | |
| Purchases | 180,000 | |
| Closing stock | 18,000 | 18,000 |
| Wages | 22,000 | |
| Auditors' fees | 5,000 | |
| Motor expenses | 6,700 | |
| Insurance | 2,000 | |
| Heat and light | 5,000 | |
| Postage | 1,500 | |
| Stationery | 4,000 | |
| Interest on debenture | 600 | |
| Depreciation | 4,500 | |
| Bad debts | 2,500 | |
| Provision for doubtful debts | | 6,160 |
| Freehold premises | 98,240 | |
| Fixtures and fittings | 10,000 | |
| Provision for depreciation on fixtures and fittings | | 500 |
| Motor lorry | 10,000 | |
| Provision for depreciation on motor lorry | | 2,000 |
| Machinery | 40,000 | |
| Provision for depreciation on machinery | | 2,000 |
| Debtors and creditors | 48,700 | 22,500 |
| Cash at bank | 16,450 | |
| Cash in hand | 50 | |
| Opening balance of profit and loss account | | 23,400 |
| Share capital:    Ordinary shares | | 77,680 |
|                 Preference shares | | 30,000 |
| | 490,240 | 490,240 |

Fig. 90. A simple example of a trial balance of a limited company.

## Directors duties regarding accounts

The directors and auditors of companies are responsible by law for compiling an annual report in a form governed by law. This is for shareholders, the public and HM Revenue and Customs (HMRC).

The annual report must include a trading, profit and loss account and balance sheet, showing fixed and current assets, all costs of current and long-term liabilities, share capital and reserves, provision for taxation and loan repayments. The report must also include any unusual financial facts, e.g. effects of any changes in accounting procedures. It must also disclose things like values of exports, donations to political parties and directors salaries, where they exceed £60,000 per annum.

The auditors report must also state the methods of depreciation used.

The combined document must give a *true and fair view* of the financial affairs of the company.

Reasons companies must publish their accounts are:

- to provide information to enable shareholders to make informed decisions on whether to invest
- to help prevent fraud and corruption.

The Companies Act 1985 gives four alternative layouts for the profit and loss account (two horizontal and two vertical) and two for the balance sheet (one horizontal and one vertical). The choice is up to the directors, but must not then be changed without good and stated reasons. Vertical layouts are the most popular in the UK, so it is those we will deal with here. Remember, though, that the trading, profit and loss account is first of all a ledger account, so it inevitably starts out in horizontal format. When we are ready to distribute it, inside or outside the firm, we can rewrite it in the more popular vertical format. The two alternative vertical formats laid down by the Companies Act 1985 are shown opposite.

## Turnover and cost of sales

Turnover means sales. Cost of sales is found by adding purchases and opening stock, plus carriage inwards costs, and deducting the value of closing stock.

## Distribution costs

Includes costs directly incurred in delivering the goods to customers.

## Administration expenses

Includes such things as wages, directors' remuneration, motor expenses (other than those included in distribution costs), auditor's fees, and so on.

## Other operating income

This means all income other than from the firm's trading activities, e.g. income from rents on property or interest on loans.

### Directors' report

A Directors' report must accompany all published accounts. 'Small' companies, however, are exempt from filing one with the Registrar of Companies; also they only have to file a modified version of their balance sheet, and do not have to file a profit and loss account at all. Medium-sized companies also have some concessions, in that a modified form of profit and loss account and accompanying notes is allowed.

### Limitations of published accounts

• Creative accounting can hide negative information.
• Not all the relevant facts have to be disclosed.

### Internal accounts

Internal accounts or management accounts are those prepared only for use within the company. Unlike published accounts, they are not required by law to be set out in a certain way. However, it pays to keep them as consistent as possible with the published accounts, so that the latter can be drawn up just by adapting the internal accounts slightly.

### A ledger account

Remember, the trading, profit and loss account is first and foremost a ledger account, so we should begin by treating it as such. Suppose we have all the accounting information ready in the trial balance: this is how we would go about preparing the final accounts.

### What you need

- the ledger (all divisions)

- the journal

- the trial balance

- details of end of year adjustments.

### Compiling company final accounts step by step

Turn back to page 95 and see the tips for preparatory work before you put together the final accounts. Remember to alter your trial balance to take account of adjustments, and to label each item in it according to where it will end up in the trading (T), profit and loss (P) account, or balance sheet (B).

1.  Journalise the ledger postings exactly according to the labelling you have just written on the trial balance. In other words, post each item labelled 'T' to the trading account and each item labelled 'P' to the profit and loss account. Post them all to the same side of such accounts (debit or credit) as those on which they appear in the trial balance. The other side of the posting, of course, goes to the account from which they are being transferred. (If you are in doubt about how to journalise, see page 51.)

2.  When you have entered all the ledger postings, write beneath them: 'To close revenue and expense accounts and transfer balances to the trading, profit and loss account'.

3.  Now post to the trading account, following exactly the instructions you have just written in the journal.

4.  Total up and balance the trading account. Bring the balance down to the profit and loss account, as 'gross profit b/d'.

5.  Now post to the profit and loss account, following exactly the instructions you have just written in the journal.

## DEBENTURE INTEREST

| Dr | | | | | Cr |
|---|---|---|---|---|---|
| **200X** | | | **200X** | | |
| Aug 31 | Bank | 600 | | | |
| Dec 31 | Accrued c/d | 450 | Dec 31 | Profit and loss | 1,050 |
| | | 1,050 | | | 1,050 |

## ELECTRICITY

| Dr | | | | | Cr |
|---|---|---|---|---|---|
| **200X** | | | **200X** | | |
| Apr 30 | EDA | 300 | Dec 31 | Profit and loss | 1,100 |
| Jul 31 | EDA | 300 | | | |
| Oct 31 | EDA | 300 | | | |
| Dec 31 | Accrued c/d | 200 | | | |
| | | 1,100 | | | 1,100 |

## INSURANCE

| Dr | | | | | Cr |
|---|---|---|---|---|---|
| **200X** | | | **200X** | | |
| Jul 31 | Bettercover | 2,000 | Dec 31 | Profit and loss | 1,000 |
| | | | Dec 31 | Prepayment c/d | 1,000 |
| | | 2,000 | | | 2,000 |

## PROVISION FOR DOUBTFUL DEBTS

| Dr | | | | | Cr |
|---|---|---|---|---|---|
| **200X** | | | **200X** | | |
| Jul 31 | | | Jan 1 | Balance b/d | 6,160 |
| | | | Jul 31 | Profit and loss | 1,540 |
| Dec 31 | Balance c/d | 7,700 | | | |
| | | 7,700 | | | 7,700 |

Fig. 91. An illustration of accounting for various end of year adjustments.

### End of year adjustments

Now things are never quite that tidy at the end of the year as to allow for merely transferring all the relevant ledger balances to the trading, profit and loss account and listing those remaining in the balance sheet. The ultimate source documents for sales and purchase records are the invoices and they do not tell the complete story.

### Accrued expenses

The company will have had bills for its electricity and gas usage but the meter reading dates are unlikely to coincide exactly with the end of the company's financial year. There will, therefore, have been some power usage that has not yet been billed. If we are going to show a true and fair view of the profit or loss, as is always the aim, we have to make adjustments in the final accounts to reflect these items of expenditure that have not yet been billed.

A similar situation may exist with loans. Supposing a firm has debenture loans payable annually but the date of the interest payment is a month after the end of the financial year. There will be a figure of $^{11}/_{12}$ of the annual interest payment to be accounted for in the final statements because that has been an expense to the firm over the past year but one which does not appear in the books to date. These items are called accrued expenses or accruals.

Other expenses which can accrue are rent, business rates, employees' wages and indeed, any service that is supplied over a period of time is likely to leave the firm some accrued expense to deal with at the end of the financial year.

An assessment needs to be made of their value. For example, if quarterly electricity usage is £1,200 and the last meter reading was a month ago then it would be reasonable to estimate that usage of £400 worth of electricity has accrued since the last bill was entered into the accounts. An adjustment has to be made in the final accounts for this. The simplest way of doing it is by entering the accrual as a c/d figure on the debit side of the ledger account for Electricity. This will increase the figure posted to the profit and loss account to the extent that it will now reflect the real usage of electricity—that which has been billed for plus that which has not. At the commencement of the next accounting year this c/d balance will be brought down to the opposite side, which will have the opposite effect, deducting that amount from the value showing for that year, thus ensuring that the amount will not be claimed twice

### Prepayments

On the other hand, there are some accounts that are paid in advance. Insurance premiums are an example. Suppose a firm pays the insurance on its premises annually and six months have elapsed since the last renewal date. It would be wrong for the firm to claim the expense of 12 months insurance against its profits if it has only used six months of the cover. It still has the other six months left so it cannot claim the cost of that six months against tax. A similar but opposite adjustment has to be made here. A carried down balance is used but on the

**ARMSTRONG ENGINEERING**
**TRIAL BALANCE**
**as at 31 December 200X**

| | £ | £ |
|---|---|---|
| Sales | | 308,000 |
| Opening stock | 15,000 | |
| Purchases | 180,000 | |
| Closing stock | 18,000 | 18,000 |
| Wages | 22,000 | |
| Auditors' fees | 5,000 | |
| Motor expenses | 6,700 | |
| Insurance | 1,000 2,000 | |
| Heat and light | 5,200 5,000 | |
| Postage | 1,500 | |
| Stationery | 4,000 | |
| Interest on debenture | 1,050 600 | |
| Depreciation | 4,500 | |
| Bad debts | 2,500 | |
| Provision for doubtful debts | | 6,160 |
| Freehold premises | 98,240 | |
| Fixtures and fittings | 10,000 | |
| Provision for depreciation on fixtures and fittings | | 500 |
| Motor lorry | 10,000 | |
| Provision for depreciation on motor lorry | | 2,000 |
| Machinery | 40,000 | |
| Provision for depreciation on machinery | | 2,000 |
| Debtors and creditors | 48,700 | 22,500 |
| Cash at bank | 16,450 | |
| Cash in hand | 50 | |
| Opening balance of profit and loss account | | 23,400 |
| Share capital: Ordinary shares | | 77,680 |
| Preference shares | | 30,000 |
| Prepayments | 1,000 | |
| Accruals | | 650 |
| Increase in provision for doubtful debts | | 1,540 |
| Profit and loss | 1,540 | |
| | 490,240 | 490,240 |
| | 492,430 | 492,430 |

Fig. 92. A trial balance adjusted to take account of accruals and prepayments.

opposite side of the ledger account for insurance. At the beginning of the new accounting year these accruals are reversed in the ledgers.

Figures 91 and 92 provide illustrations of accounting for an accrual and a prepayment in the ledger accounts.

**Making things easy for yourself**

There is no harm in making longhand adjustments in the trial balance to crystallise your thinking and relieve the demands on your memory; it is, after all, a working document rather than a document for publication. If there are many adjustments, however, it will be better to use an extended trial balance format to avoid clutter and maintain clarity. You can find an example of this in the chapter on trial balances. See Figure 52 on page 80.

## Using accruals and prepayments accounts in the ledger

Instead of simply treating accruals and prepayments as carried down balances on the relevant expense accounts some people prefer to open ledger accounts specifically for accruals and prepayments.

*Accruals*

Any additional amount of an expense debited to the profit and loss account over and above that which appeared in the ledger account for that expense, i.e. accrued usage not yet billed for, would have the counter-entry posted in the credit side of the accruals account. At the commencement of the new financial year that posting to the credit of accruals account would be reversed by debiting the account and the counter-entry posted to the credit side of the relevant expense account, so that once the next bill arrives and the amount is posted to the ledger, the balance will be reduced by the amount accounted for in last year's figures.

*Prepayments*

Any part of the balance on an expense account which is not posted to the profit and loss account, representing part of the expense paid for but not yet used would be posted to the debit side of the prepayments account, thus allowing both sides of the expense account to balance and close.

At the start of the new financial year the prepayments account would be credited and the debit entry would be posted to the relevant expense with the effect that the unused part of the prepaid expense would then appear as an expense in the period in which it would be used.

## Dealing with corporation tax in the final accounts

It is current orthodox practice to account for corporation tax in the profit and loss account, or income statement as it is increasingly being called. When all the expenses have been deducted from the gross profit you arrive at a figure of profit before taxation. The computed figure for taxation is then deducted from this to

## TRADING PROFIT AND LOSS ACCOUNT
*for the year ended 31 December 200X*

| | | | |
|---|---|---|---|
| Opening stock | 15,000 | Turnover | 308,000 |
| Purchases | 180,000 | Closing stock | 18,000 |
| Balance c/d | 131,000 | | |
| | 326,000 | | 326,000 |
| | | Gross profit b/d | 131,000 |
| Wages | 22,000 | | |
| Auditor's fees | 5,000 | | |
| Motor expenses | 6,700 | | |
| Insurance | 1,000 | | |
| Heat and light | 5,200 | | |
| Postage | 1,500 | | |
| Stationery | 4,000 | | |
| Depreciation | 4,500 | | |
| Bad debts | 2,500 | | |
| Increase in provision for bad debts | 1,540 | | |
| Loan note (debenture) interest | 1,050 | | |
| Balance c/d | 76,010 | | |
| | 131,000 | | 131,000 |

Fig. 93. The trading, profit and loss account after end of year adjustments.

## ARMSTRONG ENGINEERING
### Trading profit and loss account
*for year ended 31 December 200X*

| | | | |
|---|---|---|---|
| Turnover | | | 308,000 |
| Less cost of sales | | | |
| Stock as at 1 January 200X | | 15,000 | |
| Add purchases | | 180,000 | |
| | | 195,000 | |
| Less stock as at 31 December 200X | | 18,000 | |
| | | | 177,000 |
| Gross profit b/d | | | 131,000 |
| Less administration expenses | | | |
| Wages | | 22,000 | |
| Auditor's fees | | 5,000 | |
| Motor expenses | | 6,700 | |
| Insurance | | 1,000 | |
| Heat and light | | 5,200 | |
| Postage | | 1,500 | |
| Stationery | | 4,000 | |
| Depreciation | | 4,500 | |
| Bad debts | | 2,500 | |
| Increase in provision for bad debts | | 1,540 | 53,940 |
| | | | 77,060 |
| Loan note interest | | | 1,050 |
| Profit for year before taxation | | | 76,010 |
| Corporation tax | | | 32,000 |
| Retained profits | | | 44,010 |

| Note: Share dividends paid | | | |
|---|---|---|---|
| Preference | 5% | 1,500 | |
| Ordinary | 12% | 9,322 | |

Fig. 94. Trading, profit and loss account in vertical format

```
ARMSTRONG ENGINEERING
Trading profit and loss account
for year ended 31 December 200X

Turnover                                                   308,000
Less cost of sales                                         177,000
Gross profit                                               131,000
Less administration expenses                                53,940
                                                            77,060
Less loan note interest                                      1,050
Profit on ordinary activities before taxation               76,010
Less tax on profit from ordinary activities                 32,000
Retained profit on ordinary activities after taxation       44,010


Proposed share dividends:
Preference (5%)              1,500
Ordinary (12%)               9,322
```

Fig. 95. The same trading, profit and loss account simplified and converted
for use within the company.

```
ARMSTRONG ENGINEERING
Statement of  changes in equity
for the year ending 31 December 200X

Retained profits                                                          44,010

Less transfer to non-current assets replacement reserve      10,000

Share dividends paid:
     Preference   5%                    1,500
     Ordinary    12%                    9,322          10,822          20,822
                                                                       23,188
```

Fig. 96. Example of accounting for a  transfer to a reserve account and payment of
dividends in a statement of changes in equity.

give a figure for profit for the year after taxation (or retained profits as it is called in the new international terminology).

### Dealing with dividends

Dividends on preference shares and ordinary shares should be shown only as a note on the profit and loss account, as it is not actually an expense but rather a distribution of profit. The place where its effect on the finances of the company is shown is in the statement of changes in equity, as it represents some equity leaving the company. However, even there it is important to only show those dividends that have actually been paid and which, therefore, represent funds that have actually left the company.

### Worked example

Let's take the trial balance extracted from the books of Armstrong Engineering Ltd shown on page 142. Suppose we have to make the following adjustments before drawing up the final accounts. Debenture interest of £1,200 per annum is payable by the firm at half yearly intervals on 14 August and 14 February so there is an accrual of four and a half months' debenture interest that has to be accounted for.

Electricity usage is billed quarterly at the end of April, July, October and January. It averages out at £300 per quarter, so there is an accrual of $^2/_3$ of a quarter since the last meter reading which has not been billed and so won't be reflected in the accounts. We would be understating the expenses if we did not account for it in the final figures.

Suppose an annual insurance premium of £2,000 is paid each year on the renewal date of 1 July. Only half of this will have been used up as at the date of the final accounts so we would be overstating the expenses if we did not account for a prepayment of £1,000.

Suppose we have found that the bad debts provision we had made of £6,160, based on 2% of turnover, was insufficient to cover the value of debts that actually became uncollectable during the past year and, in view of the worsening of the economic climate that is being predicted, we have decided it would be prudent to increase the bad debts provision by a further ½% of turnover. The extra provision must be debited to the profit and loss account and credited to the provision for bad debts account. We can only charge the increase. The balance carried over from the previous year has already been charged against tax. The full amount of the debts which actually were written off in the past year have been charged against tax as bad debts so the provision that was set up and charged against tax remained intact. It can't be charged for twice. We can charge the increase, though, as that has not been claimed against tax yet.

Let's suppose corporation tax payable is computed to be £32,000 and the firm proposes to pay dividends of 5% on the preference shares and 12% on the ordinary shares.

Figures 91 to 96 provide an illustration of the accounting for all these items in the final accounts.

## No ledger posting needed

The balance sheet is not a ledger account, so there is no ledger posting to do. We simply draw up a statement showing the balances left on the ledger after we have compiled the trading, profit and loss account. Using the trial balance on page 142 we will compile a balance sheet for internal use, that also meets the requirements of the Companies Act 1985 (Format 1).

## Compiling a company balance sheet step by step

1. Make a heading: 'Fixed assets'. Allocate three cash columns on the right of a sheet of paper, and head them 'Cost', 'Less provision for depreciation', and 'Net book value'. Underneath, record the values for each fixed asset. Net book value means value after depreciation. On the left write against each the name of the asset concerned. Total up each column and cross cast (cross check).

2. Make a heading: 'Current assets'. Enter in the second column the value of stock then write against it on the left: 'Stock'. Beneath the figure enter the value of debtors, and write against it on the left: 'Debtors'. In the second column list the values of the other current assets. On the left write against each the name of the current asset concerned. Total up this column.

3. Make a heading: 'Less creditors'. In the first column list the values of creditors and accruals relating to this category. On the left, against each, write the names of each class, (i) 'Amounts falling due within one year' and (ii) 'Accruals'. Total up this column. Place the total in the second column below the total for current assets.

4. Subtract the total current liabilities (creditors) from the total current assets. Place the total in the third column below the total net book value for fixed assets. You need to place it below the level of the last total because there is an important phrase to be written against this subtotal: 'Net current assets' (in other words 'Working capital'). Add the two totals in the third column and write against that sum: 'Total net assets'. If there were any long term creditors (falling due after one year), e.g debentures, we would now list them,

| | |
|---|---|
| e.g. total net assets | 100,000 |
| Less × % debentures | 20,000 |
| | 80,000 |

but in our data there are none.

## BALANCE SHEET
### as at 31 December 200X

| | Cost | Less provision for depreciation | Net book value |
|---|---|---|---|
| **Fixed assets** | | | |
| Premises | 103,400 | | 103,400 |
| Fixtures and fittings | 10,000 | 500 | 9,500 |
| Machinery | 40,000 | 2,000 | 38,000 |
| Motor lorry | 10,000 | 2,000 | 8,000 |
| | 163,400 | 4,500 | 158,900 |
| **Current assets** | | | |
| Stock | | 18,000 | |
| Debtors | | 48,700 | |
| Cash at bank | | 19,850 | |
| Cash in hand | | 50 | |
| | | 86,600 | |
| **Less creditors** | | | |
| Amounts falling due within | | | |
| 1 year | 22,500 | | |
| Accruals | 4,000 | | |
| Proposed dividends | 34,500 | 61,000 | |
| Net current assets | | | 25,600 |
| Total net assets | | | 184,500 |
| **Provision for liabilities and charges** | | | |
| Taxation | | | 32,000 |
| **Shareholders' funds** | | | |
| Authorised share capital | | | |
| 100,000 Preference shares of £1 | 100,000 | | |
| 100,000 Ordinary shares of £1 | 100,000 | | |
| | 200,000 | | |
| **Issued share capital** | | | |
| 30,000 Preference shares of £1 | | 30,000 | |
| 90,000 Ordinary shares of £1 | | 90,000 | |
| | | 120,000 | |
| **Capital and reserves** | | | |
| Profit and loss account balance | | 32,500 | 152,500 |
| | | | 184,500 |

Fig. 97. An example of a limited company's balance sheet suitable for publication.

5. Make a heading: 'Provision for liabilities and charges'. Beneath it make a sub-heading 'Taxation'. In the third column record the value of the provision for taxation and write against it: 'Taxation'.

6. Make a subheading: 'Shareholders' funds'.

7. Underneath that make a subordinate sub-heading, 'Authorised share capital'.

8. In the first cash column list the total authorised value of each class of share, annotating accordingly, e.g. 'Preference shares of £1', 'Ordinary shares of £1'.

9. Total up this column and rule it off with a double line.

10. Make a sub-heading: 'Issued share capital'. In the second column enter the total value of shares issued in each class of share capital, annotating each, e.g. 'Preference shares of £1', 'Ordinary shares of £1'.

11. Total up this column.

12. Make a heading: 'Capital and reserves'. In the second column, list the profit and loss account balance. Add the last two figures in the second column, i.e. total issued share capital and profit and loss account balance, and place the total in the third column. Add the last two figures in the third column to arrive at the second major total, which must balance with the first (total net assets). There is room for variation in the use of columns. It depends on how many items you need to deal with in each group. But the objectives are clarity and simplicity.

### Note on terminology
Accounting in the UK is in a period of transition towards the adoption of international terminology. Public companies listed on UK or other European stock exchanges already use the international terms such as:

| UK term | International term |
| --- | --- |
| Profit and loss account | Income statement |
| Debenture | Loan note |
| Turnover | Revenue |
| Stock | Inventory |
| Debtors | Accounts receivable |
| Creditors | Accounts payable |
| Profit and loss account b/d | Retained profits |
| Provision for doubtful debts | Allowance for doubtful debts |
| Long-term liabilities | Non-current liabilities |

## ARMSTRONG ENGINEERING
### BALANCE SHEET
as at 31 Mar 200X

| | | | |
|---|---|---|---|
| **INTANGIBLE ASSETS** | | | |
| Goodwill | | | 5,000 |
| | | | |
| **FIXED ASSETS** | | | |
| Freehold premises | | 35,000 | |
| Plant and machinery | 15,000 | | |
| Less depreciation | 750 | 14,250 | |
| | | | |
| Motor van | 8,000 | | |
| Less depreciation | 1,600 | 6,400 | 55,650 |
| Total fixed assets | | | 60,650 |
| | | | |
| **CURRENT ASSETS** | | | |
| Stock | | 9,000 | |
| Debtors | 10,000 | | |
| Less provision for doubtful debts | 2,000 | 8,000 | |
| Cash at bank | | 10,000 | |
| Cash in hand | | 50 | |
| | 27,050 | | |
| | | | |
| Less **CURRENT LIABILITIES** | | | |
| Creditors | | 12,000 | |
| Working capital | | | 15,050 |
| TOTAL ASSETS | | | 75,700 |
| | | | |
| Financed by | | | |
| **CAPITAL** | | | |
| Opening balance | | | 63,050 |
| Add profit for period | | | 19,100 |
| | | 82,150 | |
| Less drawings | | | 6,450 |
| TOTAL LIABILITIES | | | 75,700 |

Fig. 98. The balance sheet of Armstrong Engineering before it became a limited company.

## Three methods of 'going limited'

A sole proprietor or partnership may wish to change the status of its business entity to that of a limited company. If so, it must draw up a balance sheet for the existing business and form a new company to purchase it at an appropriate price. The new company can pay the seller (sole proprietor or partnership) in any of three ways:

1.  Buying paid up shares. If the value of the business is say £100,000, then the share capital of the new company will be registered at at least that figure. The seller will transfer the business to the company in exchange for an equal value, not in cash, but in shares.

2.  Mixture of shares and debenture. The seller may, on the other hand, wish to accept only part of the payment in shares, and the other part in the form of a debenture. In other words, he/she would be selling the second part for money—but giving the company time to pay (debentures are a type of secured and usually long-term loan).

3.  Selling shares to other parties. Some of the extra cash raised by this means can then be used to buy some of the assets from the former owner (sole proprietor or partnership).

## Adjustments to the balance sheet

If outside parties are becoming involved, they may not agree with the various asset values shown in the business's balance sheet. They may for example disagree with the figures for bad debts provision, or with the listed value of stock or goodwill. Adjustments then need to be made to these values to satisfy everyone concerned.

You would need to make a corresponding adjustment to the capital account on the balance sheet of the business before it was bought by the limited company. When all has been agreed, we simply need to record the opening figures in the books of the new company.

There will be two fundamental differences between those entries and the details of the closing balance sheet of the business purchased:

● The capital in the opening balance sheet of the limited company will be analysed into shares (rather than into proprietor's or partners' capital). It will not show the profit or the proprietor's drawings for the period up to the takeover.

● Provision for depreciation will not feature in the opening balance sheet of the new company since it will have purchased the assets at their 'written down value'.

Armstrong, a sole proprietor, traded as Armstrong Engineering. He decided to form a limited company and transfer the assets and liabilities to it in return for ordinary shares. Assuming that the creditors had agreed to his transferring to the limited company the responsibility for the debts he had, as a sole proprietor, personally owed to them (by no means always the case), the opening balance sheet of the new company would be as shown below.

---

**ARMSTRONG ENGINEERING LTD**
**BALANCE SHEET**
as at 31 Mar 200X

| | | |
|---|---:|---:|
| INTANGIBLE ASSETS | | |
| Goodwill | | 5,000 |
| | | |
| FIXED ASSETS | | |
| Freehold premises | 35,000 | |
| Plant and machinery | 14,250 | |
| Motor van | 6,400 | 55,650 |
| Total fixed assets | | 60,650 |
| | | |
| CURRENT ASSETS | | |
| Stock | 9,000 | |
| Debtors | 8,000 | |
| Cash at bank | 10,000 | |
| Cash in hand | 50 | |
| | 27,050 | |
| | | |
| Less CURRENT LIABILITIES | | |
| Creditors | 12,000 | |
| Working capital | | 15,050 |
| | | 75,700 |
| | | |
| Financed by | | |
| *Authorised share capital* | | |
| 100,000 Ordinary shares | | |
| @ £1.00 each | 100,000 | |
| | | |
| *Issued Share Capital* | | |
| 75,700 Ordinary shares | | |
| @ £1.00 each | | 75,700 |

---

Fig. 99. The balance sheet of Armstrong Engineering after it became a limited company.

152

Here is another variation in format of final accounts. By clubs, we mean here clubs owned by their members, for example political clubs, social clubs and sports clubs. These organisations do not exist to make a 'profit'. All the revenue comes from the shareholders themselves (e.g. as members' subscriptions) and just reflects the cost of the goods and services they consume at the club. Their accounts are a matter of housekeeping, rather than 'trading'; the members contribute to an **accumulated common fund** for the common good.

### Surpluses and accumulated funds
Of course, all housekeepers like to 'put a bit by'. Committees of clubs are in effect housekeepers, too, and often develop a small excess of revenue over expenses. But this is not profit: it is merely shareholders' contributions (in various ways) left over after all expenses have been paid. In the accounts it is termed a **surplus**. It is added to the accumulated common fund to be used for the future benefit of members. It is just as an individual may save surplus income to buy things tomorrow which they could not afford today, or to make ends meet if they fall on hard times.

### Format of club accounts
Club accounts differ in format from commercial accounts, in just three ways:

- The money we call profit or loss in a partnership, sole proprietorship or limited company, we call a surplus or deficit in a club.

- Instead of a profit and loss account, clubs have an income and expenditure account.

- Instead of a capital account, clubs have an accumulated fund.

- The receipts and payments account is in effect a summary of cash and banking transactions, much like the cash book of a business.

The income and expenditure account is the equivalent of the profit and loss account of a commercial business. On the income side it shows the various sources of revenue, e.g. donations, and surpluses from activities like dances, or bingo while on the other side it analyses costs into those which can be set against income, such as bank interest, depreciation and wages (revenue expenditure) and spending on assets that will last a long time, such as buildings and equipment (capital expenditure).

Receipts and payments accounts are usually kept on a single entry basis (memorandum form) but the income and expenditure account is usually kept in double entry format.

That is not to say that no profit-making activities go on in clubs. A club may well run a bar, for example, on commercial lines. If so, a bar trading account is kept, to calculate and record gross profit; bar staff wages appear in the account along with cost of goods sold, as we dealt with on page 89. Any profit is then brought down to the club's income and expenditure account (rather than to a profit and loss account as it would be in a truly commercial business).

You can show other income-generating activities in separate trading accounts (e.g. club shop trading account), but for things like raffle and dance proceeds which do not really involve trading goods, you usually just 'net' the incomes concerned in the income and expenditure account. In other words you set against the income from the sale of tickets the cost of prizes, band hire, and so on.

**SUBSCRIPTIONS ACCOUNT**

| 200X | | | | 200X | | | |
|---|---|---|---|---|---|---|---|
| Mar 31 Balance | b/d | 100 | Mar | 31 Balance | b/d | | 50 |
| 31 Income and expenditure account | | 10,100 | | Bank | | | 10,100 |
| 31 Balance | c/d | 150 | | Balance | c/d | | 200 |
| | | 10,350 | | | | | 10,350 |

Fig. 100. Subscription fees paid by members are usually one of a club's main sources of income. This income is transferred to an 'income and expenditure account'.

| Raffle proceeds | 40.00 | |
|---|---|---|
| Less expenses | 10.00 | |
| Net proceeds | | 30.00 |
| Dance tickets | 200.00 | |
| Less expenses | 90.00 | |
| Net proceeds | | 110.00 |
| To income and expenditure account | | 140.00 |

Fig. 101. A club may also raise income by commercial activities such as raffles and dances. The income from this is also transferred to the income and expenditure account.

### Preparing final accounts

So far we have considered how to write the final accounts of profit-making organisations including sole-proprietors, partnerships and limited companies. We will now see how to write the final accounts of a non profit-making organisation, such as a club, or society.

### What you need

- receipts and payments account
- details of end of year adjustments.

### Statement of affairs

Start by drawing up a statement of affairs as at the end of the last financial year. We call it a statement of affairs rather than a balance sheet because we don't have the full records to work from and when we are working from incomplete records it is conventional to say we are drawing up a statement of affairs.

You will need details of all the fixed assets and their depreciated values, all the current assets and all the liabilities as at the end of the last financial year. The only ones of these you will get from the receipts and payments account are the cash (at bank and in hand) at the start of the period, as that account only deals with cash and what it was used to buy. It doesn't deal with any records of what is still physically present in the club's possession at any moment in time—except the cash, that is. All the other details will have to be supplied by the treasurer and/or the secretary of the club.

1. List the fixed assets in order of their permanence, e.g.
   - land
   - buildings
   - other structures
   - equipment.
2. Add them and place the sub-total in a column to the right.
3. List all the current assets in reverse order of their liquidity.
4. Add them and place the sub-total beneath the other sub-total.
5. Add both sub-totals and this will give you the total assets.
6. Now list the current liabilities and other values.
7. Add them up and place the total (total liablilites) beneath the total assets.
8. Deduct the latter from the former and you have the accumulated fund figure as at the start of the financial year.

Figure 104 provides an illustration.

### Bar trading account

The next thing to do is the bar trading account. Most of the material for this will come from the receipts and payments account, but any transactions that have not yet involved actual cash, e.g. purchases that have not yet been paid for, will have to be gleaned from the notes you have been supplied with. Draw up the bar

**TRIAL BALANCE**
of George Street Social Club
as at 31 March 200X

| | | |
|---|---:|---:|
| Opening stock | 1,000 | |
| Purchases | 30,000 | |
| Bar staff wages | 4,500 | |
| Bar sales | | 50,000 |
| Staff wages (non-bar) | 30,300 | |
| Rent and rates | 5,000 | |
| Postage | 58 | |
| Telephone | 300 | |
| Cleaning | 500 | |
| Bank charges | 150 | |
| Donations received | | 2,500 |
| Net dance and concert proceeds | | 10,000 |
| Subscriptions | | 5,000 |
| Net raffle and bingo ticket proceeds | | 500 |
| Commission on fruit machine | | 4,000 |
| Club premises | 62,000 | |
| Fixtures and fittings | 10,000 | |
| Provision for depreciation on fixtures and fittings | | 500 |
| Depreciation | 500 | |
| Bar stocks | 900 | 900 |
| Subscriptions in arrear | 250 | |
| Cash at bank | 2,200 | |
| Cash in hand | 50 | |
| Creditors | | 1,100 |
| Accumulated fund balance as at 1 April 200X | | 73,208 |
| | 147,708 | 147,708 |

Fig. 102. Typical trial balance used to prepare a bar trading account
and income and expenditure account of a social club.

trading account just as you would any trading, profit and loss account, ticking the items off in the source documents as you go to make it easy for yourself to see which items are left to deal with.

1. Deal with sales and then the cost of sales equation to find the gross profit.
2. Total up the administration costs.
3. Enter the sub-total beneath the gross profit in the right hand column.
4. Deduct the total bar administration costs from the gross profit.
5. Bring down the total to the income and expenditure account.

### Income and expenditure

Next draw up an income and expenditure account. If you are using a vertical format, you'll probably need two sub-total columns to the left of the main column for the kind of sums you will be doing.

Start with the income section and enter the subscriptions for the current year. You arrive at this by taking the subscription income for the current year from the receipts and payments account and adding the subscriptions in arrear for the current year as communicated to you by the treasurer. You then have the total value of subscription income for the current year. Just because some of it hasn't arrived in cash doesn't necessarily change the subscription income. Unless we have a sound reason to think otherwise we must assume it will be in due course. If we do have sound reason to doubt this we can write it off as a loss, in which case that member would probably be expelled. Bring down the bar profits and add in any other income, e.g. donations, legacies, etc., as listed in the receipts and payments account. Add them up to arrive at the total income.

Next list the various expense payments, those paid for, as listed in the receipts and payments account, ticking them off as you go, and any not yet paid for, as indicated in the notes you have been supplied with, e.g. bar expenses still owing.

Some expenses will not be reflected in the income and expenditure account because they are paper transactions only. Depreciation, for example, is an expense, but it won't show up in the receipts and payments account because nothing has actually been paid out in money—the expense has occurred in the form of an erosion of value. This will come from the notes you have been supplied with. Debts to write off are another example. There may be subscriptions in arrear for members who have since left the club and the committee may feel it is unlikely they will ever be paid. This writing off is also an expense that will not be reflected in the receipts and payments account.

When all the expenses have been listed and ticked off in the source documents add them up and enter the total expenses figure in the right hand column. Then deduct that from the gross profit brought down from the bar trading account and you have the *surplus income over expenditure*, which is the not-for-profit organisation equivalent of the *net profit* in a commercial firm.

You will need to write up the subscriptions account. This is drawn up in T-account or ledger format. All subscription revenue is entered on the credit side, analysed separately for the years to which each component of the total relates,

## Tanner Street Bowls Club
*Receipts and payments account for year ended 31 December 2008*

| Receipts | | Payments | |
|---|---|---|---|
| Balance at bank 01/01/08 | 440 | Bar supplies | 29,100 |
| Subscriptions received | | Groundsman's wages | 15,000 |
|    For 2006 | 760 | Bar staff wages | 6,500 |
|    For 2007 | 19,100 | Bar steward's salary | 20,000 |
| Advance payments for 2008 | 800 | Bar expenses | 300 |
| | | Repairs to fencing | 400 |
| Bar takings | 75,000 | Security expenses | 740 |
| Donations | 500 | Transport costs | 2,500 |
| Legacies | 5,000 | Cash at bank 21/12/07 | 27,060 |
| | 101,600 | | 101,600 |

*Notes*

| | 31/12/06 | 31/12/07 |
|---|---|---|
| *Bar stocks (inventory)* | *4,250* | *5,100* |
| *Creditors* | *3,900* | *4,850* |
| *Bar expenses* | *185* | *210* |
| *Transport costs* | *110* | *290* |
| *Value of land* | *110,100* | |
| *Buildings* | *27,225* | |
| *Equipment* | *4,900* | |
| | | |
| *Subscriptions in arrear as at 31/12/06* | *760* | |
| *Subscriptions in arrear as at 31/12/07* | *1,510* | |

Fig. 103. An example of a receipts and payments account for a club.

## Tanner Street Bowls Club
*Statement of affairs as at 31 December 2008*

| | | |
|---|---|---|
| Non-current assets | | |
|   Land | | 110,100 |
|   Buildings | | 27,225 |
|   Equipment | | 4,900 |
| Current assets | | |
|   Bar inventory | 4,250 | |
|   Subscriptions receivable | 760 | |
|   Cash at bank | 440 | 5,450 |
| Total assets | | 147,675 |
| Current liabilities | | |
| Accounts payable | 3,900 | |
| Bar expenses payable | 185 | |
| Transport costs payable | 110 | |
| Total liabilities | | 4,195 |
| Net assets | | 143,480 |
| Accumulated fund | | 143,480 |

Fig. 104. An example of a statement of affairs for a club.

e.g. membership subscriptions for 2005, 2006 and 2007. Now if the counter-posting on the debit side were taken as the total of the subscriptions the figure would be wrong. We have to add in the figure for those subscriptions for the current year that haven't yet been paid, because these members are obliged to pay them and unless we have a good reason to think they won't we must regard them as revenue even if it is not in hard cash. We enter them as a carried down figure 'Accounts receivable c/d'. Those parts of the total that are for previous years and those that are advance payments for future years must be posted on the debit side as balances c/d, which reduces the difference between the two sides to be carried down to the income and expenditure account.

A similar process is used where the amount paid for goods and services only tells part of the story. The amount paid for, as taken from the receipts and payments account, is posted to the debit side of the purchase control account and the amount purchased but still to be paid for is posted to the same side in order to increase the amount c/d to the income and expenditure account to reflect the full value of the goods and services purchased or consumed.

To allow for the fact that some of the payments for goods and services in the receipts and payments account were for bills outstanding at the end of the previous year (and the treasurer or secretary will, hopefully, have given you the details in the adjustment notes) the figure that represents payment for last year's bills is posted on the credit side of the purchases control account to reduce the amount that will be carried down to the income and expenditure account for purchases in the current year. If you add up the two sides the difference represents the figure to carry down to the income and expenditure account for the year for which you are accounting.

All other expenses and revenues picked up from the receipts and payments account which are complicated by the fact that part of them is for settling bills from previous years and part is perhaps advance payments for future years are unravelled in the same way—by setting up ledger type accounts for each such expense, debiting them with the cash paid, adding to the debit side the amount of any accounts or bills still to be paid to increase the figure c/d to the income and expenditure account and crediting the account with any part of the total payments that were for the previous year's bills, thus reducing the amount to be c/d to the income and expenditure account. Figure 107 gives an illustration of the subscriptions account and Figure 108 gives an illustration of the purchases control account.

If the club offers life memberships the committee may wish the fee income for this to be spread over the natural life expectancy of the member in the accounts. For example, a person joining at the age of 50 may be expected to have 30 years of life expectancy during which they will use the facilities of the club and the membership fee income should be spread over this time, bringing down decreasing portions of it each year. This is, perhaps, an unnecessarily onerous requirement though, as the fee could be much less troublesomely regarded as the fee for the privilege of joining rather than a charge for the expected number of years the facilities will be used.

**Tanner Street Bowls Club**

*Bar trading account for the year ending 31 December 2008*

| | | | |
|---|---|---|---|
| Sales | | | 75,000 |
| | | | |
| Opening inventory 01/01/2008 | | 4,250 | |
| Add purchases | | 30,050 | |
| | | 34,300 | |
| Closing inventory | | 5,100 | 29,200 |
| Gross profit | | | 45,800 |
| | | | |
| Less expenses | | | |
| Bar steward's wages | | 20,000 | |
| Bar expenses | | 325 | |
| Bar staff wages | | 6,500 | 26,825 |
| Net profit b/d to income and | | | |
| expenditure account | | | 18,975 |

Fig. 105. An example of a bar trading account for a club.

**Tanner Street Bowls Club**

*Income and expenditure account for the year ending 31 December 2008*

**Income**

| | | | |
|---|---|---|---|
| Subscription for 2008 | | | 20,610 |
| Bar profits | | | 18,975 |
| Donations received | | | 500 |
| Legacies | | | 5,000 |
| | | | 45,085 |
| | | | |
| Less expenditure | | | |
| Groundsman's wages | | 15,000 | |
| Repairs to fencing | | 400 | |
| Security expenses | | 740 | |
| Transport costs | | 2,680 | |
| Depreciation | | | |
| Buildings | 2,722 | | |
| Equipment | 980 | 3,702 | 22,522 |
| Surplus of income over expenditure | | | 22,563 |

Fig. 106. An example of an income and expediture account for a club.

| Subscriptions received | | | | |
|---|---|---|---|---|
| Balance c/d from previous year | 760 | Cash for | 2006 | 760 |
| Income and expenditure a/c | 20,610 | | 2007 | 19,100 |
| | | c/d | 2008 | 800 |
| Balance c/d (advance payments) | 800 | Balance c/d | | 1,510 |
| | 22,170 | | | 22,170 |

Fig. 107. An example of a subscriptions account.

| Purchases control | | | |
|---|---|---|---|
| Cash | 29,100 | Balance b/d (from previous year) | 3,900 |
| Balance c/d | 4,850 | Trading account | 30,050 |
| | 33,950 | | 33,950 |

Fig. 108. An example of a purchase control account for a club.

| Bar expenses | | | |
|---|---|---|---|
| Cash | 300 | Balance b/d (from previous year) | 185 |
| Balance c/d | 210 | Trading account | 325 |
| | 510 | | 510 |

| Transport costs | | | |
|---|---|---|---|
| Cash | 2,500 | Income and expenditure account | |
| Balance c/d | 290 | b/d (from previous year) | 110 |
| | | Income and expenditure a/c | 2,680 |
| | 2,790 | | 2,790 |

Fig. 109. Examples of accounting for expenditure where part is for
settling previous year's bills.

**Tanner Street Bowls Club**

*Balance sheet as at 31 December 2008*

| | | | |
|---|---|---|---|
| Non-current assets | | | |
| Land at valuation | | 110,100 | |
| Buildings at valuation | 27,225 | | |
| Less depreciation | 2,722 | 24,503 | |
| Equipment at valuation | 4,900 | | |
| Less depreciation | 980 | 3,920 | |
| Total net non-current assets | | | 138,523 |
| Current assets | | | |
| Inventory of bar stocks | 5,100 | | |
| Accounts receivable: subscriptions | 1,510 | | |
| Cash at bank | 27,060 | | |
| Total current assets | | | 33,670 |
| Total assets | | | 172,193 |
| Current liabilities | | | |
| Accounts payable (bar supplies) | 4,850 | | |
| Bar expenses | 210 | | |
| Transport costs outstanding | 290 | | |
| Subscriptions paid in advance | 800 | | |
| Total liabilities | | | 6,150 |
| Net assets | | | 166,043 |
| Accumulated fund | | | |
| Balance as at 01/01/2008 | | | 143,480 |
| Add surplus income over expenditure | | | 22,563 |
| | | | 166,043 |

Fig. 110. An example of a balance sheet of a club.

### Fixed asset register

A fixed asset register is for logging the details of each fixed asset. They include:

- the identification/serial number
- description of the asset
- date of acquisition
- cost
- how it was financed
- rate of depreciation and the method for calculating this
- annual depreciation for each year of its life
- current net book value
- date of disposal
- proceeds from disposal.

The reasons why it is important to keep a fixed asset register include:

- It details how the fixed asset figure on the balance sheet is made up.
- The business can check the presence and condition of fixed assets against their record in the register from time to time.
- It shows the current net book values, so that accurate posting can be made in the ledger at the time of disposal.
- It shows whether there is any finance on the assets, which is important at the time of disposal.

| FIXED ASSET REGISTER | |
| --- | --- |
| Identification/serial number | FM2736 |
| Description of asset | Harvey XI sheet cutter |
| Date of acquisition | 2/2/2003 |
| Cost | £6,000 |
| How financed | Cash |
| Rate and method of depreciation | Machine hours method. £1.04 per hour used |
| Annual depreciation for each year of asset's life | £1,820.00 |
| Current net book value | £2,360 |
| Date of disposal | |
| Proceeds of disposal | |

Fig. 111. Example of a fixed asset register.

163

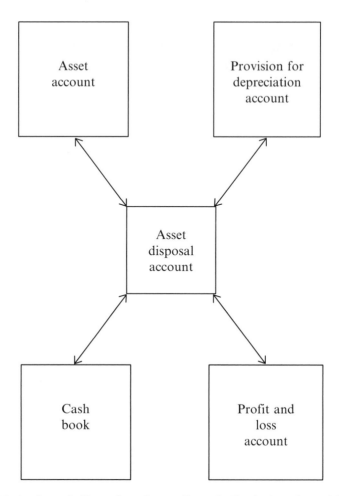

Fig. 112. A schematic illustration of asset disposal. The dual postings with the particular asset account, the account for provision for depreciation on that asset and the cash book take place when the asset is sold. The fourth does not take place until the final accounts are compiled.

## A form of final account

Asset disposal accounts are like miniature trading, profit and loss accounts: they are final accounts, and not going on any further. Once written up, with their one and only set of entries, they are balanced and carried down to show the profit or loss on the asset disposal concerned. The account will then remain untouched until such figure is transferred to the profit and loss account. The trading, profit and loss account reports all the revenues and expenses of a business at once. In contrast, asset disposal accounts only report particular transactions, in other words the disposal of individual assets. You write up a separate asset disposal account for each asset disposed of, such as a motor van or machine.

## Closing down two related accounts

The idea is not only to record the disposal of the asset, but at the same time to close down the two other accounts which relate to the asset in the books—the 'asset account' itself, and the 'provision for depreciation on asset account'. It both co-ordinates and combines the closing down of these accounts in the way it follows the double entry principle. Otherwise, recording asset disposals would be a messy business, and mistakes would be easily made.

## Three pairs of postings

With the asset disposal account you will need to make three pairs of postings:

- transfer the asset concerned from its asset account to your new asset disposal account

- transfer the provision for depreciation from its own account to your asset disposal account

- post the sale proceeds to your asset disposal account, with the counterpart posting to cash, bank, or a personal ledger account if sold on credit.

## The resulting profit or loss

The balance c/d on the asset disposal account will then represent a profit (if credit) or loss (if debit) on sale of asset. In the end, along with all the other revenue and expense account balances, it will go to the trading, profit and loss account.

## JOURNAL

| Date | Particulars | Fo. | Dr. | Cr. |
|------|-------------|-----|-----|-----|
| 200X | | | | |
| Feb 22 | Sundries | | | |
| | Asset disposal | NL40 | 10,000 | |
| |     Motor van | NL20 | | 10,000 |
| | Provision for depreciation | NL30 | 6,000 | |
| |     Asset disposal | NL40 | | 6,000 |
| | Bank | CB25 | 3,000 | |
| |     Asset disposal | NL40 | | 3,000 |
| | To record the disposal of a motor van | | | |

---

p40            **NOMINAL LEDGER**

*Asset disposal account*

| 200X | | Fo. | | 200X | | Fo. | |
|------|------|-----|------|------|------|-----|------|
| Feb 22 | Motor van | NL20 | 10,000 | Feb 22 | Provision for depreciation | NL30 | 6,000 |
| | | | | | Bank | CB25 | 3,000 |
| | | | | | Balance c/d | | 1,000 |
| | | | 10,000 | | | | 10,000 |
| Feb 23 | Balance b/d | | 1,000 | | | | |

---

p20            *Motor van account*

| 200X | | | Fo. | 200X | | Fo. | |
|------|------|-----|------|------|------|-----|------|
| Jan 1 | Balance | b/d | 10,000 | Feb 22 | Asset disposal | NL40 | 10,000 |

---

p30            *Provision for depreciation account*

| 200X | | Fo. | | 200X | | Fo. | |
|------|------|-----|------|------|------|-----|------|
| Feb 22 | Asset disposal | NL40 | 6,000 | Jan 1 | Balance | b/d | 6,000 |

---

p25            **CASH BOOK**

| 200X | | | | 200X |
|------|------|-----|------|------|
| Feb 22 | Asset disposal | NL40 | 3,000 | |

Fig. 113. An example of journalising and ledger posting for an asset disposal (a motor van originally bought for £10,000 and now sold for £3,000).

# 63  Asset disposals step by step

## What you will need
- the nominal ledger
- the journal
- the cash book.

## Step by step
1. In the next available space in the journal, write the date in the appropriate column, and the word 'Sundries' to indicate a combination posting. Below that write 'Asset disposal [name of asset]', as in the example opposite.

2. Enter the original value of the asset, i.e. the value actually recorded in the asset account, in the debit cash column (in the example, £10,000).

3. Beneath your heading, indenting slightly, write the name of the asset concerned: 'Motor van'.

4. Enter the same book value (£10,000) in the credit cash column.

5. Beneath your last entry in the particulars column, write: 'Provision for depreciation on [name of asset]'.

6. In the debit cash column, enter the balance showing on provision for depreciation account, e.g. £6,000.

7. Beneath your last entry in the particulars column, indenting slightly, write the name of the asset disposal account concerned.

8. In the credit cash column, enter the balance of the provision for depreciation account, e.g. £6,000.

9. In the particulars column write 'Cash' or 'Bank' as appropriate (or the name of a personal account if the van was sold on credit).

10. Enter sales proceeds in the debit cash column (e.g. £3,000).

11. Beneath the last entry in the particulars column, indenting slightly, write the name of the asset disposal account concerned.

12. Enter the value of sales proceeds in the credit cash column, e.g. £3,000.

13. Beneath this set of entries write: 'To record disposal of [asset concerned]'.

14. Make postings to the ledger following the instructions you have just recorded in the journal. Open new accounts where necessary.

15. Total up and balance the asset account, the provision for depreciation account and the asset disposal acount, the last of which will be the only one which may have a balance remaining. Remember, you need a separate asset disposal account for each asset disposed of.

16. Remember to complete the folio columns.

## ERRORS IN ACCOUNTS

1. *Errors of omission*
   A transaction has been missed out altogether.

2. *Errors of commission*
   A transaction has been posted to the wrong account, though to the right side. For example, posted to 'John Smith A/c' instead of 'Colin Smith A/c'.

3. *Compensation errors*
   Different errors of the same value, occurring on the opposite sides of the ledger divisions. The effect of one is obscured by the equal effect of the other, so that the trial balance still balances. There could, in fact, be more than two errors involved, the total debit errors matching the total credit errors.

4. *Errors of principle*
   Where an expense item has been posted to an asset account. Example, a 'Motor expense' has been posted to 'Motor car account'.

5. *Errors of original entry*
   The original entry was wrong. Perhaps the source document, such as an invoice, has been added up incorrectly by a sales office clerk, or misread by the book-keeper.

6. *Errors of reversal*
   Both aspects have been posted to the wrong sides: the debit aspect to the credit side, and vice versa.

7. *Posting to the wrong side of the ledger*
   Errors due to the transaction being posted to the wrong side of the ledger.

8. *Omitting one side of dual posting*
   Errors due to complete omission of one side of the dual posting.

9. *Under or overstatement*
   Errors due to under- or overstating one side of the transaction. Example: a gross invoice value, inclusive of VAT, has been posted to an asset or expense account in the ledger.

10. *Errors of summation*
    Sometimes known as 'casting errors'. Columns have been added up incorrectly, and the wrong balance carried down.

11. *Errors of transposition*
    A figure has been accidentally reversed. For example 32 has been written as 23, or 414 as 441. This error is always a multiple of 9, and if the error is one of transposition it can be spotted fairly easily.

Fig. 114. Errors in accounts.

## The right way to correct errors

No figure should ever be crossed out anywhere in the accounts. If allowed it could hide embezzlement. Of course, genuine mistakes are made, but there is a special way of putting them right. If an error is found it must be recorded in the journal, together with whatever additions or subtractions are needed to the accounts to put matters right.

## Types of error

There are 11 types of error, which we can summarise as follows:

Errors of omission

Errors of commission

Compensating errors

Errors of principle

Errors of original entry

Errors of reversal

Errors of posting to the wrong side of ledger

Errors of omitting one side of dual posting

Errors of over/understating one side

Errors of summation ('casting errors')

Errors of transposition

On the opposite page each one is explained in more detail.

Only the last five of these will be shown up by the trial balance failing to balance.

An error of commission, original entry or reversal will become apparent when a customer or supplier, whose account has been wrongly affected, informs you. They will certainly be quick to let you know if the error is to their disadvantage.

## JOURNAL

| Date | Particulars | Dr. | Cr. |
|------|-------------|-----|-----|
| 200X | | | |
| April 30 | K. Gange | 2,000.00 | |
| | Sales | | 2,000.00 |
| | To correct error of omission | | |
| 30 | Heat and light | 400.00 | |
| | Purchases | | 400.00 |
| | To correct error of principle | | |
| 30 | S. Jones | 90.00 | |
| | Motor expenses | 10.00 | |
| | Cash sales | | 100.00 |
| | To correct compensating errors due to motor expenses and cash sales both being undercast and S. Jones (debit) being omitted | | |
| 30 | A. Singer | 50.00 | |
| | A. Singh | | 50.00 |
| | To correct error of commission | | |
| 30 | Motor expenses | 15.00 | |
| | Edwards Garage | | 15.00 |
| | To correct error of original entry | | |
| 30 | Depreciation | 80.00 | |
| | Provision for depreciation | | 80.00 |
| | To correct error of reversal affecting both accounts in the sum of £40.00* | | |

Fig. 115. Accounting for errors: entries in the journal. Note: if depreciation account has been credited with £40.00, instead of debited, we must debit it with £80.00 and vice versa for provision of depreciation account.

### Identifying errors

As we saw on page 83, only the following errors will be shown up by the trial balance failing to balance:

- errors of posting one aspect of the transaction to the wrong side of the ledger

- errors of omission of one side of the dual posting

- errors of under- or overstating one side of the transaction

- errors of summation ('casting errors')

- errors of transposition of digits (e.g. 32 written as 23).

### Looking for errors in the trial balance step by step

1.   If the trial balance fails, look for a figure equal to the error amongst all the balances. If such a figure appears once only, its dual posting may have been omitted from the trial balance (though it may also be included in a larger posting), or that figure may have been missed out when summing the column.

2.   Next, divide the discrepancy by 2. Look for a figure equal to the quotient of the calculation in the trial balance. If the error is due to something being posted on the wrong side, this will show it up.

3.   Check whether the discrepancy is divisible by 9. If it is, it may be due to an error of transposition.

4.   Check your addition of the columns.

5.   Check that each of the balances in turn have been correctly copied from the ledger accounts.

6.   Check the balances of the ledger accounts.

### Treatment of minor errors

If an error reflected in the trial balance is small (e.g. £30) and it is hard to trace, it is permissible to add it to current liabilities or current assets under the heading **suspense account** just so that compilation of final accounts can go ahead. But you should never do this when the error is large. When you find the error, correct it in the journal as described (see example on opposite page).

Of course, the true profit or loss figure may be distorted as a result of this error. That is why it is only permissible to handle small errors in this way. When the error is later discovered and corrected, a statement of corrected net profit can be written up to supplement the year's final accounts.

### Correcting errors and closing the suspenses account

*Before the error is corrected*

## NOMINAL LEDGER

**Suspense account**

| | |
|---|---|
| Current assets | 30.00 |

**Current assets**

| | |
|---|---|
| Suspense account | 30.00 |

*When the error is corrected*

## JOURNAL

| | | |
|---|---|---|
| Current assets | 30.00 | |
| Suspense account | | 30.00 |
| | | |
| Name of 1st correct account | 30.00 | |
| Name of 2nd correct account | | 30.00 |
| | | |
| Correcting ledger accounts | | |

### NOMINAL LEDGER

**Current assets**

Suspense account                                   30.00

**Suspense account**

Current assets                                     30.00

**Name of 1st correct account**

Name of 2nd correct account   30.00

**Name of 2nd correct account**

Name of 1st correct account                     30.00

Fig. 116. Correcting error and closing the suspense account.

| Fashion house sells suit, for which it had paid factory £55 + VAT, to wholesaler for £100 + 17.5% VAT (collects £17.50 VAT to pay to HMRC but reclaims the £9.62 VAT it had itself paid to the fashion house). Therefore fashion house remitted a net £7.87 to HMRC. | Wholesaler sells to retailer for £140 + 17.5% VAT (collects £24.50 VAT but reclaims the £17.50 it had itself paid to the wholesaler). Therefore the wholesaler remitted £7 to HMRC. | Retailer sells suit to customer for £196 + 17.5% VAT. (Collects £34.30 VAT but reclaims the £24.50 it had itself paid to the wholesaler.) Therefore the wholesaler remitted £9.80 to HMRC. |
|---|---|---|

So in the chain from fashion house to consumer the VAT content has grown at an increasing rate and the total amount of VAT that has gone to the HMRC is £24.67 (£7.87 + £7 + £9.80 = £24.50).

Fig. 117. VAT is collected at various stages in the chain of transactions from manufacturer to end-user.

## 66  Value Added Tax

### A tax on purchases

Value Added Tax (or VAT) is very different from income tax and corporation tax. The last two are claimed at the point of income—VAT is claimed at the point of purchase. Also, a business is a source of taxation for income tax and corporation tax, but for VAT it is simply a kind of collector. A **taxable** firm has to collect VAT on the sale price of all its goods and services from its customers, and pay it over to HM Revenue and Customs (HMRC) as **output tax**. Of course, the firm is also a customer of other firms, because it needs to buy goods and services itself. But the VAT it pays on these purchases (**input tax**) can be set against the VAT it has collected from its customers; it only has to pay the balance (difference) to HMRC. (If the balance is a negative one, then HMRC refund the balance to the firm.) So in the end, it is only private individuals who actually pay VAT—plus firms too small to have to register for VAT (though they can still register if they wish).

### Which businesses need to register for VAT?

The answer is any business whose turnover in the past year was at least £67,000 unless it reasonably expects that by end of the next month the annual turnover to date will fall below that threshold figure. If a firm's sales in the next month alone are likely to be at least £67,000 it must register for VAT. If its annual turnover subsequently falls below £62,000 it can deregister if it wishes.

Registration is also compulsory without any threshold level if:

- it sells excise goods such as tobacco or alcohol;
- it makes any sales of assets on which a VAT refund has been claimed by a predecessor in the chain. These are known as Relevant Goods in VAT terminology.

### Which businesses have to keep VAT accounts?

All registered business must keep full VAT accounts. Firms that are not registered do not need to account for VAT and will ignore the fact that part of the invoice totals they enter in their purchase day books and petty cash books represent VAT. They cannot reclaim VAT they have paid to suppliers nor charge VAT on their invoices to customers. VAT does not appear anywhere in their accounts.

### VAT periods

VAT periods are normally quarterly, but a business can elect to account to HMRC on a monthly basis instead. If the business supplies mainly or exclusively exempt and /or zero-rated goods and services it will usually receive a VAT refund. In such cases it is better if the business elects to account on a monthly basis so that the refunds arrive sooner and start earning interest in the bank sooner. The managers will have to decide whether the refunds are of a significant size to warrant the extra work involved in tripling the number of VAT returns that have to be completed and filed (monthly instead of quarterly).

### VAT rates

There are a number of VAT statuses falling into two main categories:

- exempt
- taxable.

In the second category there can be an infinite number of different tax rates applying to different kinds of goods or services. The rate can be zero per cent, or any number of positive rates. 'Zero rated' does not mean 'exempt'. They are two different things.

The standard rate of VAT in the UK is currently 17½%. There is also currently a reduced rate of 5% which applies to domestic fuel and some energy-saving materials. Food and children's clothing are currently zero rated. VAT rates in existence at the time of writing are as follows:

|  | *Examples of goods and services* |
|---|---|
| Standard rate | Most goods and services |
| Reduced rate | Domestic fuel and some energy-saving materials |
| Zero rate | Food and children's clothing |

Exempt goods and services include such things as postal and banking services and any goods supplied by an exempt business.

### Keeping up to date

VAT rules and rates change from time to time and up-to-date information can be obtained from notices published on HMRC's website www.hmrc.gov.uk.

Notice no. 700 is the general VAT guide and there is a comprehensive range of booklets to cover a multitude of different subjects.

### Other terms you need to know and understand

- Inputs
- Input tax
- Outputs
- Output tax
- VAT on acquisitions from other EU states

Inputs are the taxable goods and services the business has purchased. Outputs are the taxable goods and services it has supplied to customers. Output tax is the tax it has added to its invoices to customers and for which it must remit to HMRC. Input tax is the VAT it has been charged by its suppliers and which it can deduct from the figure it has to remit to HMRC. VAT is not charged by suppliers of goods from other EU states but such a figure has to be remitted to HMRC directly by the purchaser rather than indirectly via the supplier. There is a special box on the VAT return form for such figure.

Up until recently VAT was not charged to customers in the UK by suppliers of services from other EU member states. However, the customers, themselves, had to pay such a figure to HMRC on the services they received. This was because they were deemed to have been supplied in the country of origin rather than the country of receipt, where the customers would be liable for VAT. From January 2010, the VAT rules have changed so that those provided by suppliers in another EU member state are deemed to be supplied in the country of the customer rather than the country of origin and services relating to land or property are deemed to be supplied where the land or property is located. VAT has, therefore, to be charged on them by the suppliers. Financially, it hasn't really made any difference to VAT registered customers; it has just made things simpler at the VAT return stage.

There are exceptions to this *place of supply* rule and in that respect it is complicated. Precise treatment is outside the scope of this book and readers should refer to the HMRC website for further details when required.

Further changes are due to come into effect on 1 January 2011, 1 January 2013 and 1 January 2015.

### Invoicing and VAT

VAT has to be calculated on the net amount of the income after deduction of any trade discount. Do not confuse this with early settlement discount (see page 67). That is a different issue and does not affect the VAT calculation on the invoice.

When making out the invoice:

1.   Add up all the goods and/or services being charged for.
2.   Deduct trade discount if any.
3.   Calculate VAT.

If there is a mixture of different rated goods and perhaps also some exempt goods then:

1.   List them in separate batches.
2.   Add up each batch and calculate the VAT on each total.

The calculation is easy.

### Calculating the VAT figure

There is more than one way to work out the VAT to be applied to a price. They are just looking at the same thing from different angles. The more ways you think about the same thing the more it should become understood and the more it will stick in your memory.

Here's one way:

$$\text{Net price} \times \frac{\text{VAT percentage}}{100}$$

This merely turns the VAT percentage into a decimal. When you realise this you will find it easier just to remember to multiply the net price by the VAT percentage expressed as a decimal and this means just moving the decimal point two places to the left. For example, if the VAT rate is 10% then the VAT rate expressed as a decimal is 0.10. So just think '× 0.10'.

What if there is a fraction in the percentage, e.g. as in the usual VAT rate of 17½%? It's exactly the same; just move the decimal point two places to the left. So 17½% being 17.5% in decimal, it's just × 0.75.

As mentioned earlier this is exactly the same thing as multiplying the net amount by the VAT rate/100 because dividing anything by 100 simply moves the decimal point two places to the left. This technique just cuts out the first stage of the calculation. It's easier to remember, it takes less time and uses up less paper.

Many pocket calculators have a percentage key and providing they use '*as you say it*' logic it takes the same number of steps to calculate the VAT figure:

It's just as quick and simple to multiply by the VAT rate expressed as a decimal, although you may wish to use the calculator for this simple multiplication, depending on how arithmetically skilled you are:

You then just add this figure to the net figure to arrive at the gross figure which you are asking the customer to pay.

### Cash discount or early settlement discount

Where a cash discount or early settlement discount (e.g. for settlement within 14 days) is offered VAT is calculated on the discounted figure. The VAT does not change even if settlement is not made within the stated period.

You will often see an annotation on invoices saying *deduct x% if paid within 7 days*, or words to that effect. Such discounts offered are typically figures like 2%, 2½%, 5%, etc. This discount is not deducted in the cash column of the invoice but stated as an addendum. The VAT figure shown in the cash column, however, takes into account this discount and so may at first sight appear to be an error. Take the following invoice for goods VAT rated at 17.5 %, for example:

| | |
|---|---|
| Goods total net of VAT | 100.00 |
| VAT | 16.62 |
| Total including VAT | 116.62 |

It would be tempting to jump to the conclusion that the VAT figure is wrong and that it should be £17.50. But if there is an addendum on the invoice offering a 5% discount for early settlement then the 17.5 % VAT has been calculated on £95, not £100.

### Where invoices only show the VAT-inclusive figure

Sometimes invoices for goods and services purchased will not show VAT separately from the gross total. In such cases the book-keeper must calculate the VAT content. This is an easy process – the opposite of finding the VAT inclusive, or gross figure from the net and the VAT rate.

To find the gross figure you can do one of two things.

1. Calculate the VAT and add it to the starting figure, e.g.

$$£200 \times 0.175 = 35 + 200 = £235$$

2. Or you can multiply the original figure by '1 . rate', e.g.

$$£200 \times 1.175 = £235$$

These are not fundamentally different ways, for when we multiplied £200 by 0.175 in the first example '200 × 1'was added at the end:

The second version is quicker, easier to remember and takes up less space on paper.

Suppose you have the gross figure and you wish to find the net figure. Well, if you found the gross figure from the net by multiplying by:

then it stands to reason that if you want to go in the reverse direction you just need to reverse the formula. Instead of multiplying by:

| 1 | . | VAT rate |
|---|---|----------|

divide by:

| 1 | . | VAT rate |
|---|---|----------|

That is, instead of:

it is:

All you change is this piece

When you have the net content the difference between that and the gross is the VAT.

---

**VAT summary**

| 2008 | | | 2008 | | |
|------|----|------|------|----|------|
| Input tax | Jan | 950.50 | Output tax | Jan | 1,410.32 |
| | Feb | 1,140.25 | | Feb | 2,015.35 |
| | Mar | 1,209.20 | | Mar | 2,200.95 |
| | | 3,299.95 | | | 5,626.62 |
| Add VAT allowable on acquisitions from other EU states | | 65.60 | VAT due on acquisitions from other EU states | | 65.60 |
| Deduct net input tax overclaim from previous returns | | (115.00) | Add net output tax understatement on previous returns | | 210.08 |
| Bad debt relief | | 195.75 | Annual adjustment for special retailer scheme | | 75.45 |
| Sub-total | | 3,446.30 | Sub-total | | 5,977.75 |
| Less VAT on credit notes inwards | | (35.53) | Less VAT on credit notes outwards | | (52.56) |
| Total VAT deductable | | 3,410.77 | Total VAT payable | | 5,925.19 |
| | | | Less total VAT deductable | | (3,410.77) |
| | | | VAT payable to HMRC | | 2,514.42 |

---

Fig. 118. A typical VAT summary.

# 67 Accounting for VAT

### Requirement to keep VAT records
Registered businesses have to keep records of VAT paid and received at the various rates—including zero—and also a record of all exempt supplies it makes. Different kinds of businesses record VAT differently.

### Partly exempt businesses
Where a firm sells both exempt, zero and positive-rated goods the accounting gets a bit complex. It becomes necessary to apportion their turnover. There are special schemes for retailers to make it easier to make the apportionments. However, as there are a number of such schemes they are outside the scope of this book. Here we can only focus on the mainstream VAT requirements and methods of accounting.

### VAT records
There are several ways of keeping VAT records—a basic one used by most types of business, and various special schemes for particular kinds of business.

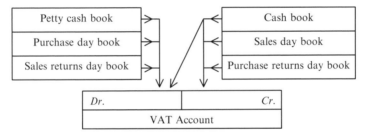

Fig. 119. Sources for the VAT account.

### The prime entries for VAT
If a business is registered for VAT it needs a place to make the prime entries for VAT. This can simply be an extra column or so in the day books (see examples on page 182). In the extra column you separately record the VAT content of purchase invoices (**inputs**) and of sales invoices (**outputs**). The petty cash book, too, can be used to record VAT in the same way; in a special column you can enter the VAT charged on petrol and other small items.

We have already come across this extra column in the day books and the petty cash book earlier on (page 46). From there it is just a matter of posting the extra column to the ledger (i.e. a 'VAT account' in the ledger) along with others, i.e. the individual, analysed 'Net amount' columns:

- you post the VAT on purchases to the debit of the VAT account
- you post the VAT on sales to the credit of the VAT account.

## SALES DAY BOOK

| Date 200X | Customer | Inv no | Gross value | Net zero R (0%) | Net rate A (8%) | Net rate B (15%) | VAT | Analysis columns |
|---|---|---|---|---|---|---|---|---|
| Jan 1 | S. Jones | 59 | 150.00 | 150.00 | | | | |
| 4 | A. Singh | 60 | 540.00 | 200.36 | 93.00 | 208.00 | 38.64 | |
| | | | 690.00 | 350.36 | 93.00 | 208.00 | 38.64 | |

## PURCHASE DAY BOOK

| Date 200X | Supplier | Inv no | Gross value | Net zero R (0%) | Net rate A (15%) | Net rate B (8%) | VAT | Analysis columns |
|---|---|---|---|---|---|---|---|---|
| Jan 4 | Entwhistle | 1/01 | 460.00 | | 400.00 | | 60.00 | |

## PETTY CASH BOOK

p50

Dr.                                                             Cr.

← Analysis columns →

| Amount | Fo. | Date 200X | Particulars | Rcp. no. | Gross value | Net exempt | Net rate A | Net rate B | VAT | Postg. | Stnry |
|---|---|---|---|---|---|---|---|---|---|---|---|
| 40.00 | | Jan 1 | Balance b/d | | | | | | | | |
| | | 28 | Stamps | 1/1 | 10.00 | 10.00 | | | | 10.00 | |
| | | | Envelopes | 1/2 | 11.50 | | 10.00 | | 1.50 | | 10.00 |
| | | | | | 21.50 | 10.00 | 10.00 | | 1.50 | 10.00 | 10.00 |
| 21.50 | CB8 | 31 | Cash | | | | | | NL30 | NL15 | NLl17 |
| | | | Balance c/d | | 40.00 | | | | | | |
| 61.50 | | | | | 61.50 | | | | | | |
| 40.00 | | Feb 1 | Balance b/d | | | | | | | | |

## LEDGER

p30

NL50

VAT

| Dr. 200X | | | | 1991 | | | Cr. |
|---|---|---|---|---|---|---|---|
| Jan 31 | Bought ledger Control | BL60 | 60.00 | Jan 1 | Balance | b/d | 30.00 |
| | Petty cash | PCB50 | 1.50 | 31 | Sales ledger Control | SL61 | 38.64 |
| 31 | Bank | CB47 | 7.14 | | | | |
| | | | 68.64 | | | | 68.64 |

Note: The entry annotated 'Bank' represents a cheque paid to HM Revenue and Customs for the balance payable for the quarter.

Fig. 120. Accounting for VAT: worked example of VAT recordings in daybook, petty cash book and ledger.

You then total up and balance the VAT account, just like any other account in the ledger. The balance represents the tax payable or repayable, depending on whether the firm has collected in more than it has paid out.

Registered businesses are also required to keep a VAT summary. This is not a ledger account but a summary or memorandum as such things are called in accounting terms. It is not part of the double entry system. Figure 118 provides an illustration.

### VAT relief on bad debts
If a debt owing to the business is more than six months old the output tax paid on the invoice can be reclaimed from HMRC. If it is in the end paid, the output tax reclaimed must be repaid to HMRC.

### VAT that cannot be reclaimed
- *VAT on cars used by the business.* Businesses cannot usually reclaim VAT on cars purchased for use in the business.
- *Goods taken from the business for private use.* If the owner of a business takes goods from the business for his or her own private use their drawings account must be debited with the full amount which the business paid for the goods, including the VAT, while, on the other hand, the purchases account must be credited with the net amount and the VAT account credited with the VAT content.

### VAT and the final accounts
The collection of VAT is not part of the essence of business transactions; it is just a duty that is imposed upon businesses by HMRC that has to be carried out alongside them. Consequently it does not figure in the profits or losses of the firm and so will not appear anywhere in the profit and loss account. It will show in the balance sheet, however, as the business, if it is registered for VAT, will almost certainly hold funds that are owed to VAT or have money owed to it in the form of a repayment of VAT at the date of the balance sheet. The latter will, therefore, be likely to contain a figure for VAT in either its current assets or its current liabilities.

At the end of the VAT period a business has to complete and send in a VAT return to HMRC (see Fig. 121). Accuracy in accounting and prompt filing of returns is required by HMRC. Penalties apply for late filing. In Figure 121:

- Boxes 1–5 are for computation of tax payable or reclaimable.
- Boxes 6–9 are for statistical purposes.

### Completing the VAT return
At the end of each of the three months, prior to the end of the current VAT period:

- The total net sales should have been posted from the sales day book to the credit side of the Sales account in the nominal ledger and the total VAT to the credit side of the VAT account in the same ledger.
- The total net sales returns should have been posted from the sales returns day book to the debit side of the Sales account in the nominal ledger and the total VAT to the debit side of the VAT account in the same ledger.
- The total net purchases should have been posted from the purchases day book to the debit side of the Purchases account in the nominal ledger and the total VAT to the debit side of the VAT account in the same ledger.
- The total net purchase returns should have been posted from the purchase returns day book to the credit side of the Purchases account in the nominal ledger and the total VAT to the credit side of the VAT account in the same ledger.
- The total net purchases should have been posted from the petty cash book to the debit side of the Purchases account in the nominal ledger and the total VAT to the debit side of the VAT account in the same ledger.

If VAT was overpaid or underpaid at the end of the last VAT period it will show in the ledger as a balance b/d at the start of the period with which you are now dealing.

If any debts have been written off during the period they will have been debited to the Sales account and the VAT content which applied debited to the VAT account, both in the nominal ledger.

The first thing to do is the VAT summary. Simply follow the format of Figure 120 on page 182 taking the figures from the Purchases, Sales and VAT accounts in the nominal ledger. The figures in the summary go on the same side as they are found in the ledger, e.g. monthly purchase totals will have been posted to the debit (left-hand) side of the Purchases account. Just copy them to the left-hand side of the VAT summary and vice versa for the monthly sales figures.

If you have any VAT due on acquisitions from other EU states it will show on the credit side of the VAT account. Copy the figure to the credit (right-hand) side of the VAT summary. If you can claim this back, as may be the case, the reclaim will appear on the debit side of the VAT account reflecting a seemingly peculiar state of affairs where you are both paying it and reclaiming it. Copy the figure to the same side of the VAT summary as it appears in the ledger.

Copy to the VAT summary any VAT underclaim or overclaim that has been carried down to the period for which you are accounting.

Copy over details of any bad debt relief you are claiming as it shows on the debit side of the VAT account.

Annual adjustments may have to be made in special retailers' schemes and if such a case applies the adjustment figure will have been posted to whatever side of the VAT account it applies. Copy it over to the VAT summary

Now you do the arithmetic. Add in the input and output tax columns. (If you are using a spreadsheet just draw a line and enter below it the formula $= sum$ and the cells concerned in brackets, e.g. $= sum(b3:b5)$.) Add all the other inputs on each side to give a sub-total and then deduct the value of credit note VAT on each side. Deduct the smaller from the larger of the two totals and you arrive at a figure for VAT payable or reclaimable.

You can now use this as the source document for completing the VAT return. The figure for box 1 is the total VAT deductible less the VAT allowable on acquisitions from other EU states if any such figure appears in the VAT summary. The latter figure goes in box 2 and box 3 is the total of these two boxes, which should be the total of the VAT deductible in the VAT summary. The figure to enter in box 4 is the total VAT payable figure from the VAT summary. Here there is no need to separate the VAT due on acquisitions figure from the rest. Box 5 is simply the difference between box 3 and box 4. Box 6 is the total value of all other outputs including any VAT. This is the total of the three months of credit postings in the Sales account of the nominal ledger, whether sold in the UK or abroad, minus any sales returns. Box 7 is same for the inputs and is the total of the three months' postings to the Purchases account, whether sold in the UK or abroad, minus any purchase returns. Box 8 requires you to provide the total value of goods net of VAT, together with any related costs, supplied to other EU countries and box 9 requires the same for acquisitions.

### Computerisation

Automatic systems and specialised tools now deal with VAT easily. For example, Sage line 50 will automatically calculate the VAT and complete a VAT return which is acceptable to HMRC as long as you simply enter the date parameters of the period for which it is to account.

There are certain differences in the format used when filing a return online to those that apply for paper returns. For example, if there is nothing to enter in a box in an online form you enter 0.00 while in a paper form you are required to write NONE. A negative value (a figure to be subtracted) must be written with a minus sign before it while a negative value on a paper form must be represented by bracketing the figure. No minus signs must appear on a paper VAT return.

After thoroughly checking the accuracy of the form write your name if you are the authorised person and sign and date it. If a payment is being sent with the form tick the box on the left of the signature. Write, or procure from the cashier, the cheque and send the form off to HMRC.

### Special arrangements for retailers

It would be a virtually impossible task for some shops to record every individual sale. Take a sweet shop, for example. It may well sell hundreds of packets of sweets or bars of chocolate a day. The proprietor simply wouldn't be able to record each item individually, so special schemes have been devised for retailers, which excuse them from having to keep itemised VAT records on sales. There are several such schemes, each with their own special return forms, and the retailer chooses one most suited to his or her kind of business.

## Online filing is becoming compulsory

New HMRC rules require that all businesses with an annual turnover of £100,000 or more and all newly registered businesses must file their VAT return and settle their VAT account online for VAT Periods that commence on or after 1 April 2010.

For those who are not yet compelled by this rule to pay online, HMRC has also changed the way payments by cheque are treated. It previously treated the receipt of the cheque as the date payment was received, but now it will regard the date the funds go into the account as the payment date. Therefore, payments may have to be sent earlier.

# Value Added Tax Return

**HM Customs and Excise**

**For the period**
**01 06 05 to 31 08 05**

For Official Use

Registration Number | Period

You could be liable to a financial penalty if your completed return and all the VAT payable are not received by the due date.

Due date: 30 09 05

For Official Use

If you have a general enquiry or need advice please call our National Advice Service on 0845 010 9000

Before you fill in this form please read the notes on the back and the VAT leaflets *"Filling in your VAT return"* and *"Flat rate scheme for small businesses"*, if you use that scheme. Fill in all boxes clearly in ink, and write 'none' where necessary. Don't put a dash or leave any box blank. If there are no pence write "00" in the pence column. **Do not** enter more than one amount in any box.

| For official use | | | £ | p |
|---|---|---|---|---|
| | VAT due in this period on **sales** and other outputs | 1 | | |
| | VAT due in this period on **acquisitions** from other **EC Member States** | 2 | | |
| | Total VAT due **(the sum of boxes 1 and 2)** | 3 | | |
| | VAT reclaimed in this period on **purchases** and other inputs (including acquisitions from the EC) | 4 | | |
| | Net VAT to be paid to Customs or reclaimed by you **(Difference between boxes 3 and 4)** | 5 | | |
| | Total value of **sales** and all other outputs excluding any VAT. **Include your box 8 figure** | 6 | | 00 |
| | Total value of **purchases** and all other inputs excluding any VAT. **Include your box 9 figure** | 7 | | 00 |
| | Total value of all **supplies** of goods and related costs, excluding any VAT, to other **EC Member States** | 8 | | 00 |
| | Total value of all **acquisitions** of goods and related costs, excluding any VAT, from other **EC Member States** | 9 | | 00 |

If you are enclosing a payment please tick this box.

DECLARATION: You, or someone on your behalf, must sign below.

I, .................................................................................................. declare that the
(Full name of signatory in BLOCK LETTERS)

information given above is true and complete.

Signature .................................................. Date................................

A false declaration can result in prosecution

**Y**

**VAT 100** (half)     Page 1                                    PT1 (September 2004)

Fig. 121. Sample VAT Form (VAT 100): Courtesy Controller of HMSO (Crown Copyright).

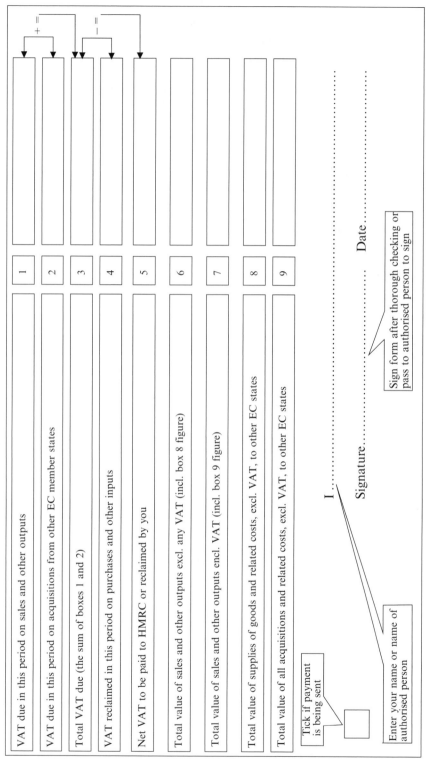

VAT due in this period on sales and other outputs | 1

VAT due in this period on acquisitions from other EC member states | 2

Total VAT due (the sum of boxes 1 and 2) | 3

VAT reclaimed in this period on purchases and other inputs | 4

Net VAT to be paid to HMRC or reclaimed by you | 5

Total value of sales and other outputs excl. any VAT (incl. box 8 figure) | 6

Total value of sales and other outputs encl. VAT (incl. box 9 figure) | 7

Total value of supplies of goods and related costs, excl. VAT, to other EC states | 8

Total value of all acquisitions and related costs, excl. VAT, to other EC states | 9

Tick if payment is being sent

Enter your name or name of authorised person

I ...........................

Signature ...........................  Date ...........................

Sign form after thorough checking or pass to authorised person to sign

Fig.122. Details needed to complete the VAT 100 form.

188

## 'Shoebox jobs'

Sometimes, small businesses neglect their book-keeping in the first year or two. They find other day-to-day business operations too demanding. The administrative side of the business seems non-productive. 'Let's make hay while the sun shines,' they say; 'we'll catch up with the book-keeping when business is slack'. But often the accounts are put off, until suddenly the proprietor receives a high income tax assessment and demand. This comes because HMRC has not received his final accounts on which to charge the correct tax. He is given 30 days to appeal against the assessment; the appeal will probably be granted, but he will only have a short time to get his records up to date and produce final accounts.

When he begins the task, he finds sales and purchase invoices all over the place, in no particular date order. Cheque book stubs have not all been filled in; he cannot find all his old bank statements; there are screwed up petrol receipts in every pocket of his working clothes and all corners of his lorry or van. He becomes bewildered, dumps everything he can find in a box and takes them along to an accountant. Little wonder accountants call these 'shoebox jobs'. Invariably some documents have been lost, so normal double entry book-keeping is impossible. A way has to be found to fill in all the gaps.

## The capital comparison method

One method is to draw up an opening and a closing statement of affairs, and deduct the opening capital from the closing capital. This is called the capital comparison method. The idea is to add together the fixed assets, the merchandise (stock), the accounts receivable (money owed to the proprietor after bad debt provision), cash in hand and cash at bank at the date in question. Deduct from that the accounts payable (money owed by the proprietor) and the difference will be capital. These statements are in effect the balance sheet, though the term balance sheet should really only be used when it has actually been drawn up from the proper ledger 'balances'.

- The difference between the capital at the end of the year, and that at the start of the year, is the net profit.

There is one big flaw in using this method alone. Some of the profit—we do not know how much—may have been taken out by the proprietor in drawings during the year; so the difference between opening and closing capitals will not itself necessarily tell us the profit. Example: suppose the opening capital was £10,000 and the closing capital £11,000. Deducting opening from closing capital suggests a net profit of £1,000. But what if the proprietor had drawn £5,000 during the year? The profit would then really have been £6,000 (£1,000 plus £5,000).

If we have accounts for drawings, however, this problem is resolved. We just add the drawings to the difference between opening and closing capitals to measure the profit.

### Capital comparison method step by step

Let us see how we might put these statements together. Remember the formula:

$$\text{Total assets} - \text{Current liabilities} = \text{Total net assets}$$

Capital plus long-term liabilities (not payable within the next year) must equal that.

1.  The first part of our closing statement of affairs will give us total net assets. We can complete it from current information, e.g. value of premises, fixtures and fittings, machinery and motor vehicles, stock (counted and valued), debtors, bank balance, cash in hand, and creditors.

2.  The first section of the second half can also be filled in from current information, i.e. the details of any longterm liabilities such as bank loans. We will have to assemble both these sections from whatever evidence is available to us, where the opening statement of affairs is concerned.

3.  We can also fill in the total for the second half of the statement. It will essentially be the same as the total net assets. Provided there are no long-term loans this figure will represent the capital. In our closing statement of affairs we will need to analyse this capital figure to show the net profit. This is found by addition and deduction, filling in the gaps as required. We will know the total: what we need are the figures to get us there. These are the steps in the calculation:

    | Example | |
    |---|---|
    | Opening capital (from opening statement of affairs) | 1,000 |
    | Add capital injections | Nil |
    | Add profit | (?) |
    | Less drawings | 4,000 |
    | Equals closing capital | 2,000 |

If the opening capital was £1,000, closing capital £2,000, no additional capital injections, and drawings of £4,000, then profit must be £5,000 (£1,000 + £0 + £5,000 − £4,000 = £2,000).

# ARMSTRONG ENGINEERING
## STATEMENT OF AFFAIRS
as at 1 July 200X

| | | | |
|---|---:|---:|---:|
| **FIXED ASSETS** | | | |
| Leasehold premises | | | 40,000 |
| Fixtures and fittings | | | 5,000 |
| Motor vehicle | | | 3,000 |
| | | | 48,000 |
| | | | |
| **CURRENT ASSETS** | | | |
| Stock | 2,500 | | |
| Debtors | 1,900 | 4,400 | |
| | | | |
| **Less CURRENT LIABILITIES** | | | |
| Creditors | 2,200 | | |
| Bank overdraft | 1,200 | 3,400 | 1,000 |
| Total net assets | | | |
| Represented by capital | | | 49,000 |

# ARMSTRONG ENGINEERING
## STATEMENT OF AFFAIRS
as at 30 June 200X

| | | | |
|---|---:|---:|---:|
| **FIXED ASSETS** | | | |
| Leasehold premises | 40,000 | | |
| Less depreciation | 2,000 | | 38,000 |
| | | | |
| Fixtures and fittings | 5,000 | | |
| Less depreciation | 250 | | 4,750 |
| | | | |
| Motor vehicle | 3,000 | | |
| Less depreciation | 1,000 | | 2,000 |
| | | | 44,750 |
| **CURRENT ASSETS** | | | |
| Stock | 3,600 | | |
| Debtors | 2,900 | 6,500 | |
| | | | |
| **Less CURRENT LIABILITIES** | | | |
| Creditors | 1,800 | | |
| Bank overdraft | 100 | 1,900 | |
| Net current assets | | | 4,600 |
| TOTAL NET ASSETS | | | 49,350 |
| | | | |
| Financed by: | | | |
| Opening capital | | | 49,000 |
| Add profit | | | *8,550* |
| Less drawings | | | (8,200) |
| | | | 49,350 |

Fig. 123. Using the capital comparison method to complete. The profit figure, given in italics, is the only figure which could fulfil the requirements of the sum.

## What you need
- Records of assets and liabilities at the start of the accounting period.

- Records of assets and liabilities at the end of the period.

- As many other records as possible for the period in question.

## Step by step
To draw up the statement of affairs at the start of the accounting period:

1.  List the fixed assets in order of permanence, and total.

2.  List and total up the current assets (in order of permanence).

3.  List and total up the current liabilities.

4.  Deduct from last total.

5.  Add to the total fixed assets.

6.  List any long-term liabilities (other than proprietor's capital) e.g. bank loans, mortgages and leases of more than a year.

7.  Enter as capital whatever figure you need to make this column exactly equal the total net assets figure.

Construct, in exactly the same way, a statement of affairs as at the end of the accounting period. Deduct the opening capital from the closing capital. Add any drawings, and deduct any capital injections by the proprietor throughout the year to arrive at the net profit for the year.

The last two steps are usually built into the format of the closing statement of affairs. In the capital section you deduct the opening capital from the closing capital, and record drawings and capital injections when arriving at and displaying the net profit. You construct the statement as far as possible in standard balance sheet format, and then fill in the missing figures by simple arithmetic.

## Example
Suppose Armstrong has failed to keep proper accounts during the last year. Faced with a tax demand, he asks us to calculate his profit for the year to 30 June 200X but he can only provide us with the following information: his leasehold premises were worth £40,000 at the start of the year, but have gone down in value by £2,000 since then. He had plant and machinery worth £5,000 which he has not added to; depreciation of £250 is assumed since then. A motor vehicle valued at £3,000 at the start of the year is now worth only £2,000. The stock level has risen from £2,500 to a present level of £3,600, the debtors figure has gone from

```
Dr.                                                    Cr.
              TOTAL DEBTORS ACCOUNT

Balance b/d        200.00    Cheques           150.00
Sales              300.00    Balance c/d       350.00
                   500.00                      500.00
```

```
              TOTAL CREDITORS ACCOUNT

Cash paid to                 Balance b/d      2,000.00
Suppliers        1,200.00    Purchases        2,200.00
Balance c/d      3,000.00
                 4,200.00                      4,200.00
```

```
                  BANK RECONCILIATION
                  as at 31 December 200X

Balance as per bank statement (overdrawn)          7,010.00

Add cheques drawn but not as yet
presented for payment:
    S. Jones                         90.00
    Frazer & Baines                 100.00            190.00
Corrected balance as per bank statement            7,200.00
    (overdrawn)
```

```
                  BANK RECONCILIATION
                  as at 31 December 200X

Balance as per bank statement (overdrawn)          6,247.00

Add cheques drawn but not as yet
presented for payment:

    A. Singh                         45.00
    Inko                            145.00            190.00
Corrected balance as per bank statement            6,437.00
    (overdrawn)
```

Fig. 124. Opening and closing bank reconciliations.

£1,900 to £2,900. The bank overdraft has gone down from £1,200 to £100 and creditors have gone down from £2,200 to £1,800. Furthermore, we know he has taken drawings of £8,200 to live on during the year. Page 193 shows how we would calculate his profit using the capital comparison method.

### Additional proof for the taxman

While the calculation of profit based on this method alone may satisfy the proprietor of a small business, the staff at HM Revenue and Customs are, understandably, likely to require additional proof that the profit figure claimed is accurate. After all, it is asking them to rely 100% on the honesty of the proprietor, not to mention the quality of his memory, in respect of the drawings he has taken.

If we have details of cash and banking transactions, plus accrued debtors and creditors for trading transactions and expenses, we can put together a trading, profit and loss account for the period, and we can use it to prove the figures in the closing statement of affairs. In fact, we could even compile the closing statement of affairs directly from those same sources, with the addition of information from the opening statement of affairs and details of any capital changes and changes in long term liabilities.

This is how to compile final accounts where many—but not all—the records are available. It involves drawing up:

- opening and closing statements of affairs
- cash and bank account analyses, which itself requires opening and closing bank reconciliations
- total debtors account
- total creditors account
- trial balance
- revenue accounts.

# A. FRAZER
## BANK ACCOUNT ANALYSIS
### for year ended 31 December 200X

| Dr. | 200X | Particulars | Motor | Wages | Rent | Heat/light | Post/tel | Drwgs | Spec items | Cr. Totals |
|---|---|---|---|---|---|---|---|---|---|---|
| 1,200.00 | Jan 1 | Balance b/d | | | | | | | | |
| | 1 | Edwards Garage | 40.00 | | | | | | | 40.00 |
| | 3 | S. Wilson | | 250.20 | | | | | | 250.20 |
| | 5 | Edwards Garage | 310.10 | | | | | | | 310.10 |
| 1,520.00 | 15 | Debtors | | | | | | | | |
| | 18 | Razi & Thaung | | | 20.70 | | | | | 20.70 |
| | 20 | A. Morris | | 31.50 | | | | | | 31.50 |
| 220.40 | 27 | Entwhistle | | | | | | | | |
| | 27 | Northern Elec | | | | 100.00 | | | | 100.00 |
| | 28 | L. Cleaves | | 30.00 | | | | | | 30.00 |
| | 31 | Cash | | | | | | 400.00 | | 400.00 |
| | 31 | Brit. Telecom | | | | | 50.00 | | | 50.00 |
| | 31 | Keele Engineering | | | | | | | 4,100.00 | 4,100.00 |
| | Feb 6 | S. Wilson | | 200.00 | | | | | | 200.00 |
| | 22 | A. Morris | | 70.00 | | | | | | 70.00 |
| 3,800.00 | 23 | Morgan & Baldwyn | | | | | | | | |
| | 28 | Northern Elec. | | | | 50.00 | | | | 50.00 |
| | 28 | Cash | | | | | | 400.00 | | 400.00 |
| | 28 | Balance c/d | | | | | | | | 714.90 |
| 6,740.40 | | Totals | 350.10 | 581.70 | 20.70 | 150.00 | 50.00 | 800.00 | 4,100.00 | 6,767.40 |
| 714.90 | Mar 1 | Balance b/d | | | | | | | | |

Fig. 125. Part of a typical bank account analysis. There would probably be many of such sheets required. This simple worked example assumes all income was banked and all expenditure was by cheque (which is highly unlikely but convenient for our purposes). If there was income and expediture in cash then a cash analysis would be desirable, but not always possible due to lack of records.

Fig. 126. Annotating the bank statements and then working from them has practical advantages.

## What you need
- Cheque book stubs, paying-in book stubs, bank statements, and any advice slips from the bank explaining entries on the bank statements. The proprietor may have to obtain duplicates of lost bank statements, and his bank will charge for these. He may also have to obtain paid (cancelled) cheques from the bank, where the counterfoils of such cheques have not been filled in.

- Several sheets of wide analysis paper with plenty of columns (e.g. up to 20), including a boldly ruled cash column on each side.

Sort the source documents into date order. Fill in any uncompleted cheque stubs after obtaining the information from cleared cheques or the proprietor's knowledge. Rule off the first bank statement at the date just before the start of the accounting period and do a bank reconciliation as at that date.

## Step by step
1. Head an analysis sheet: 'Bank account analysis for... [business name]... for period... [dates concerned]'.

2. Enter the opening balance from your reconciliation as at the last date of the previous accounting period—not the balance as per the bank statement. (Remember, if the balance is 'in favour' it will go on the left, and vice versa.)

3. Head the first column on the left 'Dr.' and the last column on the right 'Cr.'.

4. List the values of each of the lodgements in the far left hand cash column (Dr.) and the values of each of the cheques in the far right hand column (Cr.). Do this for the whole period covered by the first bank statement. You can take them directly from the bank statements to save time. If most lodgements represent sales revenue you can annotate the exceptions on the bank statement and use it also as a source for analysis later.

5. Add and balance the two columns. Bring forward your balance, just as you would any ledger account.

6. Repeat the process for the period covered by the next bank statement, and so on to the end of the accounting period.

7. Prepare a bank reconciliation statement for the final date of the accounting period.

# BANK STATEMENT

Statement as at 31 December 200X

03542256

| Date | Particulars | | Payments | Receipts | | Balance |
|------|-------------|------|----------|----------|--|---------|
| 200X | Opening balance | | | | | 350.55 |
| 12 Dec | sundry credit | | | 400.00 sales | | 750.55 |
| 15 Dec | | 543255 | 25.00 motor exp | | | 725.55 |
| 18 Dec | | 543256 | 105.10 telephone | | | 620.45 |
| 20 Dec | sundry credit | | | 350.50 rent received | | 970.95 |
| 28 Dec | | 543257 | 10.85 stationery | | | 960.10 |

Fig. 127. Example of an annotated bank statement.

| Sales | Particulars | Motor exp | Wages | Rent | Heat/ light | Post/ tel | Drawgs | Bldg reprs |
|-------|-------------|-----------|-------|------|-------------|-----------|--------|------------|
| 3,800.00 | Sheet 1 | 350.20 | 511.50 | 20.70 | 150.00 | 50.00 | 800.00 | 4,100.00 |
| 2,000.00 | 2 | 50.80 | 500.00 | 20.70 | 100.00 | 50.00 | 300.00 | |
| 1,200.00 | 3 | 19.00 | 800.00 | 20.70 | 110.00 | 10.00 | 400.00 | |
| 7,000.00 | Totals | 420.00 | 1,811.50 | 62.10 | 360.00 | 110.00 | 1,500.00 | 4,100.00 |

Fig. 128. Example of a summary of bank account analysis columns.
Note: it does not include the totals columns.

8. Extend your bank account analysis to show any extra details (leading to a different balance) shown in your bank reconciliation as at the end of the period (if, of course, the balance is different).

9. Now go back to your first analysis sheet and work your way through analysing each payment and each lodgement into an analysis column, as if it were a day book. The analysis columns for the payments will be credit columns, and those for lodgements will be debit columns: you are analysing the total credit entry to bank account that results from paying all the cheques involved. The double entry principle is not directly involved here; if it were, anlaysis of expenses would not be credit entries. The dividing line between the debit and credit columns will depend on how much of the categories apply to lodgements and payments respectively. Your list of headings, which refer to imaginary ledger accounts, will develop as you go along. You can't decide them all in advance, since you won't know the nature of each transaction until you get to it. You may well run out of analysis columns for payments. Keep one column aside as a 'miscellaneous one'; then you can record any odd bits and pieces there, and analyse them separately on another sheet. To do this, set up a supplementary sheet with the headings you need. Transfer each item by analysing it in the appropriate columns on the supplementary sheet. When all the items have been dealt with enter on the original sheet, in brackets or in red ink, in the miscellaneous column, a figure equal to the column total, to complete the transfer. In the unlikely event that you need a *misc* column on the debit side too, just follow the same procedure.

10. Sum the analysis columns for each sheet.

11. Prepare a summary of analysis column totals for each sheet.

12. Total up the summary columns.

## Finishing the job: drawing up final accounts
1. Prepare total debtors and creditors accounts.

2. Extract a trial balance.

3. Adjust for depreciation, bad and doubtful debts, accruals, prepayments, asset disposals and closing stock, obtaining details from the proprietor.

4. Draw up final accounts. Refer to appropriate chapters.

# KEY RATIOS AND WHAT THEY MEAN

| | *Concept* | *Equation* | *Optimum value* | *Diagnostic value* |
|---|---|---|---|---|
| 1. | Current ratio | $\dfrac{\text{Current assets}}{\text{Current liabilities}}$ | 2:1 | Test of solvency: i.e. a firm's ability to pay its debts |
| 2. | Acid test ratio | $\dfrac{\text{Current assets} - \text{stock}}{\text{Current liabilities}}$ | 1:1 | A refinement of the above |
| 3. | Asset turnover | $\dfrac{\text{Sales}}{\text{Net assets}}$ | * | Reveals efficiency of asset usage in terms of sales |
| 4. | Mark up | Gross profit as a percentage of cost of goods sold | * | A test of profitability. It reveals whether wholesale prices and other costs of sales are low enough to allow a good level of profit |
| 5. | Gross profit margin | Gross profit as a percentage of sales | * | As above |
| 6. | Net profit margin | Net profit as a percentage of sales | * | Shows whether overheads are too high to allow a suitable profit |
| 7. | RoCE (return on capital employed) | Net profit margin × asset turnover × 100 | * | Of special interest to investors: shows the return on investment in the company |
| 8. | Stock turnover | $\dfrac{\text{Cost of goods sold}}{\text{Average stock}}$ | * | Shows how efficiently the firm is using its asset of stock |

If average stock level throughout the year is not known it may be estimated from the average of opening and closing stocks: using closing stock alone is not satisfactory, since it may be unusually high or low depending on when the last deliveries were made in relation to the Balance Sheet date.

| | *Concept* | *Equation* | | *Diagnostic value* |
|---|---|---|---|---|
| 9. | Debt collection period | $\dfrac{\text{Debtors} \times 365}{\text{Sales}}$ | | Shows how well or badly the firm controls the amount of credit it gives. The lower the better |

*Note* *The higher the better. These optimum values are a rule of thumb only; some firms maintain very different ones without any implication of financial instability or inefficiency. It depends, in the end, on the firm and its aims.

Fig. 129. Key ratios and what they mean.

## 71   Interpreting accounts

### A variety of needs

Different people want to examine a firm's final accounts for different reasons. Final accounts are a means of proving the profits of a business to HM Revenue and Customs; but to other users they will mean much more. A purchaser of a business, an investor, a bank or other lender, or a major supplier will study them in detail to discover more information than profit alone. In fact, banks, other lenders and trade creditors will be far more interested in liquidity than profitability. Firms with high profits are not necessarily the most stable ones: often the opposite is true.

Don't confuse capital with cash either. They are different things. Capital is assets minus liabilities and even though a firm may have made high profits it could still be short of cash, because the profit simply means its net assets have increased and these may contain little or no cash.

The accounts also help the management team. Managers will study interim accounts (accounts produced more than once in the accounting year) as well as the final accounts. They need to compare actual performance and spending figures against budgeted figures, figures of previous periods, figures of competitors and average figures for the size and type of business. They, like other interested parties, will want to check the ratios between different balance sheet items because they can warn of weaknesses in the financial structure of the firm.

### Criticism of accounts

An interested party will compare this year's figures with last year's, for example sales and purchases, closing stocks and gross profit as a percentage of sales. How have the key ratios changed from one year to the next? Were changes in the first three of these due to changes in market prices or valuation changes? Or were they due to improved market share or efficiency of operation? Has gross profit as a percentage of sales remained constant in spite of increased turnover? A change in gross profit margin could be due to retail price cutting, wholesale price increase absorption (not passing it all on to customers), increases in delivery charges or reduced efficiency of the sales forces.

A change in the net profit to sales ratio will be due to increased overheads, but the firm will need to investigate which ones are to blame.

A high RoCE (return on capital employed) should be investigated: is it realistic? Profits may be inflated by simply over-valuing stocks, through poor estimating of quantities and/or values. There is more than one way of defining RoCE, but the formula shown is a common one. What matters is that the same formula is used consistently when comparing figures, from one period to the next, or one firm to another.

| Different ways of valuing assets | |
| --- | --- |
| **Asset category** | **Method** |
| **Fixed assets** | Net realisable value<br>Revenue generating capacity |
| | Historical cost less depreciation calculated by:<br>Straight line method<br>Diminishing balance method<br>Machine hours method |
| **Current assets**<br>*Stock*<br>*Debtors* | LIFO<br>Average cost method |
| *Provision for bad and doubtful debts* | The percentage allowed for bad and doubtful debts should only change for good reason and clear notification and explanation to interested parties |

Fig. 130. Different ways of valuing assets.

Failure to write down assets properly (vehicles, machinery, etc) or to make enough provision for bad debts (page 117) will also inflate the profits.

A favourable current ratio could also be due to overvaluing stocks or underassessing doubtful debts. The latter would also affect the acid test ratio.

## Consistency

It is important to people reading the accounts of a company that they are comparing like with like, e.g. that the company has not used different methods of measurement for different costs, revenues, assets or liabilities. It is also important that the same practices are used from year to year and if changed that all interested parties are clearly informed of the change. This is known as the principle of *consistency* and applies to all aspects of the accounts.

# ARMSTRONG ENGINEERING LTD
## TRADING, PROFIT & LOSS ACCOUNT
for year ended 31 December 200X

| | |
|---|---|
| Turnover | 308,000 |
| Cost of sales | 177,000 |
| Gross profit | 131,000 |
| Administration expenses | 54,500 |
| | 76,500 |
| Interest payable | 900 |
| Profit on ordinary activities before taxation | 75,600 |
| Tax on profit from ordinary activities | 32,000 |
| Profit on ordinary activities after taxation | 43,600 |
| Profit and loss account balance | |
| Undistributed profits b/f from last year | 23,400 |
| | 67,000 |
| Proposed dividends | 34,500 |
| Undistributed profits c/f to next year | 32,500 |

## BALANCE SHEET
as at 31 December 200X

| | Cost | Less provision for depreciation | Net book |
|---|---|---|---|
| Fixed assets | | | |
| Premises | 103,400 | | 103,400 |
| Fixtures and fittings | 10,000 | 500 | 9,500 |
| Machinery | 40,000 | 2,000 | 38,000 |
| Motor van | 10,000 | 2,000 | 8,000 |
| | 163,400 | 4,500 | 158,900 |
| Current assets | | | |
| Stock | 18,000 | | |
| Debtors | 48,700 | | |
| Cash at bank | 19,850 | | |
| Cash in hand | 50 | | |
| | | 86,600 | |
| Less creditors | | | |
| Amounts falling due within 1 year | 22,500 | | |
| Accruals | 4,000 | | |
| Proposed dividends | 34,500 | 61,000 | 25,600 |
| Total net assets | | | 184,500 |
| Provision for liabilities and charges | | | |
| Taxation | | | 32,000 |
| Shareholders funds | | | |
| Authorised share capital | | | |
| 100,000 Preference shares of £1 | 100,000 | | |
| 100,000 Ordinary shares of £1 | 100,000 | | |
| | 200,000 | | |
| Issued share capital | | | |
| 30,000 Preference shares of £1 | | 30,000 | |
| 90,000 Ordinary shares of £1 | | 90,000 | |
| | | 120,000 | |
| Capital and reserves | | | |
| Proft and loss account balance | | 32,500 | 152,500 |
| | | | 184,500 |

Fig. 131. Final accounts ready for interpretation.

Example of interpretation of accounts in Fig. 131 opposite.

| Information | Worked | Example | Comment |
|---|---|---|---|
| Current ratio | $\dfrac{86,600}{61,000}$ | $= 1.42/1$ | Rather low |
| Acid test ratio | $\dfrac{68,600}{61,000}$ | $= 1.12/1$ | Acceptable |
| Asset turnover | $\dfrac{308,000}{184,500}$ | $= 1.67/1$ | |
| Mark-up | $\dfrac{131,000}{177,000}$ | $\times\ 100 = 74\%$ | Very high |
| Gross profit margin | $\dfrac{131,000}{308,000}$ | $\times\ 100 = 43\%$ | Acceptable |
| Net profit margin | $\dfrac{75,600}{308,000}$ | $\times\ 100 = 25\%$ | Acceptable |
| RoCE | $0.25 \times 1.67 \times 100 = 41.75\%$ | | |
| Stock turnover | $\dfrac{177,000}{16,500}$ | $* = 11$ times | Depends on type of business |
| Debt collection period | $\dfrac{48,700}{308,000}$ | $\times\ 365 = 58$ days | |

* This average stock figure is not actually shown in the accounts, because they are *published* ones and it is not required by law to be shown. However, it can be calculated from opening stock and closing stock, both of which will appear in internal accounts. These figures have been taken from the worked example on page 142.

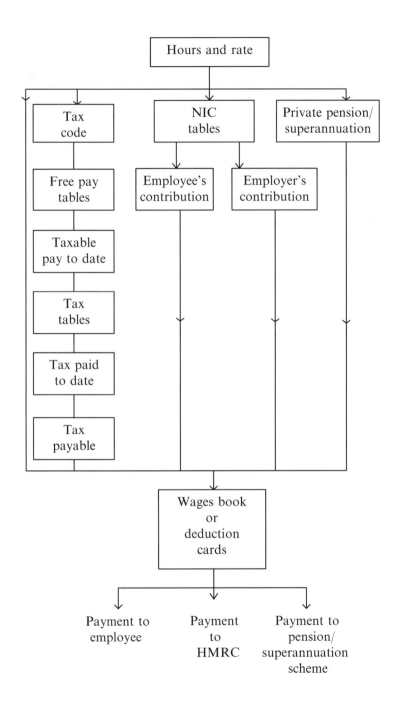

Fig. 132. Wages and salaries at a glance.

Wages and salaries are payments for people's labour. They are called **wages** when paid weekly and calculated from the number of hours worked (hourly rates) or units of production finished (piece rates). When payments are made monthly, and there is no direct relationship between them and the hours worked or units produced, they are called **salaries**. Manual and unskilled workers are paid wages; clerical workers, managers and professional people are paid monthly salaries.

Often wage earners are paid a higher hourly rate if they work after the scheduled finishing time; they may be paid an even higher one if they work very unsociable hours. For example, working after 5pm may entitle them to 50% more pay per hour, and they may receive twice the normal rate for work done on a Sunday. These rates are popularly known as 'time and a half' and 'double time'. To find a wage earner's gross pay entitlement the wages clerk multiplies the hours worked by the rate concerned (e.g. 1, 1½ or 2) and then multiplies the product by the hourly pay rate, e.g. £10.50.

Workers usually have to pay income tax on the money they earn. Everyone is entitled to some pay free from tax; the amount of exemption depends on their circumstances. For example people with dependent children have a higher level of tax exemption than those without. This level is called **free pay** and is identified by a **tax code** number. The wages clerk can simply look up the employee's code number and read off against it the cumulative free pay to date (for that tax year) to which that employee is entitled. He/she then adds this week's pay to total pay to date in the tax year, and deducts from that the free pay to date. He/she thus arrives at the taxable pay to date. He/she then calculates, by referring to a table, the cumulative tax payable on this; he/she deducts from it the tax *actually* paid to date to find out how much tax he/she must deduct this pay day.

Everyone earning more than a certain level of income (**threshold** level) must also pay regular National Insurance Contributions (NIC), to entitle them to free medical treatment and other state benefits. The wages clerk must also deduct NIC from the wages or salaries paid. The firm itself *also* has to make a contribution to each employee's NIC cover; the amount is related to level of pay.

When an employee earns above a certain figure they are charged a higher tax rate for the amount over that figure. Employee's wages are taxed at source. The company acts as a sort of sub-tax collector for HM Revenue and Customs, just as it does for collection of VAT. Income tax collected at source is called **Pay As You Earn** (PAYE).

# WAGES

Suppose Mr Jones works 50 hours, the first 40 of which are at his standard rate of £10.50 p/h, the next 5 of which amount to overtime at 'time and a half' and the next 5 after that represent Sunday work at 'double time'. Suppose also, he pays to a company pension scheme at the rate of 7% of his gross earnings. His wage slip may look something like this.

| Hours worked | Standard rate | = 40 = | 420.00 |
|---|---|---|---|
| | Standard rate × 1½ | = 5 = | 78.75 |
| | Standard rate × 2 | = 5 = | 105.00 |
| | | | 603.75 |
| Gross pay | | | |
| | Less income tax | 100.75 | |
| | NIC contribution | 66.41 | 167.16 |
| | | | 436.58 |
| | Less pension scheme contribution | | 42.26 |
| | Net pay | | 394.31 |

Fig. 133. Worked example of the completion of a wage slip.

| Wages | £20 | £10 | £5 | £1 | 50p | 20p | 10p | 5p | 2p | 1p |
|---|---|---|---|---|---|---|---|---|---|---|
| 125.39 | 120 | | 5 | | | 20 | 10 | 5 | 4 | |
| 73.40 | 60 | 10 | | 3 | | 40 | | | | |
| 101.21 | 100 | | | 1 | | 20 | | | | 1 |
| 300.00 | 280 | 10 | 5 | 4 | | 80 | 10 | 5 | 4 | 1 |

Fig. 134. A coin analysis for three wage packets.

## 74  Coin analysis and wages book

### Making up the wage packets

When all the wages have been calculated the wages clerk prepares a **coin analysis**, this is a list of all the coins needed to make up the wage packets (see opposite). Otherwise, how could he/she make them up? Let's take a simple example. Suppose there are three employees and their wages for a week are £125.39, £73.40, £101.21, a total of £300.00. If the wages clerk merely collected £300 in, say, ten pound notes from the bank he/she would not be able to make up the wages; he/she wouldn't have sufficient coins to pay out the amounts; £10s, £5s, 20ps, 10ps, 5ps, and 1ps are all needed in our example.

### Wages book/deduction cards

The wages and salaries records of the firm are kept in a **wages book** and/or on **deduction cards** supplied by the HMRC. The records show such details as gross pay to date, free pay to date, taxable pay to date, tax paid to date, and NIC contributions paid to date by employee and employer.

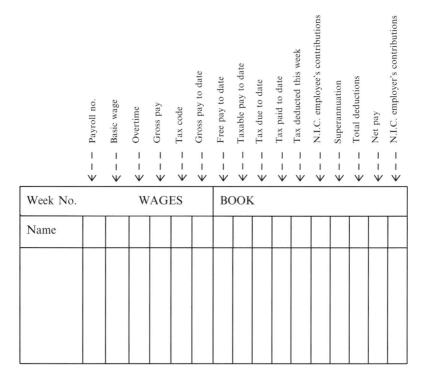

Fig. 135. Example of the layout in a typical wages book.

| £ | £ | £ | |
|---|---|---|---|
| 1st purchase | 10 @ 50 | | 500 |
| 2nd purchase | 10 @ 55 | | 550 |
| | | | 1,050 |
| | | | |
| 1st withdrawal | 2 @ 50 | | 100 |
| | | | |
| Balance | 8 @ 50 | 400 | |
| | 10 @ 55 | 550 | 950 |
| | | | |
| 2nd withdrawal | 8 @ 50 | 400 | |
| | 1 @ 55 | 55 | 455 |
| Balance | 9 @ 55 | | 495 |

Fig. 136. Illustration of stock valuation using FIFO.

|  |  | £ | £ |
|---|---|---|---|
| 1st purchase | | 10 @ 50 = | 500 |
| 2nd  " | | 10 @ 55 = | 550 |
| | | | 1,050 |

1st withdrawal from warehouse, so average
out the item costs to date, i.e. $\frac{1,050}{20}$ = £52.50 each,

| Withdrawn 2 @ £52.50 | | | |
|---|---|---|---|
| Balance 18 @ £52.50 | | | 945 |
| 3rd purchase | | 10 @ 60 = | 600 |
| | | | 1,545 |

2nd withdrawal from warehouse, so average
out the item costs to date taking the previous
average as the cost of each and every one of the
items purchased before that date, i.e. $\frac{1,545}{28}$ = £55.18

| Withdrawn 10 @ £55.18 | | | |
|---|---|---|---|
| Balance 18 @ £55.18 = | | | 993.24 |

and so it would go on.

Fig. 137. Stock valuation using 'average cost' method.

# 75  Stock records and valuation

## Basic records

Individual stock items can be quite valuable, e.g. household appliances like washing machines or tools like electric drills. In such cases the firm may well want to have a system for booking them in and out of the warehouse whenever they are bought or sold. The supplier's delivery note will be the source document for the booking in; a requisition docket of some kind will be the source document for booking out. So there will always be a record of the stock that should be in hand; periodical physical stock checks (actually going round and counting the stock) will show up any discrepancies arising from errors or pilferage.

## Stock valuation methods

At the end of the accounting period stocks have to be valued for the balance sheet. Such value is based on the cost price or replacement price, whichever is the *lower*. The idea is that the asset figures in the accounts should reflect the true values as closely as possible. Each item (or at least each group of items) should be treated separately in this valuation process.

If we are valuing the stock at cost price there may have been a number of price changes throughout the year, and if the goods are identical we may not be able to tell which ones cost which amounts. There are three main ways of dealing with this:

- FIFO (first in first out)

- LIFO (last in first out)

- average cost method.

## First in first out

FIFO assumes that the remaining stock is the subject of the most recent prices. Suppose a firm had purchased 30 televisions, the first 10 at £50, another 10 some months later at £55, and near the end of the year another 10 at £60.00. Let's suppose, also, that it sold 15 to one customer, a hotelier perhaps, just before the end of the accounting year. Since 30 had been purchased and only 15 sold there should be 15 left in stock. These 15 would be valued at the prices of the most recently purchased 15; that means all 10 of the most recent purchase at £60 each and 5 of the previous order at £55 each.

### Last in first out
LIFO does the opposite. It says that *all* remaining stock on hand is valued at the *earliest* purchase price. To value stock according to LIFO you do the same as for FIFO, using the earliest invoices, instead of the most recent.

### Average cost method
The average cost method (sometimes referred to as AVCO) requires you to divide the remaining stock (numbers of items) into the total cost of all that stock, each time an item is withdrawn from stock. You then apply the cost figure to the withdrawn stock, and to the stock remaining afterwards. When another withdrawal is made you add the last valuation to the cost of all purchases since; you then divide the total by the actual number of items in stock. Again you apply this value to the goods withdrawn *and* to the balance remaining. So the average value of remaining stock may change continuously.

### Example
Let's suppose a shop made purchases as in the example; it sells two televisions immediately after the second wholesale purchase and 10 more close to the end of the year. You would then value the stock as shown in the example in Figure 130.

FIFO is the most commonly used method. It also seems the most realistic, because businesses usually try to sell their oldest stock first.

### Advantages of FIFO method
- Unrealised profits or losses will not occur, i.e. increases in stock values due to inflation.

- Issuing the oldest items first reduces likelihood of stock perishing.

- Stock valuation will be closer to current prices than with other methods.

- This method is acceptable to HM Revenue and Customs.

- This method complies with SSAP9. This statement of standard accounting practice prescribes that stock should be valued at the lower of cost or net realisable value.

### Disadvantages
- In inflationary times costs are understated and profits overstated. This is because the cost of replacing the stock is higher than the cost of the stock used and accounted for. The reverse is true in deflationary times.

- Material issue prices vary so that it is difficult to compare prices over a range of jobs.

## Advantages of LIFO method
- It keeps stock values to a minimum.

- It causes the firm's product prices to reflect the most recent component prices.

- It could, theoretically, enable the firm to weather the storm better in times of rising component costs, because it could produce goods more cheaply than other firms when the stock in its storeroom is valued at old prices.

## Disadvantages
This method is not acceptable to HM Revenue and Customs and does not comply with SSAP9, so all consideration of its advantages is purely academic.

*Stock reorder levels*
The stock levels that trigger reordering are calculated as follows:

$$\text{buffer stock} + (\text{budgeted usage} \times \text{maximum lead time})$$

i.e. the level of stock the firm keeps as a margin of safety plus (an order figure equal to the budgeted usage per day, or week multiplied by the number of days, or weeks it takes to receive the stock after ordering).

## Computerising the stock control system
Computerised stock control systems offer many advantages over manual systems:

- Faster data processing.

- Increased accuracy.

- Savings in wages costs.

- Continuous analysis to establish economic order quantities.

- Automatic reordering made possible.

- *Just in time* stock ordering is made feasible, reducing stock holding costs to a minimum.

- More effective control of minimum and maximum levels.

- Point of sale stock control facilitated.

- Immediate and up to date reports on performance of particular stock lines made possible and easy to obtain.

- Stock keeping software can be integrated into the firm's general accounting software.

This book seeks to teach the principles of double entry book-keeping. However, readers may, in the course of their careers, come across small businesses which use single entry methods.

### The Simplex system

The most common single entry method is the **Simplex system**. This is an integrated system involving two books. One is designed for recording daily takings, daily payments and a weekly cash and bank account. All are dealt with on the same page and one page is used per week. The balances of the cash and bank accounts are carried forward to the next week, as the opening figures.

There are special VAT recording arrangements for small businesses. In corner shops for example, it would be burdensome to record each individual item of sale separately—a bar of chocolate to one customer, a newspaper to another and a ballpen to another, for example. In such cases therefore, there are special formulae for computing the VAT payable or repayable. There are a number of different schemes to suit the particular problems of different types of business. In recognition of this the Simplex range contains different versions of the daily takings and purchases book for each scheme.

The second of the two books is a sales and purchases record.

At the end of the daily takings and purchases book there is an analysis section. By following guidance notes printed on the page, owners of businesses can compile their draft profit and loss accounts and balance sheets.

### The slip system

As was pointed out on page 15, in double entry book-keeping the sources of information for posting to the ledger are the books of **prime entry**. Nothing should be posted directly from, for example, an invoice, or credit note.

However, this rule is sometimes broken. Occasionally, you'll find this stage bypassed and entries made directly into the ledger. This is called the **slip system**. It is used where accounts have to be kept very up to date, such as in banking and wherever automated systems are used. Where postings are made directly to the ledger, from invoice copies, those copies are filed to form the equivalent of the day book. This I call the **slip + 1 system**, because an extra invoice copy is needed.

In the accounts of some very small firms, the ledgers, too, are sometimes dispensed with. Instead, the invoices (or copies in the case of invoices sent out) are merely filed together with other unpaid ones, in date order. This takes the place of the personal ledger (sales and purchase). When each is paid it is stamped and removed to be filed with all the paid ones. This version I call the **slip + 2 system**, because two additional copies of each invoice are needed.

For the 'slip + 1' version a firm's invoices really need to be printed in triplicate. For the 'slip + 2' version they need to be in quadruplicate.

| A | B | C | D | E | F | G | H | I | J | K | L | M |
|---|---|---|---|---|---|---|---|---|---|---|---|---|
| Date | Particulars | Fo. | Details | Amount | | Date | Particulars | | Fo. | Details | Amount | |
| 200X | | | | | | 200X | | | | | | |
| | =IF(F7<M7,"Balance c/d"," ") | | | =IF(F7<M7,M7-F7," ") | =SUM(E3:E6) | | =IF(F7>M7,"Balance c/d"," ") | | | | =IF(M7<F7,F7-M7) | =SUM(L3:L6) |
| | | | | =SUM(E3:E7) | | | | | | | =SUM(L3:L7) | |
| | =IF(F7<M7,"Balance b/d"," ") | | | =IF(M7<F7,F7-M7," ") | | | =IF(F7>M7,"Balance b/d"," ") | | | | =IF(F7<M7,M7-F7," ") | |

Fig. 138. This is what your sheet will look like if you command your program to show the formulae you have entered. To do this, click on the Tools menu and select *Options*. Then click on *Formulae* and, finally, click the *OK* button. Don't forget to remove the tick from the *formulas* option after you are satisfied that you have entered the formulae correctly, otherwise your formulae will show instead of your figures.

| Date | Particulars | Fo. | Details | Amount | Date | Particulars | Fo. | Details | Amount |
|---|---|---|---|---|---|---|---|---|---|
| 200X | | | | | 200X | | | | |
| Jan-10 | Wood | | | 20.00 | Jan-31 | Cheque | | | 20.00 |
| Jan-15 | Nails | | | 2.00 | 31 | Balance c/d | | | 2.00 |
| | | | 22.00 | 22.00 | | | | | 22.00 |
| Feb-01 | Balance b/d | | | 2.00 | | | | | |

Fig. 139. This is what your sheet will look like when you have entered figures onto it. You will see that the formulae do not show.

## How it works

Nowadays we can use the electronic pages of a spreadsheet program if we have access to a computer. As long as you know how to write on them you can simply follow the instruction in the chapters of this book in the same way as you would for paper pages.

There are various spreadsheet packages on the market, but the differences in the way they work are not great. If you can use one you will be able to grapple with another. The examples used here relate to Microsoft Excel.

## Writing on spreadsheet pages

Just as you move to the appropriate spot on a paper page and write on it with a pen, with a spreadsheet page you move to the spot with the direction keys ← ↑ ↓ → or a mouse and type the information through the keyboard. It's as simple as that.

## Adding them up

You will need your standard and formatting toolbars showing. If they are not, click on the view menu and choose the toolbars option. Next, click in the *standard* and *formatting* boxes and then click 'OK'.

When you come to adding the columns up draw the lines of the answer boxes, using the ⊞ ↓ buttons on the formatting toolbar. Use the arrow key to select a single line for the top and a double line for the bottom. The column will add itself up if you click on the answer box and then click the $\Sigma$ button on the standard toolbar.

## Calculating the c/d balance

Where you have both debit and credit columns you will need to calculate c/d balance. To do this you have to add both sides and take the smaller figure from the larger. Then you enter the difference in the smaller column. That means you've got to jot the two totals down somewhere. Here's how you do that. First make room for a c/d balance by inserting a row if necessary above the answer boxes.

Next insert a column next to the debit column being added, by clicking on the insert menu and choosing the *columns* option while the cursor is to the right of the column. Enter in it the instruction to sum the column immediately above and to its left. To do this click on the $\Sigma$ button. ' = SUM ( )' will appear in the box. Enter in the brackets the pair of cell references which bound the column you wish to add. Separate them with a colon. Example: E3:E6.

Do the same with the credit column. Example: L3:L6. Here you will find you have to replace a cell reference already showing.

Instructions don't show up on the page – they're invisible – but the answers which they make do. This one is just a jotting though; you don't want it to show, so you must deliberately hide it. You can do this by clicking on the format menu and selecting the *columns* option, then clicking on *hide*, while the cursor is in the column concerned.

Next, enter the '*If*' command. To do this click on the *f\** button on the toolbar and choose the '*If* button while the cursor is in the last space above the total box in the debit column. Click the button labelled *Next*.

Type the first of the two cell references in which you put the column addition formula (i.e. the first of the hidden cells), followed by a < sign, and this is followed by the second of those cell references. Example F7 < M7. In the second box down, marked '*value if true*' type the reverse of this. This time the two cell references should be separated by a minus sign instead of a < symbol. In the third box down simply type a space (press the space bar once). Click the button labelled *Finish*.

Now repeat this on the credit side in the cell above the answer box, reversing the formula.

There is no point in showing zeros in these cells, so if they do appear click on the tools menu and select *options*. Make sure *Zero values* is not ticked and then press the key labelled *OK*.

Next, click in the first of the actual answer boxes and then click on the $\Sigma$ button twice. Do the same in the right hand answer box.

The balance c/d is then transferred to the opposite side after the total box, as the opening figure (Balance b/d) for the next month. To do this on the spreadsheets just type in the space below the total box on each side the formula which has been entered in the c/d balance box on the opposite side.

Click in the last available space in the particulars column (above the answer box line) and then click the *function* key. Select the *If* option and then, in the dialogue space, type the co-ordinates in which the subtotals are stored in the hidden columns, separated by a ' < ' symbol, (e.g. F7 < M7). In the second dialogue space type 'Balance c/d'. In the third dialogue box type a space (just press the space below once). Click on finish. Now do the same in the space adjacent to this one on the credit side of the sheet, reversing the formula. Lastly, enter the b/d balance narratives. Using the function key, simply enter in the particulars column, below the totals boxes on each side, the exact formula you entered in the diametrically opposite position (i.e. the space above the total box in the opposite column), but substitute the term c/d with the term b/d.

As you type in the formulae they will appear temporarily in the boxes, but will disappear as soon as you press *finish* in each case.

## Configuring a spreadsheet page for day books

It is easy to configure pages which will add themselves up and cross balance for day books. All you have to do is draw in the answer boxes, as you did for the ledger pages. Click on each answer box to highlight it and then click on the $\Sigma$ button on the toolbar.

### Making things easy for yourself

Now you don't have to go through this each month. You can keep this specimen page without any actual monthly figures in it as a template.

### Four steps for creating a template

1.   Create a single sheet workbook.
2.   Format it with the titles and formulae.
3.   Save as a template.
4.   Enter the folder in which you wish to store it.

### Speeding up ledger posting

You can keep all accounts of a single ledger division (e.g. all customer accounts) on the same sheet, one after the other, as the placing of automated summing and balancing instructions will ensure that the accounts do not get mixed up. Each ledger division becomes a different sheet (e.g. sheet 1 = Sales daybook, sheet 2 = Nominal ledger and sheet 3 = Sales ledger, and so on.) A big advantage of doing this is that you can make posting from daybooks to ledger sheets easy, by putting all the sheets involved on the screen at once. The larger your screen the easier this will be. For example:

• Sales daybook. • Nominal ledger. • Sales ledger.

Then you can simply use copy and paste across the boundaries of the sheets to do your positing. For example, to post a transaction from the Sales daybook to the relevant ledger sheets, just follow these steps:

1.   Call up all the relevant sheets on the screen at once.
2.   Click on the gross invoice value for each entry on the Sales daybook sheet.
3.   Press '**Alt**' '**E**' '**C**'.
4.   Scroll down the Sales ledger sheet to the personal account of the customer concerned.
5.   Click on the next available space in the debit column.
6.   Press '**Alt**' '**E**' '**P**'.
7.   Enter the date in the date column.
8.   When all the entries have been posted to the Sales ledger accounts, proceed as follows.
9.   Click on the net total in the Sales daybook.
10.  Press on '**Alt**' '**E**' and '**C**'.
11.  Scroll to the next available space in the credit column of the Sales account in the Nominal ledger.
12.  Press '**Alt**' '**E**' '**P**'.
13.  Click on the VAT total in the Sales daybook and press '**Alt**' '**E**' '**C**'.

14. Scroll to the next available space in the credit column of the VAT account in the Nominal ledger and press '**Alt**' '**E**' '**P**'.

## Automating depreciation calculations

Asset depreciation calculations can be done swiftly and simply, using Excel's built in functions.

## Straight line method

Click on the '***f***' tab on the menu bar (this is the toolbar which always shows at the top of the screen).

1. Select the '**Financial**' option.
2. Click, then, on the '**SLN**' option.
3. The following dialogue boxes will appear on the screen:
   asset value; estimated salvage (scrap) value; estimated useful life.
4. Enter the relevant figures and click '**OK**' to find the annual depreciation figure.

## Diminishing balance method of depreciation

1. Click on the '**Insert**' tab on the menu bar.
2. Select the '**f\***' option.
3. Then select the '**DDB**' option.
4. The following five dialogue boxes will appear.
   cost; estimated salvage value; estimated useful life; start of the period; end of the period.
5. Enter the relevant figures and click on '**OK**' to find the depreciation for the asset.

## Sum of the years (or sum of the digits) method of depreciation

Follow the same procedure as for the diminishing balance method, selecting the '**SYD**' instead of the '**DDB**' option.

In previous editions of this book I have showed readers how to make use of the electronic pages of spreadsheets. I have, however, tended to stop short of dealing with computerised book-keeping packages, as they were, hitherto, rather too complicated for many people. Things have changed though; there are now various packages on the market to suit all needs and various ability and skill levels. A comprehensive book-keeping course book must now give some attention to these too.

Their use is not a substitute for a thorough knowledge of book-keeping, however. It is not much use having accounts if you don't know what they mean and how to use them to control your business. Their use will merely speeds things up and take the donkeywork out of the job.

### The types of software available

The software packages that are available fall into two categories:

- computer-based
- web-based.

Systems can also be categorised as form-based or transaction-based.

### Form-based systems

*Sage* is an example of a form-based system. It is a comprehensive system that has been around for some time and has enjoyed the status of industry standard. It requires some degree of book-keeping knowledge and skill to use and quite a bit of setting up is required.

Another form-based system is *Simply Accounts*. This requires less setting up, less knowledge and skill to use and is less expensive than *Sage*.

### Transaction-based systems

Contrasting with form-based systems are transaction-based systems. *Accountz* is such a system. It minimises the need to get to grips with input forms by recognising that all transactions fall into one of three kinds:

- sales
- purchases
- transfers.

Only three very simple tables are used and all the transactions you have to enter can be put into one or other of these. You simply take your batch of invoices, or cheque stubs, enter them into the relevant table in any order and then move them around as required afterwards, before locking their positions.

### De-jargonated

The data input is simplified by the fact that rather than debit and credit fields, the relevant fields are labelled 'from' and 'to' – where the value is coming from and where it is going to. This further simplication will, of course, only help the novice. Each transaction is entered on a single line.

*Example*

If you have settled your credit card account you enter the value as taken from your bank account and as going to your *credit card account*. If you are recording the cash sales you enter the value as taken from your *daily takings* and as going into your *bank* account. If you are recording credit sales you enter the value as coming from *credit sales account* and as going to *unpaid invoices account*. When you settle a bill you record the value as going from the bank account and as going to the *unpaid invoices outwards account*. If VAT is applicable at standard rate you just select 'standard rate' and it will work it out for you.

The producers have done their utmost to minimise the number of key and mouse operations that you have to make.

VAT returns are quick and easy to product and this software caters for VAT accounting and production of returns for all EEC countries. All major global currencies are also provided for.

This system can cater for any kind of business unit, e.g.:

- sole trader
- partnerships
- limited company.

Report formats are infinitely changeable so that even club accounts can be produced.

It is a multiplatform product, which can be run on PCs, Applemacs or Net books.

### Web-based systems

Contrasting with computer-based systems are web-based systems. An example is a system called Fusion.

Instead of the software and the data being stored on your computer, web-based systems work from programs accessed through the internet. The user's data is also stored on the web.

There are some advantages to using this type of system. One is that as it web-based, a user can access and work on their accounts from any computer that has internet access; it doesn't have to be their own computer.

No backing up of data is required.

Upgrades are automatic and in the case of Fusion they are free, so a user will always have the latest version. Payment is by monthly subscription and the licence includes 10 users.

### Access on a need to know basis

Access can be set to restrict access by staff to only those parts of the accounting information that they need in order to perform their role in the organisation. This improves data security.

### Advantages of computerised book-keeping systems

- Some types of error will be eliminated.

- Casting (summation) is automatic.

- Posting is automatic.

- Ledger balancing is automatic.

- Extraction of trial balance can be done at any time automatically at the touch of a few keys.

- There are also many stock control advantages.

- Reduced skilled labour costs, as large amounts of data are processed by computer rather than manually.

- Easier communication of accounts, as authorised people can access them by computer.

- Live, centralised accounting is made feasible for many remote branches of firms, as happens in some pub chains, where data from tills is processed live at head office.

Computerisation of the accounts will prevent some errors, but not all types. The error types it will prevent are:

- errors of omission
- commission
- compensatory errors
- errors of original entry
- errors of principle.

The types it will not prevent are:

- errors of reversal
- posting one side to wrong side of ledger
- omission of one side only

- under/overstatement of one side
- errors of summation
- casting errors
- transposition errors.

See page 168 for an explanation of what these error terms mean.

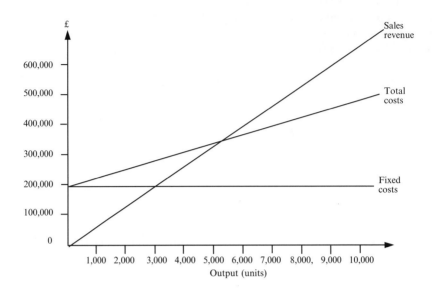

Fig. 140. Example of a break-even chart.

224

## Break-even analysis

Before a company decides to embark on a particular project break-even analysis will be carried out to predict the point below which it will cease to make a gross profit on sales—its **break-even point**.

The difference between a projected level of sales and break-even point is known as the **margin of safety**. It represents how much sales can fall short of the target before a loss is made. It therefore gives an indication of how much the project could withstand adverse trading conditions. Margin of safety can be expressed either as a percentage of sales or as units of product sold.

*To construct a break-even chart step by step*

Add up all the costs that you'll incur even if you don't sell any of your products or services, e.g. rent, administrative wages, etc. These are your **fixed costs**. Draw an *x* (horizontal) and a *y* (vertical) axis to meet each other at the bottom left hand corner. Label this point 0 (zero), because it represents no unit sales and no costs or revenues. Calibrate the *x* axis in whatever units of hypothetical sales seems appropriate, i.e. plot marks on the line representing hundreds, thousands, or any other scale of unit sales that seems appropriate.

Calibrate the *y* axis with monetary levels, i.e. mark it off in units of hundreds or thousands of pounds sterling, or whatever other scale you regard as appropriate.

Plot the total fixed costs on the *y* axis and draw a horizontal line. Label this 'Fixed costs'.

Next, add up all the costs that can be directly attributed to a single unit, or particular quantity of units sold, e.g. saleperson's commission, purchases and cost of production. Plot this figure multiplied by each quantity marked on the *x* axis vertically above that quantity and horizontally against the appropriate height on the *y* axis, after first adding the fixed cost value (which is the same regardless of how many are sold). In other words, start counting up the *y* axis, not from zero, but from the level at which fixed costs are plotted. Draw a line through the plotting. The line will be sloping and will meet the *y* axis at the point where the *fixed costs* line starts. Next plot the revenues for each volume of sales in the same way, except that here you start from the zero level. See Fig. 140 for an example.

The principle advantage of break-even analysis is that because the break-even point is presented graphically.

- The information is externalised so that it can be communicated and shared.

- The project can be handled more objectively.

Month number

| Income (£) | 1 | 2 | 3 | 4 | 5 | 6 | 7 | 8 | 9 | 10 | 11 | 12 |
|---|---|---|---|---|---|---|---|---|---|---|---|---|
| Sales | 9,000 | 9,500 | 10,000 | 10,500 | 11,000 | 11,500 | 12,000 | 12,500 | 13,000 | 13,500 | 14,000 | 14,500 |
| Income from other sources | 500 | 500 | 500 | 500 | 500 | 500 | 500 | 500 | 500 | 500 | 500 | 500 |
| (A) Total income | 9,500 | 10,000 | 10,500 | 11,000 | 11,500 | 12,000 | 12,500 | 13,000 | 13,500 | 14,000 | 14,500 | 15,000 |
| Outgoings (£) | | | | | | | | | | | | |
| Purchases | 3,000 | 3,200 | 3,300 | 3,500 | 3,700 | 3,800 | 4,000 | 4,200 | 4,300 | 4,500 | 4,700 | 4,900 |
| Overheads | 8,000 | 7,000 | 7,000 | 7,000 | 8,500 | 7,000 | 7,000 | 7,000 | 8,000 | 7,000 | 7,000 | 7,000 |
| Other outgoings | 0 | 0 | 0 | 0 | 0 | 2,000 | 0 | 0 | 0 | 2,600 | 0 | 0 |
| (B) Total outgoings | 11,000 | 10,200 | 10,300 | 10,500 | 12,200 | 12,800 | 11,000 | 11,200 | 123,00 | 14,100 | 11,700 | 11,900 |
| (A–B) Net income/outgoings | (1,500) | (200) | 200 | 500 | (700) | (800) | 2,500 | 1,800 | 1,200 | (100) | 2,800 | 3,100 |
| Add opening bank balances | 3,000 | 1,500 | 1,300 | 1,500 | 2,000 | 1,300 | 500 | 3,000 | 4,800 | 6,000 | 5,900 | 8,700 |
| Closing bank balance | 1,500 | 1,300 | 1,500 | 2,000 | 1,300 | 500 | 3,000 | 4,800 | 6,000 | 5,900 | 8,700 | 11,800 |

Fig. 141. Example of a simple cash flow projection.

*There are some disadvantages, though*

● Costs many not be linear, or only linear within a particular range. In fact economies and diseconomies of scale will, to some degree, prevent costs and revenues being linear.

● It is sometimes difficult to distinguish between fixed and variable costs.

● The use of break-even analysis assumes a single product. Most companies have a mixture of products and services for sale, so you would either need several break-even charts, or plot sales in purely monetary units, rather than units of any particular product. Then it may be difficult to accurately plot direct costs since there may be different direct costs for each sales product.

## Cash flow projection

No matter how much profit a firm is making it can still run out of cash. This can happen if, for example, it allows its customers eight weeks to pay their debts while it pays its own in four, or if it channels a lot of its sales revenues into purchasing fixed assets, leaving insufficient amounts to pay its trade creditors on time. If this happens the company may miss out on early settlement discounts or, worse still, suppliers might withdraw credit terms. Other cash commitments may be affected too—for example, the firm may be unable to pay wages on time. To avoid this happening a cash flow projection is drawn up, comparing planned inflows and outflows month by month over the period of the trading year.

*Compiling a cash flow projection step by step*

Prepare a table with 13 columns and 11 rows. Use the first column to label the meaning of the values in each row and the first row to label the months 1–12 in the trading year. This will leave 12 columns and 10 rows for data. These will, from here on, be referred to as columns 1–12 and rows 1–10 respectively. The first 3 labels down the left hand side are income categories: *Sales revenue, Income from other sources* and *Total income*. The next 4 (rows 4–7 inclusive) are outgoings: *Purchases, Overheads, Other outgoings and Total outgoings.* The next row (row 8) is for *Net income/outgoings*, i.e. the surplus of one or the other. Row 9 is for *Opening bank balance* (predicted at start of that month). The final row is for *Closing bank balance* calculated for that month, which will be the sum of rows 8 and 9.

Then you plot the figures you calculate it will be reasonable to expect. Sum rows 1 and 2 and put the answers in the total boxes in row 3. Sum rows 4–6 and enter the answers in the total boxes in row 7. Deduct row 7 from row 3 and put the differences in the answer boxes in row 8. Sum rows 8 and 9 and put the answers in the total boxes in row 10. Figure 141 is an example.

This is a general guide. In particular situations there may be more income and expenditure categories than those used here.

### Investment appraisal

Before assessing what there is to gain by investing in a project a firm needs to take the opportunity cost into account. That is the return it could expect if it placed its funds in a safe investment, like a building society account, or UK treasury bonds instead. The difference is what there is to gain from taking the risk. However, entrepreneurs need to make some other checks too. Here are four well-used strategies for investment appraisal.

- Pay back period.
- Average rate of return (ARR).
- Internal rate of return (IRR).
- Net present value.

*Pay back period*

The pay back period is the first test that is usually made. It tells you how long it will take to get your money back if things go to plan. This, in turn, says something about the risk, for the further into the future we have to extend our exposure to risk the more uncertain things become. It is often used as an initial screening strategy for investment proposals using a set maximum payback period above which rejection is automatic.

*Average rate of return*

The average rate of return is a measure of the average annual profit the firm will receive from the averaged out value the assets in the project will have over the project's lifespan. The latter is found by deducting projected residual value from initial cost to allow for depreciation. However, many firms often dispense with this deduction and just keep the assets figure at cost. This is not a bad idea, since that more accurately reflects their investment than does a depreciated figure. This, too, is often used as a screening method with a set minimum ARR below which rejection is automatic.

The weakness of this method is that it assumes that returns will not vary across the years. This might not be the case. The highest returns might not come until the later years. If an average rate of return of 30% annually actually reflects 10% in year 1, 20% in year 2 and 60% in year 3 (which still produces an average of 30% annually) then only a small portion of the total return will earn interest in the bank over the long period, but the large proportion of it will earn little or none, since it will not be earned until year 3.

It would be quite the reverse if the 60% return was expected in the first year and the 10% in the last year.

*Internal rate of return*

A method that takes this into account is the internal rate of return method. This converts the expected returns to compound interest equivalents.

The internal rate of return method considers that rate of discount which when applied to the returns of the proposed investment would result in a zero level *net present value*. (i.e. the reverse of compound interest which starts with no interest and ends with the accumulated returns). This percentage is often used as an accept or reject screening process with a minimum rate of discount being required (say, for example 18%) to avoid automatic rejection.

To find the projected internal rate of return on a project, list and sum the expected annual returns over the projected lifespan of the investment. Deduct the initial investment figure and divide the difference by the number of years. Then divide that figure by half of the initial investment figure and multiply by 100 to give an approximation to begin a trial and error process towards finding the internal rate of return.

Using a discount table select the column which most closely matches the approximation and select the figures by which to multiply each year's return to find the discounted return for that year. Then sum the products for all the years and check how close it is to the initial investment. If it is substantially more then reduce the approximation and try again, if substantially less then increase the approximation. Keep doing this until the sum of the products is more or less equal to your initial investment figure (say within 0.1% ). The discounted rate of return (column heading) you last used is the internal rate of return the investment can be expected to produce.

## Investing in company shares

Before investing in a company's shares investors compare their value with that of other similar companies and with various yardsticks. Here are the three most basic and commonly used key ratios.

Earnings per share =

$$\frac{\text{Net profit (after tax and dividend on preference shares)} \times 100}{\text{Number of ordinary shares}}$$

Price earnings ratio = $\dfrac{\text{Market price}}{\text{Earnings per share}}$

Dividend yield = $\dfrac{\text{Dividend per share} \times 100}{\text{Market price}}$

A fall in earnings per share many not in itself be sufficient reason to avoid investment, as it may mean the company has simply kept more on general reserve. However, in reality any announcements that suggest reductions on distributed profits usually have a negative effect on demand for shares, sending prices lower.

| Type of overhead £000 | Total cost £000 | Criteria for apportionment | Cost centre | Criterion values for cost centre | Workings | Overheads absorbed £000 |
|---|---|---|---|---|---|---|
| Factory rent and rates | 150 | Per cent of floor space used | Assembly line<br>Spray shop<br>Finishing | 70%<br>20%<br>10%<br>100% | 150 × 0.7 =<br>150 × 0.2 =<br>150 × 0.1 = | 105<br>30<br>25<br>150 |
| Maintenance | 200 | Maintenance staff time used | Assembly line<br>Spray shop<br>Finishing | 75%<br>20%<br>5%<br>100% | 220 × 0.75 =<br>200 × 0.2 =<br>200 × 0.05 = | 150<br>40<br>10<br>200 |
| Canteen | 80 | Number of employees | Assembly line<br>Spray shop<br>Finishing | 30<br>10<br>5<br>45 | 80 × 30/45 =<br>20 × 10/45 =<br>80 × 5/45 = | 53<br>18<br>9<br>80 |

Fig. 142.

Price/earnings ratio is commonly used as a measure of value in investment decisions. Different sectors of the stock market have different average price/earnings ratios, reflecting the different levels of risk. Both the level of risk and a share's PER is compared with others in the sector.

## Overhead absorption

A product's contribution to overheads is the net sales revenue from that product less the direct costs of production (materials and labour). See Figure 143.

| Product | Product A £ | Product B £ | Product C £ | Total £ |
|---|---|---|---|---|
| Sales revenue | 100,000 | 150,000 | 200,000 | 450,000 |
| Direct materials | 20,000 | 32,000 | 45,000 | 97,000 |
| Direct labour | 20,000 | 30,000 | 60,000 | 110,000 |
| Contribution to overheads | 60,000 | 88,000 | 95,000 | 243,000 |
| Total of overhead costs | | | | 150,000 |
| Profit | | | | 93,000 |

Fig. 143. The relationship between sales, direct costs, contribution to overheads and profit.

Overhead apportionment refers to dividing the total overhead costs in a production run by the number of units produced but this is done in a weighted way. For example if the production of **Product A** uses a machine twice as much as **Product B** then the overhead cost of that machine will be apportioned to **Products A** and **B** in the ratio of 2:1. Similarly, if the production of **Product B** requires 30% more factory space than **Product A** then the factory overhead will be apportioned to **A** and **B** in the ratio 1:1.3.

Often overheads are apportioned to cost centres and products then absorb them in the same proportions as they use those cost centres' time.

As long as you know:

• the total costs of each type of overhead
• the criteria for apportionment
• the criterion values for each cost centre

the rest is just a matter of simple ratio analysis. Figure 143 gives an example.

# THE INSTITUTE
# OF CERTIFIED
# BOOKKEEPERS

## LEVEL I CERTIFICATE IN BASIC BOOKKEEPING MOCK

### FINAL ASSIGNMENT

Successful achievement of this qualification is a mandatory part of the requirements for election to the Institute as an Associate Member.

Complete the various tasks in this booklet. Answers should be written in black or blue ink/ ballpoint pen. Please note that any work in pencil will not be marked. The use of correction fluid is not permitted. Send your completed booklet to the address at the foot of the page by no later than the deadline date indicated in the box below. A postmark on the envelope will be accepted as proof of postage by the deadline date. You are advised to obtain proof of posting from The Royal Mail. Papers posted after the deadline date will not be marked.

Name...........................................

Number......................................

Deadline Date................................

(Lee Crescent)

The Institute of Certified Bookkeepers
Wolverton Park, Wolverton, Hampshire RG26 5RU
Tel: 0845 060 2345
www.bookkeepers.org.uk

**ICB Level 1 Certificate in Basic Bookkeeping Mock Paper 2006**

## Scenario

Lee Crescent runs a mobile car valeting service, Crescent Valet Services, in a North Yorkshire coastal town. He has established a most profitable business. He operates a six-day week and provides a cleaning service to both private customers who pay by cash and corporate customers who have credit accounts.

He usually banks his cash twice per week, pays his suppliers at the month end and allows 30 days credit to his corporate customers.

You are Lee's bookkeeper and you write up Lee's books on a weekly basis.

The information that follows is for the month of June 2006. Lee's year end is 31 May.

The balances in his ledger on 1 June 2006 were:

| | |
|---|---|
| Capital | £15,900 |
| Motor Vehicle | £12,150 |
| Equipment | £6,500 |
| Stock of Materials | £500 |
| Bank | £2,100 |

| Debtors: | |
|---|---|
| Sandsend Hotel | £450 |
| Raw Lodge | £750 |

| Creditors: | | |
|---|---|---|
| Jones Garage | £400 | |
| Bank Loan | £5,900 | |
| VAT | £250 | CR |

## Task 1

Refer to the ledger accounts set out on pages 240–42 and post the opening entries as at 1 June 2006.

**(10 marks)**

**Task 2**

From the data below prepare the sales invoice to Sandsend Hotel. The charges are subject to VAT at 17½%.

Use the pro-forma invoice shown on page 236.

---

Sandsend Hotel, Back Lane, Sandsend, Whitby

Order No: 1135

Cleaning of 4 vehicles @ £7.50 each and one vehicle valet @ £25.

A trade discount of 5% is allowed.

Date: 1st June. Invoice No: 9131

---

**(5 marks)**

**Crescent Valet Services**
**Crescent Gardens**
**Whitby**
**North Yorkshire YO21 3EJ**

www.crescentvalet.co.uk          VAT Reg No:          595 9832 92

E-mail: lee@virgin.net

Mobile: 07710667188

Date: _____

Invoice No: _____

To:                              Your Order No: _____

Services supplied:                              £

_____

Less 5% trade discount          _____

VAT @ 17½%          _____

£

_____

Proprietor: Lee Crescent

## Task 3

Examine the following purchase invoice, decide whether or not you would approve it for payment and state the action you would take.

---

**Blyth Cleaning Chemicals Ltd**
**High Street**
**Blyth**
**Notts NG5 3EQ**

VAT Reg No: 612 7132 87
Date: 2 June 2006

Your Order No: 721 CV

To:  Lee Crescent
Crescent Valet Services
Crescent Gardens
Whitby YO21 3EJ

| | Unit Cost | £ |
|---|---|---|
| 4 × 5 litres of 'Bcc 1' | £12.00 (per 5L) | 48.00 |
| 4 packs of heavy duty cleaning pads | £1.50 (per pack) | 6.00 |
| | | 54.00 |
| Less 10% trade discount | | 4.50 |
| | | 58.50 |
| VAT 17½% | | 10.23 |
| | | £48.27 |

---

Pass for payment Yes/No (delete as appropriate)

Reason and state possible action:

_____

_____

_____

**(5 marks)**

## Task 4

It is 30 June and Lee has left you details of the month's transactions.

Post these to the ledger accounts detailed on pages 240–42.

(1)    Enter the invoice you prepared in Task 2 to the relevant sales ledger account, sales account (work done) and the VAT account.

Also if approved for payment enter the invoice you examined in Task 3.

(2)    Lee has approved two purchase invoices that need entering in the purchase ledger, the purchase of cleaning materials account and the VAT account.

| Whitby Motor Factors | 15 June | £352.50 |
| | | (inc. VAT) |
| Hawkser Motors | 16 June | £270.25 |
| | | (inc. VAT) |

(3)    He paid his business mobile phone bill by cheque 3 June 2006 £76.37 (inc. VAT).

Process this payment to the relevant accounts in the ledger.

(4)    His private customers cash takings for the month were: **(to which VAT needs to be added)**:

| 6th | £480 |
| 13th | £520 |
| 20th | £540 |
| 27th | £500 |

Post the above cash receipts to the relevant accounts in the ledger.

(5)    Payments made by cash:

| 7th | Petrol | £35.25 | (inc. VAT) |
| 15th | Petrol | £47.00 | (inc. VAT) |

Post these transactions to the relevant accounts in the ledger.

(6)    Lee banked the following cash during the period:

| 8th | £320 |
| 13th | £300 |
| 22nd | £500 |
| 29th | £480 |

Post these transfers.

ICB Level I Certificate in Basic Bookkeeping Mock Paper 2006   © ICB 2006

(7) Lee settled his account with Jones Garage on 25 June by cheque. Post this transaction to the relevant accounts in the ledger.

(8) Lee received a cheque from Raw Lodge in full settlement of their account on 29 June. Post this transaction to the relevant accounts.

(9) Lee sent a credit note to Sandsend Hotel for £42.80 plus VAT 17½% on 26 June.

Post this transaction to the relevant accounts.

(10) Lee had drawn a cheque from the bank on 30 June £650 for his own personal use.

**(50 marks)**

**Crescent Valet Services**

| DR | | Capital Account | | | CR |
|---|---|---|---|---|---|
| **Date** | **Details** | **£** | **Date** | **Details** | **£** |

| DR | | Motor Vehicle Account | | | CR |
|---|---|---|---|---|---|
| **Date** | **Details** | **£** | **Date** | **Details** | **£** |

| DR | | Equipment Account | | | CR |
|---|---|---|---|---|---|
| **Date** | **Details** | **£** | **Date** | **Details** | **£** |

| DR | | Stock Account | | | CR |
|---|---|---|---|---|---|
| **Date** | **Details** | **£** | **Date** | **Details** | **£** |

| DR | | Bank Account | | | CR |
|---|---|---|---|---|---|
| **Date** | **Details** | **£** | **Date** | **Details** | **£** |

| DR | | Cash Account | | | CR |
|---|---|---|---|---|---|
| **Date** | **Details** | **£** | **Date** | **Details** | **£** |

| DR | | Bank Loan Account | | | CR |
|---|---|---|---|---|---|
| **Date** | **Details** | **£** | **Date** | **Details** | **£** |

| DR | | | VAT Account | | | CR |
|---|---|---|---|---|---|---|
| Date | Details | £ | Date | Details | | £ |

| DR | | | Sales (Work Done) Account | | | CR |
|---|---|---|---|---|---|---|
| Date | Details | £ | Date | Details | | £ |

| DR | | | Purchases (Cleaning Materials) | | | CR |
|---|---|---|---|---|---|---|
| Date | Details | £ | Date | Details | | £ |

| DR | | | Postage, Telephone and Stationery Account | | | CR |
|---|---|---|---|---|---|---|
| Date | Details | £ | Date | Details | | £ |

| DR | | | Motor Vehicle Running Costs (Petrol) | | | CR |
|---|---|---|---|---|---|---|
| Date | Details | £ | Date | Details | | £ |

| DR | | | Sales (Work Done) Returns | | | CR |
|---|---|---|---|---|---|---|
| Date | Details | £ | Date | Details | | £ |

| DR | | | Drawings Account | | | CR |
|---|---|---|---|---|---|---|
| Date | Details | £ | Date | Details | | £ |

## Sales Ledger

| DR | | | Sandsend Hotel | | | CR |
|---|---|---|---|---|---|---|
| Date | Details | £ | Date | Details | | £ |

| DR | | | Raw Lodge | | | CR |
|---|---|---|---|---|---|---|
| Date | Details | £ | Date | Details | | £ |

## Purchase Ledger

| DR | | | Jones Garage | | | CR |
|---|---|---|---|---|---|---|
| Date | Details | £ | Date | Details | | £ |

| DR | | | Whitby Motor Factors | | | CR |
|---|---|---|---|---|---|---|
| Date | Details | £ | Date | Details | | £ |

| DR | | | Hawkser Motors | | | CR |
|---|---|---|---|---|---|---|
| Date | Details | £ | Date | Details | | £ |

## Task 5

Having entered the transactions for June 2006, balance off each account in the ledger and prepare the Trial Balance as at 30 June 2006.

**Trial Balance**

| | DR | CR |
|---|---|---|
| Capital Account | | |
| Motor Vehicle Account | | |
| Equipment Account | | |
| Stock Account | | |
| Bank Account | | |
| Cash Account | | |
| Bank Loan | | |
| VAT Account | | |
| Sales (Work Done) | | |
| Purchases (Cleaning Materials) | | |
| Telephone Account | | |
| Motor Vehicle Running Costs | | |
| Sales (Work Done) Returns | | |
| Drawings Account | | |
| Debtors: | | |
| | | |
| | | |
| | | |
| Creditors: | | |
| | | |
| | | |
| | | |
| | | |
| | £ | £ |

**(20 marks)**

## Task 6

Multiple Choice Questions (circle the correct answer):

(1) A business has an outstanding debtor for £500 + VAT.
    Should they decide to write it off, the entries would be: (they can reclaim the VAT)
    (a) Debit bad debts account £500, debit VAT account £87.50, credit the debtor £500.
    (b) Debit bad debts account £500, debit VAT account £87.50, credit the debtor £587.50.
    (c) Debit bad debts account £587.50, credit the debtor £587.50.
    (d) Debit bad debts account £587.50, credit the debtor £500, credit VAT account £87.50.

(2) Which of the following is not a liability:
    (a) Creditors
    (b) Bank Overdraft
    (c) Stock
    (d) Bank Loan

(3) Which of the following is considered to be capital expenditure:
    (a) Proprietor's drawings
    (b) Payment for rent
    (c) Purchase of plant and machinery
    (d) Payment of wages and salaries

(4) The owner of a business introduces a laptop computer valued at £1,100 into his business (this was his personal property).

    The entries would be:
    (a) Debit capital account
        Credit office equipment
    (b) Debit office equipment
        Credit drawings account
    (c) Debit office equipment
        Credit capital account
    (d) None of these

(5) A credit balance on the bank account (or bank column in the cash book) would indicate:
    (a) The business has cash at the bank
    (b) The business has a bank overdraft
    (c) The debit entries in the account were greater than the credits
    (d) The bookkeeper has made an error

**(10 marks)**

ICB Level 1 Certificate in Basic Bookkeeping Mock Paper 2006

## Tasks 1 and 4

| DR | | | Capital Account | | CR |
|---|---|---|---|---|---|
| Date | Details | £ | Date | Details | £ |
| 30 Jun | Balance c/d | 15,900.00 | 1 Jun | Balance b/d | 15,900.00 |
| | | | 1 Jul | Balance b/d | 15,900.00 |

| DR | | | Motor Vehicle Account | | CR |
|---|---|---|---|---|---|
| Date | Details | £ | Date | Details | £ |
| 1 Jun | Balance b/d | 12,150.00 | 30 Jun | Balance c/d | 12,150.00 |
| 1 Jul | Balance b/d | 12,150.00 | | | |

| DR | | | Equipment Account | | CR |
|---|---|---|---|---|---|
| Date | Details | £ | Date | Details | £ |
| 1 Jun | Balance b/d | 6,500.00 | 30 Jun | Balance c/d | 6,500.00 |
| 1 Jul | Balance b/d | 6,500.00 | | | |

| DR | | | Stock Account | | CR |
|---|---|---|---|---|---|
| Date | Details | £ | Date | Details | £ |
| 1 Jun | Balance b/d | 500.00 | 30 Jun | Balance c/d | 500.00 |
| 1 Jul | Balance b/d | 500.00 | | | |

| DR | | | Bank Account | | CR |
|---|---|---|---|---|---|
| Date | Details | £ | Date | Details | £ |
| 1 Jun | Balance b/d | 2,100.00 | 3 Jun | Telephone, inc. VAT | 76.37 |
| 8 Jun | Cash | 320.00 | 25 Jun | Jones Garage | 400.00 |
| 13 Jun | Cash | 300.00 | 30 Jun | Drawings | 650.00 |
| 22 Jun | Cash | 500.00 | 30 Jun | Balance c/d | 3,323.63 |
| 29 Jun | Cash | 480.00 | | | |
| 29 Jun | Raw Lodge | 750.00 | | | |
| | | 4,450.00 | | | 4,450.00 |
| 1 Jul Balance b/d | | 3,323.63 | | | |

| DR | | | Cash Account | | | CR |
|---|---|---|---|---|---|---|
| Date | Details | £ | Date | Details | | £ |
| 6 Jun | Sales (work done) | 564.00 | 7 Jun | Petrol | | 35.25 |
| 13 Jun | Sales (work done) | 611.00 | 8 Jun | Bank | | 320.00 |
| 20 Jun | Sales (work done) | 634.50 | 13 Jun | Bank | | 300.00 |
| 27 Jun | Sales (work done) | 587.50 | 15 Jun | Petrol | | 47.00 |
| | | | 22 Jun | Bank | | 500.00 |
| | | | 28 Jun | Bank | | 480.00 |
| | | | 30 Jun | Balance c/d | | 714.75 |
| | | 2,397.00 | | | | 2397.00 |
| 1 Jul Balance b/d | | 714.75 | | | | |

| DR | | | Bank Loan Account | | CR |
|---|---|---|---|---|---|
| Date | Details | £ | Date | Details | £ |
| 30 Jun | Balance c/d | 5,900.00 | 1 Jun | Balance b/d | 5,900.00 |
| | | | 1 Jul | Balance b/d | 5,900.00 |

| DR | | | VAT Account | | CR |
|---|---|---|---|---|---|
| Date | Details | £ | Date | Details | £ |
| 3 Jun | Bank/Telephone | 11.37 | 1 Jun | Balance b/d | 250.00 |
| 7 Jun | Petrol | 5.25 | 1 Jun | Sandsend Hotel | 9.14 |
| 15 Jun | Petrol | 7.00 | 6 Jun | Cash | 84.00 |
| 15 Jun | Whitby Motors | 52.50 | 13 Jun | Cash | 91.00 |
| 16 Jun | Hawkser Motors | 40.25 | 20 Jun | Cash | 94.50 |
| 26 Jun | Sandsend Hotel | 7.49 | 27 Jun | Cash | 87.50 |
| 30 Jun | Balance c/d | 492.28 | | | |
| | | 616.14 | | | 616.14 |
| | | | 1 Jul | Balance b/d | 492.28 |

| DR | | | Sales (Work Done) Account | | CR |
|---|---|---|---|---|---|
| Date | Details | £ | Date | Details | £ |
| 30 Jun | Balance c/d | 2,092.25 | 1 Jun | Sandsend Hotel | 52.25 |
| | | | 6 Jun | Cash | 480.00 |
| | | | 13 Jun | Cash | 520.00 |
| | | | 20 Jun | Cash | 540.00 |
| | | | 27 Jun | Cash | 500.00 |
| | | 2,092.25 | | | 2,092.25 |
| | | | 1 Jul Balance b/d | | 2,092.25 |

| DR | Purchases (Cleaning Materials) | | | | CR |
|---|---|---|---|---|---|
| Date | Details | £ | Date | Details | £ |
| 15 Jun | Whitby Motors | 300.00 | 30 Jun | Balance c/d | 530.00 |
| 16 Jun | Hawkser Motors | 230.00 | | | |
| | | 530.00 | | | 530.00 |
| 1 Jul | Balance b/d | 530.00 | | | |

| DR | Telephone, Postage and Stationery Account | | | | CR |
|---|---|---|---|---|---|
| Date | Details | £ | Date | Details | £ |
| 3 Jun | Bank | 65.00 | 30 Jun | Balance c/d | 65.00 |
| 1 Jul | Balance b/d | 65.00 | | | |

| DR | Motor Vehicle Running Costs (Petrol) Account | | | | CR |
|---|---|---|---|---|---|
| Date | Details | £ | Date | Details | £ |
| 7 Jun | Cash | 30.00 | 30 Jun | Balance c/d | 70.00 |
| 13 Jun | Cash | 40.00 | | | |
| | | 70.00 | | | 70.00 |
| 1 Jul | Balance b/d | 70.00 | | | |

| DR | Sales (Work Done) Returns | | | | CR |
|---|---|---|---|---|---|
| Date | Details | £ | Date | Details | £ |
| 26 Jun | Sandsend Hotel | 42.80 | 30 Jun | Balance c/d | 42.80 |
| 1 Jul | Balance b/d | 42.80 | | | |

| DR | Drawings Account | | | | CR |
|---|---|---|---|---|---|
| Date | Details | £ | Date | Details | £ |
| 30 Jun | Bank | 650.00 | 30 Jun | Balance c/d | 650.00 |
| 1 Jul | Balance b/d | 650.00 | | | |

### Sales Ledger

| DR | Sandsend Hotel | | | | CR |
|---|---|---|---|---|---|
| Date | Details | £ | Date | Details | £ |
| 1 Jun | Balance b/d | 450.00 | 26 Jun | Sales returns/VAT | 50.29 |
| 1 Jun | Sales/VAT | 61.39 | 30 Jun | Balance c/d | 461.10 |
| | | 511.39 | | | 511.39 |
| 1 Jul | Balance b/d | 461.10 | | | |

| DR | | | Raw Lodge | | CR |
|---|---|---|---|---|---|
| **Date** | **Details** | **£** | **Date** | **Details** | **£** |
| 1 Jun | Balance b/d | 750.00 | 29 Jun | Bank | 750.00 |

## Purchase Ledger

| DR | | | Jones Garage | | CR |
|---|---|---|---|---|---|
| **Date** | **Details** | **£** | **Date** | **Details** | **£** |
| 25 Jun | Bank | 400.00 | 1 Jun | Balance b/d | 400.00 |

| DR | | | Whitby Motor Factors | | CR |
|---|---|---|---|---|---|
| **Date** | **Details** | **£** | **Date** | **Details** | **£** |
| | | | 15 Jun | Purchases/VAT | 352.50 |

| DR | | | Hawkser Motors | | CR |
|---|---|---|---|---|---|
| **Date** | **Details** | **£** | **Date** | **Details** | **£** |
| | | | 16 Jun | Purchases/VAT | 270.25 |

Total 60 marks (10 for task 1 and 50 for task 4)

**Task 2**

---

**Crescent Valet Services**
**Crescent Gardens**
**Whitby**
**North Yorkshire Y021 3EJ**

www.crescentvalet.co.uk                    VAT Reg No: 595 9832 92
E-mail: lee@virgin.net
Mobile: 07710667188

|  |  |  |
|---|---|---|
| Date: | 1 June 2006 | |
| Invoice No: | 913 | |
| Your Order No: | 1135 | |
|  |  | **(1 mark)** |

To:        Sandsend Hotel
           Back Lane
           Sandsend
           Whitby                                                           **(1 mark)**
                                                            £

Services supplied:
       4 vehicles cleaned @ £7.50 each       30.00      **(½ mark)**
       1 vehicle full valet @ £25            25.00      **(½ mark)**
                                             55.00

Less 5% trade discount                        2.75      **(1 mark)**
                                             52.25

VAT @ 17½%                                    9.14      **(1 mark)**
                                            £61.39

Proprietor Lee Crescent

---

**(Total 5 marks)**

**Task 3**

Pass for payment          ~~Yes~~/No (delete as appropriate)          **(1 mark)**

Reason and state possible action:

The trade discount is incorrectly calculated.          **(1 ½ marks)**

The VAT, which has been calculated on the wrong amount, has
been deducted rather than added.          **(1 ½ marks)**

Write to Blyth Chemical asking for a revised invoice.          **(1 mark)**

**(Total 5 marks)**

**Task 5**

**Crescent Valet Services**
Trial Balance as at 30 June 2006

| | | |
|---|---|---|
| Capital Account | | 15,900.00 |
| Motor Vehicle Account | 12,150.00 | |
| Equipment Account | 6,500.00 | |
| Stock Account | 500.00 | |
| Bank Account | 3,323.63 | |
| Cash Account | 714.75 | |
| Bank Loan | | 5,900.00 |
| VAT Account | | 492.28 |
| Sales (Work Done) | | 2,092.25 |
| Purchases (Cleaning Materials) | 530.00 | |
| Telephone Account | 65.00 | |
| Motor Vehicle Running Costs | 70.00 | |
| Sales (Work Done) Returns | 42.80 | |
| Drawings Account | 650.00 | |
| Debtors: | | |
|   Sandsend Hotel | 461.10 | |
| Creditors: | | |
|   Whitby Motors | | 352.50 |
|   Hawkser Motors | | 270.25 |
| | 25,007.28 | 25,007.28 |

**(20 marks)**

**Task 6**
(1) (b)
(2) (c)
(3) (c)
(4) (c)
(5) (b)

**(10 marks)**

THE INSTITUTE
OF CERTIFIED
BOOKKEEPERS

# Level II Certificate in
# Manual Bookkeeping

## October 2007

### Time allowed: 3 hours

252

**ICB Level II Certificate in Manual Bookkeeping October 2007**

**You are a self-employed bookkeeper and all the tasks in this examination are based on scenarios regarding one of your clients.**

## Question 1

*Data*

Nigel Blyth is a self-employed plumber and heating engineer and you write up his books on a monthly basis together with preparing information for his year end for submission to his accountant.

Nigel's year end is 31 March and this scenario is based on business transactions for the month of April 2007.

On 1 April 2007 the following were the balances in Nigel's ledger:

|                    | £       |    |
|--------------------|---------|----|
| Capital            | 41,600  |    |
| Bank Loan          | 4,200   |    |
| Motor Vehicle      | 17,500  |    |
| Tools and Equipment| 20,000  |    |
| Office Equipment   | 3,600   |    |
| Stocks of Material | 1,950   |    |
| Bank               | 2,250   |    |
| Cash in Hand       | 150     |    |
|                    |         |    |
| Debtors:           |         |    |
| Bay Road School    | 1,900   |    |
| Metro Hotel        | 1,750   |    |
|                    |         |    |
| Creditors:         |         |    |
| Jessup & Smith     | 1,100   |    |
| Fletcher DIY       | 1,250   |    |
| VAT                | 950     | CR |

Nigel employs his son as a modern apprentice and has a mix of clients. Some clients pay cash on completion of the work. However, others are allowed a 30-day payment period.

He uses a number of suppliers for materials with whom he has credit accounts.

ICB Level II Certificate in Manual Bookkeeping October 2007 © ICB 2007

The following information relates to Nigel's business transactions for April 2007:

## Nigel Blyth

### Sales Day Book April 2007

| Date | Details | Net | VAT | Gross |
|------|---------|-----|-----|-------|
| 4 April | Metro Hotel | 1,400.00 | 245.00 | 1,645.00 |
| 9 April | Bay Road School | 1,150.00 | 201.25 | 1,351.25 |
| 15 April | Victoria Hotel | 1,200.00 | 210.00 | 1,410.00 |
| 22 April | Mr & Mrs Brown | 700.00 | 122.50 | 822.50 |
| 29 April | Crescent Hotel | 1,650.00 | 288.75 | 1,938.75 |
| | | £6,100.00 | £1,067.50 | £7,167.50 |

### Sales Returns Day Book

| Date | Details | Net | VAT | Gross |
|------|---------|-----|-----|-------|
| 6 April | Bay Road School | 180.00 | 31.50 | 211.50 |

### Purchase Day Book
### April 2007

| Date | Details | Net | VAT | Gross |
|------|---------|-----|-----|-------|
| 5 April | Jessup & Smith | 900.00 | 157.50 | 1,057.50 |
| 9 April | Fletcher DIY | 250.00 | 43.75 | 293.75 |
| 18 April | Whitby Plumbers Supplies | 1,400.00 | 245.00 | 1,645.00 |
| | | £2,550.00 | £446.25 | £2,996.25 |

### Purchase Returns Day Book

| Date | Details | Net | VAT | Gross |
|------|---------|-----|-----|-------|
| 7 April | Jessup & Smith | £180.00 | £31.50 | £211.50 |

ICB Level II Certificate in Manual Bookkeeping October 2007   © ICB 2007

## Extract from the Cash Book

| Date | Details | Cash £ | Bank £ | Date | Cheque no. | Details | Cash £ | Bank £ |
|---|---|---|---|---|---|---|---|---|
| 1 Apr | Balance b/d | 150.00 | 2,250.00 | 2 Apr | 700 | HMRC Customs | | 950.00 |
| 8 Apr | Bay Road School 115 | | 1,688.50 | 5 Apr | 701 | Drawings | | 1,250.00 |
| 15 Apr | Metro Hotel 116 | | 1,750.00 | 8 Apr | 702 | Jessup & Smith | | 888.50 |
| 28 Apr | Mr & Mrs Brown 117 | | 822.50 | 8 Apr | 703 | Wages | | 300.00 |
| | | | | 10 Apr | 704 | Insurance | | 1,400.00 |
| | | | | 12 Apr | | Postage | 40.00 | |
| | | | | 25 Apr | 705 | Wages | | 275.00 |
| | | | | 29 Apr | 706 | Fletcher DIY | | 625.00 |
| | | | | 30 Apr | | Balance c/d | 110.00 | 822.50 |
| | | 150.00 | 6,511.00 | | | | 150.00 | 6,511.00 |
| 1 May | Balance b/d | 110.00 | 822.50 | | | | | |

## Task 1

Post the opening entries to the general ledger, sales ledger and purchase ledger (the cash book is already written up—do not open an account for cash and bank).

Leave about six lines between each account to space them out neatly.

**(5 marks)**

## Task 2

Post from the sales day book and sales returns day book to the sales ledger accounts, the sales account, sales returns account and the VAT account in the general ledger.

**(5 marks)**

## Task 3

Post from the purchase day book and purchase returns day book to the purchase ledger accounts the purchases account (purchase of materials), purchase returns and the VAT account in the general ledger.

**(5 marks)**

## Task 4

Post the items from the cash book to the respective sales and purchase ledger accounts together with individual expense accounts in the general ledger.

**(5 marks)**

## Task 5

Balance off each account (other than the ones where there is only one entry) and prepare a trial balance as at 30 April 2007.
Don't forget that your cash and bank balances are the ones shown in the cash book extract.

**(10 marks)**

ICB Level II Certificate in Manual Bookkeeping October 2007   © ICB 2007

## Question 2

Nigel supplies you with his bank statement received at the end of April; this is shown below:

**PDM Bank Ltd**
**Low Street, Whitby**

Nigel Blyth                                     Account No: 57246661
Thorpe Lane
Robin Hoods Bay
North Yorks

| Date | Details | Receipts | Payments | Balance C/(O/D) | |
|---|---|---|---|---|---|
| 1 April | Balance | | | 2,250.00 | C |
| 6 April | CH700 | | 950.00 | 1,300.00 | C |
| 8 April | R115 | 1,688.50 | | 2,988.50 | C |
| 8 April | CH701 | | 1,250.00 | 1,738.50 | C |
| 11 April | CH702 | | 888.50 | 850.00 | C |
| 11 April | CH703 | | 300.00 | 550.00 | C |
| 13 April | CH704 | | 1,400.00 | 850.00 | O/D |
| 16 April | R116 | 1,750.00 | | 900.00 | C |
| 28 April | DD PRU (personal pension) | | 600.00 | 300.00 | C |
| 28 April | Bank Charges | | 40.00 | 260.00 | C |
| 28 April | DD Insurance (business) | | 150.00 | 110.00 | C |

*Task 1*

Using the cash book extract in Question 1, compare it with the bank statement and update the cash book balance; show this in the form of a T account. Your starting point is the bank balance shown in the cash book at 30 April.

**(5 marks)**

**Task 2**

Prepare the bank reconciliation statement at 30 April 2007.

**(5 marks)**

## Question 3

You have recently been working on Nigel's year end accounts for 31 March 2007.

The trial balance had initially failed to agree and the difference £700 CR had been posted to a suspense account. At times during the year Nigel's wife had written up the books.

On checking the records you find the following:

(1)   Nigel had paid vet fees of £500 for his daughter's horse and these had been debited to the office expenses account and credited to bank.

(2)   The purchase of new tools and equipment £850 + VAT had been posted as: debit to repairs and maintenance (net amount) and debit to the VAT account; credit the bank £998.75.

(3)   Work done during a week in June 2006 had been:
Net        £4,000
VAT      £   700
Gross    £4,700

The gross and net had been correctly posted to the accounts in the sales and general ledgers but the VAT account had been excluded.

## Task 1
Prepare journal entries to correct the errors.

**(12 marks)**

## Task 2
Post the suspense account to eliminate the balance on that account.

**(5 marks)**

## Task 3
Explain briefly to Nigel why it is so important to deal with items such as (1) in the notes above.

**(3 marks)**

ICB Level II Certificate in Manual Bookkeeping October 2007   © ICB 2007

## Question 4

You are now working on the preparation of Nigel's final accounts for year ended 31 March 2007.

Nigel's Trial Balance showed the following:

**Trial Balance as at 31 March 2007**

|  | £ | £ |
|---|---|---|
| Capital | | 29,620 |
| Bank Loan | | 4,200 |
| Motor Vehicle | 17,500 | |
| Tools and Equipment | 20,000 | |
| Office Equipment | 3,600 | |
| Stocks Materials | 1,850 | |
| Bank | 2,250 | |
| Cash | 150 | |
| Debtors | 3,650 | |
| Creditors | | 2,350 |
| VAT Account | | 950 |
| Sales (Work Done) | | 82,500 |
| Purchases (Materials) | 34,650 | |
| Repairs and Maintenance | 1,450 | |
| Motor Vehicle Running Costs | 3,350 | |
| Insurances | 1,320 | |
| Office Expenses | 650 | |
| Wages | 8,200 | |
| Drawings | 21,000 | |
| | £119,620 | £119,620 |

- Stocks of materials at 31/3/07 £1,950

## Task

Prepare the trading and profit and loss account for year ended 31 March 2007 and a balance sheet at that date.

**(20 marks)**

## Question 5

It is now the 30 June 2007 and the following information is available:

**Extract from Sales Day Book and Sales Returns Day Book, Purchase Day Book and Purchase Returns Day Book**

### Sales Day Book

| Date | Details | Net | VAT | Gross |
|------|---------|-----|-----|-------|
| Apr–Jun 2007 | Sales Work Done | £22,00.00 | £3,850.000 | £25,850.00 |

### Sales Returns Day Book

| Date | Details | Net | VAT | Gross |
|------|---------|-----|-----|-------|
| Apr–Jun | Credit Notes for Work Done | £600.00 | £105.00 | £705.00 |

### Purchase Day Book

| Date | Details | Net | VAT | Gross |
|------|---------|-----|-----|-------|
| Apr–Jun | Purchases on Credit | £9,200.00 | £1,610.00 | £10,810.00 |

### Purchase Returns Day Book

| Date | Details | Net | VAT | Gross |
|------|---------|-----|-----|-------|
| Apr–Jun | Credit Notes from Suppliers | £700.00 | £122.50 | £822.50 |

## Task 1

Prepare the VAT account, showing clearly the amount due to HM Revenue & Customs as at 30 June 2007

**(10 marks)**

## Task 2

Prepare the enclosed VAT form 100 for submission to HM Revenue & Customs.

Write your name and student number on the form and ensure that you place the loose form inside your white answer booklet to submit for marking.

**(10 marks)**

**Value Added Tax Return**
For the period
01/04/07 – 30/06/07

For Official Use

| Registration number | Period |
|---|---|
| 983172971 | 06/07 |

Nigel Blyth
Thorpe Lane
Robin Hoods Bay, Whitby

You could be liable to a financial penalty if your completed return and all the VAT payable are not received by the due date

Due date: 31/07/07

Your VAT Office telephone number is 0123-4567

For Official Use

Before you fill in this form please read the note on the back and the VAT leaflet "Filling in your VAT return". Fill in all boxes clearly in ink, and write 'none' where ... Don't put a dash or leave any box blank. If there are no pence write "00" in the pence column. Do not en... one amount in any box.

| For official use | | £ | p |
|---|---|---|---|
| VAT due in ... sales and other outputs | 1 | | 00 |
| VAT due in ... od on ... ns from other EC Member States | 2 | | |
| VAT due (the sum ... oxes 1 and ) | 3 | | 00 |
| VAT ... d in this period ... es, ... inputs (including ... quisitions from the ... | 4 | | 00 |
| Net VAT to be p... ustoms or recla... ed ... ou (Difference betwee... 3 and 4) | 5 | | 00 |
| Total value of sales and all ... outputs excluding a ... AT Include your box 8 figure | 6 | | 00 |
| Total value of purchases and all ... s excluding any V... Include your box 9 figure | 7 | | 00 |
| Total value of all supplies of goods and relate... ces, excluding any VAT, to other EC Member States | 8 | | 00 |
| Total value of all acquisitions of goods and related serv... excluding any VAT, from other EC Member States | 9 | | 00 |

Retail schemes. If you have used any of the schemes in the pe... covered by this return, enter the relevant letter(s) in this box

If you are enclosing a payment please tick this box

DECLARATION: You, or someone on your behalf, must sign below

1, _____ declare that the
(Full name of signatory in BLOCK LETTERS)

Signature _____ Date       20
A false declaration can result in prosecution

Level II Certificate in Manual Bookkeeping October 2007

**Question 1**

**Tasks 1–4**

### NIGEL BLYTH
### GENERAL/NOMINAL LEDGER

**Capital Account**

|  |  |  | 1 Apr | Balance b/d | 41,600.00 |
|---|---|---|---|---|---|

**Bank Loan**

|  |  |  | 1 Apr | Balance b/d | 4,200.00 |
|---|---|---|---|---|---|

**Motor Vehicle**

| 1 Apr | Balance b/d | 17,500.00 |  |  |  |
|---|---|---|---|---|---|

**Tools and Equipment**

| 1 Apr | Balance b/d | 20,000.00 |  |  |  |
|---|---|---|---|---|---|

**Office Equipment**

| 1 Apr | Balance b/d | 3,600.00 |  |  |  |
|---|---|---|---|---|---|

**Stocks**

| 1 Apr | Balance b/d | 1,950.00 |  |  |  |
|---|---|---|---|---|---|

**VAT Account**

| 30 Apr | SRDB | 31.50 | 1 Apr | Balance b/d | 950.00 |
|---|---|---|---|---|---|
| " | PDB | 446.25 | 30 Apr | SDB | 1,067.50 |
| " | Bank | 950.00 | " | PRDB | 31.50 |
| " | Balance c/d | 621.25 | " | Balance c/d |  |
|  |  | £2,049.00 |  |  | £2,049.00 |
|  |  |  | 1 May | Balance b/d | 621.25 |

### Drawings Account

| | | | |
|---|---|---|---|
| 5 Apr | Bank | 1,250.00 | |

### Wages Account

| | | | |
|---|---|---|---|
| 8 Apr | Bank | 300.00 | |
| 25 Apr | Bank | 275.00 | |
| | | £575.00 | |

### Insurance Account

| | | | |
|---|---|---|---|
| 10 Apr | Bank | 1,400.00 | |

### Office Expenses (Postage)

| | | | |
|---|---|---|---|
| 12 Apr | Cash | 40.00 | |

### Sales Account (Work Done)

| | | | |
|---|---|---|---|
| | | 30 Apr SDB | 6,100.00 |

### Sales Returns

| | | | |
|---|---|---|---|
| 30 Apr | SRDB | 180.00 | |

### Purchase Account

| | | | |
|---|---|---|---|
| 30 Apr | PDB | 2,550.00 | |

### Purchase Returns

| | | | |
|---|---|---|---|
| | | 30 Apr PRDB | 180.00 |

### SALES LEDGER
**Bay Road School**

| | | | | |
|---|---|---|---|---|
| 1 Apr | Balance b/d | 1,900.00 | 6 Apr SRDB | 211.50 |
| 9 Apr | SDB | 1,351.25 | 8 Apr Bank | 1,688.50 |
| | | | 30 Apr Balance c/d | 1,351.25 |
| | | £3,251.25 | | £3,251.25 |
| 1 May | Balance b/d | 1,351.25 | | |

### Metro Hotel

| | | | | | |
|---|---|---|---|---|---|
| 1 Apr | Balance b/d | 1,750.00 | 15 Apr Bank | 1,750.00 |
| 4 Apr | SDB | 1,645.00 | 30 Apr Balance c/d | 1,645.00 |
| | | £3,395.00 | | £3,395.00 |
| 1 May | Balance b/d | 1,645.00 | | |

### Victoria Hotel

| | | |
|---|---|---|
| 15 Apr | SDB | 1,410.00 |

### Mr and Mrs Brown

| | | | | |
|---|---|---|---|---|
| 22 Apr | SDB | 822.50 | 28 Apr  Bank | 822.50 |

### Crescent Hotel

| | | |
|---|---|---|
| 29 Apr | SDB | 1,938.75 |

### PURCHASE LEDGER

### Jessup & Smith

| | | | | | |
|---|---|---|---|---|---|
| 7 Apr | PRDP | 211.50 | 1 Apr | Balance b/d | 1,100.00 |
| 8 Apr | Bank | 888.50 | " | PDB | 1,057.50 |
| 30 Apr | Balance c/d | 1,057.50 | | | |
| | | £2,157.50 | | | £2,157.50 |
| | | | 1 May | Balance b/d | 1,057.50 |

### Fletcher DIY

| | | | | | |
|---|---|---|---|---|---|
| 29 Apr | Bank | 625.00 | 1 Apr | Balance b/d | 1,250.00 |
| 30 Apr | Balance c/d | 918.75 | 9 Apr | PDB | 293.75 |
| | | £1,543.75 | | | £1,543.75 |
| | | | 1 May | Balance b/d | 918.75 |

### Whitby Plumbers Supplies

| | | |
|---|---|---|
| | 18 Apr PDB | 1,645.00 |

## Model answers to ICB Level II examination paper

**Task 5 (contd)**

### Trial Balance as at 30 April 2007

| | DR £ | CR £ |
|---|---|---|
| Capital | | 41,600.00 |
| Bank Loan | | 4,200.00 |
| Motor Vehicle | 17,500.00 | |
| Tools and Equipment | 20,000.00 | |
| Office Equipment | 3,600.00 | |
| Stocks | 1,950.00 | |
| VAT Account | | 621.25 |
| Drawings | 1,250.00 | |
| Wages | 575.00 | |
| Insurances | 1,400.00 | |
| Office Expenses | 40.00 | |
| Sales | | 6,100.00 |
| Sales Returns | 180.00 | |
| Purchases | 2,550.00 | |
| Purchase Returns | | 180.00 |
| *Debtors: | | |
| Bay Road School | 1,351.25 | |
| Metro Hotel | 1,645.00 | |
| Victoria Hotel | 1,410.00 | |
| Crescent Hotel | 1,938.75 | |
| *Creditors: | | |
| Jessup & Smith | | 1,057.50 |
| Fletcher DIY | | 918.75 |
| Whitby | | 1,645.00 |
| Bank | 822.50 | |
| Cash | 110.00 | |
| | 56,322.50 | 56,322.50 |

* CANDIDATES MAY CHOOSE TO LIST TOTAL DEBTORS/CREDITORS

**Question 2**

**Task 1**

Updated Cash Book (Bank Column)

| | | | | | |
|---|---|---|---|---|---|
| 30 Apr | Balance b/d | 822.50 | 30 Apr | DD PRU | 600.00 |
| | | | " | Bank Charges | 40.00 |
| | | | " | DD Insurance | 150.00 |
| | | | " | Balance c/d | 32.50 |
| | | £822.50 | | | £822.50 |
| 1 May | Balance b/d | 32.50 | | | |

**Task 2**

BANK RECONCILIATION STATEMENT

| | | | |
|---|---|---|---|
| Balance per Bank Statement | | | 110.00 |
| Add Lodgements: | | | |
| Mr and Mrs Brown | | | 822.50 |
| | | | 932.50 |
| Less unpresented cheques: | | | |
| 705 | Wages | 275.00 | |
| 706 | Fletcher DIY | 625.00 | |
| | | | 900.00 |
| Balance per Cash Book | | | £32.50 |

## Question 3

### Task 1

| | DR | CR |
|---|---|---|
| **Journal (1)** | | |
| Drawings | 500.00 | |
| Office Expenses | | 500.00 |

Being a private item incorrectly posted to
Office Expenses Account

| | DR | CR |
|---|---|---|
| **Journal (2)** | | |
| Tools and Equipment | 850.00 | |
| Repairs and Maintenance | | 850.00 |

Being an incorrect posting, error of principle

| | DR | CR |
|---|---|---|
| **Journal (3)** | | |
| Suspense A/C | 700.00 | |
| VAT A/C | | 700.00 |

Being an error of omission

### Task 2

**Suspense Account**

| 31 Mar | Journal (3) | 700.00 | 31 Mar Balance per TB | 700.00 |
|---|---|---|---|---|
| | | 700.00 | | 700.00 |

### Task 3

The veterinary fees for Nigel's daughter's horse are a private item and must not be charged to the business as an expense.

## Question 4

**Task**

**Nigel Blyth**
**Trading and Profit and Loss Account for Year Ended 31 March 2007**

|  | £ | £ |
|---|---:|---:|
| Sales (work done) |  | 82,500 |
| Stock at 1/4/06 | 1,850 |  |
| Add purchases | 34,650 |  |
|  | 36,500 |  |
| Less stock 31/3/07 | 1,950 |  |
| Cost of materials used |  | 34,550 |
| Gross profit |  | 47,950 |
|  |  |  |
| *Expenses* |  |  |
| Repairs and maintenance | 1,450 |  |
| Motor vehicle running costs | 3,350 |  |
| Insurances | 1,320 |  |
| Office expenses | 650 |  |
| Wages | 8,200 |  |
|  |  | 14,970 |
| Net profit for year |  | 32,980 |

## Balance Sheet as at 31 March 2007

**Fixed Assets**

| | | |
|---|---|---|
| Tools and Equipment | 20,000 | |
| Motor Vehicle | 17,500 | |
| Office Equipment | 3,600 | |
| | | 41,100 |

**Current Assets**

| | | |
|---|---|---|
| Stocks | 1,950 | |
| Debtors | 3,650 | |
| Cash | 150 | |
| Bank | 2,250 | |
| | 8,000 | |

**Less Current Liabilities**

| | | |
|---|---|---|
| Creditors | 2,350 | |
| VAT Account | 950 | |
| | 3,300 | |
| Net Current Assets | | 4,700 |
| | | 45,800 |

**Less: Long-Term Liability**

| | | |
|---|---|---|
| Bank Loan | | 4,200 |
| | | £41,600 |

| | | |
|---|---|---|
| Capital at Start | 29,620 | |
| Add Profit for Year | 32,980 | |
| | 62,600 | |
| Less Drawings | 21,000 | |
| | | 41,600 |
| | | £41,600 |

## Question 5

### Task 1

**VAT Account**

| 30 Jun | PDB | 1,610.00 | 30 Jun | SDB | 3,850.00 |
|---|---|---|---|---|---|
| " | SRDB | 105.00 | " | PRDB | 122.50 |
| " | Balance c/d | 2,257.50 | | | |
| | | £3,972.50 | | | £3,972.50 |
| | | | 1 Jul | Balance b/d | 2,257.50 |

| | |
|---|---|
| **Value Added Tax Return**<br>For the period<br>01/04 – 30/07 | For Official Use |

| | Registration number | Period |
|---|---|---|
| | 983172971 | 06/07 |

Nigel Blyth
Thorpe Lane
Robin Hoods Bay, Whitby

You could be liable to a financial penalty if your completed return and all the VAT payable are not received by the due date

Due date: 31/07/07

Your VAT Office telephone number is 0123-4567

| For Official Use | |
|---|---|

Before you fill in this form please read the notes on the back and the VAT leaflet "Filling in your VAT return". Fill in all boxes clearly in ink, and write 'none' where necessary. Don't put a dash or leave any box blank. If there are no pence write "00" in the pence column. Do not enter more than one amount in any box.

| For official use | | | £ | p |
|---|---|---|---|---|
| | VAT due in this period on sales and other outputs | **1** | 3745 | 00 |
| | VAT due in this period on acquisitions from other EC Member States | **2** | NONE | |
| | Total VAT due (the sum of boxes 1 and 2) | **3** | 3745 | 00 |
| | VAT reclaimed in this period on purchases and other inputs (including acquisitions from the EC) | **4** | 1487 | 50 |
| | Net VAT to be paid to Customs or reclaimed by you (Difference between boxes 3 and 4) | **5** | 2257 | 50 |
| | Total value of sales and all other outputs excluding any VAT. Include your box 8 figure | **6** | 21400 | 00 |
| | Total value of purchases and all other inputs excluding any VAT. Include your box 9 figure | **7** | 8500 | 00 |
| | Total value of all supplies of goods and related services, excluding any VAT, to other EC Member States | **8** | NONE | 00 |
| | Total value of all acquisitions of goods and related services, excluding any VAT, from other EC Member States | **9** | NONE | 00 |
| | Retail schemes. If you have used any of the schemes in the period covered by this return, enter the relevant letter(s) in this box | | | |

If you are enclosing a payment please tick this box

DECLARATION: You, or someone on your behalf, must sign below

1, _____ NIGEL BLYTH _____ declare that the
(Full name of signatory in BLOCK LETTERS)

Signature _____ Date    20
A false declaration can result in prosecution

269

## THE INSTITUTE
## OF CERTIFIED
## BOOKKEEPERS

# Level III Diploma in
# Manual Bookkeeping

## June 2007

**Time allowed: 3 hours**

---

**INSTRUCTIONS TO CANDIDATES**

**Candidates should attempt all five questions (in any order)**

**To pass this paper, candidates must achieve a minimum of 60% overall,
<u>and</u> no less than 60% in any one question**

Answers should be **written in blue or black ink/ballpoint** and completed in
the answer book provided. Please note that any work in pencil will not be
marked.

All workings should be shown in the answer book and scrap paper should not
be used.

The use of correcting fluid is not permitted

A single line down the centre of the page is sufficient for ledger ruling. Folio
numbers are not required

For cash books and petty cash books the use of two (facing) pages in the
answer book is suggested

Calculators may be used provided that they are battery operated or solar
powered, noiseless, non-programmable and do not give a print out.

Whilst in the examination room, all mobile telephones and pagers **MUST** be
turned off.

---

**ICB Level III Diploma in Manual Bookkeeping June 2007**

## Question 1

The following trial balance has been extracted from the books of Ravenscar Ltd as at 31 December 2006:

|  | £ | £ |
|---|---|---|
| Premises at cost | 189,350 | |
| Equipment at cost | 130,000 | |
| Motor vehicles at cost | 60,000 | |
| Depreciation (accumulated): | | |
| Premises | | 40,000 |
| Equipment | | 70,000 |
| Motor vehicles | | 10,000 |
| Stocks 1/1/06 | 33,500 | |
| Debtors | 34,000 | |
| Creditors | | 13,500 |
| Bank | 7,500 | |
| Share capital (£1 each) | | 140,000 |
| Retained earnings | | 37,500 |
| Sales | | 425,000 |
| Purchases | 169,675 | |
| Carriage out | 8,000 | |
| Wages and salaries | 91,100 | |
| Heat and light | 14,100 | |
| Provision for doubtful debts | | 1,600 |
| Vehicle expenses | 2,625 | |
| Telephone, postage and stationery | 3,100 | |
| Business rates | 17,500 | |
| Carriage inward | 2,150 | |
| Bank loan | | 25,000 |
| | 762,600 | 762,600 |

Additional Information:

- A customer has recently gone into liquidation and the debt of £4,000 is to be written off.

- The provision for bad and doubtful debts is to be revised to 5% of debtors.

- Closing stocks were valued at £37,500.

- The following were the accruals and prepayments at the year end:

|  | Accruals £ | Prepayments £ |
|---|---|---|
| Business rates |  | 1,600 |
| Vehicle expenses | 1,050 |  |
| Heat and light | 375 |  |
| Telephone | 460 |  |

- The directors have declared a dividend of 8p per share.

- Loan interest of 7% is accrued due.

- On 31 December, a motor vehicle that had previously cost £10,000 with a book value of £6,400 had been disposed of for £7,500 and a cheque had been received, but no entries had been made in the books.

- Depreciation policy is as follows:
  Premises 2% on cost
  Equipment 25% reducing balance
  Motor vehicles 20% reducing balance

## Task
Prepare the company's profit and loss account for year ended 31 December 2006 and a balance sheet at that date.

**(20 marks)**

## Question 2

Steetley Sports Club has the following summary in its cash book for year ended 30 September 2006.

You are a certified bookkeeper and on the sports club committee and as the treasurer is not trained in bookkeeping and accounting you are often called upon by the chairman for your advice.

The club has recently acquired a new pavilion funded partially by a members building fund and a grant.

| Summary | £ |
|---|---:|
| Opening bank balance | 14,500 |
| **Receipts** | |
| Grant from Sports Aid | 55,000 |
| Contributions to Building Fund | 26,100 |
| Subscriptions | 18,200 |
| Interest received | 900 |
| Life membership fees | 4,000 |
| Competition receipts | 8,100 |
| Entrance fees | 3,100 |
| Sale of second-hand sports equipment (previously capitalised) | 1,100 |
| | 131,000 |

| **Payments** | |
|---|---:|
| Transport to matches | 4,200 |
| Competition prizes | 3,910 |
| Coaching fees | 2,250 |
| Equipment repairs | 910 |
| Purchase of new sports equipment | 15,200 |
| Purchase of new Pavilion | 105,000 |
| | 131,470 |

| | |
|---|---:|
| Bank overdraft | (470) |

The following information is also available:

| | 1 October 2005 | 30 September 2006 |
|---|---|---|
| Subscriptions in advance | 1,400 | 1,000 |
| Subscriptions in arrears | 400 | 600 |
| Coaching fees accrued | 140 | 160 |

The subscriptions outstanding at 1/10/05 were not received in the year and need to be written off as a bad debt. Life membership fees accrue to income over a ten-year period.

The equipment sold in the year had a NBV of £1,600 (it had previously cost £2,000).

Equipment is to be depreciated at 20% per annum on cost.

The Pavilion is to be depreciated on a straight line basis over 50 years.

Equipment at cost held at 1/10/05 was £19,500.

**Required:**

### Task 1
Explain what is meant by the term 'accumulated fund' in the accounts of a club or society.

**(2 marks)**

### Task 2
Explain the difference between a receipts and payments account and an income and expenditure account

**(2 marks)**

### Task 3
Prepare the subscriptions account for the year.

**(4 marks)**

### Task 4
Prepare the income and expenditure account for the year.

**(12 marks)**

## Question 3

Steve Pollock and Daniel Bulman are in partnership as agricultural engineers sharing profits and losses 50 : 50.

For year ended 31 December 2006 their net profit was £75,000.

Their partnership agreement included the following:

- Interest on drawings is to be charged at 5% per annum.

- Interest on capital is to be credited to each partner at a rate of 6%.

- Partnership salaries are:
  Pollock      £30,000
  Bulman      £32,000

In addition to this the following information is available:

Drawings for the year:

  Pollock      £27,500
  Bulman      £29,100

Capital account balances at 1 January 2006:

  Pollock      £25,000
  Bulman      £30,000

Current account balances at 1 January 2006:

  Pollock      £18,100
  Bulman      £19,500

## Task 1

Prepare the partnership appropriation account for year ended 31 December 2006.

**(10 marks)**

## Task 2

Write up the partners' current accounts as at 31 December 2006.

**(7 marks)**

## Task3

Explain in what circumstances a partner's current account could show a debit balance.

**(3 marks)**

## Question 4

Emma Hatchard runs a card and gift shop in rural Lincolnshire.

She has been in business for a year and presents you with the following information.

Most of her business income is in the form of cash sales but she also supplies corporate gifts to companies on credit terms.

Assets and liabilities at 31 December 2006:

|  | £ |
|---|---|
| Fixtures and fittings at cost | 80,000 |
| Motor vehicle at cost | 10,000 |
| Stocks | 11,500 |
| Debtors | 5,200 |
| Creditors for supplies | 13,200 |

The bank account summary for year ended 31 December 2006 showed:

|  | £ |
|---|---|
| Capital introduced | 81,200 |
| Receipts from sales | 195,100 |
| Wages | 16,500 |
| Heat and light | 5,150 |
| Rent and rates | 10,340 |
| Advertising | 3,950 |
| Insurances | 1,375 |
| Fixtures and fittings | 80,000 |
| Motor vehicle | 10,000 |
| Drawings | 25,700 |
| Payment to suppliers | 105,650 |
| General expenses | 3,275 |

Additional information:

* Depreciation policy:
  Fixtures and fittings 10% per annum on cost
  Motor vehicles 25% per annum on cost

* Accruals and prepayments: 31 December 2006

|  | **Accruals** | **Prepayments** |
|---|---|---|
|  | **£** | **£** |
| Heat and light | 950 | |
| Rent | 1,100 | |
| Rates | | 450 |
| Wages | 500 | |
| Advertising | | 275 |
| Insurances | | 295 |

## Task 1
Determine Emma's closing bank balance at 31 December 2006.

**(2 marks)**

## Task 2
Prepare Emma's trading and profit and loss account for the year together with a balance sheet at 31 December 2006.

**(12 marks)**

## Task 3
Comment on Emma's level of profitability in her first year of trading.

**(6 marks)**

**Question 5**

Complete the following statements.

Write the *answers* in the *answer booklet*.

(1) Define the term Capital Employed (what does it comprise on a Ltd Company Balance Sheet)?

_____

_____

(2) Define the term Shareholders' Funds (what does it comprise on a Ltd Company Balance Sheet)?

_____

_____

(3) Debentures are a less risky investment than _____ as they carry a _____ of interest.

(4) Goodwill shown on a Ltd Company Balance Sheet would be shown as an _____ asset.

(5) When comparing a Ltd Company's current assets with its current liabilities it is a measure of _____

(6) In a partnership details of interest on capital, salaries, interest on drawings and shares of profit would be stated in the_____

(7) Why would a Revaluation Reserve appear on the Balance Sheet of a Ltd Company?

_____

_____

(8) A premium arises on the issue of ordinary shares when

_____

_____

(9) Why would goodwill arise on the admission of a new partner to the business?

_____

_____

_____

(10) A Debenture is a form of _____

This is the end of the examination.

**(20 marks)**

**Level III Diploma in Manual Bookkeeping June 2007**

**Question 1**

**Ravenscar Ltd**
**Profit and Loss Account for Year Ended 31 December 2006**

|  | £ | £ |
|---|---|---|
| Sales |  | 425,000 |
| Stocks at 1/1/07 | 33,500 |  |
| Add purchases | 169,675 |  |
| Add carriage inward | 2,150 |  |
|  | 205,325 |  |
| Less stocks 3/12/07 | 37,500 |  |
| Cost of sales |  | 167,825 |
| Gross Profit |  | 257,175 |
| *Expenses:* |  |  |
| Loan Interest | 1,750 |  |
| Wages and Salaries | 91,100 |  |
| Heat and Light | 14,475 |  |
| Vehicle Expenses | 3,675 |  |
| Telephone, Post, Stationery | 3,560 |  |
| Business Rates | 15,900 |  |
| Carriage outwards | 8,000 |  |
| Bad debts w/o | 4,000 |  |
| Decrease in bad debts provision | (100) |  |
| Profit on sale of asset | (1,100) |  |
| *Depreciation:* |  |  |
| Premises | 3,787 |  |
| Equipment | 15,000 |  |
| Motor vehicles | 8,720 |  |
|  |  | 168,767 |
| Profit before tax and dividend |  | 88,408 |
| Dividend proposed |  | 11,200 |
| Profit after tax and dividend |  | 77,208 |
| P/L account b/f |  | 37,500 |
| P/L account c/f |  | £114,708 |

**Ravenscar Ltd**
**Balance Sheet as at 31 December 2006**

|  | Cost £ | Depn £ | NBV £ |
|---|---|---|---|
| Premises | 189,350 | 43,787 | 145,563 |
| Equipment | 130,000 | 85,000 | 45,000 |
| Motor vehicles | 50,000 | 15,120 | 34,880 |
|  |  |  | 225,443 |

*Current assets*
| Stocks |  | 37,500 |  |
|---|---|---|---|
| Debtors less provision for bad debt |  | 28,500 |  |
| Prepayments |  | 1,600 |  |
| Bank |  | 15,000 |  |
|  |  | 82,600 |  |

*Less current liabilities*
| Creditors |  | 13,500 |  |
|---|---|---|---|
| Accruals |  | 3,635 |  |
| Proposed dividends |  | 11,200 |  |
|  |  | 28,335 |  |
| Net current assets |  |  | 54,265 |
| Total assets less current liabilities |  |  | 279,708 |

*Less long-term liabilities*
| Bank loan |  |  | 25,000 |
|---|---|---|---|
| Net assets |  |  | 254,708 |

*Financed by*
| Capital and reserves |  |  | 140,000 |
|---|---|---|---|
| Share capital |  |  | 114,708 |
| Retained earnings |  |  | 254,708 |

## Question 2

### Task 1
The accumulated fund represents the total funds invested in the club or association and is that fund that belongs to the members.

It is simply represented by the assets less the liabilities and is similar to the concept of ownership interest.

### Task 2
A receipts and payments account is simply an account of the club or society's cash flow over a year and would show:

Opening balances and receipts
Less expenses = closing balances

An income and expenditure account on the other hand is similar to a profit and loss account of a trading entity in that it is prepared on an accruals basis and includes depreciation (a non-cash item).

The overall result over a period is either an excess or deficit often termed surplus or deficit.

### Task 3

**Subscriptions Account**

| | | | | | |
|---|---|---|---|---|---|
| 1 Oct | Balance (arrears) b/d | 400.00 | 1 Oct | Balance (adv) c/d | 1,400.00 |
| 30 Sept | Balance (adv) c/d | 1,000.00 | 30 Sept | Bank balance (arrears) c/d | 18,200.00 |
| | Income & Expenditure a/c | 19,200.00 | | Income & Expenditure a/c bad debt | 600.00 |
| | | | | | 400.00 |
| | | £20,600.00 | | | £20,600.00 |
| 1 Oct | Balance (arrears) b/d | 600.00 | 1 Oct | Balance (ADV) b/d | 1,000.00 |

## Task 4

**Steetley Sports Club**
**Income and Expenditure Account for Year Ended 2006**

|  | £ | £ |
|---|---|---|
| *Income* | | |
| Life membership (10% of £4,000) | | 400 |
| Subscriptions | | 19,200 |
| Interest received | | 900 |
| Competition receipts | 8,100 | |
| Deduct competition prizes | 3,910 | |
| | | 4,190 |
| Entrance fees | | 3,100 |
| | | 27,790 |
| | | |
| *Expenditure* | | |
| Transport to matches | | 4,200 |
| Coaching fees | | 2,270 |
| Equipment repairs | | 910 |
| Loss on sale equipment | | 500 |
| *Depreciation* | | |
| Pavilion | | 2,100 |
| Equipment | | 6,540 |
| Bad debt (subs w/o) | | 400 |
| | | 16,920 |
| Excess of income over expenditure for year | | 10,870 |

## Question 3

### Task 1

**Pollock and Bulman**
**Appropriation Account for Year Ended 31 December 2007**

|  | £ | £ |
|---|---|---|
| Net profit from trading |  | 75,000 |
| Add interest on drawings: |  |  |
| Pollock | 1,375 |  |
| Bulman | 1,455 |  |
|  |  | 2,830 |
|  |  | 77,830 |
| Less interest on capital: |  |  |
| Pollock | 1,500 |  |
| Bulman | 1,800 |  |
|  |  | 3,300 |
|  |  | 74,530 |
| Salaries: |  |  |
| Pollock | 3,000 |  |
| Bulman | 32,000 |  |
|  |  | 62,000 |
|  |  | 12,530 |
| Share of balance: |  |  |
| Pollock |  | 6,265 |
| Bulman |  | 6,265 |
|  |  | 12,530 |

## Task 2

### Pollock and Bulman

| | Pollock | Bulman | | | Pollock | Bulman |
|---|---|---|---|---|---|---|
| 31 Dec Interest on drawings | 1,375 | 1,455 | 1 Jan | Balance | 18,100 | 19,500 |
| Drawings | 27,500 | 29,100 | 31 Dec | Interest on capital | 1,500 | 1,800 |
| Balance c/d | 26,990 | 29,010 | | Salaries | 30,000 | 32,000 |
| | | | | Share of profit | 6,265 | 6,265 |
| | 55,865 | 59,565 | | | 55,865 | 59,565 |
| | | | 1 Jan | Balance b/d | 26,990 | 29,010 |

## Task 3

A partner's interest on current account would show a debit balance when drawings and interest on drawings are greater than items credited to the current account in the form of interest on capital, salaries and share of profit.

A credit balance indicates that appropriations and shares of profit have been retained in the partnership and the partners' share in the business has increased, whereas a debit balance would have an adverse effect on the partners' share in the business.

**Question 4**

**Task 1**

**Bank Balance 31 December 2006**
£14,360

**Task 2**

**Emma Hatchard**
**Trading and Profit and Loss Account for Year Ended 31 December 2007**

|  | £ | £ |
|---|---|---|
| Sales | | 200,300 |
| Purchases | 118,850 | |
| Less: Stock 31/12/07 | 11,500 | |
| Cost of goods sold | | 107,350 |
| Gross profit | | 92,950 |
| *Expenses* | | |
| Wages | 17,000 | |
| Heat and light | 6,100 | |
| Rent and rates | 10,990 | |
| Advertising | 3,675 | |
| Insurances | 1,080 | |
| General expenses | 3,275 | |
| *Depreciation* | | |
| Motor vehicle | 2,500 | |
| Fixtures and fittings | 8,000 | |
| | | 52,620 |
| Net profit for year | | 40,330 |

**Emma Hatchard**
**Balance Sheet as at 31 December 2007**

| | Cost £ | Depn £ | NBV £ |
|---|---|---|---|
| *Fixed assets* | | | |
| Fixtures and fittings | 80,000 | 8,000 | 72,000 |
| Motor vehicle | 10,000 | 2,500 | 7,500 |
| | | | 79,500 |
| *Current assets* | | | |
| Stocks | | 11,500 | |
| Debtors | | 5,200 | |
| Prepayments | | 1,020 | |
| Bank | | 14,360 | |
| | | 32,080 | |
| *Less current liabilities* | | | |
| Creditors | | 13,200 | |
| Accruals | | 2,550 | |
| | | 15,750 | |
| Net current assets | | | 16,330 |
| Net assets | | | 95,830 |
| *Financed by* | | | |
| Capital | | 81,200 | |
| Profit for year | | 40,330 | |
| | | 121,530 | |
| Less drawings | | 25,700 | 95,830 |
| | | | 95,830 |

## Task 3
Emma's profitability can be assessed by:

    GP: Sales % 46.4
    NP: Sales % 20.1

This is a most sound level of profitability. The relationship of net profit (and accounting for drawings) gives a return of:

    14,630 / 95,830 = 15.3%

She has retained £14,630 in the business.

## Question 5

Complete the following statements.

(1) Define the term Capital Employed (what does it comprise on a Ltd Company Balance Sheet)?

**Total assets less Current liabilities or Capital and Reserves plus Long-term liabilities**.

(2) Define the term Shareholders' Funds (what does it comprise on a Ltd Company Balance Sheet)?

**Share capital and reserves**

(3) Debentures are a less risky investment than **ordinary shares** as they carry a **fixed rate** of interest.

(4) Goodwill shown on a Ltd Company Balance Sheet would be shown as an **intangible asset**.

(5) When comparing a Ltd Company's current assets with its current liabilities it is a measure of **liquidity**.

(6) In a partnership details of interest on capital, salaries, interest on drawings and shares of profit would be stated in the: **partnership agreement / deed of partnership**.

(7) Why would a Revaluation Reserve appear on the Balance Sheet of a Ltd Company?

**It arises when a tangible asset is revalued at a value greater than its carrying value.**

(8) A premium arises on the issue of ordinary shares when: **the price at which the shares are offered is greater than the nominal value of the share, i.e: they are offered at a premium.**

(9) Why would goodwill arise on the admission of a new partner to the business?

**Its is a way of rewarding the existing partners for their previous effort and contribution to the business.**

(10) A debenture is a form of: **loan (long term)**.

Qualifications for business

Exam I/D 104

# QUESTION PAPER

## Qualification:
Level 1 Certificate in Book-keeping
(Qualification Accreditation Number 500/3159/4)

## Examination:
Single Unit – Keeping simple financial records

## Examination Date:
26 January 2010

**Time Allowed: 1 hour 30 minutes**

Suite 30, 40 Churchill Square, Kings Hill, West Malling, Kent, ME19 4YU
Tel: 0844 330 3527, Fax: 0844 330 3514, Email: education@iab.org.uk

# IAB Level I question paper

**INTERNATIONAL ASSOCIATION OF BOOK-KEEPERS**

**QUALIFICATION TITLE:**    **LEVEL 1 CERTIFICATE IN BOOK-KEEPING**
**SINGLE UNIT TITLE:**    **KEEPING SIMPLE FINANCIAL RECORDS**
**IAB QUALIFICATION I/D:**    **104**

## General Information and Instructions

This question paper contains FIVE questions within two Sections.  You must answer
FOUR questions as follows:

SECTION A:    Answer **both** questions in this section

- Question One carries 35 marks
- Question Two carries 15 marks

SECTION B:    Answer any **two** of the three questions in this Section

- All Questions carry 25 marks

1.    You must enter your **Student Number**, **Examination Entry Number
(Candidate Number)** and **Name of Examination Centre** in the boxes
provided on the front cover of your Answer Booklet.

2.    Time allowed : **1 hour 30 minutes**.

3.    All answers are to be written in **ink**.

4.    Cross out errors neatly, or use correcting fluid in moderation.

5.    The use of silent non-programmable calculators is permitted.

6.    If you answer or partly answer more than two questions from Section B, you
must cross out the answer you do not want marking, otherwise we will take the
marks of your first two answers.

7.    Blank pages are provided in your Answer Booklet (pages 15 and 16) for workings
if required.

8.    NOTE – this Question Paper and the Answer Booklet have information and data
printed on both sides of the pages contained within the booklets.

**Scenario**

You work for IAB Book-keeping Services, which is a small book-keeping practice offering a range of basic book-keeping services to local clients.

In this Question Paper you are presented with five different practical tasks based on the needs of those clients.

The tasks take place during the period 11 January 2010 and 15 January 2010.

**The Standard Rate of Value Added Tax (VAT) used in this examination is 17.5%.**

You are required to complete the tasks in accordance with the examination instructions, i.e.:

| | | |
|---|---|---|
| **Section A** | – | Answer **both** questions in this section |
| **Section B** | – | Answer **any two** of the three questions in this section |

**Section A** – You must answer **both** questions in this section

### Question One

The date is Monday 11 January 2010, and you are visiting Manygate Motors to assist their accounts department with various tasks. The business is registered for VAT (Value Added Tax) and the Standard Rate of VAT in use is 17.5%.

Manygate Motors purchase the parts and accessories they need from Auto Express Factors Ltd. The terms of business are 30 Days Net, with 10% Trade Discount off the list price on **all** items. You are given the current Price List (see **page 6** of this **question paper**).

You are provided with four purchase invoices recently received from Auto Express Factors Ltd (see **pages 7 to 10** of this **question paper**). Unfortunately, the invoice clerk at Auto Express Factors Ltd is careless and often makes mistakes. For this reason you must now check the four invoices for pricing or other errors before entering the correct invoices into Manygate Motors' Purchase Day Book (see your **answer booklet page 2**). Incorrect invoices and the errors must then be listed.

There was a delivery this morning from Auto Express Factors Ltd. You are provided with the delivery notes and copies of the original purchase orders (see **pages 11 and 12** of this **question paper**) in order to check that the correct items have been delivered.

Also, the following invoices and credit note from Auto Express Factors Ltd are due for settlement today:

|  |  |
|---|---|
| Invoice No. 88692 | £311.00 |
| Invoice No. 88710 | £99.70 |
| Invoice No. 88718 | £589.90 |
| Credit Note No. 2013 | (£67.60) |

Finally, the cheques and cash listed below must be banked today:

| Cheques | |
|---|---|
| G. Brown | £500.00 |
| H. Hider | £459.29 |
| A. L. Rose | £62.00 |
| T. S. Ellie | £311.61 |
| M. Jepha | £68.00 |
| P.W. Able | £263.10 |
| **Cash** | |
| **Denominations** | **Number of Notes and Coins** |
| £10 Notes | 24 |
| £5 Notes | 15 |
| £1 Coins | 17 |
| 50p Coins | 6 |
| 10p Coins | 15 |
| 5p Coins | 5 |
| 2p Coins | 7 |
| 1p Coins | 11 |

**(continues)**

## Question One (continued)

**REQUIRED:**

**A**   Check carefully the four purchase invoices received from Auto Express Factors Ltd. Invoices with pricing or other errors should be set aside. Enter correct invoices (**only**) into the Purchase Day Book.               *(4 marks)*

      ***Examination hint**: only two of the four invoices are correct.*

**B**   List any faulty invoices that you set aside in Task A, and identify the errors. State your reasons concisely – it is not necessary to recalculate and list figures affected by the errors you discover.               *(5 marks)*

**C**   Total the Purchase Day Book.               *(3 marks)*

**D**   Check the two delivery notes dated 11 January 2010 from Auto Express Factors Ltd against Manygate Motors' purchase orders 7126 and 7127 and identify any errors which might have been made by Auto Express Factors Ltd.               *(3 marks)*

**E**   Make a payment to Auto Express Factors Ltd in settlement of the invoices listed above, taking credit as shown.  The Remittance Advice and a cheque should each be dated 11 January 2010.  Note that you do not have the authority to sign the cheque.               *(9 marks)*

**F**   Prepare a Bank Paying-in Slip dated 11 January 2010 in order to deposit the cash and cheques listed above.               *(11 marks)*

**35 marks total**

The following are provided in your **answer booklet (pages 2 to 5)** for your use in completing the above tasks:

- Purchase Day Book
- Space for answers to Task B
- Space for answers to Task D
- Remittance Advice and Cheque
- Bank Paying-in Slip

**Question One (continued)**

**Auto Express Factors Ltd – Price List**

| VAT Standard Rated Items | | |
|---|---|---|
| **Details** | **Product Code** | **List Price (Standard-rated, excluding VAT)** |
| | | **£** |
| Battery: Standard 12 volt | BS208 | 49.00 |
| Battery: Heavy Duty 12 volt | BH210 | 55.00 |
| Battery: Silver 12 volt | BS316 | 65.00 |
| Battery: Calcium 12 volt | BC318 | 85.00 |
| Brake Pads Kit A | C1008 | 11.00 |
| Brake Pads Kit L | C1108 | 16.50 |
| Brake Pads Kit M | C1208 | 13.70 |
| Bulb, Headlight | 5503 | 3.20 |
| Bulb, Parking Light | 5506 | 2.20 |
| Bulb, Reversing Light | 5509 | 4.20 |
| Bulb, Fog Light | 5511 | 2.99 |
| Cable Kit A | CK1009 | 10.00 |
| Cable Kit B | CK1010 | 15.00 |
| Cable Kit C | CK1011 | 13.00 |
| Cable Kit C Plus | CK1011P | 9.00 |
| Deicer Spray 500ml | D200 | 0.90 |
| Deicer Spray 1 litre | D210 | 1.90 |
| Exhaust System (Universal) | EX666 | 47.00 |
| PowerMaster 1500 Washer | PW15 | 136.00 |
| PowerMaster 2000 Washer | PW20 | 156.00 |
| PowerMaster Hose Extension | PW15E | 32.50 |
| Satellite Navigation System | SAT60 | 89.00 |
| Satellite Navigation System Plus | SAT60P | 99.99 |
| Shock Absorber Set | 7800 | 39.90 |
| Tyre Size 215 | P0007 | 20.00 |
| Tyre Size 235 | P0015 | 25.00 |
| Universal Socket Set, 24 piece | 7778 | 14.75 |
| Universal Socket Set, 48 piece | 7780 | 19.75 |
| Wheel Trim – Alloy | WT900 | 39.00 |
| Wheel Trim – Titanium | WT700 | 45.00 |
| Wiper Blades (front) | WB192F | 6.99 |
| Wiper Blade (rear) | WB192R | 3.99 |

| VAT Zero Rated Items | | |
|---|---|---|
| **Details** | **Product Code** | **List Price (Zero-rated)** |
| | | **£** |
| Auto Express Factors Ltd 2010 Catalogue | B607 | 0.99 |
| Car Repair Manual: Volume I | B020 | 7.49 |
| Car Repair Manual: Volume II | B065 | 7.49 |
| Road Atlas, Great Britain | B111 | 11.85 |
| Road Atlas, Europe | B211 | 12.85 |

## Question One (continued)

**Manygate Motors – Purchase Invoices Received**

**Auto Express Factors Ltd**
**Unit 7, Bentley Enterprise Park, Anytown AT7 5FF**

To: Manygate Motors
43 Spa Lane
Anytown
AT6 8CV

**INVOICE No:** 88754

**Order No:** 7122      **Date (Tax Point):** 5 January 2010

| Qty | Description | Product Code | VAT rate % | Unit Price £ | p | Total £ | p |
|-----|-------------|--------------|-----------|--------------|-----|---------|-----|
| 3 | Cable Kit A | CK1009 | 17.5 | 10 | 00 | 30 | 00 |
| 3 | Cable Kit B | CK1010 | 17.5 | 15 | 00 | 45 | 00 |
| 6 | Cable Kit C | CK1011 | 17.5 | 13 | 00 | 78 | 00 |
| 10 | Cable Kit C Plus | CK1011P | 17.5 | 9 | 00 | 90 | 00 |

TERMS: 30 Days Net

| | | |
|---|---|---|
| **Goods Total** | 243 | 00 |
| **Less Trade Discount 10%** | 24 | 30 |
| **Net Goods** | 218 | 70 |
| **VAT** | 38 | 27 |
| **Invoice Total** £ | 256 | 97 |

**VAT ANALYSIS**

| VAT Rate | Total Net £ | Total VAT £ |
|----------|-------------|-------------|
| 17.5% | 218.70 | 38.27 |
| 0.0% | 0.00 | 0.00 |

E. & O.E. Carriage paid. VAT Reg No: 22 4444 33

Registered Office: Unit 7, Bentley Enterprise Park, Anytown, AT7 5FF
Company Registered in England No 6677565

## Question One (continued)

**Manygate Motors – Purchase Invoices Received (continued)**

---

### Auto Express Factors Ltd
#### Unit 7, Bentley Enterprise Park, Anytown AT7 5FF

**To:** Manygate Motors
43 Spa Lane
Anytown
AT6 8CV

**INVOICE No:** 88771

**Order No:** 7123          **Date (Tax Point):**     6 January 2010

| Qty | Description | Product Code | VAT rate % | Unit Price £ | Unit Price p | Total £ | Total p |
|-----|-------------|--------------|-----------|--------------|--------------|---------|---------|
| 15 | Shock Absorber Set | 7800 | 17.5 | 39 | 90 | 598 | 50 |
| 4 | Tyre Size 215 | P0007 | 17.5 | 39 | 90 | 159 | 60 |
| 4 | Wheel Trim – Titanium | WT700 | 17.5 | 45 | 00 | 180 | 00 |

**TERMS:** 30 Days Net

| | | |
|---|---|---|
| **Goods Total** | 938 | 10 |
| **Less Trade Discount 10%** | 93 | 81 |
| **Net Goods** | 844 | 29 |
| **VAT** | 147 | 75 |
| **Invoice Total**      £ | 992 | 04 |

**VAT ANALYSIS**

| VAT Rate | Total Net £ | Total VAT £ |
|----------|-------------|-------------|
| 17.5% | 844.29 | 147.75 |
| 0.0% | 0.00 | 0.00 |

E. & O.E.   Carriage paid.   VAT Reg No: 22 4444 33

Registered Office: Unit 7, Bentley Enterprise Park, Anytown, AT7 5FF
Company Registered in England No 6677565

---

## Question One (continued)

**Manygate Motors – Purchase Invoices Received (continued)**

---

### Auto Express Factors Ltd
#### Unit 7, Bentley Enterprise Park, Anytown AT7 5FF

| To: | Manygate Motors |  | **INVOICE No**: 88799 |
|---|---|---|---|
|  | 43 Spa Lane |  |  |
|  | Anytown |  |  |
|  | AT6 8CV |  |  |

**Order No:** 7124        **Date (Tax Point):**        7 January 2010

| Qty | Description | Product Code | VAT rate % | Unit Price £ | Unit Price p | Total £ | Total p |
|---|---|---|---|---|---|---|---|
| 11 | Battery: Standard 12 volt | BS208 | 17.5 | 49 | 00 | 539 | 00 |
| 13 | Brake Pads Kit A | C1008 | 17.5 | 11 | 00 | 143 | 00 |
| 2 | Satellite Navigation System | SAT60 | 17.5 | 89 | 00 | 178 | 00 |
| 10 | Car Repair Manual: Volume II | B065 | 0.0 | 7 | 49 | 74 | 90 |

TERMS:   30 Days Net

|  | Goods Total | 934 | 90 |
|---|---|---|---|
|  | Less Trade Discount 10% | 93 | 49 |
|  | Net Goods | 841 | 41 |
|  | VAT | 135 | 45 |
|  | Invoice Total        £ | 976 | 86 |

**VAT ANALYSIS**

| VAT Rate | Total Net £ | Total VAT £ |
|---|---|---|
| 17.5% | 774.00 | 135.45 |
| 0.0% | 67.41 | 0.00 |

E. & O.E.  Carriage paid.  VAT Reg No: 22 4444 33

Registered Office: Unit 7, Bentley Enterprise Park, Anytown, AT7 5FF
Company Registered in England No 6677565

---

**Question One (continued)**

**Manygate Motors – Purchase Invoices Received (continued)**

---

## Auto Express Factors Ltd
### Unit 7, Bentley Enterprise Park, Anytown AT7 5FF

**To:** Manygate Motors
43 Spa Lane
Anytown
AT6 8CV

**INVOICE No:** 88810

**Order No:** 7125          **Date (Tax Point):**          8 January 2010

| Qty | Description | Product Code | VAT rate % | Unit Price £ | Unit Price p | Total £ | Total p |
|-----|-------------|--------------|-----------|-----|-----|-----|-----|
| 100 | Auto Express Factors Ltd 2010 Catalogue | B607 | 0.0 | 0 | 99 | 99 | 00 |
| 10 | Road Atlas, Europe | B211 | 0.0 | 12 | 85 | 128 | 50 |
| 25 | Bulb, Headlight | 5503 | 17.5 | 3 | 20 | 80 | 00 |

**TERMS:** 30 Days Net

| | | |
|---|---|---|
| **Goods Total** | 307 | 50 |
| **Less Trade Discount 10%** | 30 | 75 |
| **Net Goods** | 276 | 75 |
| **VAT** | 12 | 60 |
| **Invoice Total**          £ | 264 | 15 |

| VAT ANALYSIS | | |
|---|---|---|
| VAT Rate | Total Net £ | Total VAT £ |
| 17.5% | 72.00 | 12.60 |
| 0.0% | 204.75 | 0.00 |

E. & O.E.   Carriage paid.   VAT Reg No: 22 4444 33

Registered Office: Unit 7, Bentley Enterprise Park, Anytown, AT7 5FF
Company Registered in England No 6677565

---

**Question One (continued)**

**Manygate Motors – Purchase Orders Sent and Delivery Notes Received**

### PURCHASE ORDER — No: 7126

**Date:** 7 January 2010

**To:** Auto Express Factors Ltd
Unit 7, Bentley Enterprise Park
Anytown
AT7 5FF

**From:** Manygate Motors
43 Spa Lane
Anytown
AT6 8CV

| Quantity | Product Code | Description |
|---|---|---|
| 10 | C1108 | Brake Pads Kit L |
| 2 | PW15 | PowerMaster 1500 Washer |
| 6 | PW15E | PowerMaster Hose Extension |
| 4 | P0015 | Tyre Size 235 |
| 5 | 7780 | Universal Socket Set, 48 piece |

### DELIVERY NOTE No: D66709

**Date:** 11 January 2010

**Purchase order no:** 7126

**To:** Manygate Motors
43 Spa Lane
Anytown
AT6 8CV

**From:** Auto Express Factors Ltd
Unit 7, Bentley Enterprise Park
Anytown
AT7 5FF

| Product Code | Quantity | Description |
|---|---|---|
| C1108 | 10 | Brake Pads Kit L |
| PW15 | 2 | PowerMaster 1500 Washer |
| PW15E | 6 | PowerMaster Hose Extension |
| P0015 | 4 | Tyre Size 235 |
| 7778 | 5 | Universal Socket Set, 24 piece |

**Question One (continued)**

**Manygate Motors – Purchase Orders Sent and Delivery Notes Received (continued)**

---

**PURCHASE ORDER**                                                   **No: 7127**

**Date:**     8 January 2010

**To:**       Auto Express Factors Ltd          **From:**   Manygate Motors
              Unit 7, Bentley Enterprise Park                43 Spa Lane
              Anytown                                        Anytown
              AT7 5FF                                        AT6 8CV

| Quantity | Product Code | Description |
|---|---|---|
| 3 | BS208 | Battery:  Standard 12 volt |
| 2 | BS316 | Battery: Silver 12 volt |
| 24 | 5503 | Bulb, Headlight |
| 24 | 5511 | Bulb, Fog Light |
|  |  |  |

---

**DELIVERY NOTE No: D66710**

**Date:**     11 January 2010          **Purchase order no:**     7127

**To:**       Manygate Motors          **From:**   Auto Express Factors Ltd
              43 Spa Lane                          Unit 7, Bentley Enterprise Park
              Anytown                              Anytown
              AT6 8CV                              AT7 5FF

| Product Code | Quantity | Description |
|---|---|---|
|  |  |  |
| BS208 | 2 | Battery:  Standard 12 volt |
| BS316 | 3 | Battery: Silver 12 volt |
| 5503 | 24 | Bulb, Headlight |
| 5511 | 24 | Bulb, Fog Light |
|  |  |  |
|  |  |  |

## Question Two

It is 12 January 2010 and you have been sent to the premises of Doncaster Plumbing Supplies where the following Memo awaits you:

---

**MEMO**                                                    **Date:** 12 January 2010
**From:**     Lucy Melenas, Finance Assistant
**To:**         Accounts Assistant
**Subject:** Sales invoice and credit note

Thank you for helping us while our book-keeper is on leave.

Doncaster Plumbing Supplies sells components on credit to trade customers.  The business is registered for VAT and the standard rate of VAT in use is 17.5%.

I attach extracts from our Price List and Customer File together with the following two items (see **pages 14 and 15** of this **question paper**):

> Purchase Order No. 2010/0099 received from RSJ Builders Ltd - the goods are in stock and will be despatched today.

> Goods Returned Note No. 777 prepared by our warehouse this morning in respect of goods returned by Friendly Plumbing.  Note that the sales invoice issued for these goods included the Trade Discount agreed with Friendly Plumbing.

You are required to complete the following tasks:

**REQUIRED**

**A**     Prepare a Sales Invoice to RSJ Builders Ltd in respect of goods supplied as per their Purchase Order No. 2010/0099.                                *(8½ marks)*

**B**     Prepare a Credit Note to Friendly Plumbing in respect of goods damaged as listed on our Goods Returned Note No. 777.                        *(6½ marks)*

Signed: *Lucy Melenas*

---

**15 marks total**

The following are provided in your **answer booklet (pages 6 and 7)** for your use in completing the above task:

- Sales Invoice
- Credit Note

# IAB Level I question paper

## Question Two (continued)

**Doncaster Plumbing Supplies – Price List (Extract)**

| VAT Standard Rated Items | | |
|---|---|---|
| **Details** | **Doncaster Plumbing Supplies Product Code** | **List Price (Standard-rated, excluding VAT)** |
| | | **£** |
| Flexible tap connector with valve 15mm | 10198 | 3.00 |
| Flexible tap connector with valve 22mm | 10199 | 3.25 |
| Domestic Central Heating Pump Standard | 10455 | 68.00 |
| Domestic Central Heating Pump Extra | 10456 | 88.00 |
| Bath Taps, Chrome (pair) | 44566 | 25.50 |
| Bath Taps, Nickel (pair) | 44567 | 27.50 |
| Bath Taps, Brass (pair) | 44568 | 29.50 |
| Basin Taps, Chrome (pair) | 44570 | 20.50 |
| Basin Taps, Nickel (pair) | 44571 | 22.50 |
| Basin Taps, Brass (pair) | 44572 | 24.50 |
| Bath Outflow Kit | 44671 | 11.90 |
| Basin Outflow Kit | 44675 | 9.90 |
| SupaFlow Shower Pump | 50876 | 55.80 |
| Washing Machine Trap 40mm | 71008 | 5.00 |

**Doncaster Plumbing Supplies – Customer File (Extract)**

| Customer | Account reference | Trade discount | Terms |
|---|---|---|---|
| Friendly Plumbing | F107 | 10% | 30 Days Net |
| RSJ Builders Ltd | R444 | 15% | 21 Days Net |

## Question Two (continued)

**RSJ Builders Ltd – Purchase Order**

| Purchase Order No: 2010/0099 | | | Date: 8 January 2010 |
|---|---|---|---|
| **To:** | Doncaster Plumbing Supplies<br>Unit 15, Riviera Industrial Estate<br>Doncaster<br>DO5 2TY | **From:** | RSJ Builders Ltd<br>40 Factory Road<br>Doncaster<br>DO4 5GG |

| Product Code | Description | Quantity |
|---|---|---|
| 44567 | Bath Taps, Nickel (pair) | 1 |
| 44571 | Basin Taps, Nickel (pair) | 2 |
| 44671 | Bath Outflow Kit | 1 |
| 44675 | Basin Outflow Kit | 2 |
| 50876 | SupaFlow Shower Pump | 1 |
| | | |

**Doncaster Plumbing Supplies – Goods Returned Note**

### Doncaster Plumbing Supplies
### Unit 15, Riviera Industrial Estate
### Doncaster DO5 2TY

#### GOODS RETURNED NOTE

| **Customer:** | Friendly Plumbing<br>17 Abbey Road<br>Doncaster<br>DO7 1SE | Goods Returned Note No: 777 |
|---|---|---|

**Customer Order No:** 10565          **Date:** 12 January 2010

| Product Code | Quantity | Description | Reason for return |
|---|---|---|---|
| 10456 | 1 | Domestic Central Heating Pump Extra | Damaged |

## Section B – You must answer **any two** of the questions in this section

### Question Three

It is 13 January 2010. You are at the premises of Western Plastics Ltd where you are presented with the following memo:

---

**MEMO**                      **Date:** 13 January 2010
**From:**     R. Hardcastle, Director, Western Plastics Ltd
**To:**        Accounts Assistant, IAB Book-keeping Services
**Subject:** Petty Cash

With this memo please find our Petty Cash Book together with eight vouchers for recent petty cash claims which have not yet been entered into the Petty Cash Book (see **page 17** of this **question paper**).

Western Plastics Ltd is registered for VAT, and it is indicated on the Petty Cash Vouchers where the expenditure includes VAT (the Standard Rate of VAT to be used is 17.5%).

Our Petty Cashier is currently on leave, as a consequence I am not sure if all transactions have been tied up correctly in his absence. In particular, I am told that yesterday Tom Sedgwick was advanced £30 from Petty Cash in order to go to our local stationery shop and purchase a new calculator.

In order that the appropriate checks can be made, I attach a list of the notes and coins in the Petty Cash Tin as at today's date (see **page 18** of this **question paper**).

You are required to complete the following tasks:

**REQUIRED**

**A**     Enter the eight Petty Cash Vouchers into the Petty Cash Book.     *(12 marks)*

**B**     Balance off the Petty Cash Book as at 13 January 2010, bringing down the balance as at that date.     *(6½ marks)*

**C**     Using the Petty Cash Reconciliation Form provided, total the list of notes and coins in the Petty Cash Tin.     *(4½ marks)*

**D**     Compare the Petty Cash Balance to the contents of the Petty Cash Tin. From the information provided, suggest the most likely reason for any difference.     *(2 marks)*

Signed: *R. Hardcastle, Director*

---

**25 marks total**

The following is provided in your **answer booklet (pages 8 and 9)** for your use in completing the above tasks:

- Petty Cash Book
- Petty Cash Reconciliation Form
- Space for answer to Task D

## Question Three (continued)

**Western Plastics Ltd – Petty Cash Vouchers**

| Petty Cash Voucher | No: 515 | AMOUNT £ | p |
|---|---|---|---|
| Date: 6 January 2010 | | | |
| Light bulbs (including VAT) | | 9 | 40 |
| | | 9 | 40 |
| Claimant: | Y Midori | | |
| Authorised by: | R Hardcastle | | |

| Petty Cash Voucher | No: 516 | AMOUNT £ | p |
|---|---|---|---|
| Date: 6 January 2010 | | | |
| Bus fare (VAT zero rated) | | 1 | 30 |
| | | 1 | 30 |
| Claimant: | D Kirwin | | |
| Authorised by: | R Hardcastle | | |

| Petty Cash Voucher | No: 517 | AMOUNT £ | p |
|---|---|---|---|
| Date: 7 January 2010 | | | |
| Postage (VAT exempt) | | 2 | 40 |
| | | 2 | 40 |
| Claimant: | D Kirwin | | |
| Authorised by: | R Hardcastle | | |

| Petty Cash Voucher | No: 518 | AMOUNT £ | p |
|---|---|---|---|
| Date: 7 January 2010 | | | |
| Carpet cleaning contractor | | 40 | 00 |
| Plus VAT | | 7 | 00 |
| | | 47 | 00 |
| Claimant: | D Lunt | | |
| Authorised by: | R Hardcastle | | |

| Petty Cash Voucher | No: 519 | AMOUNT £ | p |
|---|---|---|---|
| Date: 8 January 2010 | | | |
| Flowers for reception | | 10 | 00 |
| Plus VAT | | 1 | 75 |
| | | 11 | 75 |
| Claimant: | M E Lusardi | | |
| Authorised by: | R Hardcastle | | |

| Petty Cash Voucher | No: 520 | AMOUNT £ | p |
|---|---|---|---|
| Date: 8 January 2010 | | | |
| Magazines for reception (VAT zero rated) | | 10 | 75 |
| | | 10 | 75 |
| Claimant: | Y Midori | | |
| Authorised by: | R Hardcastle | | |

| Petty Cash Voucher | No: 521 | AMOUNT £ | p |
|---|---|---|---|
| Date: 11 January 2010 | | | |
| Refreshments (VAT zero rated) | | 1 | 73 |
| | | 1 | 73 |
| Claimant: | D Lunt | | |
| Authorised by: | R Hardcastle | | |

| Petty Cash Voucher | No: 522 | AMOUNT £ | p |
|---|---|---|---|
| Date: 12 January 2010 | | | |
| Calculator (including VAT) | | 28 | 67 |
| | | 28 | 67 |
| Claimant: | T Sedgwick | | |
| Authorised by: | R Hardcastle | | |

304

**Question Three (continued)**

**Western Plastics Ltd — Contents of Petty Cash Tin**

| Western Plastics Ltd<br>Contents of Petty Cash Tin as at 13 January 2010 | |
| --- | --- |
| **Denominations** | **Number of Notes and Coins** |
| £20 Notes | 0 |
| £10 Notes | 2 |
| £5 Notes | 5 |
| £2 Coins | 1 |
| £1 Coins | 7 |
| 50p Coins | 10 |
| 20p Coins | 6 |
| 10p Coins | 3 |
| 5p Coins | 2 |
| 2p Coins | 2 |
| 1p Coins | 3 |

## Question Four

You have received the following email:

| | | | |
|---|---|---|---|
| **From**: | 'Senior Accounts Assistant' | **Sent**: | 14 January 2010 |
| **To**: | AccountsAssistant@iabbkservs.co.uk | | |
| **Subject**: | Gifts Galore – Cash Book | | |
| **Attachment**: | Gifts Galore – list of receipts and payments | | |

Our client Gifts Galore do business on a cash and credit basis. On their behalf we maintain an analysed Cash Book with separate pages for receipts and payments. Payments are analysed into three columns: Purchases, Wages, and all other Expenses.

Gifts Galore is registered for Value Added Tax, and all sales and purchases are subject to VAT at the standard rate of 17.5%.

Gifts Galore have a policy to bank cheques immediately. However, cash (i.e. notes and coins) is held in their safe during the week so that wages and other cash expenses may be paid out. Every Monday the cash in their safe and tills is counted, an amount is held back as a float, and the balance is banked.

You are reminded that the Contra and Balances columns are there only to help with the cross-checking of totals.

Their Cash Book has been balanced off and cash and bank balances brought forward as at 5 January 2010. Gifts Galore have now sent me the attached list of receipts and payments which took place during the week ended 11 January 2010 (see **page 20** of this **question paper**).

### REQUIRED

A    Enter into the Cash Book the transactions which took place during the week
     ended 11 January 2010.                                         *(11½ marks)*

B    Balance off the Cash Book as at 11 January 2010, bringing down the balances as
     at 12 January 2010.                                            *(13½ marks)*

**25 marks total**

The following are provided in your **answer booklet (pages 10 and 11)** for your use in completing the above tasks:

- Cash Book – Receipts
- Cash Book – Payments

**Question Four (continued) – Attachment to Email**

**Gifts Galore – Receipts and Payments, week ended 11 January 2010**

| 2010 | |
|---|---|
| 5 January | Received and banked cheques totalling £1,645 (inclusive of VAT) from cash customers. |
| 5 January | Paid rent by cheque for £2,500 (exempt from VAT). |
| 6 January | Received and banked cheque for £650 from credit customer Avenue Gift Shop. |
| 6 January | Paid cheque for £999 to credit supplier Polson Ltd. |
| 7 January | Purchased stock of gifts by cash, £705 (£600 plus £105 VAT). |
| 7 January | Purchased stock of gifts by cheque, £2,350 (£2,000 plus £350 VAT). |
| 8 January | Paid cheque for £141 (£120 plus £21 VAT) for stationery. |
| 11 January | Received and banked cheques totalling for £1,128 (inclusive of VAT) from cash customers. |
| 11 January | Paid weekly staff wages by cash, £1,960. |
| 11 January | Cash sales (notes and coins) for the week totalled £5,922 inclusive of VAT. None of this has yet been banked. |
| 11 January | Paid all cash except £350 into the bank. |

## Question Five

It is 15 January 2010, and your supervisor Joanne asks you to complete some work for client Wendale Office Supplies.

Joanne provides you with the client's bank statement for the period 1-31 December 2009, together with their Cash Book which has been balanced off as at 31 December 2009 (see **pages 22 and 23** of this **question paper**).

She asks you to reconcile the bank balance per the Cash Book to the statement from the bank. The bank statement indicates that the account was overdrawn as at 31 December 2009, but Joanne reassures you that Wendale Office Supplies has a sufficient overdraft limit.

Joanne then explains that Wendale Office Supplies was started twelve months ago, and registered for Value Added Tax (VAT) in May 2009. The proprietor, Mike Tasker, has asked for some information about VAT as well as some general matters. You are to help him with his queries (see your **answer booklet page 14**).

The Standard Rate of VAT in use is 17.5%.

You are required to complete the following tasks:

### REQUIRED

**A**  Complete the Bank Reconciliation Statement to reconcile the bank balance per the Cash Book as at balance per the bank statement as at that date.                *(15 marks)*

**B**  Update the bank column of the Cash Book following the preparation of the Bank Reconciliation Stat entries 31 December 2009.                                            *(2½ marks)*

**C**  Rebalance the Cash Book and bring down the balance as at 1 January 2010.
                                                                                    *(2 marks)*

**D**  Refer to the questions in your answer booklet.        *(i)*    *(½ mark)*
                                                            *(ii)*   *(1 mark)*
                                                            *(iii)*  *(1 mark)*
                                                            *(iv)*   *(3 marks)*

                                                                    **25 marks total**

The following is provided in your **answer booklet (pages 12 to 14)** for your use in completing the above task:

- Bank Reconciliation Statement
- Cash Book (extract, bank columns only)
- Questions and space for answers to Task D

308

# IAB Level I question paper

## Question Five (continued)

**Wendale Office Supplies – Bank Statement**

**Western & City Bank Plc**
PO Box 1, London WC1X 1TY

Account Name:  Wendale Office Supplies
Branch:  Wendale 1
Sort code:  67-78-89
Account number: 10104555
Date:  31 December 2009

### Statement of Account
### 1 December 2009 – 31 December 2009

Sheet 12

| Date 2009 | Description | Payments £ | Receipts £ | Balance £ | |
|---|---|---|---|---|---|
| 1 Dec | Balance brought forward | | | 890 | |
| 3 Dec | Counter credit | | 2,400 | 3,290 | |
| 4 Dec | SO Council rates | 590 | | 2,700 | |
| 5 Dec | Cheque 100123 | 163 | | 2,537 | |
| 9 Dec | Counter credit | | 2,150 | 4,687 | |
| 9 Dec | DDR Acme Leasing | 2,109 | | 2,578 | |
| 9 Dec | Cheque 100124 | 398 | | 2,180 | |
| 10 Dec | DDR HM Revenue & Customs | 6,508 | | 4,328 | OD |
| 16 Dec | Counter credit | | 4,011 | 317 | OD |
| 16 Dec | Direct credit:  Fleming Group | | 3,500 | 3,183 | |
| 18 Dec | Cheque 100126 | 1,842 | | 1,341 | |
| 21 Dec | Cheque 100125 | 8,700 | | 7,359 | OD |
| 23 Dec | Counter credit | | 5,627 | 1,732 | OD |
| 29 Dec | Online banking:  MasterCard | 1,777 | | 3,509 | OD |
| 31 Dec | Debit card:  National Rail | 200 | | 3,709 | OD |
| 31 Dec | BP Bank charges | 18 | | 3,727 | OD |
| 31 Dec | Balance carried forward | | | 3,727 | OD |

OD – Overdrawn balance
DDR – Direct debit transaction
SO – Standing order transaction

BP – Bank payment
BACS – Bankers automated clearing service

**Question Five (continued) – Attachment to Memo**

**Wendale Office Supplies – Cash Book (extract, bank columns only)**

Wendale Office Supplies
Cash Book
(extract, bank columns only)

| RECEIPTS | | | PAYMENTS | | | |
|---|---|---|---|---|---|---|
| Date 2009 | Details | Bank £ | Date 2009 | Details | Cheque No. | Bank £ |
| 1 Dec | Balance b/f | 890 | 2 Dec | ABC Mutual | 100123 | 163 |
| 2 Dec | Sales | 2,400 | 3 Dec | British Telecom | 100124 | 398 |
| 8 Dec | Sales | 2,150 | 15 Dec | Desks UK Ltd | 100125 | 8,700 |
| 15 Dec | Sales | 4,011 | 15 Dec | Johnsons Ltd | 100126 | 1,842 |
| 22 Dec | Sales | 5,627 | 24 Dec | Wendale Wine Bar | 100127 | 520 |
| 31 Dec | Sales | 2,600 | 28 Dec | National Paper | 100128 | 1,400 |
| | | | 28 Dec | Electricity Company | 100129 | 1,208 |
| | | | 29 Dec | MasterCard | online banking | 1,777 |
| | | | 29 Dec | National Rail | debit card | 200 |
| | | | | | | |
| | | | | | | |
| | | | | | | |
| | | | 31 Dec | Balance c/d | | 1,470 |
| | | 17,678 | | | | 17,678 |
| 31 Dec | Balance b/d | 1,470 | | | | |

**IAB**
*Qualifications for business*

Exam I/D 104

# ANSWER BOOKLET

## Qualification:
Level 1 Certificate in Book-keeping
(Qualification Accreditation Number 500/3159/4)

## Examination:
Single Unit – Keeping simple financial records

## Examination Date:
26 January 2010

| | |
|---|---|
| **Student Number:** | |
| **Candidate Number:** | |
| **Name of Examination Centre:** | |

For use by assessor only:

| | Section A<br>Answer **both** questions in<br>this section | | Section B<br>Answer **any two** questions<br>in this section | | | |
|---|---|---|---|---|---|---|
| Question<br>number | 1 | 2 | 3 | 4 | 5 | Total |
| Maximum<br>marks | 35 | 15 | 25 | 25 | 25 | 100 |
| Marks<br>awarded | | | | | | |

Suite 30, 40 Churchill Square, Kings Hill, West Malling, Kent, ME19 4YU
Tel: 0844 330 3527, Fax: 0844 330 3514, Email: education@iab.org.uk

# IAB Level I answer booklet

**Section A** – You must answer **both** questions in this section

**For use in answering Question One:  Tasks A and C**

Manygate Motors – Purchase Day Book

### Purchase Day Book

| Date 2010 | Supplier | Supplier Invoice Number | Total Invoice £ | VAT £ | Net £ |
|---|---|---|---|---|---|
|  |  |  |  |  |  |
|  |  |  |  |  |  |
|  |  |  |  |  |  |
|  |  |  |  |  |  |
|  |  |  |  |  |  |

**For use in answering Question One:  Task B**

Auto Express Factors Ltd – Invoice Errors

In the space below, list any invoices that you have rejected and identify the errors that you have discovered:

| Auto Express Factors Ltd – Invoice Errors | |
|---|---|
| Invoice number | Error(s) |
|  |  |

# IAB Level I answer booklet

**For use in answering Question One: Task D**

Check the Delivery Note D66709 from Auto Express Factors Ltd against Manygate Motors' Purchase Order 7126 and explain any differences:

_____

_____

_____

_____

_____

_____

_____

Check the Delivery Note D66710 from Auto Express Factors Ltd against Manygate Motors' Purchase Order 7127 and explain any differences:

_____

_____

_____

_____

_____

_____

_____

**For use in answering Question One:  Task E**

**Manygate Motors – Remittance Advice**

| REMITTANCE ADVICE | | | |
|---|---|---|---|
| **From:** Manygate Motors 43 Spa Lane Anytown AT6 8CV | **To:** **Date:** | | |
| **Details** | | **Amount** £    p | |
|  |  |  |  |
| Cheque number: ................................ | | | |

**Manygate Motors – Cheque**

| Date: _____ Payee: _____ _____ _____ £ [_____] 104010 | **HCSB Bank Plc** Anytown, AT7 8ER  Pay _____ Date: _____ Only  Account Payee £ [_____] _____ Manygate Motors |
|---|---|
|  | 104010      12-43-66      10567894 |

12-43-66

# IAB Level I answer booklet

**For use in answering Question One:  Task F**

**Manygate Motors – Bank Paying-in Slip**

**Paying-in Slip:  Front**

**Paying-in Slip:  Reverse**

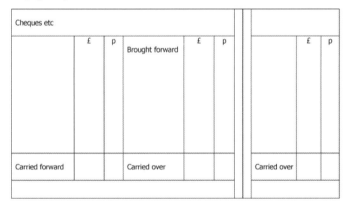

**Doncaster Plumbing Supplies – Sales Invoice**

**Doncaster Plumbing Supplies**
**Unit 15, Riviera Industrial Estate**
**Doncaster DO5 2TY**

To:

RSJ Builders Ltd
40 Factory Road
Doncaster
DO4 5GG

**INVOICE No**: 7088

**Order No:**    2010/0099              **Date (Tax Point):**    12 January 2010

| Qty | Product Code | Description | VAT rate % | Unit Price £ | p | Total £ | p |
|-----|-------------|-------------|-----------|-------------|---|---------|---|
|     |             |             |           |             |   |         |   |
|     |             |             |           |             |   |         |   |
|     |             |             |           |             |   |         |   |
|     |             |             |           |             |   |         |   |
|     |             |             |           |             |   |         |   |
|     |             |             |           |             |   |         |   |

| TERMS: | | |
|--------|--|--|
| **Goods Total** | | |
| **Less Trade Discount .....%** | | |
| **Net Goods** | | |

| VAT ANALYSIS | | | **VAT** | |
|---|---|---|---|---|
| VAT Rate | Total Net £ | Total VAT £ | **Invoice Total** | **£** |
| 17.5% | | | | |
| 0.0% | | 0.00 | | |

E. & O.E.   Carriage paid.   VAT Reg No: 67 3434 123

DPS Ltd t/a Doncaster Plumbing Supplies
Registered Office: 17 Market Chambers, Central Square, Doncaster DO5 1MM
Company Registered in England No 7867564

# IAB Level I answer booklet

**For use in answering Question Two:  Task B**

Doncaster Plumbing Supplies – Credit Note

---

### Doncaster Plumbing Supplies
### Unit 15, Riviera Industrial Estate
### Doncaster DO5 2TY

To:

Friendly Plumbing
17 Abbey Road
Doncaster
DO7 1SE

**CREDIT NOTE No:** CR199

Order No. _____ 10565 _____       Date (Tax Point): _____ 12 January 2010

| Qty | Product Code | Description | VAT rate % | Unit Price £ | p | Total £ | p |
|---|---|---|---|---|---|---|---|
|  |  |  |  |  |  |  |  |
|  |  |  |  |  |  |  |  |
|  |  |  |  |  |  |  |  |
|  |  |  |  |  |  |  |  |
|  |  |  |  |  |  |  |  |
|  |  |  |  |  |  |  |  |

REASON FOR CREDIT: _____

| **Total** | | |
|---|---|---|
| **Less Trade Discount .....%** | | |
| **Net Goods** | | |
| **VAT** | | |
| **Total Credit** | £ | |

| VAT ANALYSIS | | |
|---|---|---|
| VAT Rate | Total Net £ | Total VAT £ |
| 17.5% | | |
| 0.0% | | 0.00 |

E. & O.E.          VAT Reg No: 67 3434 123

DPS Ltd t/a Doncaster Plumbing Supplies
Registered Office: 17 Market Chambers, Central Square, Doncaster DO5 1MM
Company Registered in England No 7867564

---

# IAB Level I answer booklet

Section B – You must answer **any two** of the questions in this section

**For use in answering Question Three: Tasks A and B**

**Western Plastics Ltd – Petty Cash Book**

| Receipts £ | Date 2010 | Details | Voucher No. | Payments £ | VAT £ | Travel £ | Postage and Stationery £ | Sundries £ |
|---|---|---|---|---|---|---|---|---|
| 175.00 | 5 January | Balance b/f | | | | | | |
| | | | | | | | | |
| | | | | | | | | |
| | | | | | | | | |
| | | | | | | | | |
| | | | | | | | | |
| | | | | | | | | |
| | | | | | | | | |
| | | | | | | | | |
| | | | | | | | | |
| | | | | | | | | |
| | | | | | | | | |
| | | | | | | | | |

*Analysis columns* (VAT, Travel, Postage and Stationery, Sundries)

# IAB Level I answer booklet

**For use in answering Question Three: Task C**

**Western Plastics Ltd – Petty Cash Reconciliation Form**

**Western Plastics Ltd**
**Petty Cash Reconciliation as at**
Date: _____

|  | Amount | |
|---|---|---|
| **Notes and Coins** | **£** | **p** |
| £20 Notes | | |
| £10 Notes | | |
| £5 Notes | | |
| £2 Coins | | |
| £1 Coins | | |
| 50p Coins | | |
| 20p Coins | | |
| 10p Coins | | |
| 5p Coins | | |
| 2p Coins | | |
| 1p Coins | | |
| **Total Cash per Petty Cash Tin** £ | | |
| **Cash Balance per Petty Cash Book** £ | | |
| **Difference** £ | | |

**For use in answering Question Three: Task D**

From the information provided, suggest the most likely reason for any difference identified above between the Total Cash per Petty Cash Tin and the Cash Balance per Petty Cash Book:

_____

_____

_____

_____

_____

**Gifts Galore – Cash Book (Receipts)**

Gifts Galore
Cash Book - Receipts

| Date 2010 | Details | Cash £ | Bank £ | Debtors £ | VAT £ | Sales £ | Contra £ | Balances £ |
|---|---|---|---|---|---|---|---|---|
| 5 January | Balances b/f | 350 | 3,660 | | | | | 4,010 |

**For use in answering Question Four – Tasks A and B (continued)**

**Gifts Galore – Cash Book (Payments)**

**Gifts Galore**
**Cash Book - Payments**

| Date 2010 | Details | Cash £ | Bank £ | Creditors £ | VAT £ | Purchases £ | Wages £ | Expenses £ | Contra £ | Balances £ |
|-----------|---------|--------|--------|-------------|-------|-------------|---------|------------|----------|------------|
|           |         |        |        |             |       |             |         |            |          |            |
|           |         |        |        |             |       |             |         |            |          |            |
|           |         |        |        |             |       |             |         |            |          |            |
|           |         |        |        |             |       |             |         |            |          |            |
|           |         |        |        |             |       |             |         |            |          |            |
|           |         |        |        |             |       |             |         |            |          |            |
|           |         |        |        |             |       |             |         |            |          |            |
|           |         |        |        |             |       |             |         |            |          |            |
|           |         |        |        |             |       |             |         |            |          |            |
|           |         |        |        |             |       |             |         |            |          |            |

# IAB Level I answer booklet

**For use in answering Question Five:  Task A**

**Wendale Office Supplies – Bank Reconciliation Statement**

**Wendale Office Supplies**
**Bank Reconciliation Statement as at 31 December 2009**

| CASH BOOK ADJUSTMENTS | £ | £ | STATEMENT ADJUSTMENTS | £ | £ |
|---|---|---|---|---|---|
| Balance per Cash Book: | | | Balance per Statement: | | |
| Add Receipts on Statement not in Cash Book: | | | Add Receipts in Cash Book not on Statement: | | |
| Less Payments on Statement not in Cash Book: | | | Less Payments in Cash Book not on Statement: | | |
| Adjusted Cash Book Balance: | | | Adjusted Statement Balance | | |

# IAB Level I answer booklet

For use in answering Question Five:  Tasks B and C

Wendale Office Supplies – Cash Book (extract, bank columns only)

**Wendale Office Supplies**
**Cash Book**
**(extract, bank columns only)**

| RECEIPTS | | | PAYMENTS | | | |
|---|---|---|---|---|---|---|
| Date 2009 | Details | Bank £ | Date 2009 | Details | Chq No or Ref | Bank £ |
| 31 Dec | Balance b/f | 1,470 | | | | |
| | | | | | | |
| | | | | | | |
| | | | | | | |
| | | | | | | |
| | | | | | | |
| | | | | | | |

# IAB Level I answer booklet

### For use in answering Question Five:  Task D

The proprietor of Wendale Office Supplies, Mike Tasker, has asked for some information about VAT and some general matters.  Answer his questions as set out below.

**(i)**  Mike is confused by VAT terminology.  In December 2009 Wendale Office Supplies' sales were £16,788.00 including VAT of £2,500.34.  Is this VAT called 'input tax' or 'output tax'?

State 'input tax' or 'output tax':  _____

**(ii)**  Wendale Office Supplies has received an invoice from a supplier for £1,600 plus £280 VAT, sent an invoice to a customer for £3,000 plus £525 VAT, and sent a credit note to another customer for £800 plus £140 VAT.  Taking just these three items together, tick which of the following statements is correct.

|  |  | Tick ✓ one |
|---|---|---|
| VAT due | £105 | |
| VAT due | £385 | |
| VAT refund due | £105 | |
| VAT refund due | £385 | |

**(iii)**  Mike understands that there are other rates of VAT besides the 'Standard Rate'.  Name **two** of them for him:

1.  _____

2.  _____

**(iv)**  The following transactions have taken place recently.  Mike would like to know whether each transaction is an asset, capital, a liability, income or an expense.

|  | Enter asset, capital, liability, income or expense |
|---|---|
| £500 owed by customer B. Tyrone | |
| £1,100 owed to supplier Pen 'n Ink Ltd | |
| £10,000 of personal money introduced into the business by Mike Tasker | |
| Shelving and display units costing £8,000 bought for use in the showroom | |
| Monthly rent of £300 received from the tenant of the flat above the showroom | |
| £175 paid to waste disposal firm | |

Qualifications for business

Exam I/D 104

# MODEL ANSWERS

## Qualification:
Level 1 Certificate in Book-keeping
(Qualification Accreditation Number 500/3159/4)

## Examination:
Single Unit – Keeping simple financial records

## Examination Date:
26 January 2010

Suite 30, 40 Churchill Square, Kings Hill, West Malling, Kent, ME19 4YU
Tel: 0844 330 3527, Fax: 0844 330 3514, Email: education@iab.org.uk

# IAB Level I model answers

**Answer Question One: Tasks A and C**

**Manygate Motors – Purchase Day Book**

### Purchase Day Book

| Date 2010 | Supplier | Supplier Invoice Number | Total Invoice £ | VAT £ | Net £ |
|---|---|---|---|---|---|
| 5 Jan | Auto Express Factors Ltd | ½ 88754 | ½ 256.97 | ½ 38.27 | ½ 218.70 |
| 7 Jan | Auto Express Factors Ltd | ½ 88799 | ½ 976.86 | ½ 135.45 | ½ 841.41 |
| | | | 1  1,233.83 | 1  173.72 | 1  1,060.11 |
| | | | | | |
| | | | | | |

**For use in answering Question One: Task B**

**Auto Express Factors Ltd – Invoice Errors**

In the space below, list any invoices that you have rejected and identify the errors that you have discovered:

| Auto Express Factors Ltd – Invoice Errors | |
|---|---|
| **Invoice number** | **Error(s)** |
| 88771  1 | Item P0007 is incorrectly priced.                                          1½ |
| 88810  1 | VAT has been subtracted from the Net Goods total instead of added.    1½ |
| | |

## Answer Question One: Task D

Check the Delivery Note D66709 from Auto Express Factors Ltd against Manygate Motors' Purchase Order 7126 and explain any differences:

5 of catalogue number 7778 (Universal Socket Set, 24 piece) have been delivered

instead of 5 of catalogue number 7780 (Universal Socket Set, 48 piece) as ordered.    1

---

Check the Delivery Note D66710 from Auto Express Factors Ltd against Manygate Motors' Purchase Order 7127 and explain any differences:

2 of catalogue number BS208 (Battery: Standard 12 volt)

were delivered instead of 3 as ordered.    1

3 of catalogue number BS316 (Battery: Silver 12 volt)

were delivered instead of 2 as ordered.    1

3  marks this page
12  marks b/f
15  marks c/f

**Answer Question One: Task E**

**Manygate Motors – Remittance Advice**

| REMITTANCE ADVICE | | | |
|---|---|---|---|
| **From:** Manygate Motors 43 Spa Lane Anytown AT6 8CV | **To:** ½ Auto Express Factors Ltd | | |
| | **Date:** ½ 11 January 2010 | | |

| Details | | Amount £ | p |
|---|---|---|---|
| Invoice number 88692 | ½ | ½ 311 | 00 |
| Invoice number 88710 | ½ | ½ 99 | 70 |
| Invoice number 88718 | ½ | ½ 589 | 90 |
| Less: Credit Note number 2013 | ½ | ½ ( 67 | 60 ) * |
| Cheque number: .......104010...............½ | | 1½ 933 | 00 |

* The credit note value must be shown as negative to earn the mark, such as by including the word 'Less' in the details or placing brackets around the value or a minus sign etc.

**Manygate Motors – Cheque**

| Date: 11 Jan 2010 | **HCSB Bank Plc** Anytown, AT7 8ER | 12-43-66 |
|---|---|---|
| | Date: ½ 11 January 2010 | |
| Payee: Auto Express Factors Ltd | Pay Auto Express Factors Ltd ------------------- ½ Only | |
| | Nine hundred and thirty three | £ ½ 933.00 |
| | pounds only ---- ½ | |
| £ 933.00 | | Manygate Motors |
| 104010 | 104010 12-43-66 10567894 | |

Allow candidate's Own Figure from the Remittance Advice for the cheque amount

9 marks this page
15 marks b/f
24 marks c/f

IAB L1 Certificate Jan 2010 MA (past paper)    Page 4

328

**Answer Question One: Task F**

**Manygate Motors – Bank Paying-in Slip**

**Paying-in Slip: Front**

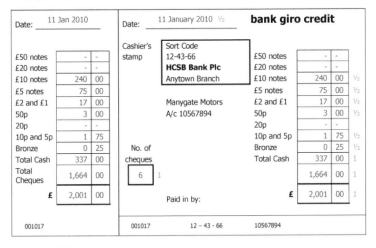

| | | | Cashier's | Sort Code | | | | |
|---|---|---|---|---|---|---|---|---|
| Date: | 11 Jan 2010 | | Date: | 11 January 2010 ½ | **bank giro credit** | | | |
| £50 notes | - | - | stamp | 12-43-66 | £50 notes | - | - | |
| £20 notes | - | - | | **HCSB Bank Plc** | £20 notes | - | - | |
| £10 notes | 240 | 00 | | Anytown Branch | £10 notes | 240 | 00 | ½ |
| £5 notes | 75 | 00 | | | £5 notes | 75 | 00 | ½ |
| £2 and £1 | 17 | 00 | | Manygate Motors | £2 and £1 | 17 | 00 | ½ |
| 50p | 3 | 00 | | A/c 10567894 | 50p | 3 | 00 | ½ |
| 20p | - | - | | | 20p | - | - | |
| 10p and 5p | 1 | 75 | | | 10p and 5p | 1 | 75 | ½ |
| Bronze | 0 | 25 | No. of | | Bronze | 0 | 25 | ½ |
| Total Cash | 337 | 00 | cheques | | Total Cash | 337 | 00 | 1 |
| Total Cheques | 1,664 | 00 | 6 | 1 | | 1,664 | 00 | 1 |
| £ | 2,001 | 00 | | Paid in by: | £ | 2,001 | 00 | 1 |
| 001017 | | | 001017 | 12 – 43 - 66 | 10567894 | | | |

**Paying-in Slip: Reverse**

Cheques etc

| | £ | p | | £ | p | | | £ | p |
|---|---|---|---|---|---|---|---|---|---|
| | | | B/forward | 1,664 | 00 | | | | |
| G Brown | 500 | 00 | ½ | | | | GB | 500 | 00 |
| H Hider | 459 | 29 | ½ | | | | HH | 459 | 39 |
| A L Rose | 62 | 00 | ½ | | | | ALR | 62 | 00 |
| T S Ellie | 311 | 61 | ½ | | | | TSE | 311 | 61 |
| M Jepha | 68 | 00 | ½ | | | | MJ | 68 | 00 |
| P W Able | 263 | 10 | ½ | | | | PWA | 263 | 10 |
| Name and figure must be correct to earn the ½ mark | | | | | | | | | |
| Carried forward | 1,664 | 00 | Carried over | ½ 1,664 | 00 | | Carried over | 1,664 | 00 |

11 marks this page
24 marks b/f
35 marks total

**Answer Question Two:  Task A**

**Doncaster Plumbing Supplies – Sales Invoice**

### Doncaster Plumbing Supplies
### Unit 15, Riviera Industrial Estate
### Doncaster DO5 2TY

To:

RSJ Builders Ltd
40 Factory Road
Doncaster
DO4 5GG

**INVOICE No**: 7088

**Order No:**    2010/0099                **Date (Tax Point):**    12 January 2010

| Qty | Product Code | Description | VAT rate % | Unit Price £ | Unit Price p | Total £ | Total p |
|-----|--------------|-------------|-----------|-----|-----|-----|-----|
| 1 | 44567 | Bath Taps, Nickel (pair) | 17.5 | 27 | 50 | ½ 27 | 50 * |
| 2 | 44571 | Basin Taps, Nickel (pair) | 17.5 | 22 | 50 | ½ 45 | 00 |
| 1 | 44671 | Bath Outflow Kit | 17.5 | 11 | 90 | ½ 11 | 90 |
| 2 | 44675 | Basin Outflow Kit | 17.5 | 9 | 90 | ½ 19 | 80 |
| 1 | 50876 | SupaFlow Shower Pump | 17.5 | 55 | 80 | ½ 55 | 80 |
| | | | | | | | |

**TERMS:**   21 Days Net   ½

| **Goods Total** | 1 160 | 00 |
|---|---|---|
| **Less Trade Discount** 15 % ½ | 1 24 | 00 |
| **Net Goods** | 1 136 | 00 |
| **VAT** | 1 23 | 80 |
| **Invoice Total**        £ | 1 159 | 80 |

| VAT ANALYSIS | | |
|---|---|---|
| VAT Rate | Total Net £ | Total VAT £ |
| 17.5% | 136.00 | 23.80 |
| 0.0% | 0.00 | 0.00 |

E. & O.E.  Carriage paid.  VAT Reg No: 67 3434 123

DPS Ltd t/a Doncaster Plumbing Supplies
Registered Office: 17 Market Chambers, Central Square, Doncaster DO5 1MM
Company Registered in England No 7867564

* All details of each line of goods must be correct to earn the mark shown.  Accept lines in any order.

8½ marks this page c/f

# IAB Level I model answers

**Answer Question Two:  Task B**

**Doncaster Plumbing Supplies – Credit Note**

<table>
<tr><td colspan="9" align="center">Doncaster Plumbing Supplies<br>Unit 15, Riviera Industrial Estate<br>Doncaster DO5 2TY</td></tr>
</table>

**To:**
Friendly Plumbing
17 Abbey Road
Doncaster
DO7 1SE

**CREDIT NOTE No:** CR199

**Order No.**    10565

**Date (Tax Point):** _____ 12 January 2010

| Qty | Product Code | Description | VAT rate % | Unit Price £ | Unit Price p | Total £ | Total p |
|-----|--------------|-------------|------------|--------------|--------------|---------|---------|
| 1 | 10456 | Domestic Central Heating Pump Extra | 17.5 | 88 | 00 | ½ 88 | 00 * |

**REASON FOR CREDIT:**    Damaged  ½

| | £ | p |
|---|---|---|
| **Total** | 1  88 | 00 |
| **Less Trade Discount** 10 % ½ | 1  8 | 80 |
| **Net Goods** | 1  79 | 20 |
| **VAT** | 1  13 | 86 |
| **Total Credit**            £ | 1  93 | 06 |

**VAT ANALYSIS**

| VAT Rate | Total Net £ | Total VAT £ |
|----------|-------------|-------------|
| 17.5% | 79.20 | 13.86 |
| 0.0% | 0.00 | 0.00 |

E. & O.E.       VAT Reg No: 67 3434 123

DPS Ltd t/a Doncaster Plumbing Supplies
Registered Office: 17 Market Chambers, Central Square, Doncaster DO5 1MM
Company Registered in England No 7867564

* All details of the line of goods must be correct to earn the ½ mark

6½  marks this page
8½  marks b/f
15   marks total

**Answer Question Three:  Tasks A and B**

**Western Plastics Ltd – Petty Cash Book**

## Western Plastics Ltd – Petty Cash Book

| Receipts £ | Date 2010 | Details | | Voucher No. | Payments £ | Analysis columns | | | |
|---|---|---|---|---|---|---|---|---|---|
| | | | | | | VAT £ | Travel £ | Postage and Stationery £ | Sundries £ |
| 175.00 | 5 January | Balance b/f | | | | | | | |
| | 6 Jan | Light bulbs | ¼ | 515 | ½ 9.40 | ½ 1.40 | | | ½ 8.00 |
| | 6 Jan | Bus fare | ¼ | 516 | ½ 1.30 | | ½ 1.30 | | |
| | 7 Jan | Postage | ¼ | 517 | ½ 2.40 | | | ½ 2.40 | |
| | 7 Jan | Carpet cleaning | ¼ | 518 | ½ 47.00 | ½ 7.00 | | | ½ 40.00 |
| | 8 Jan | Flowers | ¼ | 519 | ½ 11.75 | ½ 1.75 | | | ½ 10.00 |
| | 8 Jan | Magazines | ¼ | 520 | ½ 10.75 | | | | ½ 10.75 |
| | 11 Jan | Refreshments | ¼ | 521 | ½ 1.73 | | | | ½ 1.73 |
| | 12 Jan | Calculator | ¼ | 522 | ½ 28.67 | ½ 4.27 | | ½ 24.40 | |
| | | | | | 113.00 | 1 14.42 | 1 1.30 | 1 26.80 | 1 70.48 |
| | 13 Jan | Balance c/d | | | 1 62.00 | | | | |
| ½ 175.00 | | | | | ½ 175.00 | | | | |
| ½ 62.00 | 13 Jan | Balance c/d | | | | | | | |

Allow calculator analysed as Sundries, in which case P&S total should be £2.40 and Sundries total £94.88.

18½ marks this page c/f

**Answer Question Three: Task C**

**Western Plastics Ltd – Petty Cash Reconciliation Form**

**Western Plastics Ltd**
**Petty Cash Reconciliation as at**

Date: _____13 January 2010_____ ½

| Notes and Coins | | Amount | | |
|---|---|---|---|---|
| | | **£** | **p** | |
| £20 Notes | | 0 | 00 | |
| £10 Notes | | 20 | 00 | ¼ |
| £5 Notes | | 25 | 00 | ¼ |
| £2 Coins | | 2 | 00 | ¼ |
| £1 Coins | | 7 | 00 | ¼ |
| 50p Coins | | 5 | 00 | ¼ |
| 20p Coins | | 1 | 20 | ¼ |
| 10p Coins | | 0 | 30 | ¼ |
| 5p Coins | | 0 | 10 | ¼ |
| 2p Coins | | 0 | 04 | ¼ |
| 1p Coins | | 0 | 03 | ¼ |
| **Total Cash per Petty Cash Tin** | £ | 60 | 67 | ½ |
| **Cash Balance per Petty Cash Book** | £ | 62 | 00 | ½ |
| **Difference** | £ | 1 | 33 | ½ |

**Answer Question Three: Task D**

From the information provided, suggest the most likely reason for any difference identified above between the Total Cash per Petty Cash Tin and the Cash Balance per Petty Cash Book:

Tom Sedgwick was advanced £30.00 to purchase a calculator.  This cost £28.67

which has been entered into the Petty Cash Book (Petty Cash Voucher No. 522).

As the Petty Cash Tin is £1.33 short, from the information provided it appears

that Tom Sedgwick has not returned the £1.33 change he received from the £30

tendered in the stationery shop.

2

If an explanation is offered that is plausible but not the above explanation, award ½ mark instead of 2 marks.

6½ marks this page
18½ marks b/f
25  marks total

IAB L1 Certificate Jan 2010 MA (past paper)      Page 9

333

**Answer Question Four:  Tasks A and B**

**Gifts Galore – Cash Book (Receipts)**

Gifts Galore
Cash Book - Receipts

| Date 2010 | Details | Cash £ | Bank £ | Debtors £ | VAT £ | Sales £ | Contra £ | Balances £ |
|---|---|---|---|---|---|---|---|---|
| 5 January | Balances b/f | 350 | 3,660 | | | | | 4,010 |
| 5 Jan | Sales | | ½ 1,645 | | ¼ 245 | ¼ 1,400 | | |
| 6 Jan | Avenue Gift Shop | | ½ 650 | ¼ 650 | | | | |
| 11 Jan | Sales | | ½ 1,128 | | ¼ 168 | ¼ 960 | | |
| 11 Jan | Sales | ½ 5,922 | | | ¼ 882 | ¼ 5,040 | | |
| 11 Jan | Cash | | 1 3,257 | | | | ¼ 3,257 | |
| | | 1 6,272 | 1 10,340 | ½ 650 | ½ 1,295 | ½ 7,400 | ½ 3,257 | ½ 4,010 |
| 12 Jan | Balances b/d | 1 350 | 1 4,350 | | | | | 4,700 |

11½ marks this page c/f

334

# IAB Level I model answers

**Gifts Galore – Cash Book (Payments)**

## Gifts Galore
## Cash Book - Payments

| Date 2010 | Details | Cash £ | Bank £ | Creditors £ | VAT £ | Purchases £ | Wages £ | Expenses £ | Contra £ | Balances £ |
|---|---|---|---|---|---|---|---|---|---|---|
| 5 Jan | Rent | | ½ 2,500 | | | | | ¼ 2,500 | | |
| 6 Jan | Polson Ltd | | ½ 999 | ¼ 999 | | | | | | |
| 7 Jan | Stock | ½ 705 | | | ¼ 105 | ¼ 600 | | | | |
| 7 Jan | Stock | | ½ 2,350 | | ¼ 350 | ¼ 2,000 | | | | |
| 8 Jan | Stationery | | ½ 141 | | ¼ 21 | | | ¼ 120 | | |
| 11 Jan | Wages | ½ 1,960 | | | | | ¼ 1,960 | | | |
| 11 Jan | Bank | 1 3,257 | | | | | | | ¼ 3,257 | |
| | | 5,922 | 5,990 | ½ 999 | ½ 476 | ½ 2,600 | ½ 1,960 | ½ 2,620 | ½ 3,257 | 0 |
| 11 Jan | Balances c/d | 1 350 | 1 4,350 | | | | | | | |
| | | 1 6,272 | 1 10,340 | | | | | | | |

13½ marks this page
11½ marks b/f
25 marks total

# IAB Level I model answers

**Answer Question Five: Task A**

**Wendale Office Supplies – Bank Reconciliation Statement**

**Wendale Office Supplies**
**Bank Reconciliation Statement as at 31 December 2009**

| CASH BOOK ADJUSTMENTS | | £ | £ |
|---|---|---|---|
| Balance per Cash Book: | | 2 | 1,470 |
| Add Receipts on Statement | | | |
| Fleming Group | ½ | | ½ 3,500 |
| | | | 4,970 |
| Less Payments on Statement | | | |
| Council rates | ½ | ½ 590 | |
| Acme Leasing | ½ | ½ 2,109 | |
| HM Revenue & Customs | ½ | ½ 6,508 | |
| Bank charges | ½ | ½ 18 | |
| | | | 9,225 |
| Adjusted Cash Book Balance: | | | 1 (4,255) |

| STATEMENT ADJUSTMENTS | | £ | £ |
|---|---|---|---|
| Balance per Statement: | | 2 | (3,727) |
| Add Receipts in Cash Book | | | |
| Sales ½ | | | ½ 2,600 |
| Or counter credit, lodgement, etc | | | |
| | | | (1,127) |
| Less Payments in Cash Book | | | |
| Uncleared cheques: | | | |
| 100127 (Wendale Wine Bar) | ½ | ½ 520 | |
| 100128 (National Paper) | ½ | ½ 1,400 | |
| 100129 (Electricity Company) | ½ | ½ 1,208 | |
| Cheque no or payee acceptable | | | |
| | | | 3,128 |
| Adjusted Statement Balance | | | 1 (4,255) |

15 marks this page c/f

Negative amounts must be shown as such (by brackets, minus sign or OD) to earn the marks attaching.

# IAB Level I model answers

**Wendale Office Supplies – Cash Book (extract, bank columns only)**

**Wendale Office Supplies
Cash Book
(extract, bank columns only)**

| RECEIPTS | | | PAYMENTS | | | |
|---|---|---|---|---|---|---|
| Date 2009 | Details | Bank £ | Date 2009 | Details | Chq No or Ref | Bank £ |
| 31 Dec | Balance b/f | 1,470 | 31 Dec | Council rates | SO | ½ 590 |
| 31 Dec | Fleming Group | ½ 3,500 | 31 Dec | Acme Leasing | DDR | ½ 2,109 |
| 31 Dec | Balance c/d | ½ 4,255 | 31 Dec | HM Revenue & Customs | DDR | ½ 6,508 |
| | | | 31 Dec | Bank charges | BP | ½ 18 |
| | | ½ 9,225 | | | | ½ 9,225 |
| | | | 2010 | | | |
| | | | 1 Jan | Balance b/d | | ½ 4,255 |

Date, details and amount must all be correct to earn each ½ mark indicated above.
Ignore the Chq No or Ref column.

4½ marks this page
15 marks b/f
19½ marks c/f

## Answer Question Five: Task D

The proprietor of Wendale Office Supplies, Mike Tasker, has asked for some information about VAT and some general matters. Answer his questions as set out below.

**(i)** Mike is confused by VAT terminology. In December 2009 Wendale Office Supplies' sales were £16,788.00 including VAT of £2,500.34. Is this VAT called 'input tax' or 'output tax'?

State 'input tax' or 'output tax':    Output tax   ½

**(ii)** Wendale Office Supplies has received an invoice from a supplier for £1,600 plus £280 VAT, sent an invoice to a customer for £3,000 plus £525 VAT, and sent a credit note to another customer for £800 plus £140 VAT. Taking just these three items together, tick which of the following statements is correct.

|  |  | Tick ✓ one |
|---|---|---|
| VAT due | £105 | ✓   1 |
| VAT due | £385 |  |
| VAT refund due | £105 |  |
| VAT refund due | £385 |  |

**(iii)** Mike understands that there are other rates of VAT besides the 'Standard Rate'. Name **two** of them for him:

1.    Zero Rate          ½

2.    Reduced Rate       ½

Also accept: Exempt, Outside the Scope.
Answers may be presented in any order.

**(iv)** The following transactions have taken place recently. Mike would like to know whether each transaction is an asset, capital, a liability, income or an expense.

| | Enter asset, capital, liability, income or expense | |
|---|---|---|
| £500 owed by customer B. Tyrone | Asset | ½ |
| £1,100 owed to supplier Pen 'n Ink Ltd | Liability | ½ |
| £10,000 of personal money introduced into the business by Mike Tasker | Capital | ½ |
| Shelving and display units costing £8,000 bought for use in the showroom | Asset | ½ |
| Monthly rent of £300 received from the tenant of the flat above the showroom | Income | ½ |
| £175 paid to waste disposal firm | Expense | ½ |

5½ marks this page
19½  marks b/f
25   marks total

Exam I/D 105

# QUESTION PAPER

## Qualification:
Level 2 Certificate in Book-keeping
(Qualification Accreditation Number 500/2993/9)

## Examination:
Single Unit – Book-keeping to Trial Balance

## Examination Date:
27 January 2010

**Time Allowed: 2 hours**

Suite 30, 40 Churchill Square, Kings Hill, West Malling, Kent, ME19 4YU
Tel: 0844 330 3527, Fax: 0844 330 3514, Email: education@iab.org.uk

## INTERNATIONAL ASSOCIATION OF BOOK-KEEPERS

| | |
|---|---|
| **QUALIFICATION TITLE:** | **LEVEL 2 CERTIFICATE IN BOOK-KEEPING** |
| **SINGLE UNIT TITLE:** | **BOOK-KEEPING TO TRIAL BALANCE** |
| **IAB QUALIFICATION I/D:** | **105** |

### General Information and Instructions

This question paper contains five questions within two Sections. You must answer FOUR questions as follows:

SECTION A:      Answer **both** questions in this section

- Question One carries 35 marks
- Question Two carries 15 marks

SECTION B:      Answer any **two** of the three questions in this Section

- All Questions carry 25 marks

1.  You must enter your **Student Number, Examination Entry Number (Candidate Number)** and **Name of Examination Centre** in the boxes provided on the front cover of your Answer Booklet.

2.  Time allowed: **2 hours**.

3.  All answers are to be written in **ink**.

4.  Cross out errors neatly, or use correcting fluid in moderation.

5.  The use of silent non-programmable calculators is permitted.

6.  If you answer or partly answer more than two questions from Section B, you must cross out the answer you do not want marking, otherwise we will take the marks of your first two answers.

7.  A workings page for question one is provided on page 4 of your Answer Booklet, and a blank page for other notes/workings is provided on page 12 of your Answer Booklet.

8.  NOTE – this Question Paper and the Answer Booklet have information and data printed on both sides of the pages contained within the booklets.

# IAB Level 2 question paper

**Scenario**

IAB Accounting Services is an accounting practice offering a wide range of services to its business clients including book-keeping/accounting services, and general help and advice with day-to-day financial matters.

You are employed by IAB Accounting Services as an Accounts Assistant. You are based in the company's town centre office and carry out tasks as instructed by the Accounts Manager.

You are now presented with a series of memos, notes, emails and other relevant information, and are required to complete the tasks in accordance with the examination instructions, i.e.:

| | | |
|---|---|---|
| **Section A** | – | Answer **both** questions in this section |
| **Section B** | – | Answer **any two** of the three questions in this section |

The Standard Rate of Value Added Tax (VAT) assumed in this examination is 17.5%.

**The tasks take place during the period 11 – 15 January 2010.**

341

## Section A – You must answer **both** questions in this section

### Question One

Today's date is 11 January 2010 and you have received the following email:

| Sent: | 11 January 2010 |
|---|---|
| From: | 'Senior Accounts Assistant' |
| To: | AccountsAssistant@iabaccservs.co.uk |
| Subject: | Stackit Shelving |
| Attachments: | 📎 List of Account Balances |

Our client Stackit Shelving has provided us with a list of account balances as at 31 December 2009 (see **page 6** of this **question paper**). The business is registered for VAT, and the Standard Rate of VAT in use is 17.5%. Stackit Shelving has a bank overdraft facility of £5,000 if required.

This morning I received a further communication from the owner of the business explaining that the following omissions and errors have since been discovered:

1.  A new machine for use in the business was bought on 31 December 2009. The equipment and installation cost £9,000 plus VAT £1,575, paid by cheque. The transaction has not yet been entered in the books.

2.  Stackit Shelving sublets a spare workshop at the rear of its premises for £2,000 per quarter (exempt from VAT). The cheque received from the tenant on 24 December 2009 was entered into the books as follows:

    > Debit – Rent Receivable £2,000
    > Credit – Bank £2,000

3.  Credit note CR6777 for £387 plus VAT issued on 10 December 2009 to a trade debtor (Woking Ltd) for goods returned was debited to the Sales account instead of the Sales Returns account. The VAT was posted correctly.

4.  VAT of £16,190 due to HM Revenue & Customs was paid by cheque on 19 December 2009. The cheque was completed correctly but the transaction was entered into the books as follows:

    > Debit – VAT £16,910
    > Credit – Bank £16,910

5.  Some computer peripherals costing a total of £470 plus VAT were entered as Stationery but should instead have been posted to the Computer & IT expense account. The VAT was posted correctly.

**(continues)**

342

## Question One (continued)

6.  Two other errors have been discovered:

    A discount of £18 was correctly posted to a trade debtor's account, but no entry was made in the Discount Allowed account.

    The same day, bank interest receivable of £18 was shown as a receipt on the bank statement on 15 December 2009. This was correctly posted to Bank, but no entry was made in the Bank Interest Receivable account.

You are required to complete the following tasks:

### REQUIRED

**A**   Prepare Journal entries to correct the omissions and errors listed above. You should date your entries 31 December 2009 and include suitable narratives.

*(16½ marks)*

**B**   Using the attached list of balances and the Journal entries you prepared in Task A, prepare a Trial Balance for Stackit Shelving as at 31 December 2009.

*(18½ marks)*

**35 marks total**

The following are provided in your **answer booklet (pages 2 to 5)** for your use in completing the above tasks:

- Journal
- Working area (this will not be marked)
- Trial Balance

**Question One (continued) – Attachment to Email**

**Stackit Shelving – List of Account Balances as at 31 December 2009**

|  | £ |  |
|---|---|---|
| Accountancy | 1,800 | |
| Bank (Current Account) | 905 | (DR) |
| Bank Charges | 391 | |
| Bank Interest Receivable | 87 | |
| Bank Loan | 35,000 | |
| Capital | 90,000 | |
| Cash in hand | 422 | |
| Computers (Cost) | 4,000 | |
| Computer & IT | 2,745 | |
| Discount Allowed | 142 | |
| Gas and Electricity | 1,948 | |
| Machinery (Cost) | 7,500 | |
| Postage | 730 | |
| Purchases | 18,375 | |
| Purchase Returns | 2,065 | |
| Rent Payable | 15,800 | |
| Rent Receivable | 4,000 | |
| Sales | 31,500 | |
| Sales Returns | 3,303 | |
| Stationery | 2,201 | |
| Trade Creditors | 20,203 | |
| Trade Debtors | 18,708 | |
| Value Added Tax (VAT) | 7,145 | (CR) |
| Vehicles (Cost) | 12,030 | |
| Wages and Salaries | 99,000 | |

Please note: Page 7 of this examination is intentionally blank.

344

# IAB Level 2 question paper

## Question Two

It is Tuesday 12 January 2010 and you have been sent to the premises of Paws Pet Shop.

Paws Pet Shop makes payments to suppliers by BACS (Banker's Automated Clearing Service) on the 15th of each month. The purpose of your visit is to set up a BACS payment to their main supplier, Wessex Pet Supplies.

You are provided with the following items (see **page 9** of this **question paper**):

- Wessex Pet Supplies' personal account in Paws Pet Shop's Purchase Ledger, balanced off as at 31 December 2009
- Extract from Paws Pet Shop's Purchase Day Book for January 2010
- An extract from Paws Pet Shop's Supplier File
- Banking and BACS information required to set up a BACS payment

You are told that all of Wessex Pet Supplies' outstanding invoices are to be settled. You should take the cash discount offered, but only when payment is being made within the agreed terms of business, i.e. 14 days.

It is confirmed that all items supplied by Wessex Pet Supplies have been subject to VAT at the Standard Rate of 17.5%.

You are required to complete the following tasks:

### REQUIRED

**A**   Enter the invoices listed in the Purchase Day Book for January 2010 into Wessex Pet Supplies' Purchase Ledger account.   *(1 mark)*

**B**   Prepare a Remittance Advice dated 12 January 2010 for the BACS payment in settlement of the four outstanding invoices from Wessex Pet Supplies, i.e.:

> 3050
> 3107
> 3182
> 3207

Where cash discounts are being taken, these should be clearly shown.   *(5 marks)*

**C**   Prepare a BACS Payment Listing dated 12 January 2010, ready for the owner of Paws Pet Shop to sign and deliver to the bank, in order that the money will be paid into Wessex Pet Supplies' bank account on 15 January 2010 (the "value date").   *(7 marks)*

**D**   Update Wessex Pet Supplies' personal account in the Purchase Ledger following the BACS payment, then balance and close off the account. All entries should be dated 15 January 2010.   *(2 marks)*

**15 marks total**

The following are provided in your **answer booklet (pages 6 to 7)** for your use in completing the above tasks:

- Purchase Ledger Account
- Remittance Advice
- BACS Payment Listing

## Question Two (continued)

**Paws Pet Shop – Purchase Ledger (Extract)**

### Paws Pet Shop
### Purchase Ledger (Extract)

| DR | | | Wessex Pet Supplies | | CR |
|---|---|---|---|---|---|
| **2009** | **Details** | **£** | **2009** | **Details** | **£** |
| 15 Dec | Bank | 5.640 | 15 Dec | Balance b/d | 5,840 |
| 15 Dec | Discount Received | 200 | 18 Dec | Purchases (Invoice 3050) | 650 |
| 31 Dec | Balance c/d | 1,550 | 27 Dec | Purchases (Invoice 3107) | 900 |
| | | 7,390 | | | 7,390 |
| **2010** | | | **2010** | | |
| | | | 1 Jan | Balance b/d | 1,550 |

**Paws Pet Shop – Purchase Day Book (Extract)**

| Date 2010 | Supplier | Supplier Invoice Number | Total Invoice £ | VAT £ | Net £ |
|---|---|---|---|---|---|
| 5 Jan | Wessex Pet Supplies | 3182 | 584 | 84 | 500 |
| 11 Jan | Wessex Pet Supplies | 3207 | 1,168 | 168 | 1,000 |

**Paws Pet Shop – Extract from Supplier File**

| Payee Reference Number | Supplier | Terms of Business | Bank Sort Code | Account Number |
|---|---|---|---|---|
| 77 | Wessex Pet Supplies | 4% 14 days or net 30 days | 99-88-77 | 78780202 |

**Paws Pet Shop – Banking and BACS Information**

| Bank | Southern Bank Plc |
|---|---|
| **Bank Branch** | Redbury |
| **BACS Originator Name** | Paws Pet Shop |
| **BACS Originator Reference** | PAW3434 |
| **Account Name** | Paws Pet Shop |
| **Sort Code** | 44-55-22 |
| **Account Number** | 12340012 |

# IAB Level 2 question paper

**Section B** – You must answer **any two** of the questions in this section

### Question Three

It is Wednesday 13 January 2010 and you have been asked to visit Phil Parks and Gloria Ingham, business partners in Red Dragon, a casual clothes and sportswear shop.

#### VAT Account and VAT Return

The partnership is registered for VAT, and the first of your tasks today is to complete their VAT return. The following totals have been extracted from Red Dragon's books and show the information relating to VAT during the VAT quarter ended 31 December 2009, none of which has yet been posted to the VAT Account:

| Source | VAT £ |
|---|---|
| Sales Day Book | 21,725 |
| Sales Returns Day Book | 2,800 |
| Cash Sales | 25,700 |
| Purchase Day Book | 32,603 |
| Purchase Returns Day Book | 1,970 |
| Purchase of fixed assets | 1,175 |
| Petty Cash Expenses | 42 |

All items sold and purchased by Red Dragon during the period above were subject to VAT at the standard rate (17.5%). All the above transactions were made within the United Kingdom; there were no transactions with other EC Member States.

#### Sales Invoice

On 1st January 2010, to celebrate the 10th anniversary of their business, Phil and Gloria started selling children's clothes to complement their adult range. They realise that this makes completion of sales invoices more complicated, and they require your help to complete an invoice to credit customer All Ages Sports Club (**see page 10 of the answer booklet**). All Ages Sports Club receives a 10% trade discount and a 5% cash settlement discount.

#### Supplier Statement of Account Reconciliation

You are provided with the Statement of Account as at 31 December 2009 received from supplier Hyper Ltd, together with their personal account within Red Dragon's Purchase Ledger (see **pages 12 and 13** of this **question paper**) in order that you may reconcile the two balances.

**(continues)**

**Question Three (continued)**

You are now required to complete the following tasks:

**REQUIRED**

**A**    Enter the postings for the quarter ended 31 December 2009 to the VAT account within the General Ledger of Red Dragon. Balance off the account as at 31 December 2009, bringing down the balance as at 1 January 2010.   *(6 marks)*

**B**    Using the information prepared in Task A, complete the VAT Return for the quarter ended 31 December 2009.   *(6 marks)*

**C**    Complete the Sales Invoice to All Ages Sports Club (invoice 5602).   *(8 marks)*

**D**    Complete a Reconciliation Statement as at 31 December 2009 between the personal account of Hyper Ltd within the purchase ledger of Red Dragon, and Hyper Ltd's Statement of Account of the same date.

    **NB:** when listing adjustments, be sure to indicate clearly which figures are to be added, and which are to be subtracted.   *(5 marks)*

**25 marks total**

The following are provided in your **answer booklet (pages 8 to 11)** for your use in completing the above tasks:

- VAT account
- VAT Return
- Sales invoice
- Reconciliation statement

## Question Three (continued)

**Hyper Ltd – Supplier Statement of Account**

### STATEMENT OF ACCOUNT

| **From:** | Hyper Ltd | **To:** | Red Dragon |
| | Sportsware House | | 6 Red Dragon Yard |
| | Upper Mersey Road | | BEDDLING |
| | LIVERPOOL | | BD7 1LP |
| | L5 2EE | | |

**Date:** 31 December 2009     **Account reference:** RED015

| Date | Details | Debit £ | Credit £ | Balance £ |
|------|---------|--------|---------|----------|
| 1 Dec 2009 | Balance b/d | | | 3,073 |
| 1 Dec 2009 | Sales (Invoice 9782) | 490 | | 3,563 |
| 1 Dec 2009 | Sales Returns (Credit Note C620) | | 73 | 3,490 |
| 7 Dec 2009 | Sales (Invoice 9810) | 640 | | 4,130 |
| 12 Dec 2009 | Sales (Invoice 9860) | 219 | | 4,349 |
| 13 Dec 2009 | Sales Returns (Credit Note 638) | | 640 | 3,709 |
| 23 Dec 2009 | Sales (invoice 9899) | 710 | | 4,419 |
| 28 Dec 2009 | Payment Received – Thank You | | 1,000 | 3,419 |
| 29 Dec 2009 | Sales (Invoice 9937) | 472 | | 3,891 |
| 31 Dec 2009 | Sales Returns (Credit Note C648) | | 19 | 3,872 |
| | AMOUNT DUE | | | 3,872 |

| Current | Period 1 | Period 2 | Period 3 | Older |
|---------|----------|----------|----------|-------|
| £ 1,872 | £ 2,000 | £ 0.00 | £ 0.00 | £ 0.00 |

VAT Reg No: 789 3456 23

**Question Three (continued)**

**Red Dragon – Purchase Ledger (Extract)**

**Red Dragon**
**Purchase Ledger (Extract)**

| DR | | | Hyper Ltd | | CR |
|---|---|---|---|---|---|
| **2009** | **Details** | **£** | **2009** | **Details** | **£** |
| 3 Dec | Purchase Returns (Credit Note C620) | 73 | 1 Dec | Balance b/d | 3,073 |
| 16 Dec | Purchase Returns (Credit Note C638) | 640 | 3 Dec | Purchases (Invoice 9782) | 490 |
| 24 Dec | Bank | 1,000 | 10 Dec | Purchases (Invoice 9810) | 640 |
| 30 Dec | Bank | 2,000 | 15 Dec | Purchases (Invoice 9860) | 219 |
| 31 Dec | Balance c/d | 1,419 | 29 Dec | Purchases (Invoice 9899) | 710 |
| | | 5,132 | | | 5,132 |
| | | | **2010** | | |
| | | | 1 Jan | Balance b/d | 1,419 |

350

## Question Four

It is 14 January 2010 and you have been asked to attend the premises of Unicast Ltd.

---

**Memo**                                              **Date:** 14 January 2010

**From:**       Barbara Betzler, Accounts Assistant
**To:**         Accounts Assistant, IAB Accounting Services
**Subject:**    Purchase Day Book, Purchase Returns Day Book

Thank you for helping us complete our weekly day book procedures in my absence.

Unicast Ltd is registered for VAT, and maintains a sub-divided book-keeping system including Purchase Day Book and Purchase Returns Day Book which are totalled weekly. I have provided you with these for the week ending Friday 8 January 2010 (**see page 15 of the answer booklet**).

I have also provided you with a list of Purchase Ledger and General Ledger account codes and account balances brought down as at 4 January 2010, and an extract from the Cash Book listing cheques paid to suppliers and discounts received during the week ended 8 January 2010 (see **page 15** of this **question paper**).

You are required to complete the following tasks:

### REQUIRED

**A**    Enter the General Ledger and Purchase Ledger account balances brought down as at 4 January 2010 into the accounts provided.                                    *(5 marks)*

**B**    In the Purchase Day Book and Purchase Returns Day Book, enter the purchase ledger code against each supplier. Then enter each invoice and credit note in the appropriate Purchase Ledger account. **NB:** be sure to include the invoice number or credit note number in the details column.                                    *(6 marks)*

**C**    Code the Purchase Day Book and Purchase Returns Day Book totals, indicating whether debit or credit, then enter the totals into the General Ledger. Date your entries 8 January 2010.                                    *(9 marks)*

**D**    Enter the cheques paid to suppliers and the discounts received during the week ended 8 January 2010 into appropriate Purchase Ledger and General Ledger accounts.                                    *(4 marks)*

**E**    Balance off the Purchase Ledger Control Account, bringing down the balance as at 11 January 2010. **NB:** you are **not** required to balance off other accounts.    *(1 mark)*

**Signed:** *Barbara Betzler*

---

**25 marks**

The following are provided in your **answer booklet (pages 13 to 15)** for your use in completing the above tasks:

- General Ledger (extract)
- Purchase Ledger (complete)
- Purchase Day Book, Purchase Returns Day Book

**Question Four (continued)**

**Unicast Ltd – Account Coding and Account Balances**

| | Account Code | Balance b/d 4 January 2010 £ |
|---|---|---|
| **General Ledger (extract)** | | |
| Purchase Ledger Control | GL 2100 | 11,422 |
| Value Added Tax (VAT) | GL 2500 | 2,910 (CR) |
| Purchases | GL 5000 | 55,506 |
| Purchase Returns | GL 5100 | 8,900 |
| Discounts Received | GL 5200 | 842 |
| | | |
| **Purchase Ledger (complete)** | | |
| Alleyn Bros | PL 0010 | 1,500 |
| Norton Industries | PL 0050 | 5,125 |
| Redbridge Plc | PL 0020 | --- |
| Trend CAD | PL 0040 | 1,765 |
| Vine & Pierce Ltd | PL 0030 | 3,032 |

**Unicast Ltd – Cash Book (Extract)**

**Cheques paid to Suppliers and Discounts Received, extracted from the Cash Book for the week ended 8 January 2010**

| Date 2010 | Supplier | Cheque Payments £ | Discount Received £ |
|---|---|---|---|
| 8 Jan | Alleyn Bros | 312 | --- |
| 8 Jan | Vine & Pierce Ltd | 2,902 | 130 |
| 8 Jan | Trend CAD | 504 | 11 |
| | **Total** | 3,718 | 141 |

## Question Five

It is 15 January 2010 and you have received the following email:

| | |
|---|---|
| **Sent:** | 15 January 2010 |
| **From:** | 'Senior Accounts Assistant' |
| **To:** | AccountsAssistant@iabaccservs.co.uk |
| **Subject:** | Tasty Preserves |
| **Attachments:** | 🖹 Transactions with credit customers; 🖹 Schedule of Debtors; 🖹 General Ledger and Cash Book extracts |

### Sales Ledger Control Account Reconciliation

Jean Scurr founded her jams and pickles business Tasty Preserves seven years ago. We maintain her books of account. At the end of each month we prepare a Sales Ledger Control Account as the basis of checking total debtor balances. The balance on the Sales Ledger Control Account as at 1 December 2009 was £15,290.

I attach a list of Tasty Preserve's transactions with credit customers in December 2009 together with a Schedule of Debtors as at 31 December 2009 (see **page 18** of this **question paper**). Please complete the reconciliation specified in Tasks A and B below.

### Payroll Queries – Month 9 (December 2009)

Jean has mislaid the payroll information that we sent to her for the month of December 2009, and she has asked if we would compile the information again. I attach extracts from the relevant General Ledger accounts showing all payroll-related postings made during December 2009, from which you may obtain the information that is required (see **page 19** of this **question paper**).

I can confirm that employees at Tasty Preserves are paid monthly on the last day of each month. All items contributing to the cost of employment are processed through a Wages Control Account. There is a contributory pension scheme provided by United Pensions. When the postings to the Wages Control Account for the month are complete, the balance on the Wages Control Account is transferred to the Wages and Contributions Expense Account.

### Basic Accounting Concepts

Jean Scurr is keen to learn more about accounting, and has asked if we would give her some information about the basic accounting concepts.

**(continues)**

353

**Question Five (continued)**

You are required to complete the following tasks:

**REQUIRED**

**A**     Prepare the Sales Ledger Control Account for the month ended 31 December 2009,
bringing down the balance as at that date.                                      *(7½ marks)*

**B**     Total the personal account balances per the Sales Ledger as at 31 December 2009.
Then reconcile this total to the balance on the Sales Ledger Control Account as at 31
December 2009.                                                                  *(3 marks)*

**C**     Using the General Ledger and Cash Book extracts provided, complete the Table of
Payroll Information in your answer booklet for Month 9 (December 2009).
                                                                                *(10½ marks)*

**D**     Answer the questions in your answer booklet about the basic accounting concepts.
                                                                                *(4 marks)*

**25 marks total**

The following are provided in your **answer booklet (pages 16 to 18)** for your use in
completing the above tasks:

- Sales Ledger Control Account
- Reconciliation form
- Questions and space for answers to Task C
- Questions and space for answers to Task D

## Question Five (continued) – Attachments to Email

**Tasty Preserves – Transactions with Credit Customers, totals for month of December 2009**

|  | £ |
|---|---|
| Sales Day Book - Sales (including VAT) | 14,205 |
| Sales Returns Day Book - Sales returns (including VAT) | 1,007 |
| Cash Book - Receipts from debtors | 15,700 |
| Cash Book - Discounts Allowed | 348 |
| Journal - Customer account balance (East Bryle Village Shop) written off as a Bad Debt | 2,840 |

**Tasty Preserves – Schedule of Debtors (Complete)**

|  | 31 December 2009 |
|---|---|
|  | £ |
| Ashington Stores | 560 |
| Dingles Cafe | 140 |
| F & R Jack Ltd | 1,826 |
| Lime Street Brasserie | 2,258 |
| Peter's Place | 25 |
| Rogers Catering Company | 3,701 |
| The Speedy Sarnie Co. | 1,025 |
| Westbridge Farm Shop | 65 |

## Question Five (continued) – Attachments to Email

Tasty Preserves – General Ledger and Cash Book (Extracts)

**Tasty Preserves**
**General Ledger and Cash Book (Extracts)**

| DR | | | | Wages Control | | CR |
|---|---|---|---|---|---|---|
| **2009** | **Details** | **£** | **2009** | **Details** | | **£** |
| 31 Dec | Bank | 10,200 | 31 Dec | Wages and Contributions Expense | | 14,600 |
| 31 Dec | PAYE | 1,575 | | | | |
| 31 Dec | NIC (employee) | 650 | | | | |
| 31 Dec | NIC (employer) | 1,100 | | | | |
| 31 Dec | Pension (employee) | 450 | | | | |
| 31 Dec | Pension (employer) | 625 | | | | |
| | | 14,600 | | | | 14,600 |

| DR | | | | Wages and Contributions Expense | CR |
|---|---|---|---|---|---|
| **2009** | **Details** | **£** | **2009** | **Details** | **£** |
| 1 Dec | Balance b/d | 81,492 | 31 Dec | Balance c/d | 96,092 |
| 31 Dec | Wages Control | 14,600 | | | |
| | | 96,092 | | | 96,092 |
| **2010** | | | | | |
| 1 Jan | Balance b/d | 96,092 | | | |

| DR | | | | PAYE/NIC Creditor | CR |
|---|---|---|---|---|---|
| **2009** | **Details** | **£** | **2009** | **Details** | **£** |
| 15 Dec | Bank | 2,875 | 1 Dec | Balance b/d | 2,875 |
| 31 Dec | Balance c/d | 3,325 | 31 Dec | PAYE | 1,575 |
| | | | 31 Dec | NIC (employee) | 650 |
| | | | 31 Dec | NIC (employer) | 1,100 |
| | | 6,200 | | | 6,200 |
| | | | **2010** | | |
| | | | 1 Jan | Balance b/d | 3,325 |

| DR | | | | United Pensions Creditor | CR |
|---|---|---|---|---|---|
| **2009** | **Details** | **£** | **2009** | **Details** | **£** |
| 15 Dec | Bank | 950 | 1 Dec | Balance b/d | 950 |
| 31 Dec | Balance c/d | 1,075 | 31 Dec | Pension (employee) | 450 |
| | | | 31 Dec | Pension (employer) | 625 |
| | | 2,025 | | | 2,025 |
| | | | **2010** | | |
| | | | 1 Jan | Balance b/d | 1,075 |

| DR | | | | Cash Book (Bank Columns only) | CR |
|---|---|---|---|---|---|
| **2009** | **Details** | **£** | **2009** | **Details** | **£** |
| 1 Dec | Balance b/d | 17,899 | 15 Dec | PAYE/NIC | 2,875 |
| | | | 15 Dec | United Pensions | 950 |
| | | | 31 Dec | Wages Control | 10,200 |

*Qualifications for business*

Exam I/D 105

# ANSWER BOOKLET

### Qualification:
Level 2 Certificate in Book-keeping
(Qualification Accreditation Number 500/2993/9)

### Examination:
Single Unit – Book-keeping to Trial Balance

### Examination Date:
27 January 2010

| Student Number: | |
|---|---|
| Candidate Number: | |
| Name of Examination Centre: | |

For use by assessor only:

| | Section A<br>Answer **both** questions in this section | | Section B<br>Answer **any two** questions in this section | | | |
|---|---|---|---|---|---|---|
| Question number | 1 | 2 | 3 | 4 | 5 | Total |
| Maximum marks | 35 | 15 | 25 | 25 | 25 | 100 |
| Marks awarded | | | | | | |

Suite 30, 40 Churchill Square, Kings Hill, West Malling, Kent, ME19 4YU
Tel: 0844 330 3527, Fax: 0844 330 3514, Email: education@iab.org.uk

# IAB Level 2 answer booklet

**Section A** – You must answer **both** questions in this section

**For use in answering Question One: Task A**

**Stackit Shelving - Journal**

**Stackit Shelving**
**Journal**

| Date 2009 | Details | DR £ | CR £ |
|-----------|---------|------|------|
|           |         |      |      |
|           |         |      |      |
|           |         |      |      |
|           |         |      |      |
|           |         |      |      |

# IAB Level 2 answer booklet

**For use in answering Question One: Task A (continued)**

**Stackit Shelving - Journal**

**Stackit Shelving**
**Journal**

| Date 2009 | Details | DR £ | CR £ |
|-----------|---------|------|------|
|           |         |      |      |
|           |         |      |      |
|           |         |      |      |

# IAB Level 2 answer booklet

**Candidates may find it helpful to use this workings area to set out the ledger account balances before redrafting the Trial Balance.**

| Ledger Account | DR £ | CR £ |
|---|---|---|
| Accountancy | | |
| Bank (Current Account) | | |
| Bank Charges | | |
| Bank Interest Receivable | | |
| Bank Loan | | |
| Capital | | |
| Cash in hand | | |
| Computers (Cost) | | |
| Computer & IT | | |
| Discount Allowed | | |
| Gas and Electricity | | |
| Machinery (Cost) | | |
| Postage | | |
| Purchases | | |
| Purchase Returns | | |
| Rent Payable | | |
| Rent Receivable | | |
| Sales | | |
| Sales Returns | | |
| Stationery | | |
| Trade Creditors | | |
| Trade Debtors | | |
| Value Added Tax (VAT) | | |
| Vehicles (Cost) | | |
| Wages and Salaries | | |
| | | |

# IAB Level 2 answer booklet

**For use in answering Question One: Task B**

Stackit Shelving – Trial Balance as at 31 December 2009

**Stackit Shelving**
**Trial Balance as at 31 December 2009**

| Ledger Account | DR £ | CR £ |
|---|---|---|
| Accountancy | | |
| Bank (Current Account) | | |
| Bank Charges | | |
| Bank Interest Receivable | | |
| Bank Loan | | |
| Capital | | |
| Cash in hand | | |
| Computers (Cost) | | |
| Computer & IT | | |
| Discount Allowed | | |
| Gas and Electricity | | |
| Machinery (Cost) | | |
| Postage | | |
| Purchases | | |
| Purchase Returns | | |
| Rent Payable | | |
| Rent Receivable | | |
| Sales | | |
| Sales Returns | | |
| Stationery | | |
| Trade Creditors | | |
| Trade Debtors | | |
| Value Added Tax (VAT) | | |
| Vehicles (Cost) | | |
| Wages and Salaries | | |
| | | |

**For use in answering Question Two: Tasks A and D**

**Paws Pet Shop – Purchase Ledger (Extract)**

**Paws Pet Shop**
**Purchase Ledger (Extract)**

| DR | | | Wessex Pet Supplies | | CR |
|---|---|---|---|---|---|
| **2010** | **Details** | **£** | **2010** | **Details** | **£** |
| | | | 1 Jan | Balance b/d | 1,550 |

**For use in answering Question Two: Task B**

**Paws Pet Shop – Remittance Advice**

| | REMITTANCE ADVICE | | |
|---|---|---|---|
| **From:** Paws Pet Shop<br>The Arcade<br>Redbury<br>RE56 7WQ | **To:** _____ | | |
| | **Date:** _____ | | |
| | | Amount | |
| **Details** | | **£** | **p** |
| | | | |
| | | | |
| Payment by: **BACS** | | | |

# IAB Level 2 answer booklet

**For use in answering Question Two:  Task C**

**Paws Pet Shop – BACS Payment Listing**

## SOUTHERN BANK PLC - BACS PAYMENT LISTING

Bank Branch: _____

BACS Originator Name: _____

BACS Originator Reference: _____

Date: _____

| Payee Name | Payee Reference Number | Bank Sort Code | Account Number | Amount £ | p |
|---|---|---|---|---|---|
|  |  |  |  |  |  |
|  |  |  |  |  |  |
|  |  |  |  |  |  |
|  |  |  |  |  |  |
|  |  |  |  |  |  |
|  |  | **BATCH TOTAL** |  |  |  |

Value date _____

Account Name _____

Sort Code _____

Account Number _____

Authorised Signature(s) _____

_____

# IAB Level 2 answer booklet

**Section B** – You must answer **any two** of the questions in this section

**For use in answering Question Three:  Task A**

**Red Dragon – VAT account**

Red Dragon
General Ledger (Extract)

| DR | | | Value Added Tax (VAT) | | CR |
|---|---|---|---|---|---|
| **Date** | **Details** | **£** | **Date** | **Details** | **£** |
| 2009 | | | 2009 | | |
| 20 Oct | Bank | 11,305 | 1 Oct | Balance b/d | 11,305 |

# IAB Level 2 answer booklet

**For use in answering Question Three: Task B**

**Red Dragon – VAT Return for the Quarter ended 31 December 2009**

|  | BOX | £ | P |
|---|---|---|---|
| VAT due in this period on sales | 1 |  |  |
| VAT due in this period on EC acquisitions | 2 |  |  |
| Total VAT due (sum of boxes 1 and 2) | 3 |  |  |
| VAT reclaimed in this period on purchases | 4 |  |  |
| **Net VAT to be paid to H.M. Revenue & Customs or reclaimed by you** | 5 |  |  |
| Total value of sales, excluding VAT | 6 |  | 00 |
| Total value of purchases, excluding VAT | 7 |  | 00 |
| Total value of EC sales, excluding VAT | 8 |  | 00 |
| Total value of EC purchases, excluding VAT | 9 |  | 00 |

**Notes:**

1. The Box 1 figure above (VAT due in this period on sales) is the total of all output tax in the period less the VAT debited to the VAT account in respect of VAT refunded to customers on credit notes for sales returns.

2. The Box 4 figure above (VAT reclaimed in this period on purchases) is the total of all input tax in the period less the VAT credited to the VAT account in respect of VAT refunded by suppliers on credit notes for purchase returns.

365

**For use in answering Question Three: Task C**

**Red Dragon – Sales Invoice**

**NB:** 13 figures must be entered to complete this invoice correctly

## INVOICE

### 'Red Dragon'
Est. 2000
**6 Red Dragon Yard, Beddling
BD7 1LP**

**To:**
All Ages Sports Club
Beddling Leisure Centre
The Roundabout
Beddling
BD8 6CD

**Invoice number**   5602

**Order No:**   2010 / 27          **Date (Tax Point):**          13 January 2010

| Qty | Description | VAT rate % | Unit Price £ | Unit Price p | Total £ | Total p |
|---|---|---|---|---|---|---|
| 15 | Men's 'Cobra' Cotton T-Shirt, Size L | 17.5 | 14 | 50 | | |
| 15 | Ladies' 'Zebra' Cotton T-Shirt, Size M | 17.5 | 11 | 50 | | |
| 10 | Unisex Hi-Visibility Sports Fleece, Size ML | 17.5 | 33 | 00 | | |
| 20 | Child's 'Zig' Polyester Cotton T-Shirt, 8-10 | 0 | 8 | 99 | | |
| 10 | Child's 'Zag' Polyester Cotton T-Shirt, 8-10 | 0 | 7 | 99 | | |

**TERMS:** 5% 14 days / 30 days net

| **Goods Total** | | |
| **Less Trade Discount: 10%** | | |
| **Net Goods** | | |
| **VAT** | | |
| **Invoice Total** | £ | |

| VAT ANALYSIS | | |
|---|---|---|
| VAT Rate | Total Net £ | Total VAT £ |
| 17.5% | | |
| 0.0% | | 0.00 |

E. & O.E.  Carriage paid.  VAT Reg No: 321 4321 56

Partners: P Parks, G Ingham

# IAB Level 2 answer booklet

**For use in answering Question Three: Task D**

**Red Dragon – Reconciliation Statement**

**Red Dragon**
**Reconciliation of Purchase Ledger Account**
**to Supplier Statement of Account**
**(Hyper Ltd)**
**as at 31 December 2009**

| | £ |
|---|---|
| Balance per supplier account in Purchase Ledger | |
| Adjustments – unticked items on Statement: | |
| | |
| Adjustments – unticked items in Purchase Ledger: | |
| | |
| Balance per Supplier Statement | |

Please note: Page 12 of this answer booklet is intentionally blank.

# IAB Level 2 answer booklet

**For use in answering Question Four: Tasks A, C, D and E**

Unicast Ltd – General Ledger (extract)

**Unicast Ltd**
**General Ledger (extract)**

| DR | | | Purchase Ledger Control (GL 2100) | | | CR |
|---|---|---|---|---|---|---|
| **2010** | **Details** | **£** | **2010** | **Details** | | **£** |
| | | | | | | |

| DR | | | Value Added Tax (GL 2500) | | | CR |
|---|---|---|---|---|---|---|
| **2010** | **Details** | **£** | **2010** | **Details** | | **£** |
| | | | | | | |

| DR | | | Purchases (GL 5000) | | | CR |
|---|---|---|---|---|---|---|
| **2010** | **Details** | **£** | **2010** | **Details** | | **£** |
| | | | | | | |

| DR | | | Purchase Returns (GL 5100) | | | CR |
|---|---|---|---|---|---|---|
| **2010** | **Details** | **£** | **2010** | **Details** | | **£** |
| | | | | | | |

| DR | | | Discount Received (GL 5200) | | | CR |
|---|---|---|---|---|---|---|
| **2010** | **Details** | **£** | **2010** | **Details** | | **£** |
| | | | | | | |

# IAB Level 2 answer booklet

**For use in answering Question Four: Tasks A, B, D and E**

Unicast Ltd - Purchase Ledger (complete)

**Unicast Ltd**
**Purchase Ledger (complete)**

| DR | | | Alleyn Bros (PL 0010) | | | CR |
|---|---|---|---|---|---|---|
| 2010 | Details | £ | 2010 | Details | | £ |

| DR | | | Norton Industries (PL 0050) | | | CR |
|---|---|---|---|---|---|---|
| 2010 | Details | £ | 2010 | Details | | £ |

| DR | | | Redbridge Plc (PL 0020) | | | CR |
|---|---|---|---|---|---|---|
| 2010 | Details | £ | 2010 | Details | | £ |

| DR | | | Trend CAD (PL 0040) | | | CR |
|---|---|---|---|---|---|---|
| 2010 | Details | £ | 2010 | Details | | £ |

| DR | | | Vine & Pierce Ltd (PL 0030) | | | CR |
|---|---|---|---|---|---|---|
| 2010 | Details | £ | 2010 | Details | | £ |

**For use in answering Question Four: Tasks B and C**

Unicast Ltd – Purchase Day Book and Purchase Returns Day Book

### Unicast Ltd - Purchase Day Book

| Invoice Date 2010 | Supplier | Purchase Ledger Code | Supplier's Invoice Number | Total £ | VAT £ | Net £ |
|---|---|---|---|---|---|---|
| 4 Jan | Redbridge Plc | | 7895 | 4,700 | 700 | 4,000 |
| 5 Jan | Vine & Pierce Ltd | | 1054 | 1,399 | 199 | 1,200 |
| 6 Jan | Trend CAD | | INV899 | 936 | 136 | 800 |
| 8 Jan | Norton Industries | | 66003 | 282 | 42 | 240 |
| | | | **TOTALS** | 7,317 | 1,077 | 6,240 |
| | | **GENERAL LEDGER CODE** | | | | |
| | | **DEBIT OR CREDIT** | | | | |

### Unicast Ltd - Purchase Returns Day Book

| Invoice Date 2010 | Supplier | Purchase Ledger Code | Supplier's Credit Note Number | Total £ | VAT £ | Net £ |
|---|---|---|---|---|---|---|
| 6 Jan | Alleyn Bros | | CR682 | 188 | 28 | 160 |
| 7 Jan | Norton Industries | | 5043 | 282 | 42 | 240 |
| | | | **TOTALS** | 470 | 70 | 400 |
| | | **GENERAL LEDGER CODE** | | | | |
| | | **DEBIT OR CREDIT** | | | | |

**For use in answering Question Five:  Task A**

Tasty Preserves – Sales Ledger Control Account

**Tasty Preserves**
**General Ledger (Extract)**

| DR | | | | Sales Ledger Control | | | | CR |
|---|---|---|---|---|---|---|---|---|
| 2009 | Details | | £ | | 2009 | Details | | £ |

**For use in answering Question Five:  Task B**

**Tasty Preserves - Reconciliation of Personal Account Balances per Sales Ledger as at 31 December 2009 to Sales Ledger Control Account Balance as at that Date**

| | £ | DR/CR |
|---|---|---|
| Total debtors per Sales Ledger – 31 December 2009 | | |
| Balance per Sales Ledger Control Account – 31 December 2009 | | |
| Difference | | |

# IAB Level 2 answer booklet

**For use in answering Question Five: Task C**

**Tasty Preserves – Table of Payroll Information, Month 9 (December 2009)**

### Table of Payroll Information
### Month 9 (December 2009)

| | | |
|---|---|---|
| **Net Pay** | | £ |
| PAYE | £ | |
| Employee National Insurance | £ | |
| Employee Pension | £ | |
| Total Employee Deductions | | £ |
| **Gross Pay** | | £ |
| Employer National Insurance | £ | |
| Employer Pension | £ | |
| Total Employer Contributions | | £ |
| **Cost of Employment for Month** | | £ |
| Due to H M Revenue & Customs | | £ |
| Due to United Pensions | | £ |
| Total Cost of Employment, Year to Date | | £ |

# IAB Level 2 answer booklet

**For use in answering Question Five:  Task D**

**Tasty Preserves – Basic Accounting Concepts**

Jean Scurr's jams and pickles business Tasty Preserves has been very successful, despite her having no detailed knowledge of book-keeping or accounting.

She is now showing more interest in the work of IAB Accounting Services and has heard that 'accounting concepts' are the principles which underpin the books of account.

Examine her comments below, and state which of the **four basic accounting concepts** is being referred to in each case.

**i)**  Jean Scurr is very proud of her staff whose hard work and loyalty is vital to the continuing success of Tasty Preserves.  State the basic accounting concept which prevents these attributes from being recorded in the books of account:

_____

**ii)**  Jean frequently complains that IAB Accounting Services keeps the business transactions of Tasty Preserves separate from her own private financial affairs.  State the basic accounting concept which IAB Accounting Services is following:

_____

**iii)**  Jean has noticed that her cooking, canning and packaging machinery is shown in the books of account at the cost that she bought it some years ago, rather than at today's prices.  State the basic accounting concept which IAB Accounting Services is following:

_____

**iv)**  Jean has been told that IAB Accounting Services enter every transaction into her books twice, as a debit and as a credit.  State the basic accounting concept behind this double entry procedure:

_____

Exam I/D 105

# MODEL ANSWERS

### Qualification:
Level 2 Certificate in Book-keeping
(Qualification Accreditation Number 500/2993/9)

### Examination:
Single Unit – Book-keeping to Trial Balance

### Examination Date:
27 January 2010

Suite 30, 40 Churchill Square, Kings Hill, West Malling, Kent, ME19 4YU
Tel: 0844 330 3527, Fax: 0844 330 3514, Email: education@iab.org.uk

# IAB Level 2 model answers

**Answer Question One:  Task A**

**Stackit Shelving - Journal**

### Stackit Shelving
### Journal

| Date 2009 | Details | | DR £ | | CR £ | |
|---|---|---|---|---|---|---|
| 31 Dec | Machinery (Cost) | ½ | ½ | 9,000 | | |
| | VAT | ½ | ½ | 1,575 | | |
| | Bank | ½ | | | ½ | 10,575 |
| | Purchase of machine for use in the business. ½ | | | | | |
| | Allow 'error of omission' | | | | | |
| 31 Dec | Bank | ¼ | ¼ | 2,000 | | |
| | Rent receivable | ¼ | | | ¼ | 2,000 |
| | Bank | ¼ | ¼ | 2,000 | | |
| | Rent receivable | ¼ | | | ¼ | 2,000 |
| | Correction of error of reversal. Rent received posted with debit and credit entries reversed. ½ | | | | | |
| | **Alternative:** | | | | | |
| | Bank | ½ | ½ | 4,000 | | |
| | Rent receivable | ½ | | | ½ | 4,000 |
| 31 Dec | Sales Returns | ½ | ½ | 387 | | |
| | Sales | ½ | | | ½ | 387 |
| | Correction of allocation error.  Sales Returns debited to Sales in error. ½ | | | | | |
| | Allow 'error of commission' | | | | | |

Usual journal marking rules apply, i.e. marks can be given for correct account names with incorrect figures, but correct figures will only receive the marks if the account names are correct.

8½ marks this page c/f

**Answer Question One:  Task A (continued)**

**Stackit Shelving - Journal**

Stackit Shelving
Journal

| Date 2009 | Details | | DR £ | CR £ |
|---|---|---|---|---|
| 31 Dec | Bank | ¼ | ¼ 16,910 | |
| | VAT | ¼ | | ¼ 16,910 |
| | VAT | ¼ | ¼ 16,190 | |
| | Bank | ¼ | | ¼ 16,190 |
| | Correction of transposition error, VAT payment of £16,190 entered as £16,910.   ½ | | | |
| | Alternative: | | | |
| | Bank | ½ | ½ 720 | |
| | VAT | ½ | | ½ 720 |
| 31 Dec | Computer & IT | ½ | ½ 470 | |
| | Stationery | ½ | | ½ 470 |
| | Correction of allocation error.  Computer & IT equipment put to Stationery.   ½ | | | |
| | Allow 'error of commission'  Also allow 'error of principle' because candidate may have treated Computer & IT as a cost account rather than expenses account. | | | |
| 31 Dec | Discount Allowed | ½ | ½ 18 | |
| | Bank Interest Receivable | ½ | | ½ 18 |
| | Correction of compensating errors. *   ½ Discount Allowed debit entry omitted, and Bank Interest Receivable credit entry omitted.   ½ | | | |
| | * Award this additional ½ mark if narrative shows awareness that these are compensating errors. | | | |

8   marks this page
8½   marks b/f
16½   marks c/f

IAB L2 Certificate Jan 2010  MA (past paper)                 Page 3

376

**Answer Question One:  Task B**

**Stackit Shelving – Trial Balance as at 31 December 2009**

### Stackit Shelving
### Trial Balance as at 31 December 2009

| Ledger Account | | | DR £ | CR £ | |
|---|---|---|---|---|---|
| Accountancy | | ½ | 1,800 | | |
| Bank (Current Account) | 10,575CR  2,000DR  2,000DR  16,910DR  16190CR | | | 4,950 | 1 |
| Bank Charges | | ½ | 391 | | |
| Bank Interest Receivable | 18CR | | | 105 | 1 |
| Bank Loan | | | | 35,000 | ½ |
| Capital | | | | 90,000 | ½ |
| Cash in hand | | ½ | 422 | | |
| Computers (Cost) | | ½ | 4,000 | | |
| Computer & IT | 470DR | 1 | 3,215 | | |
| Discount Allowed | 18DR | 1 | 160 | | |
| Gas and Electricity | | ½ | 1,948 | | |
| Machinery (Cost) | 9,000DR | 1 | 16,500 | | |
| Postage | | ½ | 730 | | |
| Purchases | | ½ | 18,375 | | |
| Purchase Returns | | | | 2,065 | ½ |
| Rent Payable | | ½ | 15,800 | | |
| Rent Receivable | 2,000CR  2,000CR | | | 8,000 | 1 |
| Sales | 387CR | | | 31,887 | 1 |
| Sales Returns | 387DR | 1 | 3,690 | | |
| Stationery | 470CR | 1 | 1,731 | | |
| Trade Creditors | | | | 20,203 | ½ |
| Trade Debtors | | ½ | 18,708 | | |
| Value Added Tax (VAT) | 1,575DR  16,910CR  16,190DR | | | 6,290 | 1 |
| Vehicles (Cost) | | ½ | 12,030 | | |
| Wages and Salaries | | ½ | 99,000 | | |
| | | ½ | 198,500 | 198,500 | ½ |

18½ marks this page
16½ marks b/f
35   marks total

IAB L2 Certificate Jan 2010  MA (past paper)          Page 4

## Answer Question Two: Tasks A and D

### Paws Pet Shop – Purchase Ledger (Extract)

**Paws Pet Shop**
**Purchase Ledger (Extract)**

| DR | | | | | Wessex Pet Supplies | | | CR |
|---|---|---|---|---|---|---|---|---|
| **2010** | **Details** | | **£** | **2010** | **Details** | | | **£** |
| 15 Jan | Bank | ½ | 3,242 | 1 Jan | Balance b/d | | | 1,550 |
| 15 Jan | Discount Received | ½ | 60 | 5 Jan | Purchases (Inv. 3182) | | ½ | 584 |
| | | | | 11 Jan | Purchases (Inv. 3207) | | ½ | 1,168 |
| | | ½ | 3,302 | | | | ½ | 3,302 |

Allow Discount Received split into two
postings of £20 and £40 for the same half
mark.

## Answer Question Two: Task B

### Paws Pet Shop – Remittance Advice

| | | **REMITTANCE ADVICE** | | |
|---|---|---|---|---|
| **From:** | Paws Pet Shop | | | |
| | The Arcade | **To:** | | |
| | Redbury | | Wessex Pet Supplies ½ | |
| | RE56 7WQ | | | |
| | | **Date:** | | |
| | | | 12 January 2010 ½ | |

| Details | | Amount | |
|---|---|---|---|
| | | **£** | **p** |
| Invoice 3050 | ½ | 650 | 00 * |
| Invoice 3107 | ½ | 900 | 00 |
| Invoice 3182 | ½ | 584 | 00 |
| Less: Cash Discount | ½ | ( 20 | 00 ) |
| Invoice 3207 | ½ | 1,168 | 00 |
| Less: Cash Discount | ½ | ( 40 | 00 ) |
| Payment by: **BACS** | 1 | 3,242 | 00 |

* Details must be correct as well as the value to earn each mark shown.

Cash Discounts must be shown clearly (not just subtracted from the invoice total) and indicated as
negative in some way in either details or value - otherwise the mark is forfeit.

Allow Cash Discounts to be combined into a single figure of £60 (award 1 mark).

8 marks this page c/f

# IAB Level 2 model answers

**Answer Question Two: Task C**

**Paws Pet Shop – BACS Payment Listing**

## SOUTHERN BANK PLC - BACS PAYMENT LISTING

| | | |
|---|---|---|
| Bank Branch: | Redbury | ½ |
| BACS Originator Name: | Paws Pet Shop | ½ |
| BACS Originator Reference: | PAW3434 | ½ |
| Date: | 12 January 2010 | ½ |

| Payee Name | Payee Reference Number | Bank Sort Code | Account Number | Amount £ | p |
|---|---|---|---|---|---|
| Wessex Pet Supplies ½ | 77  ½ | 99-88-77  ½ | 78780202  ½ | ½  3,242 | 00 |
| | | | | | |
| | | | | | |
| | | | | | |
| | | | | | |
| | | | **BATCH TOTAL** | ½  3,242 | 00 |

| | | |
|---|---|---|
| Value date | 15 January 2010 | ½ |
| Account Name | Paws Pet Shop | ½ |
| Sort Code | 44-55-22 | ½ |
| Account Number | 12340012 | ½ |
| Authorised Signature(s) | | |

Allow candidate's Own Figure from the Remittance Advice on previous page.

379

**Answer Question Three:  Task A**

**Red Dragon – VAT account**

Red Dragon
General Ledger (Extract)

| DR | | | Value Added Tax (VAT) | | | CR |
|---|---|---|---|---|---|---|
| **Date** | **Details** | £ | **Date** | **Details** | | £ |
| **2009** | | | **2009** | | | |
| 20 Oct | Bank | 11,305 | 1 Oct | Balance b/d | | 11,305 |
| 31 Dec | Sales Returns Day Book | ½  2,800 | 31 Dec | Sales Day Book | ½ | 21,725 |
| 31 Dec | Purchase Day Book | ½  32,603 | 31 Dec | Cash Sales | ½ | 25,700 |
| 31 Dec | Purchase of Fixed Assets | ½  1,175 | 31 Dec | Purchase Returns Day Book | ½ | 1,970 |
| 31 Dec | Petty Cash Expenses | ½  42 | | | | |
| 31 Dec | Balance c/d | ½  12,775 | | | | |
| | | ½  60,700 | | | ½ | 60,700 |
| | | | **2010** | | | |
| | | | 1 Jan  ½ | Balance b/d | ½ | 12,775 |

# IAB Level 2 model answers

**Red Dragon – VAT Return for the Quarter ended 31 December 2009**

|  | BOX | £ | P | |
|---|---|---|---|---|
| VAT due in this period on sales | 1 | 44,625 | 00 | 1 |
| VAT due in this period on EC acquisitions | 2 | 0 | 00 | |
| Total VAT due (sum of boxes 1 and 2) | 3 | 44,625 | 00 | 1 |
| VAT reclaimed in this period on purchases | 4 | 31,850 | 00 | 1 |
| **Net VAT to be paid to H.M. Revenue & Customs or reclaimed by you** | 5 | 12,775 | 00 | 1 |
| Total value of sales, excluding VAT | 6 | 255,000 | 00 | 1 |
| Total value of purchases, excluding VAT | 7 | 182,000 | 00 | 1 |
| Total value of EC sales, excluding VAT | 8 | 0 | 00 | |
| Total value of EC purchases, excluding VAT | 9 | 0 | 00 | |

**Notes:**

1. The Box 1 figure above (VAT due in this period on sales) is the total of all output tax in the period less the VAT debited to the VAT account in respect of VAT refunded to customers on credit notes for sales returns.

2. The Box 4 figure above (VAT reclaimed in this period on purchases) is the total of all input tax in the period less the VAT credited to the VAT account in respect of VAT refunded by suppliers on credit notes for purchase returns.

For clarity, do NOT allow candidate's Own Figures from the VAT ledger account.

6 marks this page
6 marks b/f
12 marks c/f

381

## Answer Question Three: Task C

**Red Dragon – Sales Invoice**

**NB:** 13 figures must be entered to complete this invoice correctly

**INVOICE**

**'Red Dragon'**
Est. 2000
**6 Red Dragon Yard, Beddling**
**BD7 1LP**

To:
All Ages Sports Club
Beddling Leisure Centre
The Roundabout
Beddling
BD8 6CD

**Invoice number** 5602

**Order No:** 2010 / 27          **Date (Tax Point):** 13 January 2010

| Qty | Description | VAT rate % | Unit Price £ | Unit Price p | Total £ | Total p |
|---|---|---|---|---|---|---|
| 15 | Men's 'Cobra' Cotton T-Shirt, Size L | 17.5 | 14 | 50 | ½ 217 | 50 |
| 15 | Ladies' 'Zebra' Cotton T-Shirt, Size M | 17.5 | 11 | 50 | ½ 172 | 50 |
| 10 | Unisex Hi-Visibility Sports Fleece, Size ML | 17.5 | 33 | 00 | ½ 330 | 00 |
| 20 | Child's 'Zig' Polyester Cotton T-Shirt, 8-10 | 0 | 8 | 99 | ½ 179 | 80 |
| 10 | Child's 'Zag' Polyester Cotton T-Shirt, 8-10 | 0 | 7 | 99 | ½ 79 | 90 |

| | | £ | p |
|---|---|---|---|
| **Goods Total** | | ½ 979 | 70 |
| **Less Trade Discount:** 10% | | ½ 97 | 97 |
| **Net Goods** | | ½ 881 | 73 |
| **VAT** | | ½ 107 | 73 |
| **Invoice Total** | £ | 2 989 | 46 |

**TERMS:** 5% 14 days / 30 days net

**VAT ANALYSIS**

| VAT Rate | Total Net £ | Total VAT £ |
|---|---|---|
| 17.5% | ½ 648.00 | ½ 107.73 |
| 0.0% | ½ 233.73 | 0.00 |

E. & O.E.  Carriage paid.  VAT Reg No: 321 4321 56

Partners: P Parks, G Ingham

8 marks this page
12  marks b/f
20  marks c/f

**Answer Question Three: Task D**

**Red Dragon – Reconciliation Statement**

**Red Dragon**
**Reconciliation of Purchase Ledger Account**
**to Supplier Statement of Account**
**(Hyper Ltd)**
**as at 31 December 2009**

| | £ | |
|---|---|---|
| Balance per supplier account in Purchase Ledger | 1,419 | ¼ |
| Adjustments – unticked items on Statement: | | |
| Add Invoice 9937 ¼ | 472 | ¼ |
| Less Credit Note C648 ¼ | ( 19 ) | ¼ |
| | | |
| Adjustments – unticked items in Purchase Ledger: | | |
| Add Bank Payment ¼ | 2,000 | ¼ |
| Bonus marks if there are no spurious or incorrect entries | | 3 |
| Balance per Supplier Statement | 3,872 | ¼ |

If a value is negative it must be indicated as negative in some way, in either details or value, otherwise both marks on that line are forfeit.

5 marks this page
20 marks b/f
25 marks total

IAB L2 Certificate Jan 2010  MA (past paper)          Page 10

383

**Answer Question Four: Tasks A, C, D and E**

**Unicast Ltd – General Ledger (extract)**

## Unicast Ltd
### General Ledger (extract)

**DR** | | | **Purchase Ledger Control (GL 2100)** | | | **CR**

| 2010 | Details | | £ | 2010 | Details | | £ |
|------|---------|------|-------|------|---------|------|-------|
| 8 Jan | Purchase Returns Day Book | ½ | 470 | 4 Jan | Balance b/d | 1 | 11,422 |
| 8 Jan | Bank | ½ | 3,718 | 8 Jan | Purchase Day Book | ½ | 7,317 |
| 8 Jan | Discount Received | ½ | 141 | | | | |
| 8 Jan | Balance c/d | ½ | 14,410 | | | | |
| | | | 18,739 | | | | 18,739 |
| | | | | 11 Jan | Balance b/d | ½ | 14,410 |

**DR** | | | **Value Added Tax (GL 2500)** | | | **CR**

| 2010 | Details | | £ | 2010 | Details | | £ |
|------|---------|------|-------|------|---------|------|-------|
| 8 Jan | Purchase Day Book | ½ | 1,077 | 4 Jan | Balance b/d | ½ | 2,910 |
| | | | | 8 Jan | Purchase Returns Day Book | ½ | 70 |

**DR** | | | **Purchases (GL 5000)** | | | **CR**

| 2010 | Details | | £ | 2010 | Details | | £ |
|------|---------|------|-------|------|---------|------|-------|
| 4 Jan | Balance b/d | ½ | 55,506 | | | | |
| 8 Jan | Purchase Day Book | ½ | 6,240 | | | | |

**DR** | | | **Purchase Returns (GL 5100)** | | | **CR**

| 2010 | Details | | £ | 2010 | Details | | £ |
|------|---------|------|-------|------|---------|------|-------|
| | | | | 4 Jan | Balance b/d | ½ | 8,900 |
| | | | | 8 Jan | Purchase Returns Day Book | ½ | 400 |

**DR** | | | **Discount Received (GL 5200)** | | | **CR**

| 2010 | Details | | £ | 2010 | Details | | £ |
|------|---------|------|-------|------|---------|------|-------|
| | | | | 4 Jan | Balance b/d | ½ | 842 |
| | | | | 8 Jan | Cash Book * | ½ | 141 |

\* Discount Received of £141 must be presented as a single figure

8½ marks this page c/f

384

# IAB Level 2 model answers

**Unicast Ltd - Purchase Ledger (complete)**

### Unicast Ltd
### Purchase Ledger (complete)

**DR**           Alleyn Bros (PL 0010)           **CR**

| 2010 | Details | £ | | 2010 | Details | £ | |
|------|---------|---|---|------|---------|---|---|
| 6 Jan | Purchase Returns (Credit Note CR682) | ½ | 188 | 4 Jan | Balance b/d | ½ | 1,500 |
| 8 Jan | Bank | ½ | 312 | | | | |

**DR**           Norton Industries (PL 0050)           **CR**

| 2010 | Details | £ | | 2010 | Details | £ | |
|------|---------|---|---|------|---------|---|---|
| 7 Jan | Purchase Returns (Credit Note 5043) | ½ | 282 | 4 Jan | Balance b/d | ½ | 5,125 |
| | | | | 8 Jan | Purchases (Invoice 66003) | ½ | 282 |

**DR**           Redbridge Plc (PL 0020)           **CR**

| 2010 | Details | £ | | 2010 | Details | £ | |
|------|---------|---|---|------|---------|---|---|
| | | | | 4 Jan | Purchases (Inv. 7895) | ½ | 4,700 |

**DR**           Trend CAD (PL 0040)           **CR**

| 2010 | Details | £ | | 2010 | Details | £ | |
|------|---------|---|---|------|---------|---|---|
| 8 Jan | Bank | ½ | 504 | 4 Jan | Balance b/d | ½ | 1,765 |
| 8 Jan | Discount Received | ½ | 11 | 6 Jan | Purchases (Invoice Inv. 899) | ½ | 936 |

**DR**           Vine & Pierce Ltd (PL 0030)           **CR**

| 2010 | Details | £ | | 2010 | Details | £ | |
|------|---------|---|---|------|---------|---|---|
| 8 Jan | Bank | ½ | 2,902 | 4 Jan | Balance b/d | ½ | 3,032 |
| 8 Jan | Discount Received | ½ | 130 | 5 Jan | Purchases (Inv. 1054) | ½ | 1,399 |

7½ marks this page
8½ marks b/f
16 marks c/f

385

**Answer Question Four: Tasks B and C**

**Unicast Ltd – Purchase Day Book and Purchase Returns Day Book**

### Unicast Ltd - Purchase Day Book

| Invoice Date 2010 | Supplier | Purchase Ledger Code | Supplier's Invoice Number | Total £ | VAT £ | Net £ |
|---|---|---|---|---|---|---|
| 4 Jan | Redbridge Plc | ½ PL0020 | 7895 | 4,700 | 700 | 4,000 |
| 5 Jan | Vine & Pierce Ltd | ½ PL0030 | 1054 | 1,399 | 199 | 1,200 |
| 6 Jan | Trend CAD | ½ PL0040 | INV899 | 936 | 136 | 800 |
| 8 Jan | Norton Industries | ½ PL0050 | 66003 | 282 | 42 | 240 |
| | | **TOTALS** | | 7,317 | 1,077 | 6,240 |
| | | **GENERAL LEDGER CODE** | | ½ GL2100 | ½ GL2500 | ½ GL5000 |
| | | **DEBIT OR CREDIT** | | ½ CR | ½ DR | ½ DR |

### Unicast Ltd - Purchase Returns Day Book

| Invoice Date 2010 | Supplier | Purchase Ledger Code | Supplier's Credit Note Number | Total £ | VAT £ | Net £ |
|---|---|---|---|---|---|---|
| 6 Jan | Alleyn Bros | ½ PL0010 | CR682 | 188 | 28 | 160 |
| 7 Jan | Norton Industries | ½ PL0050 | 5043 | 282 | 42 | 240 |
| | | **TOTALS** | | 470 | 70 | 400 |
| | | **GENERAL LEDGER CODE** | | ½ GL2100 | ½ GL2500 | ½ GL5100 |
| | | **DEBIT OR CREDIT** | | ½ DR | ½ CR | ½ CR |

9 marks this page
16 marks b/f
25 marks total

## Answer Question Five: Task A

**Tasty Preserves – Sales Ledger Control Account**

**Tasty Preserves**
**General Ledger (Extract)**

| DR | | | Sales Ledger Control | | | CR |
|---|---|---|---|---|---|---|
| **2009** | **Details** | | **£** | **2009** | **Details** | **£** |
| 1 Dec | Balance b/d | 1 | 15,290 | 31 Dec | Sales Returns Day Book | 1  1,007 |
| 31 Dec | Sales Day Book | 1 | 14,205 | 31 Dec | Cash Book – Receipts | 1  15,700 |
| | | | | 31 Dec | Cash Book – Discount Allowed | 1  348 |
| | | | | 31 Dec | Journal – Bad Debt Write Off | 1  2,840 |
| | | | | 31 Dec | Balance c/d | 1  9,600 |
| | | | 29,495 | | | 29,495 |
| 31 Dec | Balance b/d | ½ | 9,600 | | | |

## Answer Question Five: Task B

**Tasty Preserves - Reconciliation of Personal Account Balances per Sales Ledger as at 31 December 2009 to Sales Ledger Control Account Balance as at that Date**

| | £ | DR/CR |
|---|---|---|
| Total debtors per Sales Ledger – 31 December 2009 | ½  9,600 | ½  DR |
| Balance per Sales Ledger Control Account – 31 December 2009 | ½  9,600 | ½  DR |
| Difference | 1  0 * | |

* award mark for zero, nil, dash – anything (other than left blank) that indicates a nil value

10½ marks this page c/f

**Answer Question Five:  Task C**

Tasty Preserves – Table of Payroll Information, Month 9 (December 2009)

---

**Table of Payroll Information
Month 9 (December 2009)**

| | | | | | | |
|---|---|---|---|---|---|---|
| **Net Pay** | | | | £ | 1 | 10,200 |
| PAYE | £ | ½ | 1,575 | | | |
| Employee National Insurance | £ | ½ | 650 | | | |
| Employee Pension | £ | ½ | 450 | | | |
| Total Employee Deductions | | | | £ | 1 | 2,675 |
| **Gross Pay** | | | | £ | 1 | 12,875 |
| Employer National Insurance | £ | ½ | 1,100 | | | |
| Employer Pension | £ | ½ | 625 | | | |
| Total Employer Contributions | | | | £ | 1 | 1,725 |
| **Cost of Employment for Month** | | | | £ | 1 | 14,600 |
| Due to H M Revenue & Customs | | | | £ | 1 | 3,325 |
| Due to United Pensions | | | | £ | 1 | 1,075 |
| Total Cost of Employment, Year to Date | | | | £ | 1 | 96,092 |

---

IAB L2 Certificate Jan 2010  MA (past paper)          Page 15

10½ marks this page
10½ marks b/f
21  marks c/f

388

## Answer Question Five:  Task D

### Tasty Preserves – Basic Accounting Concepts

Jean Scurr's jams and pickles business Tasty Preserves has been very successful, despite her having no detailed knowledge of book-keeping or accounting.

She is now showing more interest in the work of IAB Accounting Services and has heard that 'accounting concepts' are the principles which underpin the books of account.

Examine her comments below, and state which of the **four basic accounting concepts** is being referred to in each case.

**i)**  Jean Scurr is very proud of her staff whose hard work and loyalty is vital to the continuing success of Tasty Preserves.  State the basic accounting concept which prevents these attributes from being recorded in the books of account:

| Money measurement | 1 |
|---|---|

**ii)**  Jean frequently complains that IAB Accounting Services keeps the business transactions of Tasty Preserves separate from her own private financial affairs.  State the basic accounting concept which IAB Accounting Services is following:

| Business entity | 1 |
|---|---|

**iii)**  Jean has noticed that her cooking, canning and packaging machinery is shown in the books of account at the cost that she bought it some years ago, rather than at today's prices.  State the basic accounting concept which IAB Accounting Services is following:

| Historic cost | 1 |
|---|---|

**iv)**  Jean has been told that IAB Accounting Services enter every transaction into her books twice, as a debit and as a credit.  State the basic accounting concept behind this double entry procedure:

| Dual aspect | 1 |
|---|---|

4 marks this page
21 marks b/f
25 marks total

Qualifications for business

Exam I/D 106

# QUESTION PAPER

## Qualification:
Level 3 Diploma in Accounting & Advanced Book-keeping
(Qualification Accreditation Number 500/3022/x)

Record Adjustments and Prepare Financial Statements

## Examination:
Paper One

## January 2010
## Morning Sitting

**Time Allowed: 2 hours**

Suite 30, 40 Churchill Square, Kings Hill, West Malling, Kent ME19 4U
Tel: 0844 330 3527, Fax: 0844 330 3514, e-mail:mail@iab.org.uk

**THE INTERNATIONAL ASSOCIATION OF BOOK-KEEPERS**

**IAB LEVEL 3 DIPLOMA IN ACCOUNTING AND ADVANCED BOOK-KEEPING**

**UNIT TITLE:** **RECORD ADJUSTMENTS AND PREPARE FINANCIAL STATEMENTS**

**PAPER ONE**

**GENERAL INFORMATION AND INSTRUCTIONS**

- THIS QUESTION BOOKLET CONTAINS FIVE QUESTIONS WITHIN TWO SECTIONS. YOU MUST ANSWER **FOUR** QUESTIONS AS FOLLOWS:

SECTION A   -   ANSWER **BOTH** QUESTIONS IN THIS SECTION

- Question One Carries 25 Marks
- Question Two Carries 15 Marks

SECTION B   -   ANSWER **ANY TWO** OF THE QUESTIONS IN THIS SECTION

- All Questions Carry Equal Marks – 30 Marks Each

- In addition to this Question Paper you are also provided with an Answer Booklet.

- You must enter your **Student Number, Candidate Number** and **Name of Examination Centre** in the boxes provided on the front cover of your **Answer Booklet**.

- **Time allowed : Two Hours.** It is recommended that this time be allocated as follows:

- SECTION A QUESTIONS – 40 Minutes
- SECTION B QUESTIONS – 80 Minutes

- All answers are to be written in **ink**.

- Correction fluid can be used in moderation, otherwise cross out errors neatly.

- The use of silent non-programmable calculators is permitted.

- If you answer three questions from Section B, you must cross out the answer you do not want marking, otherwise we will take the marks of your first two answers.

- **NOTE – This question booklet has information and data printed on both sides of the pages contained within the booklet.**

# IAB Level 3 question paper

**Section A** – You must answer **both** questions in this section

## Question One

Double entry books are kept on behalf of Fourseasons Foods. Sales Ledger Control and Purchase Ledger Control Accounts are kept in the main ledger and are part of the double entry book-keeping system. The personal accounts of trade debtors and trade creditors are kept in the Sales Ledger and Purchase Ledger respectively, these ledgers are kept as subsidiary ledgers with the personal accounts being maintained as memorandum accounts.

As at 1 January 2009 the main ledger included a Provision for Doubtful Debts Account carrying a balance of £4,620, being the account balance brought forward from the previous year end (31 December 2008).

As at 31 December 2009 the following two accounts also appeared in the main ledger:

| Account | Balance £ |
|---|---|
| Sales Ledger Control | 416,480 |
| Bad Debts | 6,210 |

The balance on the Bad Debts account represents trade debtor balances already written off as bad in the year ended 31 December 2009.

Following a further review of trade debtor balances at 31 December 2009 it was agreed that the balance of £1,480 on the account of Fieldside Bakeries should now also be written off as a bad debt. It was further agreed that following the write off the balance brought forward on the Provision for Doubtful Debts Account be adjusted to represent an amount equivalent to 1% of the remaining trade debtors.

---

**REQUIRED:**

**Task A**    Show the balance brought forward on the Provision for Doubtful Debts Account as at 1 January 2009 (½ mark)

**Task B**    Show the balances brought forward on the Sales Ledger Control Account and Bad Debts Account as at 31 December 2009 (1 mark)

**Task C**    Prepare the Journal entry to write off the balance on the account of Fieldside Bakeries. Date your Journal entry 31 December 2009 and include a suitable narrative (3 marks)

**Task D**    Post the Journal entry prepared in Task C above to relevant accounts in the main ledger (2 marks)

---

**Task E**   Prepare the Journal entry required to account for the adjustment to the balance on the Provision for Doubtful Debts Account as at 31 December 2009. Date your Journal entry 31 December 2009 and include a suitable narrative (7½ marks)

**Task F**   Post from the Journal entry prepared in Task E above to the Provision for Doubtful Debts Account in the main ledger (1½ marks)

**Task G**   Prepare the Journal entry necessary to transfer the balance on the Bad Debts Account as at 31 December 2009 to the Profit and Loss Account. Date your Journal entry 31 December 2009 and include a suitable narrative (2 marks)

**Task H**   Post from the Journal entry prepared in Task G above to the Bad Debts Account in the main ledger and close off the account (1½ marks)

**Task I**   Balance off the Provision for Doubtful Debts Account and Sales Ledger Control Account as at 31 December 2009, bringing down the account balances as at that date (4 marks)

**Task J**   Using the Balance Sheet (extract) provided show the net debtors as they would appear on the Balance Sheet as at 31 December 2009 (2 marks)

**(Total 25 Marks)**

**Note:**   The following proformas are provided for your use in completing the above tasks:

- Main Ledger Accounts – Provision for Doubtful Debts, Sales Ledger Control and Bad Debts (see **page 1** of your **Answer Booklet**)
- Journal (see **page 2** of your **Answer Booklet**)
- Balance Sheet (extract) (see **page 2** of your **Answer Booklet**)

**Question Two**

As at 31 December 2009 the book-keeper extracted a Trial Balance from the books of account of Metalmex.

On totalling the Trial Balance the book-keeper found debit (DR) balances totalled £1,462,620 whilst credit (CR) balances totalled £1,467,720.

On reviewing postings to the books of account for the year ended 31 December 2009 the following book-keeping errors were discovered.

a   A cheque in payment for repairs to a delivery vehicle (vehicle running costs) had been posted in the books as follows:

>        DR – Vehicle (cost) £800
>        DR – VAT £140
>        CR – Bank £940

b   At 31 December 2009 the net goods total (value of goods excluding VAT) of £146,180 had been transferred from the Sales Day Book to the Sales Account as £141,680.

c   A cheque received from the local authority in respect of a rates rebate, had been posted in the books as follows:

>        CR – Rates £4,800
>        CR – Bank £4,800

---

**REQUIRED:**

**Task A**   Post the difference in books balance as at 31 December 2009 to a Suspense Account (1 mark)

**Task B**   Prepare the Journal entries necessary to correct the book-keeping errors given above.   Date your Journal entries 31 December 2009 and include suitable narratives (11½ marks)

**Task C**   Show the elimination of the Suspense Account balance as at 31 December 2009 and close off the account (2½ marks)

**(Total 15 Marks)**

---

**Note:**   The following proformas are provided for your use in completing the above tasks:

- Suspense Account (see **page 4** of your **Answer Booklet**)
- Journal (see **page 4** of your **Answer Booklet**)

**Section B** – You must answer **any two** questions from this section

## Question Three

Lilly Potter operates as a market trader. She sells a variety of plants, shrubs and fresh flowers and trades in the name of Heaven's Scent.

The following is the Balance Sheet of the business as at 31 December 2008:

### Heaven's Scent
### Balance Sheet as at 31 December 2008

|  | £ | £ | £ |
|---|---|---|---|
| **Fixed Assets** |  |  |  |
| Market stall and equipment (net book value) |  | 1,800 |  |
| Van (net book value) |  | 10,500 |  |
|  |  |  | 12,300 |
| **Current Assets** |  |  |  |
| Stock | 1,800 |  |  |
| Operating expenses prepaid | 500 |  |  |
| Bank | 4,000 |  |  |
| Cash | 200 |  |  |
|  |  | 6,500 |  |
| **Less Current Liabilities** |  |  |  |
| Trade creditors | 1,300 |  |  |
| Operating expenses accrued | 700 |  |  |
|  |  | 2,000 |  |
| Working capital |  |  | 4,500 |
|  |  |  | 16,800 |
| **Financed by:** |  |  |  |
| Opening capital | 14,200 |  |  |
| **Add** Net profit | 15,800 |  |  |
|  |  | 30,000 |  |
| **Less** Drawings |  | 13,200 |  |
|  |  |  | 16,800 |

The following is a summary of the transactions processed through the business Bank Account in the year ended 31 December 2009:

### Heaven's Scent
### Bank Account

| Receipts | £ | Payments | £ |
|---|---|---|---|
| Balance b/f (31/12/2008) | 4,000 | Van running costs | 4,840 |
| Cash | 85,464 | Trade creditors | 47,120 |
|  |  | Operating expenses | 10,460 |
|  |  | Drawings | 14,000 |
|  |  | New equipment | 2,000 |
|  |  | Balance c/d (31/12/2009) | 11,044 |
|  | 89,464 |  | 89,464 |
| Balance b/d (31/12/2009) | 11,044 |  |  |

You are also provided with the following additional information as at 31 December 2009:

1    All customers are cash customers.

2    At the close of business each day takings from cash sales are banked after making up the following days cash float and paying various business expenses in cash. At close of business on 31 December 2009 the cash float of the business was £250. In the year ended 31 December 2009 the following payments were made in cash:

- Operating expenses £1,200
- Wages £4,800
- Cash purchases (goods for resale) £6,200

3    Fixed assets are to be depreciated as follows in the year ended 31 December 2009:

- Market stall and equipment £1,000 (includes depreciation on new equipment)
- Van £3,000

4    On 31 December 2009 £2,120 was owed to trade creditors in respect of goods supplied in the year ended 31 December 2009.

5    Operating expenses of £900 were prepaid at 31 December 2009, at the same date there were operating expenses accrued of £1,650.

6    Stock of the business as at 31 December 2009 was valued at £2,150.

---

**REQUIRED:**

**Task A**    Prepare the Trading and Profit and Loss Account of the business for the year ended 31 December 2009 (16 marks)

**Task B**    Prepare the Balance Sheet of the business as at 31 December 2009 (14 marks)

**(Total 30 Marks)**

---

**Note:** The following proformas are provided for your use in completing the above tasks:

- Trading and Profit and Loss Account (see **page 6** of your **Answer Booklet**)
- Balance Sheet (see **page 7** of your **Answer Booklet**)

## Question Four

Freda and Tina have been in partnership for several years. The financial year of their business ends on 31 December. As at 1 January 2009 the balances on the Capital Accounts and Current Accounts of Freda and Tina were:

|  | **Capital Accounts** £ | **Current Accounts** £ |
|---|---|---|
| Freda | 120,000 | 1,250 (CR) |
| Tina | 80,000 | 1,860 (DR) |

On formation of the partnership a Partnership Agreement was drawn up and included the following terms:

- No interest would be charged on partners' drawings
- Partners would be given interest on capital at the rate of 6% per year
- Tina would be given a partnership salary of £6,000 per year
- Remaining profits and losses would be shared 60% Freda and 40% Tina

As from 1 July 2009 it was decided that the profit sharing ratio within the original agreement be revised, but that the terms relating to interest charged on drawings, interest paid on capital and the salary paid to Tina would remain as originally agreed. As from 1 July 2009 the profit sharing ratio was revised as follows:

- Freda 50%
- Tina 50%

On changing the profit sharing ratio a valuation of £60,000 was placed on the goodwill of the existing business. A goodwill account is not to be maintained in the books of the business.

In the year ended 31 December 2009 the partnership business generated a net profit of £74,800. The profit was earned uniformly over the period of the year of trading 1 January 2009 to 31 December 2009.

In the year ended 31 December 2009 Freda and Tina took drawings from their business as follows:

|  | **Drawings** £ |
|---|---|
| Freda | 36,000 |
| Tina | 32,000 |

**REQUIRED:**

**Task A**     Prepare the Capital Account of each partner for the year ended 31 December 2009 (6½ marks)

**Task B**     Prepare the Current Account of each partner for the year ended 31 December 2009 (9½ marks)

**Task C**     Prepare the Partnership Appropriation Account for the year ended 31 December 2009 (14 marks)

**(Total 30 Marks)**

**Note:** The following proformas are available for your use in completing the above tasks:

- Capital Accounts (see **page 9** of your **Answer Booklet**)
- Current Accounts (see **page 9** of your **Answer Booklet**)
- Appropriation Account (see **page 10** of your **Answer Booklet**)

## Question Five

You are employed by D B Interiors as a book-keeper.  The following transactions took place recently:

**Transaction Number**

| | |
|---|---|
| 1 | David Bryant, the proprietor of D B Interiors introduced a further £25,000 as additional capital to finance expansion of the business. |
| 2 | Office furniture costing £2,500 was purchased for use in the administration office. |
| 3 | A heat and light bill of £750 was paid by cheque. |
| 4 | Goods for resale were purchased costing £7,200, payment was made by cheque. |
| 5 | A loan of £10,000 was received from the bank as additional funds to finance the expansion of business. |
| 6 | A delivery vehicle costing £20,000 was purchased for use in the business.  Payment was made by cheque. |
| 7 | Rent and rates of £12,600 were paid by cheque. |
| 8 | Amounts totalling £19,600 were received by cheque in respect of sales to customers. |
| 9 | A cheque for £850 was paid in respect of road tax and insurance on the new delivery vehicle. |
| 10 | Rent of £1,200 was received by cheque from a tenant in respect of office space sub-let to them. |
| 11 | Bank charges of £60 were debited by the bank to the Bank Account of D B Interiors. |

**REQUIRED:**

**Task A**   Comment **briefly** on each of the following terms:

Capital income
Revenue income
Capital expenditure
Revenue expenditure    (11 marks)

**Task B**   Using the table provided on **page 14** of your **Answer Booklet**, showing each of the above transactions by number, categorise each of the transactions as being either Income (capital or revenue) or Expenditure (capital or revenue). Show also where each item of income or expenditure would be used in preparing financial statements (Trading Account, Profit and Loss Account or Balance Sheet) for D B Interiors.

You would complete this task by ticking (✓) the relevant boxes next to each transaction number. The first transaction has been processed for you by way of an example. (19 marks)

**(Total 30 Marks)**

**Note:**   The following proformas are provided for your use in completing the above tasks:

• Lined pages for the purpose of answering Task A (see **pages 12 and 13** of your **Answer Booklet**)
• Table for categorising items of income and expenditure (see **page 14** of your **Answer Booklet**)

# IAB
*Qualifications for business*

Exam I/D 106

# ANSWER BOOKLET

## Qualification:
Level 3 Diploma in Accounting & Advanced Book-keeping
(Qualification Accreditation Number 500/3022/x)

Record Adjustments and Prepare Financial Statements

## Examination:
**Paper One**

## January 2010
## Morning Sitting

| | |
|---|---|
| **Student Number:** | |
| **Candidate Number:** | |
| **Name of Examination Centre:** | |

For use by assessor only:

| | Section A | | Section B | | | |
|---|---|---|---|---|---|---|
| **Question** | 1 | 2 | 3 | 4 | 5 | **Total** |
| **Marks** | | | | | | |

Suite 30, 40 Churchill Square, Kings Hill, West Malling, Kent, ME19 4YU
Tel: 0844 330 3527, Fax: 0844 330 3514, e-mail: mail@iab.org.uk

# IAB Level 3 answer booklet

**Section A** – You must answer **both** questions in this section

**Question One**

**Fourseasons Foods**

**Tasks A, B, D, F, H & I Main Ledger Accounts**

### Main Ledger (Extract)

| DR | | | Provision for Doubtful Debts | | | CR |
|---|---|---|---|---|---|---|
| 2009 | Details | £ | 2009 | Details | | £ |

| DR | | | Sales Ledger Control | | | CR |
|---|---|---|---|---|---|---|
| 2009 | Details | £ | 2009 | Details | | £ |

| DR | | | Bad Debts | | | CR |
|---|---|---|---|---|---|---|
| 2009 | Details | £ | 2009 | Details | | £ |

# IAB Level 3 answer booklet

**Tasks C, E & G – Journal**

## Journal

| 2009 | Details | DR £ | CR £ |
|---|---|---|---|
|  |  |  |  |
|  |  |  |  |
|  |  |  |  |
|  |  |  |  |
|  |  |  |  |
|  |  |  |  |
|  |  |  |  |
|  |  |  |  |

**Task J – Balance Sheet (Extract)**

### Fourseasons Foods
### Balance Sheet (Extract) as at 31 December 2009

**Current Assets**  £  £  £

Trade debtors
**Less** Provision for doubtful debts
Net debtors

Please note: Page 3 of this examination paper was left intentionally blank.

**Question Two**

**Metalmex**

**Tasks A & C – Suspense Account**

### Ledger (Extract)

| DR | | | Suspense | | CR |
|---|---|---|---|---|---|
| 2009 | Details | £ | 2009 | Details | £ |
| | | | | | |

**Task B – Journal**

### Journal

| 2009 | Details | DR £ | CR £ |
|---|---|---|---|
| | | | |
| | | | |
| | | | |
| | | | |
| | | | |
| | | | |
| | | | |
| | | | |
| | | | |

Please note: Page 5 of this examination paper was left intentionally blank.

# IAB Level 3 answer booklet

**Section B** – You must answer **any two** questions from this section

**Question Three**

**Heaven's Scent**

**Task A – Trading and Profit and Loss Account**

| Heaven's Scent<br>Trading and Profit and Loss Account for the Year Ended 31 December 2009 | £ | £ | £ |
|---|---|---|---|
| | | | |
| | | | |
| | | | |
| | | | |
| | | | |
| | | | |
| | | | |
| | | | |
| | | | |
| | | | |
| | | | |
| | | | |
| | | | |
| | | | |
| | | | |
| | | | |
| | | | |
| | | | |
| | | | |
| | | | |
| | | | |
| | | | |

**Task B – Balance Sheet**

| Heaven's Scent<br>Balance Sheet at 31 December 2009 | | | |
|---|---|---|---|
| | £ | £ | £ |
| | | | |
| | | | |
| | | | |
| | | | |
| | | | |
| | | | |
| | | | |
| | | | |
| | | | |
| | | | |
| | | | |
| | | | |
| | | | |
| | | | |
| | | | |
| | | | |
| | | | |
| | | | |
| | | | |
| | | | |
| | | | |
| | | | |
| | | | |
| | | | |
| | | | |
| | | | |
| | | | |

Please note: Page 8 of this examination paper was left intentionally blank.

**Question Four**

**Freda and Tina – Trading in Partnership**

**Task A – Capital Accounts**

DR                                                   Capital Accounts                                                   CR

| 2009 | Details | Freda £ | Tina £ | 2009 | Details | Freda £ | Tina £ |
|------|---------|---------|--------|------|---------|---------|--------|
|      |         |         |        |      |         |         |        |
|      |         |         |        |      |         |         |        |
|      |         |         |        |      |         |         |        |
|      |         |         |        |      |         |         |        |
|      |         |         |        |      |         |         |        |
|      |         |         |        |      |         |         |        |
|      |         |         |        |      |         |         |        |
|      |         |         |        |      |         |         |        |

**Task B – Current Accounts**

DR                                                   Current Accounts                                                   CR

| 2009 | Details | Freda £ | Tina £ | 2009 | Details | Freda £ | Tina £ |
|------|---------|---------|--------|------|---------|---------|--------|
|      |         |         |        |      |         |         |        |
|      |         |         |        |      |         |         |        |
|      |         |         |        |      |         |         |        |
|      |         |         |        |      |         |         |        |
|      |         |         |        |      |         |         |        |
|      |         |         |        |      |         |         |        |
|      |         |         |        |      |         |         |        |
|      |         |         |        |      |         |         |        |
|      |         |         |        |      |         |         |        |
|      |         |         |        |      |         |         |        |

**Task C – Appropriation Account**

| | 1/1/2009<br>to<br>30/6/2009<br>£ | 1/7/2009<br>to<br>31/12/2009<br>£ | Total<br>£ |
|---|---|---|---|
| **Freda and Tina**<br>**Appropriation Account for the Year Ended 31 December 2009** | | | |
| | | | |
| | | | |
| | | | |
| | | | |
| | | | |
| | | | |
| | | | |
| | | | |
| | | | |
| | | | |
| | | | |
| | | | |
| | | | |
| | | | |
| | | | |
| | | | |
| | | | |
| | | | |

Please note: Page 11 of this examination paper was left intentionally blank.

**Question Five**

**D B Interiors – Categorising Income and Expenditure**

**Task A – Comments on Accounting Terms – Capital Income, Revenue Income, Capital Expenditure and Revenue Expenditure**

409

**Comments (continued)**

410

## Task B – Table Categorising Items of Income and Expenditure

| Table Categorising Items of Income and Expenditure and Showing the Use of Income and Expenditure in the Preparation of Financial Statements | | | | | | | |
|---|---|---|---|---|---|---|---|
| Transaction Number | Income | | Expenditure | | Use in the Preparation of Financial Statements | | |
| | Capital | Revenue | Capital | Revenue | Trading Account | Profit and Loss Account | Balance Sheet |
| 1 | ✓ | | | | | | ✓ |
| 2 | | | | | | | |
| 3 | | | | | | | |
| 4 | | | | | | | |
| 5 | | | | | | | |
| 6 | | | | | | | |
| 7 | | | | | | | |
| 8 | | | | | | | |
| 9 | | | | | | | |
| 10 | | | | | | | |
| 11 | | | | | | | |

411

**IAB**
*Qualifications for business*

Exam I/D 106

# MODEL ANSWERS

## Qualification:
Level 3 Diploma in Accounting & Advanced Book-keeping
(Qualification Accreditation Number 500/3022/x)

Record Adjustments and Prepare Financial Statements

## Examination:
**Paper One**

## January 2010
## Morning Sitting

Suite 30, 40 Churchill Square, Kings Hill, West Malling, Kent, ME19 4YU
Tel: 0844 330 3527, Fax: 0844 330 3514, e-mail: mail@iab.org.uk

**Section A**

**Answer Question One**

**Fourseasons Foods**

**Tasks A, B, D, F, H & I Main Ledger Accounts**

### Main Ledger (Extract)

| DR | | | Provision for Doubtful Debts | | | CR |
|---|---|---|---|---|---|---|
| **2009** | **Details** | | **£** | **2009** | **Details** | **£** |
| 31 Dec | Profit and loss ½ | 1 | 470 | 1 Jan | Balance b/f ½ | 4,620 |
| 31 Dec | Balance c/d | 2 | 4,150 | | | |
| | | ¼ | 4,620 | | | ¼ 4,620 |
| | | | | 31 Dec | Balance b/d ¼ | 4,150 |

| DR | | Sales Ledger Control | | | | CR |
|---|---|---|---|---|---|---|
| **2009** | **Details** | **£** | **2009** | **Details** | | **£** |
| 31 Dec | Balance b/f | ½ 416,480 | 31 Dec | Bad debts ½ | ½ | 1,480 |
| | | | 31 Dec | Balance c/d | ½ | 415,000 |
| | | ¼ 416,480 | | | ¼ | 416,480 |
| 31 Dec | Balance b/d | ¼ 415,000 | | | | |

| DR | | | Bad Debts | | | CR |
|---|---|---|---|---|---|---|
| **2009** | **Details** | | **£** | **2009** | **Details** | **£** |
| 31 Dec | Balance b/f | ½ | 6,210 | 31 Dec | Profit and loss ½ | ½ 7,690 |
| 31 Dec | Sales ledger control ½ | ½ | 1,480 | | | |
| | | ¼ | 7,690 | | | ¼ 7,690 |

10½ Marks this page C/F

**Tasks C, E & G – Journal**

### Journal

| 2009 | Details | DR £ | CR £ |
|---|---|---|---|
| 31 Dec | Bad debts ½<br>Sales ledger control 1<br><br>Balance on account of Fieldside Bakeries written off as a bad debt ½ | ½ 1,480 | ½ 1,480 |
| 31 Dec | Provision for doubtful debts ½<br>Profit and loss ½<br><br>Decrease in provision for doubtful debts at year end ½ | 3   470 | 3   470 |
| 31 Dec | Profit and loss ¼<br>Bad debts ¼<br><br>Transfer of balance on Bad Debts Account to Profit and Loss Account at year end ½ | ½ 7,690 | ½ 7,690 |

**Task J – Balance Sheet (Extract)**

### Fourseasons Foods
### Balance Sheet (Extract) as at 31 December 2009

| Current Assets | £ | £ | £ |
|---|---|---|---|
| Trade debtors | ½ 415,000 | | |
| **Less** Provision for doubtful debts | ½ 4,150 | | |
| Net debtors | | 1 410,850 | |

14½ Marks this page
10½ Marks b/f
25 Total Marks

**Workings**

**Provision for Doubtful Debts Adjustment**

**Provision for Doubtful Debts to Be**

Trade debtors £416,480 - £1,480 = £415,000 x 1% = £4,150

**Provision for Doubtful Debts (Increase/(Decrease)**

|  | £ |
|---|---|
| Provision for doubtful debts to be | 4,150 |
| Provision for doubtful debts b/f (1/1/2009) | <u>4,620</u> |
| Provision for doubtful debts adjustment | <u>(470)</u>  (Decrease) |

Dr – Provision for Doubtful Debts Account

Cr – Profit and Loss Account

**Answer Question Two**

**Metalmex**

**Tasks A & C – Suspense Account**

### Ledger (Extract)

| DR | | | | Suspense | | | CR |
|---|---|---|---|---|---|---|---|
| **2009** | **Details** | | **£** | **2009** | **Details** | | **£** |
| 31 Dec | Difference in books | 1 | 5,100 | 31 Dec | Bank | 1 | 9,600 |
| 31 Dec | Sales | 1 | 4,500 | | | | |
| | | ¼ | 9,600 | | | ¼ | 9,600 |

**Task B – Journal**

### Journal

| 2009 | Details | DR £ | | CR £ | |
|---|---|---|---|---|---|
| 31 Dec | Vehicle running costs ½<br>Vehicle (cost) ½<br><br>Correction of error of principle ½ | 1 | 800 | 1 | 800 |
| 31 Dec | Suspense ½<br>Sales ½<br><br>Correction of transposition error ½ | 1 | 4,500 | 1 | 4,500 |
| 31 Dec | Bank ½<br>Suspense ½<br><br>Correction of error of reversal of entry ½ | 1½ | 9,600 | 1½ | 9,600 |

15 Total Marks

**Section B**

**Answer Question Three**

**Heaven's Scent**

**Task A – Trading and Profit and Loss Account**

**Heaven's Scent**
**Trading and Profit and Loss Account for the Year Ended 31 December 2009**

|  | | £ | | £ | | £ |
|---|---|---|---|---|---|---|
| Sales | | | | | 2 | 97,714 |
| **Less Cost of Goods Sold** | | | | | | |
| Opening stock | 1 | 1,800 | | | | |
| **Add** Purchases | 2 | 54,140 | | | | |
| | | | | 55,940 | | |
| **Less** Closing stock | | | 1 | 2,150 | | |
| Cost of Sales | | | | | 1 | 53,790 |
| **Gross Profit** | | | | | 1 | 43,924 |
| **Less Expenses** | | | | | | |
| Van running costs | | | 1 | 4,840 | | |
| Operating expenses | | | 2 | 12,210 | | |
| Wages | | | 1 | 4,800 | | |
| Depreciation (£1,000 £3,000) | | | 2 | 4,000 | | |
| | | | | 25,850 | | |
| **Net Profit** | | | | | 2 | 18,074 |

16 Marks this page C/F

## Task B – Balance Sheet

**Heaven's Scent**
**Balance Sheet at 31 December 2009**

| | £ | £ | £ |
|---|---|---|---|
| **Fixed Assets** | | | |
| Market stall and equipment (net book value) | | 1  2,800 | |
| Van | | 1  7,500 | |
| | | | 10,300 |
| **Current Assets** | | | |
| Stock | 1  2,150 | | |
| Operating expenses prepaid | 1  900 | | |
| Bank | 1  11,044 | | |
| Cash | 1  250 | | |
| | | 14,344 | |
| **Less Current Liabilities** | | | |
| Trade creditors | 1  2,120 | | |
| Operating expenses accrued | 1  1,650 | | |
| | | 3,770 | |
| Working capital | | | 1  10,574 |
| | | | 1  20,874 |
| **Financed By** | | | |
| Opening capital | 1  16,800 | | |
| **Add** Net profit | 1  18,074 | | |
| | | 34,874 | |
| **Less** Drawings | | 1  14,000 | |
| | | | 1  20,874 |

14 Marks this page
16 Marks b/f
30 Total Marks

# IAB Level 3 model answers

## Workings

| DR | Cash | | CR |
|---|---|---|---|
| | £ | | £ |
| Balance b/f | 200 | Bank | 85,464 |
| Sales | 97,714 | Operating exp's | 1,200 |
| | | Wages | 4,800 |
| | | Purchases | 6,200 |
| | | Balance c/d | 250 |
| | 97,914 | | 97,914 |
| Balance b/d | 250 | | |

| DR | Sales | | CR |
|---|---|---|---|
| | £ | | £ |
| Trading | 97,714 | Cash | 97,714 |

| DR | Purchases | | CR |
|---|---|---|---|
| | £ | | £ |
| Cash | 6,200 | Trading | 54,140 |
| Trade creditors | 47,940 | | |
| | 54,140 | | 54,140 |

| DR | Trade Creditors | | CR |
|---|---|---|---|
| | £ | | £ |
| Bank | 47,120 | Balance b/f | 1,300 |
| Balance c/d | 2,120 | Purchases | 47,940 |
| | 49,240 | | 49,240 |
| | | Balance b/d | 2,120 |

| DR | Operating Expenses | | CR |
|---|---|---|---|
| | £ | | £ |
| Balance b/f | 500 | Balance b/f | 700 |
| Cash | 1,200 | Profit and loss | 12,210 |
| Bank | 10,460 | Balance c/d | 900 |
| Balance c/d | 1,650 | | |
| | 13,810 | | 13,810 |
| Balance b/d | 900 | Balance b/d | 1,650 |

**Answer Question Four**

**Freda and Tina – Trading in Partnership**

**Task A – Capital Accounts**

| DR | | | | Capital Accounts | | | CR |
|---|---|---|---|---|---|---|---|
| **2009** | **Details** | **Freda £** | **Tina £** | **2009** | **Details** | **Freda £** | **Tina £** |
| 1 July | Goodwill adjm't | - | 1½ 6,000 | 1 Jan | Balance b/f | ½ 120,000 | ½ 80,000 |
| 31 Dec | Balance c/d | 1 126,000 | 1 74,000 | 1 July | Goodwill adjm't | 1½ 6,000 | - |
| | | 126,000 | 80,000 | | | 126,000 | 80,000 |
| | | | | 31 Dec | Balance b/d | ¼ 126,000 | ¼ 74,000 |

**Task B – Current Accounts**

| DR | | | | Current Accounts | | | CR |
|---|---|---|---|---|---|---|---|
| **2009** | **Details** | **Freda £** | **Tina £** | **2009** | **Details** | **Freda £** | **Tina £** |
| 1 Jan | Balance b/f | - | ½ 1,860 | 1 Jan | Balance b/f | ½ 1,250 | - |
| 31 Dec | Drawings | ½ 36,000 | ½ 32,000 | 31 Dec | Interest on capital | 1 7,380 | 1 4,620 |
| 31 Dec | Balance c/d | 1 3,870 | 1 2,320 | 31 Dec | Salary | - | 1 6,000 |
| | | | | 31 Dec | Share of profit | 1 31,240 | 1 25,560 |
| | | 39,870 | 36,180 | | | 39,870 | 36,180 |
| | | | | 31 Dec | Balance b/d | ¼ 3,870 | ¼ 2,320 |

16 Marks this page C/F

## Task C – Appropriation Account

<table>
<tr><td colspan="4">Freda and Tina<br>Appropriation Account for the Year Ended 31 December 2009</td></tr>
<tr><td></td><td>1/1/2009<br>to<br>30/6/2009<br>£</td><td>1/7/2009<br>to<br>31/12/2009<br>£</td><td>Total<br>£</td></tr>
<tr><td>Net profit</td><td>½ 37,400</td><td>½ 37,400</td><td>½ 74,800</td></tr>
<tr><td>Less: Interest on capital – Freda</td><td>1   3,600</td><td>1   3,780</td><td>½   7,380</td></tr>
<tr><td>– Tina</td><td>1   2,400</td><td>1   2,220</td><td>½   4,620</td></tr>
<tr><td></td><td>31,400</td><td>31,400</td><td>62,800</td></tr>
<tr><td>Less: Salary – Tina</td><td>1   3,000</td><td>1   3,000</td><td>½   6,000</td></tr>
<tr><td></td><td>28,400</td><td>28,400</td><td>56,800</td></tr>
<tr><td>Less: Share of profit – Freda</td><td>1   17,040</td><td>1   14,200</td><td>½   31,240</td></tr>
<tr><td>– Tina</td><td>1   11,360</td><td>1   14,200</td><td>½   25,560</td></tr>
<tr><td></td><td>-</td><td>-</td><td>-</td></tr>
</table>

## Workings

### Goodwill

| | Creation<br>£ | | Deletion<br>£ | | Net<br>Adjustment<br>£ | |
|---|---|---|---|---|---|---|
| Freda | 36,000 | (CR) | 30,000 | (DR) | 6,000 | (CR) |
| Tina | 24,000 | (CR) | 30,000 | (DR) | 6,000 | (DR) |
| | 60,000 | (CR) | 60,000 | (DR) | - | |

### Interest on Capital

Freda - £120,000 x 6% x ½ = £3,600 (1/1/2009 – 30/6/2009)
    - £126,000 x 6% x ½ = £3,780 (1/7/2009 – 31/12/2009)
                 £7,380

Tina  - £80,000 x 6% x ½ = £2,400 (1/1/2009 – 30/6/2009)
    - £74,000 x 6% x ½ = £2,220 (1/7/2009 – 31/12/2009)
               £4,620

### Share of Profit

1/1/2009 – 30/6/2009 £28,400 = Freda 60% £17,040, Tina 40% £11,360
1/7/2009 – 31/12/2009 £28,400 = Freda 50% £14,200, Tina 50% £14,200

14 Marks this page
16 Marks b/f
30 Total Marks

**Answer Question Five**

**D B Interiors – Categorising Income and Expenditure**

**Task A – Comments on Accounting Terms – Capital Income, Revenue Income, Capital Expenditure and Revenue Expenditure**

**Capital Income** – income borrowed by the business and invested in the business long-term 1. Such income includes capital invested by the owner(s) of the business 1 and finance taken from other external sources 1. = 3 marks

**Revenue Income** – income earned by the business 1, generated from either its trading or non-trading activities 1. = 2 marks

**Capital Expenditure** – expenditure which has a long-term effect on the profit making capacity of the business 1. Capital expenditure includes the cost of acquiring fixed assets 1, together with other costs incurred when installing, modifying or improving such assets 1. = 3 marks

**Revenue Expenditure** – expenditure which has only a short-term effect on the profit making capacity of the business 1. Benefit is derived from such expenditure in one accounting period 1. Revenue expenditure constitutes the day to day costs and expenses incurred in generating sales and running a business 1. = 3 marks

11 Marks this page C/F

## Task B – Table Categorising Items of Income and Expenditure

| Transaction Number | Income | | Expenditure | | Use in the Preparation of Financial Statements | | |
|---|---|---|---|---|---|---|---|
| | Capital | Revenue | Capital | Revenue | Trading Account | Profit and Loss Account | Balance Sheet |
| 1 | ✓ | | | | | | ✓ |
| 2 | | | 1 ✓ | | | | 1 ✓ |
| 3 | | | | 1 ✓ | | 1 ✓ | |
| 4 | | | | 1 ✓ | 1 ✓ | | |
| 5 | 1 ✓ | | | | | | 1½ ✓ |
| 6 | | | ½ ✓ | | | | ½ ✓ |
| 7 | | | | 1 ✓ | | 1 ✓ | |
| 8 | | 1 ✓ | | | 1 ✓ | | |
| 9 | | | | ½ ✓ | | ½ ✓ | |
| 10 | | 1 ✓ | | | | 1½ ✓ | |
| 11 | | | | 1 ✓ | | 1 ✓ | |

Title row: Table Categorising Items of Income and Expenditure and Showing the Use of Income and Expenditure in the Preparation of Financial Statements

19 Marks this page
11 Marks b/f
30 Total Marks

*Qualifications for business*

Exam I/D 107

# QUESTION PAPER

## Qualification:

Level 3 Diploma in Accounting & Advanced Book-keeping
(Qualification Accreditation Number 500/3022/x)

Record Adjustments and Prepare Financial Statements

## Examination:
Paper Two

## January 2010
## Afternoon Sitting

**Time Allowed: 2 hours**

Suite 30, 40 Churchill Square, Kings Hill, West Malling, Kent ME19 4U
Tel: 0844 330 3527, Fax: 0844 330 3514, e-mail:mail@iab.org.uk

# IAB Level 3 question paper

**THE INTERNATIONAL ASSOCIATION OF BOOK-KEEPERS**

**IAB LEVEL 3 DIPLOMA IN ACCOUNTING AND ADVANCED BOOK-KEEPING**

**UNIT TITLE:**  **RECORD ADJUSTMENTS AND PREPARE FINANCIAL STATEMENTS**

**PAPER TWO**

**GENERAL INFORMATION AND INSTRUCTIONS**

- THIS QUESTION BOOKLET CONTAINS FIVE QUESTIONS WITHIN TWO SECTIONS. YOU MUST ANSWER **FOUR** QUESTIONS AS FOLLOWS:

SECTION A  -  ANSWER **BOTH** QUESTIONS IN THIS SECTION

- Question One Carries 25 Marks
- Question Two Carries 15 Marks

SECTION B  -  ANSWER **ANY TWO** OF THE QUESTIONS IN THIS SECTION

- All Questions Carry Equal Marks – 30 Marks Each

- In addition to this Question Paper you are also provided with an Answer Booklet.

- You must enter your **Student Number, Candidate Number** and **Name of Examination Centre** in the boxes provided on the front cover of your **Answer Booklet**.

- **Time allowed : Two Hours**. It is recommended that this time be allocated as follows:

- SECTION A QUESTIONS – 40 Minutes
- SECTION B QUESTIONS – 80 Minutes

- All answers are to be written in **ink**.

- Correction fluid can be used in moderation, otherwise cross out errors neatly.

- The use of silent non-programmable calculators is permitted.

- If you answer three questions from Section B, you must cross out the answer you do not want marking, otherwise we will take the marks of your first two answers.

- **NOTE – This question booklet has information and data printed on both sides of the pages contained within the booklet.**

**Section A** – You must answer **both** questions in this section

**Question One**

The Belles is a ladies football club which plays in division one of the local ladies amateur football league. The Balance Sheet of the club as at 31 December 2008 is given below:

**The Belles**
**Balance Sheet as at 31 December 2008**

|  | £ | £ | £ |
|---|---|---|---|
| **Fixed Assets** |  |  |  |
| Minibus (net book value) |  | 12,000 |  |
| Club equipment (net book value) |  | 2,500 |  |
|  |  |  | 14,500 |
| **Current Assets** |  |  |  |
| Subscriptions (in arrears) | 180 |  |  |
| Ground rent (prepaid) | 300 |  |  |
| Bank and cash | 1,620 |  |  |
|  |  | 2,100 |  |
| **Less Current Liabilities** |  |  |  |
| Subscriptions (received in advance) |  | 360 |  |
|  |  |  | 1,740 |
|  |  |  | 16,240 |
| **Represented by** |  |  |  |
| Opening accumulated fund |  | 16,880 |  |
| **Less** deficit in year |  | (640) |  |
| Accumulated fund at 31/12/2008 |  |  | 16,240 |

The treasurer of the club has kept a cash book on behalf of the club in which all receipts and payments in the year ended 31 December 2009 have been recorded. The following is a summary of receipts and payments for the year ended 31 December 2009:

**The Belles**
**Receipts and Payments Account for the Year Ended 31 December 2009**

**Bank and Cash Account**

| Receipts | £ | Payments | £ |
|---|---|---|---|
| Balance b/f (31 December 2008) | 1,620 | Minibus running costs | 1,820 |
| Match day gate receipts | 6,680 | Ground maintenance | 1,500 |
| Subscriptions | 2,080 | Insurances | 600 |
| Raffle ticket sales | 3,140 | New club equipment | 2,000 |
| Donations | 1,800 | Ground rent | 2,400 |
|  |  | League affiliation fees | 250 |
|  |  | Referee and linesmen fees | 1,400 |
|  |  | Raffle prizes | 1,200 |
|  |  | Balance c/d (31 December 2009) | 4,150 |
|  | 15,320 |  | 15,320 |
| Balance b/d (31 December 2009) | 4,150 |  |  |

The club treasurer has also provided the following additional information as at 31 December 2009:

1     All subscriptions in arrears at 31 December 2008 were received in the year ended 31 December 2009.

2     At 31 December 2009 subscriptions received in advance were £480, subscriptions in arrears at 31 December 2009 amounted to £120.

3     Ground rent of £400 was prepaid as at 31 December 2009.

4     Depreciation for the year ended 31 December 2009 is to be accounted for as follows:

- Minibus £3,000
- Club equipment £900 (includes depreciation on new club equipment purchased in the year)

---

**REQUIRED:**

**Task A**     Prepare the Income and Expenditure Account of The Belles for the year ended 31 December 2009 (12 marks)

**Task B**     Prepare the Balance Sheet of The Belles as at 31 December 2009 (13 marks)

**(Total 25 Marks)**

---

**Note:** The following proformas are provided for your use in completing the above tasks:

- Income and Expenditure Account (see **page 1** of your **Answer Booklet**)
- Balance Sheet (see **page 2** of your **Answer Booklet**)

**Question Two**

The books of account of World of Beds are kept on a double entry basis and include separate accounts kept for the purpose of accounting for adjustments made in respect of prepayments and accruals.

As at 1 January 2009 the balances brought forward from the previous year end (31 December 2008) on the prepayments and accruals accounts were:

- Prepayments   £1,600
- Accruals      £880

The prepayments account balance brought forward at 1 January 2009 related to two months rent prepaid on the premises occupied by World of Beds, whereas the accruals account balance represented an accrual made in respect of heat and light bills (gas and electricity) used in the quarter ended 31 December 2008 but unpaid at the year end.

In the year ended 31 December 2009 payments in respect of rent and heat and light were made from the business bank account by direct debit as follows:

**2009**

| | |
|---|---|
| 20 January | Paid £880 in respect of gas and electricity used in the quarter ended 31 December 2008 |
| 20 February | Paid rent of £4,800 for the six months period ended 31 August 2009 |
| 20 April | Paid £950 in respect of gas and electricity used in the quarter ended 31 March 2009 |
| 20 July | Paid £780 in respect of gas and electricity used in the quarter ended 30 June 2009 |
| 20 August | Paid rent of £5,400 for the six months period ending 28 February 2010 |
| 20 October | Paid £800 in respect of gas and electricity used in the quarter ended 30 September 2009 |

The following additional information is also available:

i)     The rent on the premises occupied by World of Beds increased from £800 per month to £900 per month as from 1 September 2009.

ii)    Gas and electricity used in the quarter ended 31 December 2009 was 15% higher than usage in the previous quarter.

428

**REQUIRED**

**Task A** Bring forward the balances as at 1 January 2009 on the Prepayments Account and Accruals Account (1 mark)

**Task B** Prepare the Journal entries necessary to clear the prepayment and accruals account balances to their respective expense accounts as at 1 January 2009. Date your Journal entries 1 January 2009 and include suitable narratives (2½ marks)

**Task C** Post the Journal entries prepared in Task B above into the ledger accounts (1 mark)

**Task D** Post the payments made in respect of rent and heat and light in the year ended 31 December 2009 to the expense accounts of Rent and Heat and Light in the ledger (1½ marks)

**Task E** Prepare the Journal entries to account for rent prepaid and heat and light accrued as at the year end 31 December 2009. Date your Journal entries 31 December 2009 and include suitable narratives (3½ marks)

**Task F** Post the Journal entries prepared in Task E above into the ledger accounts (1 mark)

**Task G** Prepare the Journal entries necessary to transfer the expenses of rent and heat and light to the Profit and Loss Account at the year end 31 December 2009. Date your Journal entries 31 December 2009 and include suitable narratives (3½ marks)

**Task H** Post the Journal entries prepared in Task G above into the Rent account and Heat and Light account in the ledger and close off these two accounts at the year end (1 mark)

**NB:** There is no requirement to balance off the Prepayments and Accruals accounts at the year end

**(Total 15 Marks)**

**Note:** The following proformas are provided for your use in completing the above tasks:

- Prepayments Account, Accruals Account, Rent Account and Heat and Light Account (see **page 4** of your **Answer Booklet**)
- Journal (see **page 5** of your **Answer Booklet**)

# IAB Level 3 question paper

**Section B** – You must answer **any two** questions from this section

**Question Three**

Amy and Beth have been in partnership for several years trading as A&B (Wholesale) Fashions. The following Trial Balance was extracted from books of account kept on behalf of the business as at the year ended 31 December 2009:

### A&B (Wholesale) Fashions
### Trial Balance as at 31 December 2009

|  | DR £ | CR £ |
|---|---|---|
| Capital Accounts (31 December 2009) – Amy |  | 140,000 |
| – Beth |  | 80,000 |
| Current Accounts (31 December 2008) – Amy | 1,250 |  |
| – Beth |  | 2,960 |
| Drawings (31 December 2009) – Amy | 20,000 |  |
| – Beth | 18,000 |  |
| Sales |  | 403,440 |
| Purchases | 227,630 |  |
| Returns | 2,260 | 4,060 |
| Carriage inwards | 5,790 |  |
| Stock (31 December 2008) | 114,520 |  |
| Trade debtors and creditors | 128,160 | 79,270 |
| Office expenses | 18,550 |  |
| Salaries and wages | 56,480 |  |
| Discounts allowed | 4,820 |  |
| Rent and rates | 23,600 |  |
| Motor expenses | 8,950 |  |
| Heating and lighting | 4,200 |  |
| General expenses | 7,720 |  |
| Fixtures and fittings (cost) | 25,000 |  |
| - Provision for depreciation – 31 December 2008 |  | 7,500 |
| Motor vehicles (cost) | 40,000 |  |
| - Provision for depreciation – 31 December 2008 |  | 16,400 |
| Bank | 27,580 |  |
| Provision for doubtful debts – 31 December 2008 |  | 880 |
|  | 734,510 | 734,510 |

430

# IAB Level 3 question paper

The following additional information is also available as at 31 December 2009:

1   Stock at 31 December 2009 was originally valued at £115,600. Since the original valuation was carried out however, it has been discovered that one stock line, included in the original valuation at a value of £9,000, had in fact been valued at retail selling price. The selling price of the stock line concerned is calculated by using a mark up of 50%.

2   Rent and rates of £5,800 are prepaid at 31 December 2009.

3   An amount of £1,200 is to be accrued for heating and lighting bills unpaid at 31 December 2009.

4   General expenses includes a payment of £1,200 in respect of insurances. The invoice from the insurer was paid on 10 September 2009 and is for the year 1 September 2009 to 31 August 2010.

5   Depreciation for the year ended 31 December 2009 is to be provided for as follows:

    - Fixtures and fittings – 10% per year using the straight line method applied on a full year basis
    - Motor vehicles – 20% per year using the diminishing balance method applied on a full year basis

6   The balance of £2,160 on the account of a trade debtor is to be written off as a bad debt as at 31 December 2009. The balance on the Provision for Doubtful Debts Account is then to be adjusted to an amount equivalent to 1% of the value of the remaining trade debtors.

An extract from the Partnership Agreement drawn up on behalf of the partnership requires that profits or losses of the business be appropriated as follows:

a   Each partner be charged interest on drawings at a rate of 2% based on the balance on their Drawings Accounts at the year end.

b   Each partner be given interest on capital at the rate of 4% based on the balance on their Capital Accounts at the year end.

c   Amy is to be given a partnership salary of £10,000 per year, Beth is to be given a partnership salary of £8,000 per year.

d   Remaining profits or losses are to be shared equally between the partners.

**REQUIRED**

**Task A** Prepare the Trading and Profit and Loss Account of A&B (Wholesale) Fashions for the year ended 31 December 2009 (17 marks)

**Task B** Prepare the Appropriation Account of A&B (Wholesale) Fashions for the year ended 31 December 2009 (5 marks)

**Task C** Prepare the Current Accounts of Amy and Beth for the year ended 31 December 2009 (8 marks)

**NB:** A Balance Sheet is **NOT** required

**(Total 30 Marks)**

**Note:** The following proformas are provided for your use in completing the above tasks:

- Trading and Profit and Loss Account (see **page 7** of your **Answer Booklet**)
- Appropriation Account (see **page 8** of your **Answer Booklet**)
- Current Accounts (see **page 8** of your **Answer Booklet**)

432

**Question Four**

Fixed assets owned by Fivestar Engineering are categorised for accounting purposes as follows:

- Fixtures and Fittings
- Plant and Machinery
- Vehicles

A separate cost account and provision for depreciation account is kept in the books for each category of fixed asset. As at 1 January 2009 the balances on the cost and provision for depreciation accounts were:

- Fixtures and Fittings (Cost) £8,000
- Plant and Machinery (Cost) £284,000
- Vehicles (Cost) £120,000
- Fixtures and Fittings (Provision for Depreciation) £3,000
- Plant and Machinery (Provision for Depreciation) £113,600
- Vehicles (Provision for Depreciation) £52,500

A Fixed Asset Disposal account is kept in the ledger for the purpose accounting for fixed assets disposed of. A Depreciation Expense Account is also kept in the ledger for the purpose of accounting for the depreciation of fixed assets.

It is the policy of Fivestar Engineering to depreciate its fixed assets as follows:

- Fixtures and fittings are depreciated by 12.5% per year using the straight line method applied on a full year basis

- Plant and machinery is depreciated by 20% per year using the diminishing balance method applied on a full year basis

- Vehicles are depreciated by 20% per year using diminishing balance method applied on a month for month basis

**NB:** None of the fixed assets currently held by the business have been written down to a nil residual value. Fivestar Engineering acquired and disposed of several fixed assets in the year ended 31 December 2009 as follows:

**Acquisitions**

- Fixtures and fittings at a cost of £2,400 were acquired on 1 March 2009. The fixtures and fittings were paid for by cheque.
- Plant and machinery at a cost of £20,000 was acquired on 1 May 2009. The plant and machinery was paid for by cheque
- A vehicle costing £36,000 was acquired on 1 September 2009. The vehicle was paid for by cheque

**Disposals**

- Fixtures and fittings which had originally cost £1,600 were disposed of on 31 March 2009. A cheque for £400 was received on disposal. At the time of disposal the fixtures and fittings disposed of had a net book value of £800.

---

**REQUIRED**

**Task A**     Bring forward as at 1 January 2009 the balances on each of the fixed asset cost, and fixed asset provision for depreciation accounts in the ledger (3 marks)

**Task B**     Post the transactions necessary to account for the acquisition of fixed assets in the year ended 31 December 2009 to the relevant fixed assets cost accounts in the ledger (1½ marks)

**Task C**     Post the cheques received on disposal of fixtures and fittings to the Fixed Asset Disposal Account (½ mark)

**Task D**     Prepare the Journal entries required to account for the disposal of fixtures and fittings in the year ended 31 December 2009. Date your Journal entries 31 December 2009 and include suitable narratives (3½ marks)

**Task E**     Post the Journal entries prepared in Task D above to relevant accounts in the ledger (2 marks)

**Task F**     Prepare the Journal entries to account for the depreciation of fixed assets as at the year end 31 December 2009. Date your Journal entries 31 December 2009 and include suitable narratives (7¼ marks)

**Task G**     Post the Journal entries prepared in Task F above to relevant accounts in the ledger (3 marks)

**Task H**     Prepare the Journal entry as at 31 December 2009 necessary to transfer the profit and loss on disposal of fixed assets at the year end to the Profit and Loss Account. Date your Journal entry 31 December 2009 and include a suitable narrative (1¾ marks)

**Task I**     Post from the Journal entry prepared in Task H above to the Fixed Asset Disposal Account and close the Fixed Asset Disposal Account (½ mark)

---

**Task J** Balance off each of the fixed asset cost accounts and fixed asset provision for depreciation accounts as at 31 December 2009, bringing down the account balances at that date (4½ marks)

**Task K** Prepare the Journal entry as at 31 December 2009 necessary to transfer the depreciation expense to the Profit and Loss Account. Date your Journal entry 31 December 2009 and include a suitable narrative (2 marks)

**Task L** Post from the Journal entry prepared in Task K above to the Depreciation Expense Account and close the account (½ mark)

**(Total 30 Marks)**

**Note:** The following proformas are provided for your use in completing the above tasks:

- Ledger Accounts (see **pages 10 and 11** of your **Answer Booklet**)
- Journal (see **pages 12 and 13** of your **Answer Booklet**)

435

## Question Five

Provided below is an Extended Trial Balance prepared as at the year end 31 December 2009 on behalf of Alison West, who trades in the name of Direct Catering Supplies.

| Direct Catering Supplies – Extended Trial Balance as at 31 December 2009 | | | | | | | | |
|---|---|---|---|---|---|---|---|---|
| Ledger Account | Trial Balance | | Adjustments | | Profit & Loss | | Balance Sheet | |
| | DR | CR | DR | CR | DR | CR | DR | CR |
| | £ | £ | £ | £ | £ | £ | £ | £ |
| Capital | | 32685 | | | | | | 32685 |
| Drawings | 17000 | | | | | | 17000 | |
| Fixtures and fittings (cost) | 8000 | | | | | | 8000 | |
| Fixt's and fittings (acc'd dep'n) | | 2820 | | 1036 | | | | 3856 |
| Office equipment (cost) | 4500 | | | | | | 4500 | |
| Office equipm't (acc'd dep'n) | | 900 | | 450 | | | | 1350 |
| Sales | | 207656 | | | | 207656 | | |
| Purchases | 118848 | | | | 118848 | | | |
| Sales returns | 1560 | | | | 1560 | | | |
| Purchase returns | | 1810 | | | | 1810 | | |
| Stock – 31/12/2008 | 21650 | | | | 21650 | | | |
| Wages and salaries | 38975 | | | | 38975 | | | |
| Warehouse rent | 12600 | | | 200 | 12400 | | | |
| Warehouse rates | 9800 | | | 1400 | 8400 | | | |
| Insurances | 1400 | | | | 1400 | | | |
| Heat and light | 2150 | | 300 | | 2450 | | | |
| Office and admin expenses | 1065 | | | | 1065 | | | |
| Advertising | 1500 | | | | 1500 | | | |
| Bad debts | 600 | | 380 | | 980 | | | |
| Discount allowed | 1280 | | | | 1280 | | | |
| Discount received | | 1620 | | | | 1620 | | |
| Cleaning and maintenance | 673 | | | | 673 | | | |
| Cash | 560 | | | | | | 560 | |
| Bank | 5760 | | | | | | 5760 | |
| Trade debtors | 6880 | | | 380 | | | 6500 | |
| Trade creditors | | 7310 | | | | | | 7310 |
| | 254801 | 254801 | | | | | | |
| Closing stock – P&L | | | | 19980 | | 19980 | | |
| Closing stock – balance sheet | | | 19980 | | | | 19980 | |
| Warehouse rent prepaid | | | 200 | | | | 200 | |
| Warehouse rates prepaid | | | 1400 | | | | 1400 | |
| Heat and light accrued | | | | 300 | | | | 300 |
| Depreciation in year | | | 1486 | | 1486 | | | |
| Net profit | | | | | 18399 | | | 18399 |
| | | | | | | | | |
| | | | 23746 | 23746 | 231066 | 231066 | 63900 | 63900 |

# IAB Level 3 question paper

---

**REQUIRED**

**Task A**   Prepare the Trading and Profit and Loss Account of Direct Catering Supplies for the year ended 31 December 2009 (14 marks)

**Task B**   Prepare the Balance Sheet of Direct Catering Supplies as at 31 December 2009 (16 marks)

**(Total 30 Marks)**

---

**Note:**   The following proformas are provided for your use in completing the above tasks:

- Trading and Profit and Loss Account (see **page 15** of your **Answer Booklet**)
- Balance Sheet (see **page 16** of your **Answer Booklet**)

**IAB**

*Qualifications for business*

Exam I/D 107

# ANSWER BOOKLET

## Qualification:
### Level 3 Diploma in Accounting & Advanced Book-keeping
(Qualification Accreditation Number 500/3022/x)

Record Adjustments and Prepare Financial Statements

## Examination:
**Paper Two**

## January 2010
## Afternoon Sitting

| | |
|---|---|
| **Student Number:** | |
| **Candidate Number:** | |
| **Name of Examination Centre:** | |

For use by assessor only:

| | Section A | | Section B | | | |
|---|---|---|---|---|---|---|
| **Question** | 1 | 2 | 3 | 4 | 5 | **Total** |
| **Marks** | | | | | | |

Suite 30, 40 Churchill Square, Kings Hill, West Malling, Kent, ME19 4YU
Tel: 0844 330 3527, Fax: 0844 330 3514, e-mail: mail@iab.org.uk

438

# IAB Level 3 answer booklet

**Section A** – You must answer **both** questions in this section

**Question One**

**The Belles**

**Task A – Income and Expenditure Account**

| The Belles<br>Income and Expenditure Account for the Year Ended 31 December 2009 | £ | £ | £ |
|---|---|---|---|
| | | | |
| | | | |
| | | | |
| | | | |
| | | | |
| | | | |
| | | | |
| | | | |
| | | | |
| | | | |
| | | | |
| | | | |
| | | | |
| | | | |
| | | | |
| | | | |
| | | | |
| | | | |
| | | | |
| | | | |

**Task B – Balance Sheet**

| The Belles<br>Balance Sheet as at 31 December 2009 | | | |
|---|---|---|---|
| | £ | £ | £ |
| | | | |
| | | | |
| | | | |
| | | | |
| | | | |
| | | | |
| | | | |
| | | | |
| | | | |
| | | | |
| | | | |
| | | | |
| | | | |
| | | | |
| | | | |
| | | | |
| | | | |
| | | | |
| | | | |
| | | | |
| | | | |
| | | | |
| | | | |
| | | | |
| | | | |
| | | | |

Please note: Page 3 of this examination paper is intentionally blank.

# IAB Level 3 answer booklet

**Question Two**

**World of Beds**

Tasks A, C, D, F and H – Ledger Accounts

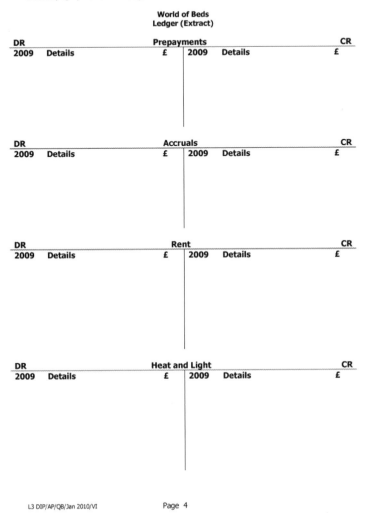

World of Beds
Ledger (Extract)

| DR | | Prepayments | | | CR |
|----|---------|---|------|---------|----|
| **2009** | **Details** | **£** | **2009** | **Details** | **£** |

| DR | | Accruals | | | CR |
|----|---------|---|------|---------|----|
| **2009** | **Details** | **£** | **2009** | **Details** | **£** |

| DR | | Rent | | | CR |
|----|---------|---|------|---------|----|
| **2009** | **Details** | **£** | **2009** | **Details** | **£** |

| DR | | Heat and Light | | | CR |
|----|---------|---|------|---------|----|
| **2009** | **Details** | **£** | **2009** | **Details** | **£** |

# IAB Level 3 answer booklet

**Tasks B, E and G – Journal**

**World of Beds**
**Journal**

| 2009 | Details | DR £ | CR £ |
|------|---------|------|------|
|      |         |      |      |

Please note: Page 6 of this examination paper is intentionally blank.

# IAB Level 3 answer booklet

**Section B** – You must answer **any two** questions from this section

**Question Three**

**A & B (Wholesale) Fashions**

**Task A – Trading and Profit and Loss Account**

| A & B (Wholesale) Fashions Trading and Profit and Loss Account for the Year Ended 31 December 2009 | | | |
|---|---|---|---|
| | £ | £ | £ |
| | | | |
| | | | |
| | | | |
| | | | |
| | | | |
| | | | |
| | | | |
| | | | |
| | | | |
| | | | |
| | | | |
| | | | |
| | | | |
| | | | |
| | | | |
| | | | |
| | | | |
| | | | |
| | | | |
| | | | |
| | | | |
| | | | |
| | | | |
| | | | |
| | | | |
| | | | |

**Task B – Appropriation Account**

| A & B (Wholesale Fashions) Appropriation Account for the Year Ended 31 December 2009 | | |
|---|---|---|
| | £ | £ |
| | | |
| | | |
| | | |
| | | |
| | | |
| | | |
| | | |
| | | |
| | | |
| | | |
| | | |
| | | |
| | | |
| | | |
| | | |
| | | |
| | | |
| | | |
| | | |

**Task C – Current Accounts**

| Details | Amy £ | Beth £ | 2009 | Details | Amy £ | Beth £ |
|---|---|---|---|---|---|---|
| | | | | | | |
| | | | | | | |
| | | | | | | |
| | | | | | | |
| | | | | | | |
| | | | | | | |
| | | | | | | |
| | | | | | | |

Current Accounts / CR

Page 9 of this examination paper is intentionally blank.

**Question Four**

**Fivestar Engineering**

**Tasks A, B, C, E, G, I, J and L – Ledger Accounts**

**Ledger (Extract)**

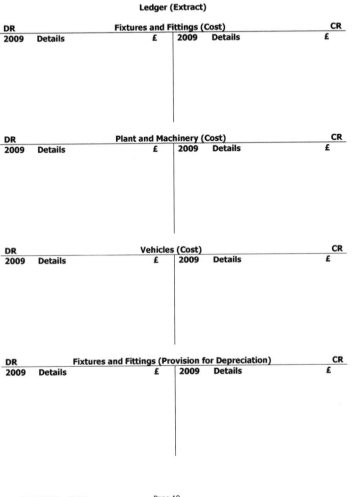

| DR | | Fixtures and Fittings (Cost) | | | CR |
|----|---------|---:|------|---------|---:|
| 2009 | Details | £ | 2009 | Details | £ |

| DR | | Plant and Machinery (Cost) | | | CR |
|----|---------|---:|------|---------|---:|
| 2009 | Details | £ | 2009 | Details | £ |

| DR | | Vehicles (Cost) | | | CR |
|----|---------|---:|------|---------|---:|
| 2009 | Details | £ | 2009 | Details | £ |

| DR | | Fixtures and Fittings (Provision for Depreciation) | | | CR |
|----|---------|---:|------|---------|---:|
| 2009 | Details | £ | 2009 | Details | £ |

**Ledger Accounts (continued)**

| DR | | Plant and Machinery (Provision for Depreciation) | | CR |
|---|---|---|---|---|
| 2009 | Details | £ | 2009 Details | £ |

| DR | | Vehicles (Provision for Depreciation) | | CR |
|---|---|---|---|---|
| 2009 | Details | £ | 2009 Details | £ |

| DR | | Fixed Asset Disposal | | CR |
|---|---|---|---|---|
| 2009 | Details | £ | 2009 Details | £ |

| DR | | Depreciation Expense | | CR |
|---|---|---|---|---|
| 2009 | Details | £ | 2009 Details | £ |

# IAB Level 3 answer booklet

**Tasks D, F, H and K – Journal**

**Journal**

| 2009 | Details | DR £ | CR £ |
|------|---------|------|------|
|      |         |      |      |
|      |         |      |      |
|      |         |      |      |
|      |         |      |      |
|      |         |      |      |
|      |         |      |      |
|      |         |      |      |
|      |         |      |      |
|      |         |      |      |
|      |         |      |      |
|      |         |      |      |
|      |         |      |      |
|      |         |      |      |

447

**Journal (continued)**

**Journal**

| 2009 | Details | DR £ | CR £ |
|------|---------|------|------|
|      |         |      |      |
|      |         |      |      |
|      |         |      |      |
|      |         |      |      |
|      |         |      |      |
|      |         |      |      |
|      |         |      |      |
|      |         |      |      |
|      |         |      |      |
|      |         |      |      |
|      |         |      |      |

Page 14 of this examination paper is intentionally blank.

**Question Five**

**Direct Catering Supplies**

Task A – Trading and Profit and Loss Account

| Direct Catering Supplies Trading and Profit and Loss Account for the Year Ended 31 December 2009 | £ | £ | £ |
|---|---|---|---|
| | | | |
| | | | |
| | | | |
| | | | |
| | | | |
| | | | |
| | | | |
| | | | |
| | | | |
| | | | |
| | | | |
| | | | |
| | | | |
| | | | |
| | | | |
| | | | |
| | | | |
| | | | |
| | | | |
| | | | |
| | | | |
| | | | |
| | | | |
| | | | |
| | | | |
| | | | |
| | | | |
| | | | |

**Task B – Balance Sheet**

| Direct Catering Supplies Balance Sheet as at 31 December 2009 | | | |
|---|---|---|---|
| | £ | £ | £ |
| | | | |
| | | | |
| | | | |
| | | | |
| | | | |
| | | | |
| | | | |
| | | | |
| | | | |
| | | | |
| | | | |
| | | | |
| | | | |
| | | | |
| | | | |
| | | | |
| | | | |
| | | | |
| | | | |
| | | | |
| | | | |
| | | | |
| | | | |
| | | | |
| | | | |
| | | | |
| | | | |
| | | | |

Page 17 of this examination paper is intentionally blank.

**IAB**
*Qualifications for business*

Exam I/D 107

# MODEL ANSWERS

## Qualification:
Level 3 Diploma in Accounting & Advanced Book-keeping
(Qualification Accreditation Number 500/3022/x)

Record Adjustments and Prepare Financial Statements

## Examination:
Paper Two

## January 2010
Afternoon Sitting

Suite 30, 40 Churchill Square, Kings Hill, West Malling, Kent, ME19 4YU
Tel: 0844 330 3527, Fax: 0844 330 3514, e-mail: mail@iab.org.uk

**Section A**

**Answer Question One**

**The Belles**

**Task A – Income and Expenditure Account**

**The Belles**
**Income and Expenditure Account for the Year Ended 31 December 2009**

| Income | | £ | | £ | | £ |
|---|---|---|---|---|---|---|
| Match day gate receipts | | | ½ | 6,680 | | |
| Subscriptions | | | 2 | 1,900 | | |
| Raffle ticket sales | ½ | 3,140 | | | | |
| **Less** Raffle prizes | ½ | 1,200 | | | | |
| Profit on raffles | | | ½ | 1,940 | | |
| Donations | | | ½ | 1,800 | | |
| | | | | | | 12,320 |
| **Expenditure** | | | | | | |
| Minibus running costs | | | ½ | 1,820 | | |
| Ground maintenance | | | ½ | 1,500 | | |
| Insurances | | | ½ | 600 | | |
| Ground rent | | | 2 | 2,300 | | |
| League affiliation fees | | | ½ | 250 | | |
| Referee and linesmen fees | | | ½ | 1,400 | | |
| Depreciation (£3,000 + £900) | | | 1 | 3,900 | | |
| | | | | | | 11,770 |
| **Surplus of income over expenditure** | | | | | 2 | 550 |

12 Marks this page C/F

**Task B – Balance Sheet**

**The Belles**
**Balance Sheet as at 31 December 2009**

| Fixed Assets | | £ | | £ | | £ |
|---|---|---|---|---|---|---|
| Minibus (net book value) | | | 2 | 9,000 | | |
| Club equipment (net book value) | | | 3 | 3,600 | | |
| | | | | | | 12,600 |
| **Current Assets** | | | | | | |
| Subscriptions (in arrears) | 1 | 120 | | | | |
| Ground rent (prepaid) | 1 | 400 | | | | |
| Bank and cash | 1 | 4,150 | | | | |
| | | | | 4,670 | | |
| **Less Current Liabilities** | | | | | | |
| Subscriptions (received in advance) | | | 1 | 480 | | |
| | | | | | | 4,190 |
| | | | | | 1 | 16,790 |
| **Represented By** | | | | | | |
| Opening accumulated fund | | | 1 | 16,240 | | |
| **Add** surplus in year | | | 1 | 550 | | |
| Accumulated fund at 31/12/2009 | | | | | 1 | 16,790 |

13 Marks this page
12 Marks b/f
25 Total Marks

# IAB Level 3 model answers

**Workings**

| DR | Subscriptions | | CR | DR | Ground Rent | | CR |
|---|---|---|---|---|---|---|---|
| | £ | | £ | | £ | | £ |
| Balance b/f | 180 | Balance b/f | 360 | Balance b/f | 300 | Income Exp A/C | 2,300 |
| Income & Exp A/C | 1,900 | Bank | 2,080 | Bank | 2,400 | Balance c/d | 400 |
| Balance c/d | 480 | Balance c/d | 120 | | | | |
| | 2,560 | | 2,560 | | 2,700 | | 2,700 |
| Balance b/d | 120 | Balance b/d | 480 | Balance b/d | 400 | | |

**Answer Question Two**

**World of Beds**

**Tasks A, C, D, F and H – Ledger Accounts**

World of Beds
Ledger (Extract)

| DR | | | Prepayments | | | CR |
|---|---|---|---|---|---|---|
| **2009** | **Details** | | **£** | **2009** | **Details** | **£** |
| 1 Jan | Balance b/f | ½ | 1,600 | 1 Jan | Rent | ¼ 1,600 |
| 31 Dec | Rent | ¼ | 1,800 | | | |

| DR | | | Accruals | | | CR |
|---|---|---|---|---|---|---|
| **2009** | **Details** | | **£** | **2009** | **Details** | **£** |
| 1 Jan | Heat and light | ¼ | 880 | 1 Jan | Balance b/f | ½ 880 |
| | | | | 31 Dec | Heat and light | ¼ 920 |

| DR | | | Rent | | | CR |
|---|---|---|---|---|---|---|
| **2009** | **Details** | | **£** | **2009** | **Details** | **£** |
| 1 Jan | Prepayments | ¼ | 1,600 | 31 Dec | Prepayments | ¼ 1,800 |
| 20 Feb | Bank | ¼ | 4,800 | 31 Dec | Profit and loss | ½ 10,000 |
| 20 Aug | Bank | ¼ | 5,400 | | | |
| | | | 11,800 | | | 11,800 |

| DR | | | Heat and Light | | | CR |
|---|---|---|---|---|---|---|
| **2009** | **Details** | | **£** | **2009** | **Details** | **£** |
| 20 Jan | Bank | ¼ | 880 | 1 Jan | Accruals | ¼ 880 |
| 20 Apr | Bank | ¼ | 950 | 31 Dec | Profit and loss | ½ 3,450 |
| 20 Jul | Bank | ¼ | 780 | | | |
| 20 Oct | Bank | ¼ | 800 | | | |
| 31 Dec | Accruals | ¼ | 920 | | | |
| | | | 4,330 | | | 4,330 |

5 ½ Marks this page C/F

**Tasks B, E and G – Journal**

## World of Beds
## Journal

| 2009 | Details | DR £ | CR £ |
|---|---|---|---|
| 1 Jan | Rent ¼ <br> Prepayments ¼ <br><br> Reversal of adjustment for rent prepaid at year end 31 December 2008 ¼ | ¼ 1,600 | ¼ 1,600 |
| 1 Jan | Accruals ¼ <br> Heat and light ¼ <br><br> Reversal of adjustment for heat and light accrued at year end 31 December 2008 ¼ | ¼ 880 | ¼ 880 |
| 31 Dec | Prepayments ¼ <br> Rent ¼ <br><br> Adjustment for rent prepaid at year end 31 December 2009 ¼ | ½ 1,800 | ½ 1,800 |
| 31 Dec | Heat and light ¼ <br> Accruals ¼ <br><br> Adjustment for heat and light accrued at year end 31 December 2009 ¼ | ½ 920 | ½ 920 |
| 31 Dec | Profit and loss ¼ <br> Rent ¼ <br><br> Expense of rent at year end 31 December 2009 transferred to Profit and Loss Account ¼ | ½ 10,000 | ½ 10,000 |
| 31 Dec | Profit and loss ¼ <br> Heat and light ¼ <br><br> Expense of heat and light at the year end 31 December 2009 transferred to Profit and Loss Account ¼ | ½ 3,450 | ½ 3,450 |

9½ Marks this page
5½ Marks b/f
15 Total Marks

**Workings**

**Rent Prepaid**

£5,400 ÷ 6 = £900 x 2 = £1,800 prepaid

**Heat and Light Accrued**

£800 x 115% = £920 accrued

## Section B

## Question Three

## A & B (Wholesale) Fashions

### Task A – Trading and Profit and Loss Account

**A & B (Wholesale) Fashions**
**Trading and Profit and Loss Account for the Year Ended 31 December 2009**

| | | £ | £ | £ |
|---|---|---|---|---|
| Sales | | ½ 403,440 | | |
| **Less** Sales returns | | ½ 2,260 | | |
| Net Sales | | | | ½ 401,180 |
| **Less Cost of Goods Sold** | | | | |
| Opening stock | ½ 114,520 | | | |
| **Add** Purchases | ½ 227,630 | | | |
| **Add** Carriage inwards | 1 5,790 | | | |
| **Less** Purchase returns | ½ 4,060 | | | |
| | | 343,880 | | |
| **Less** Closing stock (£115,600 - £3,000) | | 2 112,600 | | |
| Cost of sales | | | 1 231,280 | |
| **Gross Profit** | | | 1 169,900 | |
| **Less Expenses** | | | | |
| Office expenses | | ½ 18,550 | | |
| Salaries and wages | | ½ 56,480 | | |
| Discounts allowed | | ½ 4,820 | | |
| Rent and rates (£23,600 - £5,800) | | 1 17,800 | | |
| Motor expenses | | ½ 8,950 | | |
| Heating and lighting (£4,200 + £1,200) | | 1 5,400 | | |
| General expenses (£7,720 - £800) | | 1 6,920 | | |
| Depreciation (£2,500 + £4,720) | | 1 7,220 | | |
| Bad debts | | 1 2,160 | | |
| Provision for doubtful debts (increase) | | 1 380 | | |
| | | | 128,680 | |
| **Net Profit** | | | 1 41,220 | |

17 Marks this page C/F

## Task B – Appropriation Account

**A & B (Wholesale Fashions)**
**Appropriation Account for the Year Ended 31 December 2009**

| | | £ | | £ |
|---|---|---|---|---|
| Net profit | | | ½ | 41,220 |
| **Add:** Interest on Drawings – Amy | ½ | 400 | | |
| – Beth | ½ | 360 | | |
| | | | | 760 |
| | | | | 41,980 |
| **Less:** Interest on Capital – Amy | ½ | 5,600 | | |
| – Beth | ½ | 3,200 | | |
| | | | | 8,800 |
| | | | | 33,180 |
| **Less:** Salaries – Amy | ¼ | 10,000 | | |
| – Beth | ¼ | 8,000 | | |
| | | | | 18,000 |
| | | | | 15,180 |
| **Less:** Share of profit – Amy | 1 | 7,590 | | |
| – Beth | 1 | 7,590 | | |
| | | | | 15,180 |
| | | | | - |

5 Marks

## Task C – Current Accounts

**Current Accounts**     **CR**

| Details | Amy £ | | Beth £ | | 2009 | Details | Amy £ | | Beth £ | |
|---|---|---|---|---|---|---|---|---|---|---|
| Balance b/f | ¼ | 1,250 | | - | 1 Jan | Balance b/f | | - | ¼ | 2,960 |
| Interest on drawings | ½ | 400 | ½ | 360 | 31 Dec | Interest on capital | ½ | 5,600 | ½ | 3,200 |
| Drawings | ½ | 20,000 | ½ | 18,000 | 31 Dec | Salaries | ½ | 10,000 | ½ | 8,000 |
| Balance c/d | 1 | 1,540 | 1 | 3,390 | 31 Dec | Share of profit | ½ | 7,590 | ½ | 7,590 |
| | | 23,190 | | 21,750 | | | | 23,190 | | 21,750 |
| | | | | | 31 Dec | Balance b/d | ¼ | 1,540 | ¼ | 3,390 |
| | | | | | | | 8 Marks | | | |

13 Marks this page
17 Marks b/f
30 Total Marks

**Answer Question Four**

**Fivestar Engineering**

**Tasks A, B, C, E, G, I, J & L – Ledger Accounts**

### Ledger (Extract)

**DR**         Fixtures and Fittings (Cost)         **CR**

| 2009 | Details | | £ | 2009 | Details | | £ |
|---|---|---|---|---|---|---|---|
| 1 Jan | Balance b/f | ½ | 8,000 | 31 Dec | Fixed asset disposal | ½ | 1,600 |
| 1 Mar | Bank | ½ | 2,400 | 31 Dec | Balance c/d | ½ | 8,800 |
| | | | 10,400 | | | | 10,400 |
| 31 Dec | Balance b/d | ¼ | 8,800 | | | | |

**DR**         Plant and Machinery (Cost)         **CR**

| 2009 | Details | | £ | 2009 | Details | | £ |
|---|---|---|---|---|---|---|---|
| 1 Jan | Balance b/f | ½ | 284,000 | 31 Dec | Balance c/d | ½ | 304,000 |
| 1 May | Bank | ½ | 20,000 | | | | |
| | | | 304,000 | | | | 304,000 |
| 31 Dec | Balance b/d | ¼ | 304,000 | | | | |

**DR**         Vehicles (Cost)         **CR**

| 2009 | Details | | £ | 2009 | Details | | £ |
|---|---|---|---|---|---|---|---|
| 1 Jan | Balance b/f | ½ | 120,000 | 31 Dec | Balance c/d | ½ | 156,000 |
| 1 Sept | Bank | ½ | 36,000 | | | | |
| | | | 156,000 | | | | 156,000 |
| 31 Dec | Balance b/d | ¼ | 156,000 | | | | |

**DR**         Fixtures and Fittings (Provision for Depreciation)         **CR**

| 2009 | Details | | £ | 2009 | Details | | £ |
|---|---|---|---|---|---|---|---|
| 31 Dec | Fixed asset disposal | ½ | 800 | 1 Jan | Balance b/f | ½ | 3,000 |
| 31 Dec | Balance c/d | ½ | 3,300 | 31 Dec | Depreciation expense | ½ | 1,100 |
| | | | 4,100 | | | | 4,100 |
| | | | | 31 Dec | Balance b/d | ¼ | 3,300 |

8 Marks this page C/F

**Tasks C, E, I & L – Ledger Accounts (continued)**

| DR | Plant and Machinery (Provision for Depreciation) | | | | CR |
|---|---|---|---|---|---|
| **2009** | **Details** | **£** | **2009** | **Details** | **£** |
| 31 Dec | Balance c/d | ½ 151,680 | 1 Jan | Balance b/f | ½ 113,600 |
| | | | 31 Dec | Depreciation expense | ½ 38,080 |
| | | 151,680 | | | 151,680 |
| | | | 31 Dec | Balance b/d | ¼ 151,680 |

| DR | Vehicles (Provision for Depreciation) | | | | CR |
|---|---|---|---|---|---|
| **2009** | **Details** | **£** | **2009** | **Details** | **£** |
| 31 Dec | Balance c/d | ½ 68,400 | 1 Jan | Balance b/f | ½ 52,500 |
| | | | 31 Dec | Depreciation expense | ½ 15,900 |
| | | 68,400 | | | 68,400 |
| | | | 31 Dec | Balance b/d | ¼ 68,400 |

| DR | Fixed Asset Disposal | | | | CR |
|---|---|---|---|---|---|
| **2009** | **Details** | **£** | **2009** | **Details** | **£** |
| 31 Dec | Fixtures and fittings (cost) | ½ 1,600 | 31 Mar | Bank | ½ 400 |
| | | | 31 Dec | Fixtures and fittings (dep'n) | ½ 800 |
| | | | 31 Dec | Profit and loss | ½ 400 |
| | | 1,600 | | | 1,600 |

| DR | Depreciation Expense | | | | CR |
|---|---|---|---|---|---|
| **2009** | **Details** | **£** | **2009** | **Details** | **£** |
| 31 Dec | Fixtures and fittings (dep'n) | ½ 1,100 | 31 Dec | Profit and loss | ½ 55,080 |
| 31 Dec | Plant and machinery (dep'n) | ½ 38,080 | | | |
| 31 Dec | Vehicles (dep'n) | ½ 15,900 | | | |
| | | 55,080 | | | 55,080 |

7½ Marks this page
8 Marks b/f
15½ Marks C/F

**Tasks D, F, H and K – Journal**

## Journal

| 2009 | Details | DR £ | CR £ |
|---|---|---|---|
| 31 Dec | Fixed asset disposal ¼ <br> Fixtures and fittings (cost) ¼ <br><br> Transfer of cost of fixtures and fittings cost following disposal ¼ | ½ 1,600 | ½ 1,600 |
| 31 Dec | Fixtures and fittings (provision for depreciation) ¼ <br> Fixed asset disposal ¼ <br><br> Transfer of accumulated depreciation on fixtures and fittings following disposal ¼ | ½ 800 | ½ 800 |
| 31 Dec | Depreciation expense ¼ <br> Fixtures and fittings (provision for depreciation) ¼ <br><br> Depreciation on fixtures and fittings at year end ¼ | ½ 1,100 | ½ 1,100 |
| 31 Dec | Depreciation expense ¼ <br> Plant and machinery (provision for depreciation) ¼ <br><br> Depreciation on plant and machinery at year end ¼ | 1 38,080 | 1 38,080 |
| 31 Dec | Depreciation expense ¼ <br> Vehicles (provision for depreciation) ¼ <br><br> Depreciation on vehicles at year end ¼ | 1 15,900 | 1 15,900 |
| 31 Dec | Profit and loss ¼ <br> Fixed asset disposal ¼ <br><br> Loss on disposal transferred to Profit and Loss Account at year end ¼ | ½ 400 | ½ 400 |

12 ½ Marks this page
15 ½ Marks b/f
28   Marks C/F

# IAB Level 3 model answers

**Journal (continued)**

## Journal

| 2009 | Details | DR £ | CR £ |
|------|---------|------|------|
| 31 Dec | Profit and loss ¼<br>Depreciation expense ¼<br><br>Transfer of depreciation expense to Profit and<br>Loss Account at year end ½ | ½ 55,080 | ½ 55,080 |

**Workings**

**Depreciation Fixtures and Fittings**

Cost £8,000 + £2,400 - £1,600 = £8,800 x 12.5% = £1,100 depreciation

**Depreciation Plant and Machinery**

Net Book Value £284,000 + £20,000 (-) £113,600 = £190,400 x 20% = £38,080
depreciation

**Depreciation Vehicles**

Net book value (old vehicles) £120,000 - £52,500 = £67,500

New vehicle purchased 1 September 2009 therefore owned four months at
31 December 2009

Depreciation (old vehicles) £67,500 x 20% = £13,500

Depreciation (new vehicle) £36,000 x 20% = £7,200 ÷ 3 = <u>£2,400</u>

Depreciation in year <u>15,900</u>

L3 DIP/AP/MA/Jan 2010/VI          Page 12

**Answer Question Five**

**Direct Catering Supplies**

Task A – Trading and Profit and Loss Account

**Direct Catering Supplies**
**Trading and Profit and Loss Account for the Year Ended 31 December 2009**

|  | £ | £ | £ |
|---|---|---|---|
| Sales |  | ½ 207,656 |  |
| **Less** Sales returns |  | ½ 1,560 |  |
| Net Sales |  |  | ½ 206,096 |
| **Less Cost of Goods Sold** |  |  |  |
| Opening stock | ½ 21,650 |  |  |
| **Add** Purchases | ½ 118,848 |  |  |
| **Less** Purchase returns | ½ 1,810 |  |  |
|  |  | 138,688 |  |
| **Less** Closing stock |  | ½ 19,980 |  |
| Cost of Sales |  |  | 1 118,708 |
| **Gross Profit** |  |  | 1 87,388 |
| **Add Other Income** |  |  |  |
| Discount received |  |  | 1 1,620 |
|  |  |  | ½ 89,008 |
| **Less Expenses** |  |  |  |
| Wages and salaries |  | ½ 38,975 |  |
| Warehouse rent |  | ½ 12,400 |  |
| Warehouse rates |  | ½ 8,400 |  |
| Insurances |  | ½ 1,400 |  |
| Heat and light |  | ½ 2,450 |  |
| Office and admin expenses |  | ½ 1,065 |  |
| Advertising |  | ½ 1,500 |  |
| Bad debts |  | ½ 980 |  |
| Discount allowed |  | 1 1,280 |  |
| Cleaning and maintenance |  | ½ 673 |  |
| Depreciation |  | ½ 1,486 |  |
|  |  |  | 70,609 |
| **Net Profit** |  |  | 1 18,399 |

14 Marks this page C/F

**Task B – Balance Sheet**

**Direct Catering Supplies**
**Balance Sheet as at 31 December 2009**

| | £ | | £ | | £ | |
|---|---|---|---|---|---|---|
| | **Cost** | | **Less Dep'n to Date** | | **NBV** | |
| **Fixed Assets** | | | | | | |
| Fixtures and fittings | ½ | 8,000 | ½ | 3,856 | ½ | 4,144 |
| Office equipment | ½ | 4,500 | ½ | 1,350 | ½ | 3,150 |
| | | 12,500 | | 5,206 | 1 | 7,294 |
| **Current Assets** | | | | | | |
| Stock | 1 | 19,980 | | | | |
| Trade debtors | ½ | 6,500 | | | | |
| Prepayments | 1 | 1,600 | | | | |
| Bank | ½ | 5,760 | | | | |
| Cash | ½ | 560 | | | | |
| | | | ½ | 34,400 | | |
| **Less Current Liabilities** | | | | | | |
| Trade creditors | ½ | 7,310 | | | | |
| Accruals | ½ | 300 | | | | |
| | | | ½ | 7,610 | | |
| Working capital | | | | | 1 | 26,790 |
| | | | | | 2 | 34,084 |
| **Financed By:** | | | | | | |
| Capital | ½ | 32,685 | | | | |
| **Add** Net profit | ½ | 18,399 | | | | |
| | | | | 51,084 | | |
| **Less** Drawings | | | ½ | 17,000 | | |
| | | | | | 2 | 34,084 |

16 Marks this page
14 Marks b/f
30 Total Marks

Exam I/D 108

# QUESTION PAPER

## Qualification:
Level 4 Diploma in Accounting to International
Standards
(Qualification Accreditation Number 500/3370/0)

## Examination:
Single unit: Prepare and Appraise Financial Statements

## January 2010

**Time Allowed: 3 hours**

Suite 30, 40 Churchill Square, Kings Hill, West Malling, Kent ME 19 4YU
Tel: 0844 330 3527, Fax: 0844 330 3514, e-mail:mail@iab.org.uk

# IAB Level 4 question paper

**IAB LEVEL 4 DIPLOMA IN ACCOUNTING TO INTERNATIONAL STANDARDS**

**UNIT TITLE: PREPARE AND APPRAISE FINANCIAL STATEMENTS**

**GENERAL INFORMATION AND INSTRUCTIONS**

- THIS QUESTION BOOKLET CONTAINS FIVE QUESTIONS WITHIN TWO SECTIONS. YOU MUST ANSWER **FOUR** QUESTIONS AS FOLLOWS:

  SECTION A   -   ANSWER **BOTH** QUESTIONS IN THIS SECTION

  - Question One Carries 25 Marks
  - Question Two Carries 15 Marks

  SECTION B   -   ANSWER **ANY TWO** OF THE QUESTIONS IN THIS SECTION

  - All Questions Carry Equal Marks – 30 Marks Each

- In addition to this Question Paper you are also provided with an Answer Booklet.

- You must enter your **Student Number, Candidate Number** and **Name of Examination Centre** in the boxes provided on the front cover of your **Answer Booklet**.

- **Time Allowed: Three hours.** It is recommended that this time be allocated as follows:

  - SECTION A QUESTIONS   -   80 Minutes
  - SECTION B QUESTIONS   -   100 Minutes

- All answers are to be written in **ink**.

- Blank pages are provided in your **Answer Booklet** for notes/workings

- Correcting fluid can be used in moderation, otherwise cross out errors neatly.

- The use of silent non-programmable calculators is permitted.

- If you answer three questions from Section B, you must cross out the answer you do not want marking, otherwise we will take the marks of your first two answers.

- **NOTE – This question paper has information and data printed on both sides of the pages.**

**Section A** – You must answer **both** questions in this section

**Question One**

The following Trial Balance has been extracted from the books of Hudson Ltd at 31 December 2009:

**Trial Balance as at 31 December 2009**

|  | DR £'000 | CR £'000 |
|---|---|---|
| Share capital (ordinary shares of £1 each) | | 2,000 |
| Share premium | | 500 |
| Retained earnings (31/12/2008) | | 580 |
| Land and buildings – cost | 2,500 | |
| Land and buildings – accumulated depreciation (31/12/2009) | | 250 |
| Plant and machinery – cost | 2,175 | |
| Plant and machinery – accumulated depreciation (31/12/2009) | | 1,230 |
| 8% Loan stock (2015) | | 500 |
| Revenue | | 16,127 |
| Purchases | 10,490 | |
| Accruals | | 62 |
| Prepayments | 56 | |
| Inventories (31/12/2008) | 1,120 | |
| Provision for doubtful receivables (31/12/2009) | | 22 |
| Trade receivables | 1,270 | |
| Trade payables | | 1,050 |
| Loan stock interest paid | 20 | |
| Interim dividend paid | 180 | |
| Distribution costs | 1,040 | |
| Administrative expenses | 2,180 | |
| Cash and cash equivalents | 1,290 | |
| | 22,321 | 22,321 |

You are also provided with the following additional information as at 31 December 2009:

i   Inventories as at 31 December 2009 were valued at cost of £1,300,000.

ii  An accrual for the balance of annual interest on the loan stock is to be provided for.

iii Land included in the land and buildings at cost figure on the Trial Balance above and valued at £500,000 is to be revalued at 31 December 2009 at £800,000. Company policy is not to depreciate land.

iv  The corporation tax expense for the year ended 31 December 2009 is estimated to be £650,000.

V     Administrative expenses of £15,000 are prepaid at 31 December 2009.

Vi    All operations are continuing operations.

---

**REQUIRED:**

**Task A**   Prepare the Income Statement of Hudson Ltd for the year ended 31 December 2009 in accordance with IAS 1

**Task B**   Prepare the Balance Sheet of Hudson Ltd at 31 December 2009 in accordance with IAS 1

             Notes to the financial statements are not required but detailed workings should be shown where appropriate

**(Total 25 Marks)**

---

**Note:**  The following proformas are provided for your use in completing the above tasks:

- Income statement (see **page 1** of your **answer booklet**)
- Balance Sheet (see **page 2** of your **answer booklet**)

**Question Two**

There are a wide range of users who are interested in the financial statements of limited companies.

---

**REQUIRED:**

Explain the scope of interest in the financial statements of a company of each of the following users:

- Investors
- Lenders
- Suppliers

**(Total 15 Marks)**

---

**Note:** You are presented with the following proforma for your use in completing the above task:

- Ruled/lined area (see **pages 4 and 5** of your **answer booklet**)

**Section B** – You must answer **any two** questions from this section

## Question Three

The draft Balance Sheets of Don plc and Nile Ltd for the year ended 31 December 2009 are set out below:

### Balance Sheets at 31 December 2009

| | Don plc £'000 | Don plc £'000 | Nile Ltd £'000 | Nile Ltd £'000 |
|---|---|---|---|---|
| **ASSETS** | | | | |
| Non-current assets | | | | |
| Property, plant and equipment | 16,899 | | 2,282 | |
| Investment in Nile Ltd (at cost) | 2,570 | | - | |
| | | 19,469 | | 2,282 |
| | | | | |
| Current assets | | | | |
| Inventories | 4,462 | | 666 | |
| Trade and other receivables | 3,050 | | 496 | |
| Cash and cash equivalents | 110 | | 130 | |
| | | 7,622 | | 1,292 |
| **Total assets** | | 27,091 | | 3,574 |
| | | | | |
| **EQUITY AND LIABILITIES** | | | | |
| Equity | | | | |
| Issued share capital | 10,000 | | 1,200 | |
| Share premium | 2,000 | | 250 | |
| Retained earnings | 11,522 | | 1,010 | |
| | | 23,522 | | 2,460 |
| Non-current liabilities | | | | |
| Long-term loan | | - | | 500 |
| | | | | |
| Current liabilities | | | | |
| Trade and other payables | 2,704 | | 359 | |
| Taxation | 865 | | 255 | |
| | | 3,569 | | 614 |
| **Total equity and liabilities** | | 27,091 | | 3,574 |

The following information is also available:

i     Don plc acquired 960,000 of the shares in Nile Ltd on 31 December 2008.

ii     The share capital of both Don plc and Nile Ltd consists of ordinary shares of £1 each. There have been no changes to the balances of share capital or share premium during the year to 31 December 2009.

iii     At 31 December 2008 the balance on the retained earnings account of Nile Ltd was £760,000.

iv    As at 31 December 2008 the property plant and equipment of Nile Ltd was
      professionally revalued. It was established that the fair value of property
      plant and equipment was £2,000,000. At the date the revaluation was
      carried out the net book value of the property, plant and equipment of
      Nile Ltd was £1,500,000. The revaluation has not yet been reflected in the
      Balance Sheet of Nile Ltd.

v     There was no impairment of goodwill in the year ended 31 December
      2009.

---

**REQUIRED:**

Prepare the Consolidated Balance Sheet of Don plc and its subsidiary for the
year ended 31 December 2009.

You should show any workings used in completing the above task.

**(Total 30 Marks)**

---

**Note:**   The following proforma is provided for your use in completing the above
task:

- Consolidated Balance Sheet (see **page 6** of your **answer booklet**)

## Question Four

Derwent Ltd has prepared the following draft financial statements:

**Derwent Ltd**
**Balance Sheets at 31 December**

| | 2009 | 2008 |
|---|---|---|
| **ASSETS** | £'000 | £'000 |
| **Non-current assets** | | |
| Property, plant and equipment | 4,365 | 3,555 |
| | | |
| **Current assets** | | |
| Short-term investments at cost | 903 | 828 |
| Inventories | 1,080 | 745 |
| Trade and other receivables | 970 | 747 |
| Cash and cash equivalents | - | 216 |
| | | |
| **Total assets** | 7,318 | 6,091 |
| | | |
| **EQUITY AND LIABILITIES** | | |
| **Capital and reserves** | | |
| Share capital | 855 | 675 |
| Share premium | 792 | 525 |
| Retained earnings | 3,562 | 2,856 |
| **Total shareholders' funds** | 5,209 | 4,056 |
| | | |
| **Non-current liabilities** | | |
| 10% Loan stock | 465 | 575 |
| | | |
| **Current liabilities** | | |
| Bank overdraft | 84 | - |
| Trade and other payables | 835 | 644 |
| Income tax payables | 725 | 816 |
| | | |
| **Total equity and liabilities** | 7,318 | 6,091 |

**Derwent Ltd**
**Income Statement for the year ended 31 December 2009**

| | £'000 |
|---|---|
| **Revenue** | 4,132 |
| Cost of sales | 2,064 |
| **Gross profit** | 2,068 |
| Distribution costs | 151 |
| Administrative expenses | 331 |
| **Profit from operations** | 1,586 |
| Finance costs | 57 |
| **Profit before tax** | 1,529 |
| Income tax expense | 574 |
| **Profit for the year** | 955 |

The following data is relevant to the year ended 31 December 2009:

(a) Depreciation charged for the year was £512,000

(b) Dividends paid during the year amounted to £249,000.

(c) Leasehold premises costing £488,000 were acquired during the year.

(d) Plant and equipment with a net book value of £104,000, was sold for £63,000, giving a loss on disposal of £41,000

---

**REQUIRED:**

Prepare the Cash Flow Statement of Derwent Ltd for the year ended 31 December 2009 in accordance with the requirements of IAS 7.

You should show any workings used in completing the above task.

**(Total 30 Marks)**

---

**Note:** You are provided with the following proforma for your use in completing the above task:

- Cash Flow Statement (see **page 8** of your **answer booklet**)

## Question Five

Set out below are the draft Balance Sheets and Income Statements for Tyne plc and Wear Ltd, for the year ended 31 December 2009:

**Balance Sheets at 31 December 2009**

| | Tyne plc £'000 | Wear Ltd £'000 |
|---|---|---|
| **ASSETS** | | |
| **Non-current assets** | | |
| Property, plant and equipment | 2,280 | 9,380 |
| | | |
| **Current assets** | | |
| Inventories | 144 | 315 |
| Trade receivables | 450 | 1,260 |
| Cash and cash equivalents | 6 | 264 |
| | 600 | 1,839 |
| **Total assets** | 2,880 | 11,219 |
| | | |
| **EQUITY AND LIABILITIES** | | |
| **Capital and reserves** | | |
| Share capital – ordinary shares of £1 each | 1,600 | 1,800 |
| Retained earnings | 690 | 4,207 |
| **Total shareholders' funds** | 2,290 | 6,007 |
| | | |
| **Non-current liabilities** | | |
| Long-term borrowings | 120 | 3,000 |
| | | |
| **Current liabilities** | | |
| Trade payables | 271 | 1,412 |
| Income tax payables | 199 | 800 |
| | 470 | 2,212 |
| **Total equity and liabilities** | 2,880 | 11,219 |

**Income Statements for the year ended
31 December 2009**

|  | Tyne plc £'000 | Wear Ltd £'000 |
|---|---|---|
| Revenue | 1,800 | 8,400 |
| Cost of sales | 720 | 2,520 |
| **Gross profit** | 1,080 | 5,880 |
| Distribution costs | 156 | 864 |
| Administrative expenses | 180 | 420 |
| **Profit from operations** | 744 | 4,596 |
| Finance costs | 6 | 144 |
| **Profit before tax** | 738 | 4,452 |
| Income tax | 199 | 1,202 |
| **Net profit for the period** | 539 | 3,250 |

---

**REQUIRED:**

**Task A** Calculate the following ratios for Tyne plc and Wear Ltd for the year ended 31 December 2009:

- Return on capital employed (at 31 December 2009)
- Gross profit margin
- Net profit margin
- Current ratio
- Acid test (quick) ratio

**NB:** Display your ratios using the table provided in your answer booklet. Use the workings area below the table to show the formulae used in calculating the ratios and your workings. Express your ratios to two decimal places.

**Task B** Briefly explain the purpose of each of the ratios calculated above and comment on the relative performance of each company in terms of profitability and liquidity for the year ended 31 December 2009.

**(Total 30 Marks)**

---

**Note:** You are provided with the following proformas for your use in completing the above tasks:

- Table of ratios (see **page 10** of your **answer booklet**)
- Workings area to show the formula and workings used in calculating each ratio (see **pages 10 and 11** of your **answer booklet**)
- Ruled/(lined) area to be used for the purpose of presenting your comments (see **pages 12 and 13** of your **answer booklet**)

Exam I/D 108

# ANSWER BOOKLET

## Qualification:

Level 4 Diploma in Accounting to International Standards

(Qualification Accreditation Number 500/3370/0)

## Examination:

Single unit: Prepare and Appraise Financial Statements

## January 2010

| Student Number: | |
|---|---|
| Candidate Number: | |
| Name of Exam Centre: | |

For use by assessor only:

| | Section A | | Section B | | | |
|---|---|---|---|---|---|---|
| Question | 1 | 2 | 3 | 4 | 5 | Total |
| Marks | | | | | | |

Suite 30, 40 Churchill Square, Kings Hill, West Malling, Kent ME 19 4YU
Tel: 0844 330 3527, Fax: 0844 330 3514, e-mail:mail@iab.org.uk

# IAB Level 4 answer booklet

**Section A** – You must answer **both** questions in this section

**For Use in Answering Question One**

**Task A – Income Statement**

**Hudson Ltd**
**Income Statement**
**For the Year Ended 31 December 2009**

| Continuing operations | £'000 |
|---|---|
| Revenue | |
| Cost of Sales | |
| **Gross profit** | _____ |
| Distribution costs | |
| Administrative expenses | |
| **Profit from operations** | _____ |
| Finance costs | |
| **Profit before tax** | _____ |
| Income tax expense | |
| **Net profit for the period from continuing operations** | _____ |
| | _____ |

# IAB Level 4 answer booklet

**Task B – Balance Sheet**

**Hudson Ltd**
**Balance Sheet at 31 December 2009**

| | £'000 |
|---|---|
| **Assets** | |
| **Non-current assets** | |
| | |
| **Current assets** | |
| | |
| **Total assets** | ———— |
| **Equity and Liabilities** | |
| **Share capital and reserves** | |
| | |
| **Total shareholders' funds** | |
| **Non-current liabilities** | |
| | |
| **Current liabilities** | |
| | |
| **Total equity and liabilities** | ———— |

Please note: Page 3 of this answer booklet is intentionally blank.

# IAB Level 4 answer booklet

**For Use in Answering Question Two**

**Scope of interest in the financial statements of a company**
**Users – Investors, Lenders and Suppliers:**

# IAB Level 4 answer booklet

**Section B** – You must answer **any two** questions from this section

**For Use in Answering Question Three**

**Don plc - Consolidated Balance Sheet**

**Don plc**
**Consolidated Balance Sheet at 31 December 2009**

| ASSETS | £'000 | £'000 |
|---|---|---|
| Non-current assets | | |

Current assets

| Total assets | | |
|---|---|---|

**EQUITY AND LIABILITIES**
**Capital and reserves**

Minority interest

**Non-current liabilities**

**Current liabilities**

| Total equity and liabilities | | |
|---|---|---|

Please note: Page 7 of this answer booklet is intentionally blank.

# IAB Level 4 answer booklet

**For Use in Answering Question Four**

**Derwent Ltd – Cash Flow Statement**

| Derwent Ltd<br>Cash Flow Statement<br>For the Year Ended 31 December 2009 | £'000 | £'000 |
|---|---|---|
| **Cash flows from operating activities** | | |
| | | |
| | | |
| | | |
| | | |
| | | |
| | | |
| | | |
| | | |
| | | |
| | | |
| Net cash from/(used in) operating activities | | |
| **Cash flows from investing activities** | | |
| | | |
| | | |
| | | |
| Net cash from/(used in) investing activities | | |
| **Cash flows from financing activities** | | |
| | | |
| | | |
| Net cash from/(used in) financing activities | | |
| **Net increase/(decrease) in cash and cash equivalents** | | |
| **Cash and cash equivalents at beginning of period** | | |
| **Cash and cash equivalents at end of period** | | |

Please note: Page 9 of this answer booklet is intentionally blank.

**For Use in Answering Question Five**

**Tyne plc and Wear Ltd**

**Task A – Table of Ratios**

<table>
<tr><td colspan="3" align="center">Tyne plc and Wear Ltd<br>Table of Financial Ratios<br>For the Year Ended 31 December 2009</td></tr>
<tr><td>Ratio</td><td>Tyne plc</td><td>Wear Ltd</td></tr>
<tr><td>Return on capital employed</td><td></td><td></td></tr>
<tr><td>Gross profit ratio</td><td></td><td></td></tr>
<tr><td>Net profit ratio</td><td></td><td></td></tr>
<tr><td>Current ratio</td><td></td><td></td></tr>
<tr><td>Acid test (quick) ratio</td><td></td><td></td></tr>
</table>

**Task A – Workings Area (to show Formulae Used and Workings)**

**Return on capital employed (at 31 December 2009)**

**Gross profit ratio**

**Net profit ratio**

**Current ratio**

**Acid test (quick) ratio**

485

# IAB Level 4 answer booklet

Task B  —  Tyne plc and Wear Ltd

The purpose of each of the ratios calculated above and comments on the relative performance of each of the companies in terms of profitability and liquidity for the year ended 31 December 2009.

Please note: Page 14 of this answer booklet is intentionally blank.

Qualifications for business

Exam I/D 108

# MODEL ANSWERS

## Qualification:
Level 4 Diploma in Accounting to International Standards
(Qualification Accreditation Number 500/3370/0)

## Examination:
Single unit: Prepare and Appraise Financial Statements

## January 2010

Suite 30, 40 Churchill Square, Kings Hill, West Maling, Kent ME 19 4YU
Tel: 0844 330 3527, Fax: 0844 330 3514, e-mail:mail@iab.org.uk

488

## Answer Question One

**Hudson Ltd**
**Income Statement for the Year Ended 31 December 2009**

| Continuing operations | | £'000 |
|---|---|---|
| Revenue | ½ | 16,127 |
| Cost of sales | 2 | 10,310 |
| **Gross profit** | ½ | 5,817 |
| Distribution costs | ½ | 1,040 |
| Administrative expenses | 2 | 2,165 |
| **Profit from operations** | | 2,612 |
| Finance costs | 2 | 40 |
| **Profit before tax** | | 2,572 |
| Income tax expense | ½ | 650 |
| **Net profit for the period from continuing operations** | 1 | 1,922 |

9 marks this page c/f

**Workings £'000**

| Cost of sales | £'000 |
|---|---|
| Opening inventories | 1,120 |
| Purchases | 10,490 |
| | 11,610 |
| Closing inventories | (1,300) |
| | 10,310 |

**Administrative expenses**

£2,180 - £15 = £2,165

**Finance costs**

£20 + £20 = £40

**Hudson Ltd**
**Balance Sheet at 31 December 2009**

|  |  | £'000 |
|---|---|---|
| **Assets** |  |  |
| **Non-current assets** |  |  |
| Property, plant and equipment | 2 | 3,495 |
|  |  |  |
| **Current assets** |  |  |
| Inventories | 1 | 1,300 |
| Trade and other receivables | 2 | 1,319 |
| Cash and cash equivalents | 1 | 1,290 |
|  |  | 3,909 |
|  |  |  |
| **Total assets** | 1 | 7,404 |
|  |  |  |
| **Equity and Liabilities** |  |  |
| **Share capital and reserves** |  |  |
| Share capital | 1 | 2,000 |
| Share premium | 1 | 500 |
| Revaluation reserve | 1 | 300 |
| Retained earnings | 2 | 2,322 |
|  |  |  |
| **Total shareholders' funds** |  | 5,122 |
|  |  |  |
| **Non-current liabilities** |  |  |
| 8% Loan stock (2015) | 1 | 500 |
|  |  |  |
| **Current liabilities** |  |  |
| Trade and other payables | 1 | 1,132 |
| Income tax payable | 1 | 650 |
|  |  | 1,782 |
|  |  |  |
| **Total equity and liabilities** | 1 | 7,404 |

16 marks this page
9 marks b/f
25 Total marks

# IAB Level 4 model answers

**Workings (£'000)**
**Property, plant and equipment**

| | Cost £'000 | Acc'd Dep'n £'000 | NBV £'000 |
|---|---|---|---|
| Land and buildings (£2,500 + £300) | 2,800 | 250 | 2,550 |
| Plant and machinery | 2,175 | 1,230 | 945 |
| | 4,975 | 1,480 | 3,495 |

**Trade and other receivables**

£1,270 - £22 + £56 + £15 = £1,319

**Retained earnings**

| | £'000 |
|---|---|
| Net profit in period | 1,922 |
| Retained earnings (31/12/2008) | 580 |
| Interim dividends paid | (180) |
| Retained earnings (31/12/2009) | 2,322 |

**Trade and other payables**

£1,050 + £62 + £20 = £1,132

**Answer Question Two**

## Users of financial statements

There are a wide range of users who are interested in the financial statements of limited companies. This includes the following:

- Investors will use financial statements to determine whether to buy, hold or sell shares(2). They will also use financial statements to assess the ability of the entity to pay dividends(2). Potential investors use financial statements to help determine whether or not they should buy shares(2). They will be interested in the stability of a company, its future potential and the stewardship of its management(3). (9 marks)

- Lenders will use financial statements to assess the ability of a company to meet interest payments and repay capital. (3 marks)

- Suppliers will use financial statements to assess the liquidity position of a company to determine whether amounts owing to them will be paid when they fall due (3 marks)

(Total 15 Marks)

**Answer Question Three**

**Don plc and Nile Ltd**

**Consolidated Balance Sheet**

**Don plc**
**Consolidated Balance Sheet at 31 December 2009**

| | £'000 | £'000 |
|---|---|---|
| **Assets** | | |
| **Non-current assets** | | |
| Goodwill (W4) | 3    402 | |
| Property, plant and equipment | 3 19,681 | |
| | | 20,083 |
| **Current assets** | | |
| Inventories | 2   5,128 | |
| Trade and other receivables | 2   3,546 | |
| Cash and cash equivalents | 2     240 | |
| | | 8,914 |
| **Total assets** | | 3 28,997 |
| | | |
| **Equity and Liabilities** | | |
| Equity | | |
| Share capital | 1  10,000 | |
| Share premium | 1   2,000 | |
| Consolidated retained earnings (W6) | 3  11,722 | |
| Equity attributable to holders of the parent | | 23,722 |
| Minority interest (W5) | | 3     592 |
| | | 24,314 |
| **Long-term liabilities** | | |
| Long-term loan | | 500 |
| **Current liabilities** | | |
| Trade and other payables | 2   3,063 | |
| Taxation | 2   1,120 | |
| | | 4,183 |
| **Total equity and liabilities** | | 3 28,997 |
| | | 30 Total marks |

**Don plc and Nile Ltd**

**Workings**

**W1 Group Structure**

| | | | | |
|---|---|---|---|---|
| Parent | 80% | Shares acquired by parent | 960,000 | = 80% |
| Subsidiary | 20% | Share capital of subsidiary | 1,200,000 | |
| | 100% | | | |

**W2 Revaluation Reserve**

| | £'000 |
|---|---|
| Fair value of property, plant and equipment | 2,000 |
| Less Book value | 1,500 |
| Revaluation (increase) | 500 |

Consolidated property, plant and equipment.

| | £000 |
|---|---|
| Don plc - property, plant and equipment | 16,899 |
| Nile Ltd - property, plant and equipment  (£2,282 + £500) | 2,782 |
| Consolidated property, plant and equipment | 19,681 |

**W3 Net Assets of Subsidiary**

| | At Date of Acquisition £'000 | At Balance Sheet Date £'000 |
|---|---|---|
| Share capital | 1,200 | 1,200 |
| Share premium | 250 | 250 |
| Revaluation reserve | 500 | 500 |
| Retained earnings | 760 | 1,010 |
| | 2,710 | 2,960 |

**W4 Goodwill**

| | £'000 | |
|---|---|---|
| Cost of investment in subsidiary | 2,570 | |
| Share of net assets in subsidiary | 2,168 | (£2,710 x 80%) |
| Goodwill | 402 | |

**W5 Minority Interest**

Net assets of subsidiary at Balance Sheet date
£2,960 x 20% = £592

**W6 Consolidated Retained Earnings**

|  | £'000 |
|---|---|
| Retained earnings of parent (100%) | 11,522 |
| Post acquisition retained earnings of subsidiary £250 x 80% | 200 |
| Group retained earnings | 11,722 |

**Answer Question Four**

**Derwent Ltd**
**Cash Flow Statement**
**for the year ended 31 December 2009**

|  | £'000 | £'000 |
|---|---|---|
| **Cash flows from operating activities** | | |
| Operating profit (before interest and tax) | 1 1,586 | |
| Adjustments for: | | |
| Depreciation | 1  512 | |
| Loss on disposal of non-current assets | 1   41 | |
|  | 2,139 | |
| Increase in trade and other receivables | 2 (223) | |
| Increase in inventories | 2 (335) | |
| Increase in trade and other payables | 2  191 | |
| Cash generated from operations | 1,772 | |
| Interest paid | 1  (57) | |
| Income taxes paid (working 2) | 3 (665) | |
| **Net cash flow from operating activities** | | 1 1,050 |
| | | |
| **Cash flows from investing activities** | | |
| Payments to acquire property, plant and equipment (working 1) | 2 (1,426) | |
| Proceeds from the sale of property, plant and equipment | 1   63 | |
| *Net cash used in investing activities* | | 1(1,363) |
| | | |
| **Cash flows from financing activities** | | |
| Proceeds from the issue of share capital | 2  447 | |
| Repayment of loan stock | 2 (110) | |
| Dividends paid | 1 (249) | |
| *Net cash used in financing activities* | | 1  88 |
| **Net decrease in cash and cash equivalents** | | 2 (225) |
| **Cash and cash equivalents at beginning of period** | | 2 1,044 |
| **Cash and cash equivalents at end of period** | | 2  819 |

30 Total marks

*Working 1*

| DR | | | Property, Plant and Equipment (NBV) | | CR |
|---|---|---|---|---|---|
| **Date** | **Details** | **£000** | **Date** | **Details** | **£000** |
| 01/01/09 | Balance b/d | 3,555 | 31/12/09 | Disposal | 104 |
| 31/12/09 | *Additions (total)* | 1,426 | 31/12/09 | Depreciation expense | 512 |
| | | | 31/12/09 | Balance c/d | 4,365 |
| | | 4,981 | | | 4,981 |
| 31/12/09 | Balance b/d | 4,365 | | | |

*Working 2*

| DR | | | Income Tax Payables | | CR |
|---|---|---|---|---|---|
| **Date** | **Details** | **£000** | **Date** | **Details** | **£000** |
| 31/12/09 | *Cash paid* | 665 | 01/01/09 | Balance b/d | 816 |
| 31/12/09 | Balance c/d | 725 | 31/12/09 | Income tax (I/S) | 574 |
| | | 1,390 | | | 1,390 |
| | | | 31/12/09 | Balance b/d | 725 |

**Answer Question Five**

**Tyne plc and Wear Ltd**

**Task A – Table of ratios**

| Tyne plc and Wear Ltd<br>Table of Financial Ratios<br>For the Year Ended 31 December 2009 | | |
|---|---|---|
| **Ratio** | **Tyne plc** | **Wear Ltd** |
| Return on capital employed | 30.87% | 51.03% |
| Gross profit ratio | 60.00% | 70.00% |
| Net profit ratio | 41.33% | 54.71% |
| Current ratio | 1.28:1 | 0.83:1 |
| Acid test (quick) ratio | 0.97:1 | 0.69:1 |

(15 marks – see workings)

**Formulae and workings**

**Return on Capital Employed**     1     $\dfrac{\text{Profit from operations}}{\text{Capital employed}}$  x 100

    **Tyne plc**                                **Wear Ltd**

$\dfrac{\text{¼  £744}}{\text{¼ £2,410}}$  x 100 = 30.87% ½      $\dfrac{\text{¼ £4,596}}{\text{¼ £9,007}}$  x 100 = 51.03 ½

**Gross profit margin**     1     $\dfrac{\text{Gross profit}}{\text{Revenue}}$  x 100

    **Tyne plc**                                **Wear Ltd**

$\dfrac{\text{¼£1,080}}{\text{¼£1,800}}$  x 100 = 60.00% ½      $\dfrac{\text{£5,880}}{\text{£8,400}}$  x 100 = 70.00%  ½

**Net profit margin**     1     $\dfrac{\text{Profit from operations}}{\text{Revenue}}$  x 100

    **Tyne plc**                                **Wear Ltd**

$\dfrac{\text{¼  £744}}{\text{¼ £1,800}}$  x 100 = 41.33% ½      $\dfrac{\text{¼£4,596}}{\text{¼£8,400}}$  x 100 = 54.71% ½

9 marks this page c/f

497

**Current ratio**    1    $\dfrac{\text{Current assets}}{\text{Current liabilities}}$

| Tyne plc | Wear Ltd |
|---|---|
| ¼ $\dfrac{£600}{£470}$ = 1.28:1 ½ | ¼ $\dfrac{£1,839}{£2,212}$ = 0.83:1 ½ |

**Acid test ratio**    1    $\dfrac{\text{Current assets - inventories}}{\text{Current liabilities}}$

| Tyne plc | Wear Ltd |
|---|---|
| ¼ $\dfrac{£456}{£470}$ = 0.97 :1 ½ | ¼ $\dfrac{£1,524}{£2,212}$ = 0.69:1 ½ |

## Task B - The purpose of each of the ratios calculated above and comment on the relative performance of each company

### Profitability

The return on capital employed (ROCE) shows how much profit is being generated per £1 of capital invested in the business long-term(1). In the financial year to 31 December 2009 Wear Ltd performed better than Tyne plc(1). Wear Ltd generated a return on capital employed of £51 for every £100 of capital employed, by comparison Tyne plc only generated a return of £31 per £100 of capital employed(1). = 3 marks

The gross profit margin indicates how much profit is being generated per £1 of revenue after taking into account the direct costs of generating the revenue(1). The ratio indicates how effectively a company is controlling its direct costs(1). In the year ended 31 December 2009 Wear Ltd generated a gross profit margin of £70 for every £100 of revenue, whereas, Tyne plc generated a gross profit margin of £60 per £100 of revenue. Again Wear Ltd outperformed Tyne plc(1).
= 3 marks

The net profit margin ratio shows how much profit is being generated by the company for every £1 of revenue having accounted for all expenses other than finance costs and income tax(1). Wear Ltd was able to generate a net profit £54.71 per £100 of revenue by comparison Tyne plc generated £41.33 in net profit per £100 of revenue(1). Wear Ltd was better able to control not only its costs in proportion to revenue but also its expenses than Tyne plc(1).

= 3 marks
15 marks this page
9 marks b/f
24 marks c/f

## Liquidity

Liquidity ratios measure the ability of a company to manage its short-term liabilities and give an indication of the solvency of the company(1). The current ratio indicates how well the current liabilities of a company are covered by its current assets. The ideal ratio is dependent upon the nature of the business but a general rule is that a company ought to have a current asset ratio of between 1.5 and 2(1). Neither company meets this criteria but while Tyne plc has sufficient current assets to cover current liabilities, Wear Ltd does not and may have significant cash flow problems if it experiences difficulty in collecting from its credit customers(1).  = 3 marks

The acid test ratio is a more stringent measure of liquidity as it recognises that it takes time to convert inventories into cash. The ratio is calculated by deducting inventories from current assets and comparing these (quick) assets to current liabilities(1). Ideally this ratio (other than for a cash based business) should be no lower than 1:1 as a lower figure would indicate that a company cannot meet its current liabilities without converting some of its inventories to cash quickly(1). Tyne plc has 97p of current assets for every £1 of current liability which is acceptable. Wear Ltd, however only has 69p of current asset for every £1 of current liability which could place a severe strain on its cash flow(1).  = 3 marks

6 marks this page
24  marks b/f
30 Total marks

## OCR Advanced Subsidiary GCE *Accounting Principles*
## 2005 Specimen Paper

Gemma Bay started business on 1 January 1998. The following information is available for the purchases of machinery and office equipment.

### Machinery
1 January 1998 – three machines purchased, M1 and M2 costing £15,000 each, and M3 costing £20,000.

1 January 2000 – two machines purchased, M4 and M5 costing £12,000 each.

1 October 2000 – two machines purchased, M6 costing £15,000 and M7 costing £25,000.

### Office equipment
1 January 1998 – office equipment purchased costing £25,000. Machinery is depreciated at the rate of 20% per annum by the reducing balance method. Office equipment is depreciated by the straight line method over an estimated life of 10 years, taking into account a residual value of 10% on cost price. Machine M2 was disposed of on 30 June 1999 for £10,200 and Machine M3 was disposed of on 30 September 2000 for £13,000. No office equipment was disposed of during the period.

A full year's depreciation is provided in the year that machinery is purchased. No depreciation is provided in the year of disposal. The financial year end is 31 December.

### Required
**(a)** Prepare the following accounts for each of the years 1998, 1999 and 2000:
  **(i)** Machinery Account
  **(ii)** Provision for Depreciation of Machinery Account.          [19]

**(b)** Prepare the Machinery Disposals Account for each of the years 1999 and 2000.          [8]

**(c)** Prepare the Balance Sheet extract as at 31 December 2000 for Machinery and Office Equipment.          [4]

**(d)** Evaluate the choice of depreciation methods used by the business for these types of fixed asset.          [8]

**[Total: 39]**

© OCR 2000

**OCR Advanced Subsidiary GCE Accounting** *Accounting Principles*
**2005 Specimen Paper**

Dragon Ltd manufactures a single product. Its costs and sales for the year ended 30 November 2000 were as follows:

| | |
|---|---|
| Units sold | 21,000 |
| Selling price per unit | £40 |
| Variable costs per unit | |
|    Wages | £8 |
|    Materials | £18 |
|    Overheads | £4 |
|    Fixed costs | £187,000 |

To improve profit for the year commencing 1 December 2000 the following changes are expected to take place.

Units to be sold are 22,500.

Selling price is to be maintained at £40 per unit.

Wages are to be increased by 5% per unit.

Material costs are to be reduced by 10% per unit, this being achieved by committing to a long-term contract with a single supplier only.

Variable overheads are to be reduced by £0.10 per unit.

Fixed costs are to increase by £20,000.

### Required

**(a)** Using the data for the year commencing 1 December 2000, calculate:
   **(i)** the break-even in units and sales value;
   **(ii)** the profit for the year;
   **(iii)** the margin of safety in units and as a percentage;
   **(iv)** the sales in units required to maintain the profit level of the
   year ended 30 November 2000. **[24]**

**(b)** Explain what you understand by the term 'margin of safety'. **[4]**

**(c)** Evaluate its usefulness to a company. **[4]**

**(d)** Briefly outline two advantages and two limitations of break-even
   analysis. **[4]**

**[Total: 36]**

© OCR 2000

**OCR Advanced Subsidiary GCE Accounting** *Final Accounts*
**2502  Specimen Paper**

On 28 February 1999 the following balances were extracted from the books of
Barber Manufacturing, a local business solely owned by Ken Barber.

|  | £ |
|---|---|
| Stocks – 1 March 1998 | |
| Raw materials | 38,300 |
| Work in progress | 40,200 |
| Finished goods | 58,590 |
| Purchases – raw materials | 573,000 |
| Direct expenses | 63,100 |
| Direct wages | 146,200 |
| Indirect wages | 38,300 |
| Sales | 1,163,400 |
| Debtors | 93,600 |
| Loan interest | 500 |
| Rent and rates | 16,100 |
| Insurance | 920 |
| Sundry office expenses | 15,760 |
| Premises at cost | 120,000 |
| Provision for depreciation – premises | 24,000 |
| Plant and machinery at cost | 80,000 |
| Provision for depreciation – plant and machinery | 52,560 |
| Provision for unrealised profit and goods manufactured | 2,790 |
| Bad debts | 720 |
| Provision for doubtful debts | 3,120 |
| Loan (10% p.a. interest) | 10,000 |

The following information is also relevant:

- Stocks as at 28 February 1999:
  - raw materials £35,40
  - work in progress £36,476
  - finished goods £74,340.

- The business transfers finished goods from the factory to the Trading Account
  at factory cost plus 5% profit on manufacture.

- A provision is to be made for unrealised profit on the stock of finished goods
  on 28th February 1999 of £3,540.

- The loan was taken out on 1 March 1997 and is for a five-year period.

- Rent and rates are apportioned between the factory and office on the basis 5:1.

- Rent of £1,900 is outstanding.

- Insurance, which includes a prepayment of £80, is apportioned between factory and office on the basis 6:1.

- Provision for depreciation is to be made as follows:
  - premises: 5% on cost, to be apportioned 5:1 between factory and office
  - plant and machinery: 30% on the reducing balance basis, to be apportioned 6:1 between factory and office
  - provision for doubtful debts is to be provided at 4% of debtors.

## Required

**(a)** A Manufacturing, Trading and Profit and Loss Account for the
year ended 28 February 1999 (for internal use only)                      **[28]**

**(b)** An explanation of the advantages and disadvantages for
Barber Manufacturing of changing from a sole trader
business to a partnership in terms of ownership and finance.      **[8]**
                                                            **[Total: 36]**

© OCR 2000

**OCR Advanced Subsidiary GCE Accounting** *Final Accounts*
**2502 Specimen Paper**

Nick Morgan, a member of Sandfields Sports Club, has taken over the duties of Treasurer of the Club, the previous Treasurer having recently moved away from the area. The following statement has been prepared for presentation to members at the Club's annual general meeting.

Balance Sheet for the year end 31 December 1999

| **Balances for 1998** | £ | | **Payments** | £ |
|---|---|---|---|---|
| Premises | 12,000 | | Equipment | 1,100 |
| Equipment | 2,400 | | Donations | 250 |
| Bank | 810 | | Rates and insurance | 1,840 |
| | 15,210 | | Postage | 235 |
| | | | Depreciation and equipment | 480 |
| Subscriptions received | | | Part-time wages | 2,707 |
| 1998 | 279 | | | |
| 1999 | 4,314 | | | |
| 2000 | 168 | 4,761 | | |
| | | | **Balances to 2000** | |
| | | | Premises | 12,000 |
| Life membership | 600 | | Equipment | 1,920 |
| | | | Bank | 1,439 |
| Premises sub-let | 1,300 | | | |
| Premises sub-let | | | | |
| advance payment | 100 | | | |
| | | 21,971 | | 21,971 |

- A life membership scheme was introduced during 1999 and any such fees received are to be capitalised and transferred to income over five years by equal installments each year, commencing in the year received.

- Premises are not depreciated, while equipment is depreciated by 20% of the balance brought forward from the year before. Provision should be made on new equipment bought during the year. The depreciation rate is applied for the full year irrespective of date of purchase. No assets were disposed of during the year.

- At 31 December 1999 £40 was owing for part-time wages, and rates of £110 had been prepaid.

**Required**

**(a)** An Income and Expenditure Account for the year ending
31 December 1999, together with a Balance Sheet as at that date,
to good accounting format, for submission to members. **[28]**

**(b)** Explain to the new Treasurer the differences between a
Receipts and Payments Account, and an Income and Expenditure
Account. Indicate when one would be used in preference to
the other. **[12]**

**[Total 40 marks]**

© OCR 2000

**OCR Advanced GCE** Accounting *Company Accounts and Interpretation*
**2505 Specimen Paper**

The summarised Balance sheets at the end of the last two years for Tyler plc are shown below

| | 30 April 1998 | | | 30 April 1999 | | |
|---|---|---|---|---|---|---|
| | £'000 | £'000 | £'000 | £'000 | £'000 | £'000 |
| Fixed assets | Cost | Depreciation | Net | Cost | Depreciation | Net |
| Premises | 100 | – | 100 | 100 | – | 100 |
| Plant and machinery | 80 | 18 | 62 | 105 | 24 | 81 |
| Motor vehicles | 30 | 12 | 18 | 30 | 16 | 14 |
| | 210 | 30 | 180 | 235 | 40 | 195 |
| | | | | | | |
| *Current assets* | | | | | | |
| Stock | | 38 | | | 79 | |
| Debtors | | 52 | | | 49 | |
| Bank | | 56 | | | 25 | |
| | | 146 | | | 153 | |
| *Current liabilities* | | | | | | |
| Trade creditors | 62 | | | 71 | | |
| **Corporation Tax** | 11 | | | 12 | | |
| **Dividends** | 8 | 81 | 65 | 9 | 92 | 61 |
| | | | 245 | | | 256 |
| **Capital and reserves** | | | | | | |
| **Ordinary shares** | | | 200 | | | 210 |
| **6% Redeemable preference shares** | | | 20 | | | |
| **Capital redemption Reserve** | | | – | | | 10 |
| **Profit and loss** | | | 25 | | | 36 |
| | | | 245 | | | 256 |

(i)   Plant and machinery costing £25,000 was sold during the year at a loss of £3,000. The depreciation charge for the year on plant and machinery was £16,000. No motor vehicles were disposed of or bought during the year.
(ii)  The 6% redeemable preference shares were redeemed at par on 1 May 1998.
(iii) Interest received from short term investments purchased and sold between 1 January to 31 March 1999 amounted to £2,000.

## Required
(a)  A Cash Flow Statement in accordance with FRS 1 (revised) for the year ended 30 April 1999.                                      [31]
(b)  A major shareholder is concerned about a reduction in the bank balance of Tyler plc although a profit has been made for the year. How would the directors explain this situation?                                       [4]

**[Total marks 35]**

© OCR 2000

**OCR Advanced GCE Accounting Company** *Accounts and Interpretation*
**2505 Specimen Paper**

The issued share capital of Cowbridge plc consists of 400,000 Ordinary Share of £1 each, and 80,000 7% Preference Shares of £1 each. If offered a further 150,000 Ordinary Shares to the public at a price of £1.80 each.

The terms of the issue were:

|  | £ |
|---|---|
| Payable on application | 0.50 |
| Payable on allotment (including the premium) | 0.80 |
| First call | 0.50 |

Applications were received for 165,000 shares. It was decided to return application monies to applicants for 15,000 shares, and the remaining applicants were allotted shares to exactly the full issue amount.

All money due on allotment was duly received and the first call was to be made at a later date.

**Required**

(a) Prepare the following ledger accounts to record the above transactions. (Note: balancing of accounts is not required.)
      Bank Account
      Application and Allotment Account
      Ordinary Share Capital Account
      Share Premium Account                                              **[14]**

(b) Explain the term 'authorised share capital'. How is the authorised share capital of a company authorised? Why could this capital differ from the issued capital?                     **[6]**

                                                                   **[Total: 20]**

© OCR 2000

## AQA GCE Accounting Foundation Tier Paper 2 3122/2F
## 24 June 2003

David Ford is an electrical wholesaler. Information about some of the businesses transactions for February 2003 is given below.

On 8 February 2003 David Ford sent two invoices to customers, the details were as follows:

|  | £ |
|---|---:|
| Invoice number 00121 to Melchester Electrical Supplies | |
| 10 personal stereos model A43 at £40 each | 400.00 |
| plus VAT | 70.00 |
| | 470.00 |
| Invoice number 00122 to Town Traders Ltd. | |
| 12 personal stereos model AT79 at £70 each | 840.00 |
| 6 micro hi-fis model T24 at £90 each | 540.00 |
| | 1,380.00 |
| Less trade discount 20% | 276.00 |
| plus VAT | 193.20 |
| | 1,297.20 |

(a) Record the information from the two invoices in the sales journal

| Date | Customer | Invoice No | Goods | | VAT | | Total | |
|---|---|---|---|---|---|---|---|---|
| | | | £ | p | £ | p | £ | p |
| | | | | | | | | |
| | | | | | | | | |
| | | | | | | | | |

PCD Manufactures Ltd is one of David Ford's suppliers. The following information relates to the account for this creditor.

Feb 1   Balance, amount owed to PCD Manufactures Ltd by David Ford £600

     14   David Ford settled his account with PCD Manufacture Ltd by cheque £600

     23   Invoice sent by PCD Manufactures Ltd to David Ford for goods £1,000 plus VAT £175

     27   David Ford received a credit note from PCD Manufactures Ltd for £160 plus VAT £28, for goods returned.

(b) Record the above information in the account of PCD Manufactures Ltd. Bring down the balance on the account at March 2003.

PCD Manufacturing Ltd Account

| Date | | £ | p | Date | | £ | p |
|------|---|---|---|------|---|---|---|
| | | | | | | | |
| | | | | | | | |
| | | | | | | | |
| | | | | | | | |
| | | | | | | | |

**(6 marks)**

David Ford maintains a three-column cash book. The transactions for March 2003 have been recorded.

| Date | Details | Folio | Discount £ | Cash £ | Bank £ | Date | Details | Folio | Discount £ | Cash £ | Bank £ |
|------|---------|-------|-----------|--------|--------|------|---------|-------|-----------|--------|--------|
| Mar 1 | Balance | B/d | | 800 | | Mar 1 | Balance | B/d | | | 3,000 |
| Mar 5 | T Wolf | | 75 | | 1,425 | Mar 3 | Cleaning | | | 40 | |
| Mar 8 | Sales | | | | 2,025 | Mar 8 | A Kalifa | | 100 | | 1,900 |
| Mar 17 | F Townsend | | 250 | | 4,750 | Mar 11 | Motor expenses | | | 30 | |
| Mar 18 | Cash | C | | | 700 | Mar 18 | Bank | C | | 700 | |
| Mar 30 | Sales | | | 55 | | Mar 20 | Wages | | | | 350 |
| | | | | | | Mar 23 | B Hughes | | 40 | | 760 |
| | | | | | | Mar 27 | Drawings | | | | 400 |
| | | | | | | Mar 31 | Balance | C/d | | 85 | 2,490 |
| | | | 325 | 855 | 8,900 | | | | 140 | 855 | 8,900 |
| April | Balance | B/d | | 85 | 2,490 | | | | | | |

(c) What does the balance b/d of £3,000 on 1 March represent? **(1 mark)**

(d) (i) Do the columns headed 'Discount' refer to cash discount or trade discount? **(1 mark)**

   (ii) Give a reason for your choice of answer in (d) (i) **(2 marks)**

(e) (i) Is the discount on 5 March discount allowed or discount received? **(1 mark)**

(ii) Give a reason for your choice of answer in (e) (i) **(2 marks)**

(iii) What percentage is the discount in (e) (i)? **(1 mark)**

(f) (i) Is the discount on 8 March discount allowed or discount received? **(1 mark)**

(ii) give a reason for your choice of answer in (f) (i) **(2 marks)**

(g) (i) What does the C in the Folio column on 18 March stand for **(1 mark)**

(ii) Explain why there are two entries in the Cash Book on 18 March **(1 mark)**

(h) What do the drawings on 27 march represent? **(2 marks)**

(i) Name and complete the following accounts to show where the totals of £325 and £140 will be transferred to at the end of March.

| | | | | Account | | |
|---|---|---|---|---|---|---|
| Date | | £ | p | Date | £ | p |
| | | | | | | |
| | | | | | | |

| | | | | Account | | |
|---|---|---|---|---|---|---|
| Date | | £ | p | Date | £ | p |
| | | | | | | |
| | | | | | | |

**(4 marks)**

## AQA GCE Accounting Foundation Tier Paper 2 3122/2F
## 24 June 2003

The following list of balances appeared in the books of W. Boardman at 31 March 2003.

|                        | £       |
|------------------------|--------:|
| Sales                  | 492,700 |
| Purchases              | 250,000 |
| Carriage inwards       | 1,200   |
| Carriage outwards      | 1,500   |
| Discounts allowed      | 2,800   |
| Discounts received     | 2,400   |
| Returns inwards        | 7,000   |
| Returns outwards       | 8,000   |
| Vehicles at cost       | 70,000  |
| Trade debtors          | 50,000  |
| Motor expenses         | 24,000  |
| Insurance              | 12,000  |
| Stock at 1 April 2002  | 33,000  |
| Electricity            | 16,000  |
| Salaries               | 102,000 |
| Sundry expenses        | 4,850   |
| Rent received          | 7,000   |

The following additional information is also available.

- Stock at 31 March 2003 was £35,000.

- Provide for depreciation on cost as follows: vehicles 20% p.a.

- Electricity of £4,000 was outstanding at 31 March 2003.

- Insurance of £3,000 was prepaid at 31 March 2003.

Prepare W. Boardman's trading and profit and loss accounts for the year ended 31 March 2003. **(21 marks)**

© AQA 2003

## AQA GCE Accounting Foundation Tier Paper 2 3122/2F
### 24 June 2003

RolHoMa Ltd has prepared the following balance sheet which contains a number of errors.

### RolHoMa Ltd Balance Sheet
### for the year ended 31 December 2002

| | £ | | £ |
|---|---|---|---|
| Share capital and reserves | 123,000 | Premises | 110,000 |
| Motor vehicles | 28,000 | Stock at 31 December 2002 | 11,000 |
| Debentures | 55,000 | Stock at 1 January 2002 | 16,000 |
| Cash | 1,000 | Machinery | 40,000 |
| Bank loan repayable 2005 | 6,000 | Retained profit | 23,500 |
| Trade debtors | 10,000 | Balance at bank | 4,000 |
| | | Expenses owing | 500 |
| | | Trade creditors | 7,000 |
| | | Fixtures and fittings | 11,000 |
| | 223,000 | | 223,000 |

(a) Explain briefly what is meant by:
   (i)  Fixed assets                                         **(2 marks)**
   (ii)  Current assets                                      **(2 marks)**
   (iii) Current liabilities                             **(2 marks)**
   (iv) Long-term liabilities                            **(2 marks)**

(b) Prepare a corrected balance sheet for RolHoMa Ltd. showing clearly:
   (i)  Fixed assets
   (ii)  Current assets
   (iii) Current liabilities
   (iv) Long-term liabilities
   (v)  Share capital and reserve

**(22 marks)**

### AQA GCE Accounting Higher Tier Paper 1 3122/1H
### 18 June 2003

The following information was taken from the accounting records of J. Bells Ltd.

#### Sales Journal (Day Books)

| Date 2003 | Customer | Goods £ | VAT £ | Net £ |
|---|---|---|---|---|
| 14 May | A. Dancer & Co Ltd | 2,600 | 455 | 3,055 |

At 1 May 2003 A. Dancer and Co Ltd owed J. Bells Ltd £4,650.

On 18 May 2003 A. Dancer and Co Ltd sent a cheque for £4,570 to J. Bells Ltd claiming £80 discount.

Using the ledger account below write up the account for A. Dancer and Co Ltd as it would appear in the books of J. Bells Ltd. Bring down the balance on 1 June 2003.

#### A. Dancer and Co Ltd Account

| Date | Details | | Date | Details | |
|---|---|---|---|---|---|
| | | | | | |
| | | | | | |
| | | | | | |
| | | | | | |
| | | | | | |
| | | | | | |
| | | | | | |

**(6 marks)**

A trial balance has been prepared but the following items have not been included:

|  | £ |
|---|---|
| Purchases | 235,000 |
| Machinery | 120,000 |
| Bank overdraft | 53,000 |
| Provision for doubtful debts | 4,000 |
| Returns inwards | 2,000 |
| Carriage outwards | 3,000 |
| Rent received | 25,000 |
| Bad debts written off | 10,000 |
| Carriage inwards | 20,000 |

From the list above complete and total the following trial balance by inserting the appropriate amount in the correct column.

### Trial balance as at 31 March 2003

|  |  | Dr £ | Cr £ |
|---|---|---|---|
| Total of trial balance entries made so far |  | 325,000 | 633,000 |
| (a) | Purchases |  |  |
| (b) | Machinery |  |  |
| (c) | Bank overdraft |  |  |
| (d) | Provision for doubtful debts |  |  |
| (e) | Returns inwards |  |  |
| (f) | Carriage outwards |  |  |
| (g) | Rent received |  |  |
| (h) | Bad debts written off |  |  |
| (i) | Carriage inwards |  |  |
|  |  |  |  |
|  |  |  |  |

**(9 marks)**

© AQA 2003

### AQA GCE Accounting Higher Tier paper 1 13122/1H
### 18 June 2003

Select the information required from the following list of balances to produce a Balance Sheet as at 31 May 2003 for United Boxes plc. The Balance Sheet should show a figure for working capital.

|  | £ |
|---|---|
| Machinery (at cost) | 80,000 |
| Issued ordinary shares | 75,000 |
| Vehicles (at cost) | 50,000 |
| Opening stock | 10,000 |
| General reserve | 25,000 |
| Debtors | 30,000 |
| Closing stock | 15,000 |
| Bank overdraft | 2,000 |
| Creditors | 17,000 |
| Provision for depreciation | |
|   Machinery | 20,000 |
|   Vehicles | 15,000 |
| Provision for doubtful debts | 500 |
| Proposed dividends | 10,000 |
| Profit and Loss Account balance as at 31 May 2003 | 10,500 |

**(17 marks)**

© AQA 2003

**AQA GCE Accounting** *Unit 2 Financial Accounting: Introduction to Published Accounts of Limited Companies* **14 January 2004**

The following balances have been extracted form the books of Positive Advertising Plc at 31 December 2003.

|  | £000 |
|---|---|
| Issued share capital |  |
| Ordinary shares of £1 each fully paid | 2,000 |
| 6% Preference shares of £1 each fully paid | 500 |
| Profit and loss account balance as at 1 January 2003 | 65 |
| Revaluation reserve | 70 |
| Trade creditors and accrued expenses | 35 |
| Profit before tax for the year ended 31 December 2003 | 694 |
| Taxation for the year ended 31 December 2003 | 208 |

The directors propose the following:

A full year's dividend on the preference shares.
An ordinary share dividend of 4% per share.

## Required

(a) Prepare the profit and loss appropriation account for the year
ended 31 December 2003 **(8 marks)**

(b) Prepare the capital and reserves section of the balance sheet **(5 marks)**

(c) Prepare the current liabilities section of the balance sheet **(4 marks)**

When preparing a balance sheet it is important to distinguish between long-term and current liabilities.

(d) Give **one** example of a long-term liability **(1 mark)**

(e) Explain why it is important to distinguish between long-term
and current liabilities. **(4 marks)**

© AQA 2004

**AQA Advanced Subsidiary GCE Accounting** *Unit 2 Financial Accounting: Introduction to Published Accounts of Limited Companies* **14 January 2004**

The managing director of Supermarket Supreme Plc has asked you to prepare a short report explaining to shareholders the purpose of producing a cash flow statement each year.

To..................................................................................................

From ..............................................................................................

Date ...............................................................................................

Subject ...........................................................................................

(Heading **1 mark**)
(Report **7 marks**)

© AQA 2004

**AQA Advanced Subsidiary GCE Accounting** *Unit 2 Financial Accounting: Introduction to Published Accounts of Limited Companies* **14 January 2004**

In the books of Jones and Simpson Ltd the following errors have been discovered after preparing the draft accounts for the year ended 31 October 2003.

1   The purchase of a machine costing £4,000 has been included in the total for purchases.

2   Returns inwards of £640 have been omitted completely from the accounts.

3   The sales day book was undercast by £7,800.

4   The wages were incorrectly stated as £89,000. The correct figure was £98,000.

The draft profit calculated was £67,000.

**Required**

(a)   Calculate the corrected net profit for the year ended 31 October 2003                                                                       **(6 marks)**

(b)   State any changes, as a result of these corrections, which will have to be made to the balance sheet. Identify each sub-heading, item and amount involved.                                       **(6 marks)**

© AQA 2004

**AQA Advanced Subsidiary GCE Accounting** *Unit 2 Financial Accounting: Introduction to Published Accounts of Limited Companies* **14 Jan 2004**

Both directors and auditors have duties with regard to the accounts of limited companies. Explain what their duties are.

Directors' duties are ...................................................................................
................................................................................................................
................................................................................................................
................................................................................................................
................................................................................................................
................................................................................................................

**(3 marks)**

Auditors' duties are..................................................................................
................................................................................................................
................................................................................................................
................................................................................................................
................................................................................................................
................................................................................................................

**(3 marks)**

© AQA 2004

**AAT NVQ/SVQ Level 2 in Accounting** *Preparing Ledger Balances and an Initial Trial Balance (PLB)* **(2003 standards) 30 November 2004**

## Task 2.1
The following document has been received by Special Events from its customer PKG Limited.

| BACS REMITTANCE ADVICE | |
|---|---|
| To: Special Events | From: PKG Limited |
| *Your ref: SE102* | *Our ref:1650* |

| 30 November 2004 | BACS Transfer | £1,410 |
|---|---|---|

Payment has been made by BACS and will be paid directly into your bank account on the date shown above

(a) What accounts in the main (general) ledger will be used to record this transaction?

(b) Give ONE advantage to Special Events of being paid by BACS transfer.

(c) Give ONE advantage to PKG Limited of paying by BACS transfer.

## Task 2.2
What documents would Special Events send out:

(a) with a cheque to pay an account?

(b) to list unpaid invoices and ask for payment each month?

(c) to correct an overcharge on an invoice issued?

## Task 2.3
Special Events keeps a small amount of petty cash in the office to purchase miscellaneous items during the month. The imprest level is £100. The following purchases were made during November.

| | | |
|---|---|---|
| 15 November Window Cleaning | £30.00 |
| 22 November Postage | £25.00 |
| 29 November Stationery | £28.00 |

(a) Make the relevant entries in the petty cash control account showing clearly the balance carried down at 30 November (closing balance) and brought down at 1 December (opening balance).

(b) What will be the amount required to restore the imprest level?

(c) Name ONE precaution that should be taken to ensure the petty cash is safe and secure.

## Task 2.4

Keith Boxley has just learned that a customer, Bibby and Company, has ceased trading and the outstanding amount on its account will have to be written off as a bad debt. What accounting entries must you make in the main (general) ledger to write off the net amount of £500 and the VAT?

| Account name | Dr £ | Cr £ |
| --- | --- | --- |
|  |  |  |
|  |  |  |
|  |  |  |

## Task 2.5

Keith Boxley needs advice about the most efficient way of organising the filing system. Suggest one efficient way of filing each of the following documents, giving a different method for each.

(a) Sales invoices _____

(b) Purchase invoices _____

(c) Bank statements _____

## Task 2.6

Within a computerised accounting system code numbers will be used, for instance customer account codes.

Give TWO other examples of the use of code numbers in a computerised accounting system.

## Task 2.7

Keith Boxley is purchasing a computer and hopes to change from a manual to a computerised accounting system. He already has a keyboard and mouse.

Name ONE other item of hardware and one item of software that he will also need to operate the system.

## Task 2.8

The following information has become available.

(a) An amount of £45 has been credited to the discounts allowed account instead of the discounts received account.

(b) An amount paid by cheque for insurance has been recorded as £120 instead of the correct amount of £180.

(c) A credit purchase of £600 plus VAT for stationery has been incorrectly recorded as £200 plus VAT.

Record the journal entries needed in the main (general) ledger, to deal with the above. Narratives are not required.

## Task 2.9

This is a summary of transactions with suppliers during the month of November.

|  | £ |
|---|---|
| Balance of creditors at 1 November 2004 | 30,260 |
| Goods bought on credit | 11,500 |
| Money paid to credit suppliers | 9,357 |
| Discounts received | 170 |
| Goods returned to credit suppliers | 125 |

(a) Prepare a purchases ledger control account from the above details. Show clearly the balance carried down at 30 November (closing balance) and brought down at 1 December (opening balance).

The following closing credit balances were in the subsidiary (purchases) ledger on 30 November.

|  | £ |
|---|---|
| Williams and Whale | 15,400 |
| Jacksons Limited | 3,500 |
| Conference Caterers | 11,218 |
| Fine Foods | 1,900 |
| J. Wilson | 215 |

(b) Reconcile the balances shown above with the purchases ledger control account balance you have calculated in part (a).

(c) What may have caused the difference you calculated in part (b)?

## Task 2.10

On 29 November Special Events received the following bank statement as at 22 November: The cash book as at 29 November is shown below.

**CENTREPOINT BANK Plc**
**High Street, Bedford BF13 8RF**

To Special Events      Account No 34287280      22 November 2004

**STATEMENT OF ACCOUNT**

| Date 2004 | Details | Paid out | Paid in | Balance | |
|---|---|---|---|---|---|
| 01 Nov | Balance b/f | | | 10,4000 | C |
| 05 Nov | Cheque 006165 | 3,500 | | 6,900 | C |
| 08 Nov | Cheque 006166 | 2,100 | | 4,800 | C |
| 11 Nov | Bank Giro Credit | | | | C |
| | L Smith | | 5,000 | 9,800 | C |
| 11 Nov | Bank Giro Credit | | | | C |
| | B Roberts | | 7,500 | 17,300 | C |
| 12 Nov | Cheque 006168 | 380 | | 16,920 | C |
| 15 Nov | Direct Debit | | | | C |
| | Bedford CC | 186 | | 16,734 | C |
| 19 Nov | Direct Debit | | | | C |
| | Myers Insurance | 45 | | 16,689 | C |
| 22 Nov | Overdraft facility fee | 40 | | 16,489 | C |
| 22 Nov | Bank charges | 50 | | 15,599 | C |

### CASH BOOK

| Date 2004 | Details | Bank £ | Date 2004 | Cheque number | Details | Bank £ |
|---|---|---|---|---|---|---|
| 01 Nov | Balance b/f | 10,400 | 01 Nov | 006165 | LLB Limited | 3,500 |
| 11 Nov | L Smith | 5,000 | 01 Nov | 006166 | Down and Daly | 2,100 |
| 11 Nov | B Roberts | 7,500 | 05 Nov | 006167 | Hobbs Limited | 4,600 |
| 15 Nov | G Brown | 1,700 | 05 Nov | 006168 | H & H Limited | 380 |
| 22 Nov | B Singh | 4,550 | 22 Nov | 006169 | Eddies Bar | 500 |
| | | | | | | |
| | | | | | | |
| | | | | | | |
| | | | | | | |
| | | | | | | |
| | | | | | | |
| | | | | | | |
| | | | | | | |

(a) Check the items on the bank statement against the items in the cash book.

(b) Update the cash book as needed.

(c) Total the cash book and clearly show the balance carried down at 29 November (closing balance) and brought down at 30 November (opening balance). Note: you do not need to adjust the accounts in Section 1.

(d) Using the information prepare a bank reconciliation statement as at 29 November.

© AAT 2004

**AAT NVQ/SVQ Level 3 in Accounting** *Recording and Evaluating Costs and Revenues (ECR)* **(2003 standards) 29 November 2004**

China Ltd manufactures and sells pottery made from clay. You work as an accounting technician at China Ltd, reporting to the Finance Director. The company operates an integrated absorption costing system. Stocks are valued on a first in first out (FIFO) basis. The Finance Director has given you the following tasks.

## Task 1.1

Complete the following stock card for clay using the FIFO method for valuing issues to production and stocks of materials.

| STOCK CARD Product: Clay | | | | | | | | | |
|---|---|---|---|---|---|---|---|---|---|
| | Receipts | | | Issues | | | Balance | | |
| Date | Quantity kgs | Cost per kg £ | Total cost £ | Quantity kgs | Cost per kg £ | Total cost £ | Quantity kgs | Cost per kg £ | Total cost £ |
| B/f at 1 Nov | | | | | | | 15, 000 | 0.50 | 7,500 |
| 8 Nov | 60,000 | 0.45 | | | | | | | |
| 9 Nov | | | 45,000 | | | | | | |
| 16 Nov | 40,000 | 0.55 | | | | | | | |
| 17 Nov | | | 50,000 | | | | | | |

## Additional data

The company's production budget requires 25,000 kgs of clay to be used each week. The company plans to maintain a buffer stock of clay equivalent to one week's budgeted production. It takes between one and two weeks for delivery of clay from the date the order is placed with the supplier.

## Task 1.2

Calculate the reorder level for clay.

© AAT 2004

**AAT NVQ/SVQ Level 3 in Accounting *Maintaining Financial Records and Preparing Accounts (FRA)* (2003 standards) 1 December 2004**

Frank Khan owns Fixit, a business that repairs and maintains properties. There are no credit sales. The business operates from small rented premises where the plant and equipment are stored. Frank Khan does not keep a double entry book-keeping system. You are an accounting technician at Harper and Co., the accounting firm that prepares the final accounts for Fixit. You are working on the accounts for Fixit for the year ending 30 September 2004. Your colleague has already summarised the cash and bank accounts.

**Fixit**
**Cash and bank summary for the year ended 30 September 2004**

|  | Cash £ | Bank £ |  | Cash £ | Bank £ |
|---|---|---|---|---|---|
| Balance b/d | 560 | 2,310 | Rent |  | 2,600 |
| Sales | 17,400 | 32,000 | Wages | 20,500 |  |
| Bank | 10,000 |  | Materials | 2,600 |  |
|  |  |  | Creditors for materials |  | 11,005 |
|  |  |  | Travel expenses | 2,470 |  |
|  |  |  | Administration expenses | 1,990 |  |
|  |  |  | Cash |  | 10,000 |
|  |  |  | Balance c/d | 400 | 10,705 |
|  | 27,960 | 34,310 |  | 27,960 | 34,310 |

The following balances are also available:

| Assets and liabilities as at: | 30 September 2003 £ | 30 September 2004 £ |
|---|---|---|
| Plan and equipment at cost | 19,000 | 19,000 |
| Plant and equipment accumulated depreciation | 5,600 | Not yet available |
| Stocks of materials at cost | 2,890 | 1,940 |
| Prepayment for rent | 550 | Not yet available |
| Creditors for materials | 1,720 | 1,835 |
| Accrual for travel expenses | 380 | 425 |

## Task 1.1
Calculate the figure for capital as at 30 September 2003.

## Task 1.2

Calculate the total sales for the year ended 30 September 2004.

## Task 1.3

Prepare the purchases ledger control account for the year ended 30 September 2004, showing clearly the credit purchases of materials.

## Task 1.4

Calculate the total purchases of materials for the year ended 30 September 2004.

## Task 1.5

Depreciation is provided at 25% per annum on a reducing balance basis.

(a) Calculate the depreciation charge for the year ended 30 September 2004.

(b) Calculate the revised accumulated depreciation as at 30 September 2004.

## Task 1.6

Calculate the travel expenses for the year ended 30 September 2004.

## Task 1.7

The figure for rent in the cash and bank summary includes £650 for the quarter starting 1 October 2004.

Prepare the rent account for the year ended 30 September 2004, showing clearly the rent for the year.

## Task 1.8

Frank Khan has given you a closing stock figure of £1,940 at cost. He has also told you that he has a supply of bricks which he acquired free of charge. He is confident that he will be able to sell these bricks for at least £500. These are not included in the stock valuation of £1,940. What figure for closing stock should be included in the accounts of Fixit? (Circle only one answer.)

**£1,440 / £1,940 / £2,440 / None of these**

## Task 1.9

Complete the following trial balance as at 30 September 2004, taking into account your answers to the above tasks, and all the other information you have been given.

**Fixit**

*Trial balance as at 30 September 2004*

| | Dr £ | Cr £ |
|---|---|---|
| Plant and equipment | | |
| Plant and equipment accumulated depreciation | | |
| Opening stock | | |
| Prepayment | | |
| Creditors for materials | | |
| Accrual | | |
| Bank | | |
| Cash | | |
| Capital | | |
| Sales | | |
| Purchases | | |
| Wages | | |
| Depreciation charge for the year | | |
| Travel expenses | | |
| Rent | | |
| Administration expenses | | |
| Closing stock – profit and loss account | | |
| Closing stock – balance sheet | | |
| | | |
| **Total** | | |

## Task 1.10

Frank Khan has told you he is concerned about the figure in the trial balance for fixed assets. He knows that it includes all the plant and equipment that he has bought over a number of years but he does not have a list of the items. It is possible that some are broken or missing. He needs your advice. Write a memo to Frank Khan:

- List SIX items of information that a fixed assets register should contain.

- Give THREE reasons why he should keep a fixed assets register.

© AAT 2004

### AAT NVQ/SVQ  (2003 standards) 1 December 2004

Henry and James are the owners of HJ Cleaning, a partnership business that sells industrial cleaning equipment. You are an accounting technician at Harper and Co., the accounting firm that prepares the final accounts for HJ Cleaning.

- The financial year end is 30 September.
- The partners maintain an integrated accounting system consisting of a main ledger, a purchases ledger, a sales ledger and a stock ledger.
- Stock records are maintained at cost in the stock ledger which is updated every time a sale or stock purchase is made.
- HJ Cleaning is registered for VAT.
- The proforma extended trial balance for the year ended 30 September 2004 is shown below.

At the end of the financial year on 30 September 2004, the following trial balance was taken from the main ledger:

|  | Dr £ | Cr £ |
|---|---|---|
| Administration expenses | 88,014 | |
| Bank | 106,571 | |
| Capital account – Henry | | 50,000 |
| Capital account – James | | 50,000 |
| Cash | 165 | |
| Closing stock | 69,580 | 69,580 |
| Current account – Henry | | 3,600 |
| Current account – James | | 4,200 |
| Depreciation charge for the year | 8,750 | |
| Opening stock | 75,150 | |
| Purchases | 185,400 | |
| Purchases ledger control account | | 16,200 |
| Rent | 14,000 | |
| Sales | | 450,800 |
| Sales ledger control account | 53,000 | |
| Selling expenses | 43,970 | |
| VAT | | 10,200 |
| Vehicles at cost | 35,000 | |
| Vehicles accumulated depreciation | | 25,000 |
| Total | 679,600 | 679,600 |

### Additional data

Most of the year-end adjustments have been entered, but there are some adjustments you now need to make:

(a)  Accountancy fees of £1,900 need to be accrued. Ignore VAT.

(b) A provision for doubtful debts of 1.5% of the value of the sales ledger control account needs to be introduced.

(c) The total value of a purchase invoice for electricity for £329, including VAT of 17.5%, was debited to selling expenses. Electricity should be charged to administration expenses.

(d) A credit note from a supplier for purchases was entered into the ledgers as a purchase invoice. The credit note was for £470 including VAT at 17.5%.

## Task 2.1
Prepare journal entries to account for the above. Dates and narratives are not required.

## Task 2.2
Enter your journal entries into the adjustment columns of the extended trial balance.

## Task 2.3
Extend the profit and loss and balance sheet columns of the extended trial balance. Make entries to record the net profit or loss for the year ended 30 September 2004.

### HJ Cleaning Extended trial balance as at 30 September 2004

| | Ledger balances | | Adjustments | | Profit and loss account | | Balance sheet | |
|---|---|---|---|---|---|---|---|---|
| | Dr £ | Cr £ | Dr £ | Cr £ | Dr £ | Cr £ | Dr £ | Cr £ |
| Administration expenses | 88,014 | | | | | | | |
| Bank | 106,571 | | | | | | | |
| Capital account – Henry | | 50,000 | | | | | | |
| Capital account – James | | 50,000 | | | | | | |
| Cash | 165 | | | | | | | |
| Closing stock | 69,580 | 69,580 | | | | | | |
| Current account – Henry | | 3,600 | | | | | | |
| Current account – James | | 4,200 | | | | | | |
| Depreciation charge for the year | 8,750 | | | | | | | |
| Opening stock | 74,150 | | | | | | | |
| Purchases | 185,400 | | | | | | | |
| Purchases ledger control account | | 16,200 | | | | | | |
| Rent | 14,000 | | | | | | | |
| Sales | | 450,800 | | | | | | |
| Sales ledger control account | 53,000 | | | | | | | |
| Selling expenses | 43,970 | | | | | | | |
| VAT | | 10,220 | | | | | | |
| Vehicles at cost | 35,000 | | | | | | | |
| Vehicles accumulated depreciation | 25,000 | 679,600 | | | | | | |
| | TOTAL | 679,600 | | | | | | |

## Additional data

Henry and James share the profits of the partnership equally.

## Task 2.4

Update the partners' current accounts to account for the profit or loss for the year ended 30 September 2004. Balance off the accounts and bring the balances down.

*Current accounts*

| | Henry £ | James £ | | | Henry £ | James £ |
|---|---|---|---|---|---|---|
| | | | 30 September 2004 | Balance b/d | 3,600 | 4,200 |
| | | | | | | |
| | | | | | | |
| | | | | | | |
| | | | | | | |

## Task 2.5

Prepare a balance sheet for HJ Cleaning as at 30 September 2004.

| Workings | HJ Cleaning Balance sheet as at 30 Septmber 2004 | £ | £ | £ |
|---|---|---|---|---|
| | | | | |
| | Fixed assets | | | |
| | Vehicles | | | |
| | | | | |
| | Current assets | | | |
| | Stock | | | |
| | Debtors | | | |
| | Bank | | | |
| | Cash | | | |
| | | | | |
| | Current liabilities | | | |
| | Creditors | | | |
| | VAT | | | |
| | Accruals | | | |
| | | | | |
| | Net current assets | | | |
| | | | | |
| | Net assets | | | |
| | | | | |
| | Capital employed | Henry | James | Total |
| | Capital accounts | | | |
| | Current accounts | | | |
| | Total | | | |

## Additional data

On 1 October 2004 Charles was admitted to the partnership.

- He introduced £100,000 to the bank account.
- Goodwill was valued at £220,000 on 30 September 2004.
- Goodwill is to be eliminated from the accounts.
- The new profit sharing percentages are:
  Henry 40%
  James 40%
  Charles 20%

## Task 2.6

Update the capital accounts for the partnership, showing clearly the introduction and elimination of goodwill. Balance off the accounts.

*Capital accounts*

| | | Henry £ | James £ | Charles £ | | | Henry £ | James £ | Charles £ |
|---|---|---|---|---|---|---|---|---|---|
| | | | | | 1 October 2004 | Balance b/d | 50,000 | 50,000 | |
| | | | | | | | | | |
| | | | | | | | | | |
| | | | | | | | | | |
| | | | | | | | | | |

*Note the style difference between the OCR and AQA papers in displayed maximum marks for each question is deliberate and reflects the differences in styles on the actual papers. AAT papers do not display maximum marks.*

© AAT 2004

**Accounting ratios**. Statistical measures taken from the accounts of a business to aid financial assessment and control.

**Accruals**. Expenses incurred, but not yet billed to the firm.

**Amalgamation**. Joining two firms into one.

**Assets**. The term comes from the word 'assez', meaning 'enough'. It is used because the property of a proprietor is judged in terms of whether it is sufficient to discharge his/her liabilities, i.e.: to settle his/her debts.

**Assets: fixed and current**. Assets are classified into fixed assets and current assets. The former are those which will be retained in the business, e.g.: machines, motor vehicles, etc; the latter, it is assumed, will be consumed in the business within the fiscal year and includes: stock, debtors, cash in hand and cash at bank.

**Average cost method**. A method of stock valuation in which remaining stock values are averaged out every time a withdrawal is made.

**Bad debts**. Debts which a firm regards as uncollectable.

**Balance**. This term is used in 3 different ways in double entry book-keeping.
1. For the debit and credit column totals
2. For the balancing item required to equalise the two column totals (balance c/d)
3. For that balancing item transferred as the opening figure for the subsequent accounting period (balance b/d).

**Balance sheet**. A listing of the ledger balances remaining after compilation of the revenue account. (It is not, as some think, called a balance sheet merely because it balances.)

**Bank reconciliation**. A standardised format statement explaining a discrepancy between the bank statement balance and the cash book balance.

**Bought ledger**. That division of the ledger which contains personal accounts of suppliers. It is also sometimes referred to as the purchase ledger or creditors account.

**Cash book**. The book in which records of cash and banking transactions are made.

**Credit note**. A document which reverses the effect of an invoice.

**Creditors**. People or firms to whom the business owes money.

**Capital**. This term derives from the latin words 'Capitalis', meaning 'chief' and 'capitali', meaning 'property', giving us the combined meaning of 'property of the chief'. The chief of a business is, of course, the proprietor.

**Control account**. An account in a ledger division which amounts to a mini trial balance for that division. It consists of aggregates of each type of posting therein, e.g.: the sales ledger control account will be posted with the aggregate value of cheques received, the aggregated invoice totals for the month, and so on. It is used both as a check on the accuracy and as a means of making the compilation of the overall trial balance easier.

**Debtors**. People or firms who owe money to the business.

**Depreciation**. The writing down of an asset's value in the books of a business to allow for wear and tear.

**Dividends**. Shares of profit paid to shareholders.

**Drawings**. The retrieval of capital by a proprietor or partners for private use.

**Early settlement discount**. A discount allowed to customers as an enticement to pay their bills on time.

**Expenses**. Purchases of goods or services for consumption by the business within the financial year. They do not enhance the value of any fixed assets though they may include repairs to them. Examples are: goods for resale, wages, repairs, heat and lighting costs, petrol and professional fees.

**FIFO**. First In First Out. A method of stock valuation based on the assumption that the latest cost prices prevail.

**Final accounts**. The revenue accounts and balance sheet of a firm at a particular moment in time and covering a particular financial period, e.g.: a financial year.

**Goodwill**. The intangible fixed asset of a business's reputation.

**Gross profit**. Sales revenue minus cost of sales.

**Gross profit margin**. Gross profit as a percentage of sales.

**Imprest system**. A system of managing petty cash in which a fund is regularly replenished to a set amount by the cashier.

**Income and expenditure account**. A non-profit-making club's equivalent of a business's profit and loss account.

**Input tax**. VAT charged by a supplier on goods or services it has supplied and which will be subsequently reclaimed by the business from HM Revenue and Customs.

**Interim accounts**. Revenue accounts and balance sheet drawn up at intervals more frequent than each financial year and used for management purposes.

**Invoice**. A bill for goods or services rendered.

**Journal**. A book of prime entry in debit and credit format used for initial entries of a miscellany of transactions for which no other book exists. E.g.: the intial recording of opening figures, bad debt, depreciation and the correction of errors. However, some people refer to the day books as journals too, e.g.: sales journal, purchase journal, etc. and the journal as defined above is then referred to as the 'Journal Proper'.

**Ledger**. The ledger is the essential double entry accounting system and consists of a number of divisions, e.g.: the general ledger, personal ledger, cash book and petty cash book. Since each of these divisions is often kept in a separate bound book it is not surprising that people tend to think of them as separate ledgers, but this is not truly the case, they are all divisions of the one ledger system.

**Liabilities**. Financial obligations to others—debts owed out. Capital too is listed under liabilities in the balance sheet since it is owed to the proprietor by the business.

**LIFO**. Last In First Out. A method of stock valuation based on the assumption that the earliest cost prices prevail.

**Limited company**. A business entity which has its own rights and obligations under the law. Its capital is divided into shares and the liability of the shareholders in the event of a liquidation is limited to the value of shares held.

**Liquidity**. The ability of a firm to pay its debts.

**Net profit**. Gross profit minus overhead expenses.

**Nominal ledger**. That division of the ledger in which impersonal accounts are kept.

**Output tax**. VAT charged to customers by a business and which it will have to subsequently remit to HM Revenue and Customs.

**Overhead expenses**. Expenses which cannot be directly related to turnover.

**Partnership**. An unlimited business unit owned by more than one proprietor.

**Personal ledger**. That division of the ledger which contains personal accounts of suppliers and customers. It is divided into 2 sub-divisions—bought ledger and sales ledger.

**Petty cash book**. The book of prime entry in which records of small cash transactions are kept.

**Postage book**. A book in which records of stamps purchased and used are made.

**Private ledger**. A separate division of the ledger in which capital items are posted.

**Private limited company**. A limited liability company whose share dealings are restricted and cannot be quoted on the stock exchange. It only has to have two shareholders and one director to comply with company law, though that director could not also act as company secretary.

**Profit**. The reward to the proprietor, partners or shareholders for the business risk they have taken.

**Profit and loss account**. That section of the revenue accounts which shows the calculation of net profit, by deduction of overhead expenses from gross profit.

**Profit and loss appropriation account**. That part of the revenue accounts of a partnership or limited company which explains how the net profit is to be appropriated.

**Provision for bad debts**. A suitable provision set against the value of debtors to allow for some which will become uncollectable.

**Provision for depreciation**. An allowance set against an asset for wear and tear.

**Public company**. A limited liability company which is empowered to sell its shares freely and have them quoted on the stock exchange. It must have a minimum of 7 shareholders and 2 directors.

**Purchase day book**. A book of prime entry in which the inital record of purchases is made prior to posting to the ledger.

**Purchase returns day book**. A book of prime entry in which the intial record of goods returned to suppliers is made prior to posting to the ledger.

**Receipts and payments book**. The main accounting book used by many club stewards in non-profit-making clubs.

**Revenues**. Inflows of money or money's worth to the firm, e.g. sales figures, rents, discounts received, etc. They must be distinguished from proceeds of sale of fixed assets, which is capital income rather than revenue income and is ultimately shown in the balance sheet rather than the trading, profit and loss account.

**Revenue accounts**. The set of accounts which shows the net profit earned by a business, how it is calculated and how it is to be distributed. Typically they include the trading account and the profit and loss account. For a partnership or limited company they will also include an appropriation account, for a manufacturing business, they will include the manufacturing account and for a club they will include an income and expenditure account.

**Sales day book**. The book of prime entry in which the initial record of all sales is made prior to posting to the ledger.

**Sales ledger**. That division of the ledger which contains personal accounts of customers. It is also sometimes referred to as the debtors ledger.

**Sales return day book**. The book of prime entry in which the initial record of goods returned by customers is made prior to posting to the ledger.

**Share capital**.

*Authorised share capital* The amount of capital a company is permitted to raise by means of issuing shares.

*Issued share capital* The nominal value of shares actually issued by a company.

*Ordinary shares* Shares in a company which earn the holders a percentage of profits. In the event of a liquidation this category of investors will be the last in the queue for recovery of their investment.

*Preference shares* Shares which entitle the holders to a fixed rate of dividend on profits. Their claim on profits comes before ordinary shareholders as would their claim on residual assets in the event of a liquidation.

*Redeemable shares* Shares which the company is empowered to buy back.

**Sole proprietorship**. An unlimited firm owned solely by one person.

**Statement of affairs**. A description and valuation of the assets and liabilities of a business and the way the net assets are represented by capital at a particular moment in time. In effect, it is the same as a balance sheet, but not called so because the source used for compilation is not the ledger balances, but rather a series of inventories.

**Stock**. Goods for resale or for use in a manufacturing process for the production of goods for resale.

**Suspense account**. An account into which a value equal to an error can be posted temporarily in order to make the books balance while the source of the error is being sought.

**Trading account**. That section of the revenue accounts which explains the calculation of gross profit.

**Trial balance**. A listing and summing of all the ledger balances at a particular moment in time to confirm that the total debits equal the total credits and, thus, provide some measure of confidence in the accuracy of the ledger posting.

**Value Added Tax (VAT)**. A tax on goods and services. Businesses act as sub-collectors by charging VAT on goods they sell and remitting it to HM

Revenue and Customs after deducting the VAT they, themselves, have been charged on their purchases from other firms.

**Working capital.** The difference between current assets and current liabilities.